AF352688

TEACHER OF THE LOGOS

TEACHER OF THE LOGOS

ESSAYS ON ORIGEN'S REDISCOVERED LAST WORK

EDITED BY

Joseph W. Trigg and Robin Darling Young

The Catholic University of America Press
Washington, D.C.

Copyright © 2025
The Catholic University of America Press
All rights reserved.
Copyright claim excludes previously published materials,
as listed in the Acknowledgments.
The paper used in this publication meets the minimum
requirements of American National Standards for Information
Science—Permanence of Paper for Printed Library Materials,
ANSI Z39.48-1992.

∞

Cataloging-in-Publication Data is available
from the Library of Congress
ISBN (hardcover): 978-0-8132-3966-8
ISBN (ebook): 978-0-8132-3967-5

CONTENTS

TO THE MEMORY OF JUDITH LEE KOVACS
(1944–2020)

Joseph W. Trigg and Robin Darling Young

INTRODUCTION

Origen of Caesarea is one of the few teachers of early Christianity who has trained not one or two generations of scholars, but over fifteen-hundred years of men and women both fascinated and persuaded by his approach to philosophy, scriptural exegesis, and ethical training. This astounding man, a genius whose prodigious work made possible all later Christian thought, intended and planned to set his work upon a secure foundation, consciously imitating the Logos whose *oikonomia*—the benevolent arrangement of the cosmos and its inhabitants—he was the first to describe in full. His plans succeeded, and yielded not only the work of numerous fourth-century writers, who themselves as teachers spread his way of thinking through their own published thought; it yielded a way of looking at the world under the aegis of the Logos that not only imitated that Logos' charm in discourse, but shaped the way in which those who wanted to understand at the most profound level would have to discipline themselves in order to understand both Origen's thinking and the Logos' work—both evident and elusive. Through Jerome, Augustine, Cassian, and their readers, Origen's approach streamed into the Latin West, later to provide the basis for both Thomas Aquinas in the thirteenth and Erasmus in the sixteenth century; and despite the hostility of its sixth-century enemies living in Palestine and Constantinople, Origen's thought permeated Greek, Syriac, and Armenian ascetic communities through Evagrius of Pontus, and Greek theology through Gregory of Nazianzus and Gregory of Nyssa. His thought remained, in these crucial areas, a fundamental approach both to philosophy in Christianity, to scriptural exegesis, and to the understanding of human psychology upon which a benignly stringent moral discipline was based.

Generations of beneficiaries of Origen's work continued both in Europe and the Mediterranean, —wherever the theological and historical faculties of universities carried along the study of this third-century master. The heirs of Origen continue to read his works today, and not only for historical information—they read him because he inspires an intelligent understanding of the biblical text and of the perceptible and intelligible worlds described by philosophy; both satisfy attentive readers, even as they understand that the account of physical reality or the church structure that Origen took for granted, must have evolved and changed since his era.

Two of those later students, graduate-school colleagues, had rejoined each other's company after forty years—and had begun to read his first, programmatic *On First Principles* (written around 220–230, in Alexandria), working through a comparison of Rufinus' Latin translation and what was left of the original Greek, dictated by Origen to those scribes memorably described in Eusebius of Caesarea's *Ecclesiastical History*. But we had hardly begun to cover Book 4 when news arrived of the discovery of a large portion of Origen's massive treatment of the Psalms, in the form of homilies delivered to the congregation of Caesarea and, very likely, some of his own advanced students there. Like the rest of the scholarly world, we saw the following announcement, distributed first from the museum where it was found and then disseminated through websites and other public media:

Spectacular Find: Homilies by Origen of Alexandria discovered in original Greek.

A spectacular discovery was recently made during the cataloguing of Greek manuscripts from the Johan Jacob Fugger Collection in the Bayerischen Staatsbibliothek. In the course of cataloging, the philologist Marina Molin Pradel identified the manuscript of numerous texts, hitherto unknown in the original Greek, of Homilies on the Psalms by Origen of Alexandria (185–253/54 AD), the most significant theologian of early Christianity before Augustine. The importance of this find cannot be overestimated. The internationally recognized Origen expert, Lorenzo Perrone of the University of Bologna, has confirmed the very high likelihood of the attribution to Origen.[1]

---

1. Translated by the authors, last accessed in https://www.merkur.de/lokales/muenchen/stadt-muenchen/spektakulaerer-fund-griechische-predigten-origenes-entdeckt-meta-2350564.html.

So read the press release on June 12, 2012 from the Bayerischen Staatsbibliothek in Munich. Codex Monacensis Graecus 314 (CMG 314) is a parchment manuscript with 371 leaves upon which a twelfth-century monk had copied, in a clear middle-Byzantine hand, twenty-nine Greek homilies on the Psalms. The author or authors remained unspecified in the manuscript. A month earlier, in May of 2012, Marina Molin Pradel, the first librarian since the seventeenth century to examine the manuscript closely, was on the verge of experiencing an archivist's dream, recovering a seemingly lost work by a major author in the collection under her care. Dr. Molin Pradel had strong reason to believe that at least four homilies were Origen's and that, in all likelihood, all of them were, yet only a scholar familiar with Origen's work could verify that, and she turned to Professor Lorenzo Perrone of the University of Bologna. He was one of the initiators of an Italian study group on Origen that brought Origen studies to a new level with the publication of an annual journal, *Adamantius*, of which he was editor, and the *Dizionario Origene*,[2] to which he contributed. He had published widely on Origen and had recently completed a magisterial book on Origen's understanding of prayer.[3] Even before the discovery, he had already decided to work on the meager remains of Origen's extensive work on the Psalms.

Perrone learned about the find on May 21, 2012, the day after Bologna had been shaken by its first serious earthquake in many years. Aftershocks did not distract him from studying CMG 314 on the Staatsbibliothek website. He was confident, within three weeks, that all twenty-nine homilies in GMS 314 were by Origen. Nine homilies survived in Latin translations by Rufinus. CMG 314 contained the originals of four of these nine, Homilies 1–4 on Psalm 37 and of a passage from Homily 1 on Psalm 15 quoted in Book 1 of Pamphilus's *Apology for Origen*, which Rufinus had also translated into Latin. All twenty-nine were also attested in Jerome's Epistle 33; they were among the one-hundred-twenty homilies on selected psalms among the works by Origen still accessible in the episcopal library of Caesarea toward the end of the fourth century. Only fragments of the Greek original existed, but brief comments attributed to the work remain in Byzantine commentaries.

Having vouched for their authenticity, Perrone, assisted by other members of the Italian Study Group, began editing the manuscript for the venerable series

2. *Origene Dizzionario: la cultura, il pensiero, le opere* (Rome: Città Nuova, 2000).
3. *La preghiera secondo Origene: l'impossibilità donata* (Brescia: Morcelliana, 2011).

publishing critical editions of early Christian works since 1891, *Die Griechische Christlichen Schriftsteller*. There it appeared, in 2015, as *Origenes Werke*, Band 13 (GCS O13). The speed of publication was remarkable. By contrast, the only comparable discovery of works by Origen in modern times, ancient papyrus codices discovered at Tura in Egypt in 1942, were not fully accessible for over a generation.[4] Introductory essays by Pradel and Perrone discuss the manuscript and its discovery; Perrone explains the evidence for its authenticity; and Emanuela Prinzivalli, who had earlier edited the nine Homilies on the Psalms translated by Rufinus,[5] explains what can be learned by comparing Rufinus's translation to the Greek original of Homilies 1–4 on Psalm 36. Perrone and two other members of the Italian Study Group, Emanuela Prinzivalli and Antonio Cacciari, edited the text of the twenty-nine homilies. A passage from Homily 1 on Psalm 15 that Rufinus preserved in his translation of Pamphilus appears printed side by side with the Greek in the main body of the edition. The team indicated in bold text the Greek fragments from the Homilies. An appendix sets the Greek and Latin of these four homilies side by side, and an index of scripture lists approximately three thousand citations and allusions. Two more indices list approximately two thousand parallel passages elsewhere in Origen's work and around two hundred fifty in other ancient authors. The editorial standards of the GCS dictate the inclusion of such citations, but few volumes quote from them as liberally alongside the text itself. The labor that went into producing GCS O13 and the care to make it useful as an instrument of study testify to Perrone and his team's generosity of spirit and love of Origen.

Twenty-nine homilies, occupying five hundred twenty-three pages in GCS O13, is indeed a "spectacular find." Origen's works constitute a large portion of Christian literature surviving from the period before Constantine. Although his influence was immense, as we have indicated above, his work had challenged many early Christian teachers even in his own lifetime, and some challenged him openly. Opposition to his thought peaked at two moments: at the end of the fourth century, after the slanders of Epiphanius of Salamis, aided by Jerome; and in the mid-sixth century, when a heated controversy over his legacy began among certain monks of Palestine and led to his condemnation at the highest level of imperial government. In the East, his works

---

4. *On the Passover*, the last works by Origen discovered at Tura to be edited, became available in 1979 as Origène, *Sur la Pâque: Traité inédit publié d'après un papyrus de Toura*, ed. Octave Guérand and Pierre Nautin (Paris: Beauchesne, 1979).

5. Origene, *Omelie sui Salmi* (Florence: Nardini, 1991).

ceased to be copied or were erased and copied over; some were deliberately destroyed. The remaining works of Origen constitute only the fraction of his work that has happened to survive a thousand years of neglect and deliberate destruction (including the burning of the Library of Caesarea containing his works, in the Arab invasion of 638). Now, about half of Origen's work is accessible only in early Latin translations that are sadly deficient by comparison to their original Greek versions. Before the identification of CNG 314, twenty homilies of Origen in the original Greek were our only transcripts of Christian preaching from the pre-Constantinian period. Now there are forty-nine.

It is particularly welcome that these homilies are on the Psalms, the book of the Hebrew Scriptures/Old Testament most frequently cited from its Greek version, the Septuagint, in the New Testament. Papyrological evidence suggests that, already before Origen's time, the Psalms had a privileged role in Christian prayer and worship; Christians occasionally owned their own copies, and, perhaps because Jesus quoted them, they began to be regarded as utterances supplemental to quotations in the Gospels.[6] Later, in the fourth century, the Psalms would be central both to developing worship of both cathedral and monastery, and also to personal use in private worship. They were also a site of biblical exegesis: Christian authors followed Origen's example in devoting extensive commentaries and homilies to interpret the Psalms both for learned readers and for ordinary Christian gatherings. For Origen, the Psalms had been a lifelong focus of work, he devoted two commentaries as well as homilies to their explanation. Like Marina Molin Pradel, Origen himself was as a philologist and watched for hitherto neglected texts and, in an early example of biblical archeology, found a hitherto unknown Greek translation of them in a jar at Jericho.[7] The work of Marie-Josèphe Rondeau on early Christian commentaries on the Psalms demonstrates the great importance of Psalm commentaries to early Christian thought; how vital Origen's contribution had to have been; and how frustrating it has been, up to now, to be aware of that contribution without being able to know it adequately.[8]

---

6. Colin Roberts in *Manuscript, Society and Belief in Early Christian Egypt* (London: The British Academy, 1979), 53 stated that, on the basis of papyri, the Psalter was "more used and read than any book of the Old Testament, perhaps more than any book of the Bible, throughout the Christian centuries in Egypt."

7. See Eusebius, *Ecclesiastical History*, 6.16.2–3.

8. *Les commentaires patristiques du Psautier (IIIe - Ve siècles)* (Rome: Pont. Institutum Studiorum Orientalium, 1982), "Au total, ce qu'on peut réunir d'Origène sur les Psaumes n'est … qu'une faible part de se qui fut," 62.

In addition to the partial restoration of his last work, there is still more reason for celebration; as our title indicates, Lorenzo Perrone, as he prepared GCS O13, discovered that these homilies are, very likely, the last of Origen's works. They give us Origen's mature judgment and final appraisal of all the topics that they touch. Thanks to the diligent work of Perrone and his colleagues, GCS O13 becomes the capstone of Origen's work. The thousands of biblical citations in Perrone's apparatus are a mute testimony to Origen's intimate knowledge of the Bible and his ability to interpret it as a coherent whole. The astonishingly large number of parallel passages from Origen's own work, embracing all periods of his life, testify to the remarkable consistency and coherence of that work.

Although consistent with the rest of Origen's work, these homilies exhibit his deepening insight into the Incarnation; the church; and the process of divinization, particularly the divinization of the body; and human psychology, where Origen posits something like what is now called the "adaptive unconscious."[9] They provide deeper insight, too, into Origen's understanding of the cosmos as a revelation of the divine Logos, his use and understanding of prayer, his relationship to Jews and Judaism, his understanding of sound and music. They help us better assess Origen's biblical interpretation including the format and function of the *Hexapla*, and his use of rhetoric. They also provide fascinating glimpses of life in the third century in Caesarea: Origen describes domestic difficulties, games, athletic training, the theater, wine connoisseurship, and the distribution of imperial honors.

Many of these themes are explored in the essays in this volume. They are the fruit of a one-day colloquium at The Catholic University of America, held on May 22–23, 2017. We had been reading the Homilies several years before the conference; once we had fully grasped their importance, we decided to ask Professor William E. Klingshirn, Director of the Center for the Study of Early Christianity, whether the Center would be willing to support a colloquium. He readily agreed, and the Center generously supported the gathering. Professor Lorenzo Perrone graciously agreed to come to Washington to give a public lecture and to participate in the colloquium. We then invited both beginning and established scholars of Origen to meet at CUA for the day-long

---

9. In PS15H2.3 the "kidneys" that discipline the soul in Ps 15.7 (LXX) are "ways of thinking and seeds of rationalizations before they arise in the heart." They "already exist potentially within." On the adaptive unconscious see Timothy D. Wilson, *Strangers to Ourselves: Discovering the Adaptive Unconscious* (Cambridge, MA: Harvard University Press, 2002).

colloquium. Their essays follow Professor Perrone's public lectures in Washington at the Catholic University of America.

Those who took part in the colloquium did not always agree with each other's conclusions, but we all enjoyed the excitement of sharing observations about a text that was new to us and still largely unknown. In "Origen in the Light of the New Homilies on the Psalms," Professor Perrone opened the colloquium with the public lecture in the May Gallery of CUA's Mullen Library; it became our first chapter. He introduced the features of the collection of homilies discovered in 2012: their selection and composition compared with a series assembled and translated by Rufinus in the early fifth century, Eusebius and Jerome's knowledge of the homilies, their transmission and composition, and Origen's procedure introducing individual homilies. Perrone concluded that Origen, trained as a grammarian and philosopher, was foremost a "teacher of the Logos," assisting both bishops and communities as one who "unveils the mysteries of God," detecting Scripture's hidden meanings and showing how the biblical text is worthy of the Logos.

Alex Poulos, now a recent PhD but at the time a doctoral student in Greek and Latin at CUA, presented our second chapter. He considers Origen's understanding of the soul: what is consistent, from *Peri Archōn* forward, and what has changed in Origen's thinking? He argues that the relationship between spirit, mind, soul and body has become more complicated, just as his understanding of both angels and the natural world has deepened. Jesus himself, if the evangelists are to be believed,[10] already took an interest in the exegetical issue that Marie-Josèphe Rondeau made the guiding thread of her investigation of early Christian interpretation of the Psalms. She called this the "*exégèse prosopologique*," the identification of the *persona/ prosōpon*, the voice speaking in the Psalm. In her presentation, our third chapter, Miriam J. DeCock, then a doctoral student but now an Assistant Professor of Biblical Studies at Dublin City University, applies and vindicates Rondeau's approach, showing how and when Origen was able to identify the speaker in a Psalm as Christ. Professor Elizabeth Dively Lauro of Loyola-Marymount University, an invitee to the colloquium, contributed another discussion of *prosōpon*, our chapter four. In the two homilies on Psalm 15 that she examines, the *prosōpon* of Christ engages in an act of submission but at the same time is equal to the Father. The Son needs the Father for his existence, she argues,

---

10. See Mt 22.43–45, Mk 35–37, Lk 20.41–44.

but is equal to the Father in nature and power. The Son, and Scripture as well, thus have salvific power for the believer, and make possible humans' *telos*—union with Christ in his union with the Father. In his presentation, our chapter five, Mark Randall James, instructor at Fordham University and Hunter College, deepened the investigation of his doctoral research in his contribution on "performing the scriptures" in the Psalms homilies. Origen, James proposes, should be seen not as a text scholar, but as someone like a linguist, who understands the Psalms as a linguistic performance that Christians can make their own, in order to perform scripture accurately.

In her presentation, chapter six, Professor Margaret M. Mitchell of the University of Chicago examines the new homilies for their teaching on Christ, the Law, and the Jewish people. She argues that Origen departs from the apostle Paul's more positive views of the status of the Jewish people and grounds his views almost exclusively in the Letter to the Galatians. Origen thought that Christians must not participate in Jewish feasts; he thought that the exile from Jerusalem was a sign of divine punishment of the Jews for their killing Christ. Christians, too, could lose divine favor; but Jews already, and inasmuch as they remained Jews, irreversibly had lost it, according to Origen.

In chapter seven, Professor Robin Darling Young of CUA, co-editor of the volume, looks at the reception of Origen's Psalms homilies. An important commentator on the Psalms in the fourth century was the Origenist thinker Evagrius of Pontus. Do his *Scholia on the Psalms* reflect an acquaintance with these homilies of Origen's? A comparison of Evagrius' scholia on Psalm 76, as identified by Marie-Josèphe Rondeau, shows that each of the scholia has a corresponding section in Origen's homilies on that psalm, with one intriguing exception: the final scholion reflects a section of Clement's *Stromateis*. Now that they have been published in a critical edition, we can see just how closely Evagrius adhered to Origen's overall interpretation of the Psalms, and to determine the degree to which Evagrius' composition aligns with the translations and compositions of his contemporaries among the followers of Origen—Rufinus and, earlier, Jerome. The scholia are an important means by which the teaching of Origen passed into the broader, and later, Christian exegetical tradition.

In chapter two, our other co-editor, Joseph Trigg, a retired Episcopal minister who has published extensively on Origen, discusses issues raised by his current project, translating the homilies for a volume to appear presently in the Fathers of the Church series. He begins by showing how CNG 314 now helps us better understand Origen's own theory of translation. He also shows how the challenges that faced Rufinus, laid out by Emmanuela Prinzivalli in GCS O13, to a large extent still confront us today: handling biblical citations, making the transcript of a speech accessible to those who were not there when it was delivered, expressing in a new language thoughts that are intimately connected with Origen's carefully precise Greek, dealing with changed cultural assumptions that distort how the text is perceived. He argues that facing these challenges in a range of actual choices a translator has to make about style, vocabulary, even punctuation, gives us insight into Origen's thought.

We invite the readers of this volume to share the excitement we experienced in each other's company for an all-too-short time. We all recognized that our investigations took place both in response to this new text, and to invite further study. All of us regarded it as a great privilege to be among the first people to examine a newly discovered treasure. We offer this volume as an invitation to read further in these rediscovered works of the first great teacher to shape Christianity after the Apostle Paul.

Lorenzo Perrone

1. ORIGEN IN THE LIGHT OF THE NEW *HOMILIES ON THE PSALMS*

The discovery of the Munich codex: questions on the new collection of Origen's homilies

Five years after the discovery by Marina Molin Pradel of a Munich manuscript with twenty-nine homilies of Origen on the Psalms,[1] and two years after the publication of the critical edition,[2] this is already the second conference on the collection of Codex Monacensis Graecus 314. In the wake of the first, that was held in Bologna in 2013,[3] research on the new texts has been going on and the present occasion will further foster it. It is not my intention today to present an overview of it, inasmuch as a Paris colleague, Marie-Odile Boulnois, has recently accomplished this task in an accurate manner.[4] Rather, I would like to continue to develop my observations on the new *Homilies on the Psalms* to better grasp their distinctive profile from the literary and the exegetical point of view. By doing so, my aim is not simply to show once more what is the specific contribution that they offer to our knowledge of the

1. Marina Molin Pradel, "Novità origeniane dalla Staatsbibliothek di Monaco di Baviera: il Cod. graec. 314." *Adamantius* 18 (2012): 16–40.

2. *HPs.* I shall quote Origen's writings according to the abbreviations adopted in the edition.

3. For the proceedings of the conference, see C. Barilli and L Perrone, "Origene commentatore dei Salmi: dai frammenti catenari al Codice di Monaco." *Adamantius* 20 (2014): 173–286.

4. Marie-Odile Boulnois, "Chronique d'une découverte et de ses retombées scientifiques: les nouvelles Homélies sur les Psaumes d'Origène" *Revue des Études Tardo-Antiques* 5 (2015–2016): 351–62. For further studies see now Lorenzo Perrone, *«Meine Zunge ist mein Ruhm»: Studien zu den neuen Psalmenhomilien des Origenes*, (Münster: Aschendorff, 2021).

Alexandrian, as I did on other occasions, but rather to share with you some of my questions in view of the novel evidence at our disposal. These interrogations should hopefully help to reach a deeper understanding of Origen's homiletic performance and of his role as teacher.

To begin, let us go back for a moment to the discovery itself. My friend Marina Molin Pradel, who had never read a line of Origen before coming across our codex, achieved a masterly work. As you probably know, the anonymous manuscript from the beginning of the 12th century is erroneously introduced by the note of a copyist, in the first folio, as "Interpretation of the Gospel, the Apostles, and the Psalter,"[5] despite the fact that the next line clearly indicates the text which follows under the title: "1st Homily on Psalm 15."[6] No less misleading is the mention of Michael Psellos, the Byzantine polymath of the 11th century, as "commentator of the Psalter," appended to the last folio by a later hand (between the 14th and the 15th centuries) and subsequently added also in the upper margin of the first folio, as if Psellos was the author.[7] Apart from the possible explanation of such inaccurate information, these features are of no help in order to identify the author. By the same token they raise the problem of the transmission of Origen's writings, and of the milieus which were responsible for it, more specifically as far as the *Homilies* are concerned.

On this point, happily, we have a unique source for retracing the literary *corpus* of the Alexandrian and the process of transmission, so to say, from its beginnings: Jerome's *Letter 33* to Paula, resting on the catalogue of the library of Caesarea that Eusebius appended to his *Life of Pamphilus*.[8] Marina Molin Pradel checked its evidence almost immediately, after she overcame another disturbing element: the previous catalogue by Ignaz Hardt, from the beginning of the 19th century, was in its turn misleading, because it recorded in the Munich codex four homilies "on Psalm 31," instead of Psalm 36. So, Jerome's list, indicating five homilies on this psalm, and their Latin translation by Rufinus provided the first key to detect the author of the Greek sermons. Moreover, it was possible to extend their attribution to Origen also thanks to the excerpts preserved in the exegetical *catenae* on the Psalter, at

5. *H15Ps* I Tit. in app. (73): Ἑρμηνεία τοῦ εὐα‹γγελίου›, τ‹ῶν› ἀπο‹στόλων› κ‹αὶ› τοῦ ψαλτηρί‹ου›.

6. *H15Ps* I Tit. (73): Εἰς τὸν ιε´ ψαλμὸν ὁμιλία α´.

7. See the presentation by Molin Pradel in *HPs*, 29–30.

8. Pierre Nautin, *Origène: sa vie et son œuvre* (Paris: Beauchesne, 1977), 225–60 and Andrew Carriker, *The Library of Eusebius of Caesarea* (Leiden: Brill, 2003), 8–22.

least for a considerable lot of the *Homilies*, not to mention an extract from the *2nd Homily on Psalm 15* in the *Apology for Origen* by Pamphilus and Eusebius of Caesarea. At the same time, the inner criteria consisting in the examination of language, style, exegetical approach and doctrinal contents, definitively assured the authorship of the Alexandrian.[9]

If there are no more doubts concerning the attribution of the texts in the Munich codex to Origen, many questions remain open with regard to the composition of the collection and its transmission. A comparison with the similar series assembled by Rufinus in his precious selection of nine homilies on Psalms 36–38 is unfortunately not very helpful.[10] It is indeed a shorter and a more homogeneous collection than our codex, as the translator himself states in his preface. It consists of nine sermons on three Psalms that not only lead Origen essentially to develop a moral interpretation, but also to draw with their coherent sequence the spiritual itinerary from conversion and penance of the sinner to the perfection of the righteous.[11] On the contrary, when we look at its content, the Munich series presents a more complex and varied visage: two homilies on Psalm 15, four on Psalm 36, two on Psalm 67, three on Psalm 73, one on Psalm 74, one on Psalm 75, four on Psalm 76, nine on Psalm 77, two on Psalm 80 and one on Psalm 81. The only unifying aspect of external nature, at least for the greater part of this *corpus*, is the fact that most of the sermons deal with the Psalms of Asaph (Pss 73–77, 80–81). Yet the manuscript does not include the complete series of the sermons on these Psalms (Pss 49 and 72–82), although according to Jerome's catalogue Origen preached on all of them, with the only exception of Psalm 79. Since we miss one homily on Psalm 49, three homilies on Psalm 72, four on Psalm 78 and three on Psalm 82, we have to exclude that the Psalms of Asaph dictated alone the assemblage of the sermons. In addition, the *1st Homily on Psalm 73* presents the figure of Asaph as a prophet without alluding to previous explanations, even if the treatment of the rubrics by Origen should not be regarded as too strict.[12]

9. Lorenzo Perrone, "Origenes rediuiuus: La découverte des homélies sur les Psaumes dans le Cod. Gr. 314 de Munich," *Revue d'études augustiniennes et patristiques* 59 (2013): 55–93 and Lorenzo Perrone, "Discovering Origen's Lost Homilies on the Psalms," *Auctores Nostri* 15 (2015): 19–46.

10. Cf. *H36–38PsL*.

11. E. Prinzivalli, "Vinea. spiritualis intellegentiae. L'interpretazione omiletica dei salmi in Origene. Un'indagine a partire dalle omelie sui salmi 36 37 38," *Annali di storia dell'esegesi* 7 (1990): 397–416.

12. *H73Ps* I, 1 (225:8–10): Ὡς ἐπιγέγραπται δὲ ὁ ψαλμός, οὐκέτι τοῦ Δαυὶδ ἀλλὰ τοῦ Ἀσάφ, καὶ αὐτοῦ προφητεύσαντος ἐν τοῖς ἐπιγεγραμμένοις αὐτοῦ ψαλμοῖς, "the Psalm is no longer inscribed 'of David,' but '*of Asaph*' and because he is prophesying in the Psalms inscribed to him" (p. 179). The translations are generally taken from Joseph W. Trigg, *Homilies on the Psalms: Codex Monacensis Graecus 314* (Washington, DC: The Catholic University of America Press, 2020) (occasionally with modifications).

Psalms of Asaph	Jerome, *Ep.* 33	Codex Graecus 314
Ps 49	1 homily	—
Ps 72	3 homilies	—
Ps 73	3 homilies	3 homilies
Ps 74	1 homily	1 homily
Ps 75	1 homily	1 homily
Ps 76	3 homilies	4 homilies
Ps 77	9 homilies	9 homilies
Ps 78	—	—
Ps 79	4 homilies	—
Ps 80	2 homilies	2 homilies
Ps 81	1 homily	1 homily
Ps 82	3 homilies	—

Eusebius, who commented upon the whole series in his *Commentary on the Psalms*, reports in the *Ecclesiastical History* an interesting fragment from one of Origen's homilies on Psalm 82.[13] It deals with the heresies of the Elkesaites, and the critique of their doctrines, which the preacher summarizes for his audience, could fit quite well with the heresiological concerns often emerging in the Munich codex, especially with regard to the Ebionites or the judaizing (and anti-Pauline) tendencies within the Christian communities of Caesarea and Palestine in the middle of the third century. However, our collection did not include these homilies, so that at all events it is reductive to assume the heresiological aspects as its unifying principle. Not even a quantitative criterion helps to explain the preference accorded to some homilies instead of others, if the selection was meant to give at least some pieces from the largest groups of sermons. Jerome, for instance, lists three homilies on Psalm 72 and four on Psalm 79, but the collection omits both series; on the other hand, it skips precisely the latter of them in the continuous series of the sermons delivered by Origen on Psalms 73–81.

The *catenae* fragments still wait for more reliable editions, although they may transmit some authentic excerpts for the missing sermons on Psalms 49,

---

For the mentions of Asaph, see further *H74Ps* 1 (269:5); *H76Ps* I, 1 (294:1–14); *H77Ps* I, 1 (351:5–17); *H80Ps* II, 1 (496:18–19).

13. Eusebius of Caesarea, *Hist. Eccl.* VI, 38: ὁμιλῶν ἐπὶ τοῦ κοινοῦ εἰς τὸν πβ΄ ψαλμόν, "preaching in public on Ps 82." Apart from the qualification of the fragment as homiletic, Eusebius does not indicate the number of the homily among the three on Ps 82.

72, 78 and 82 among the group of the Asaph Psalms.[14] As a sort of counter-balance, we can check the list of the Munich codex over against the double series of Jerome's *Tractatus in Psalmos*, a work that scholars have long held as being simply a translation and adaptation of homilies preached by Origen.[15] Now, the *Tractatus* likewise has no homily on Psalm 49, but includes one on Psalm 78 and two on Psalm 82, while it substantially reflects the list of the Munich collection: in fact, there is only the omission of the homilies on Psalm 73, since the *Homilies on Psalm 36* (also missing in the *Tractatus*) were translated by Rufinus. As a consequence, we can first of all rely on the external similarity of the two series to assert a proximity of the *Tractatus* to the *Homilies*. Moreover, preliminary investigations point to Jerome's acquaintance with some of the Munich sermons, even if his dependence upon them is neither servile nor restricted to the corresponding homily of Origen, inasmuch as Jerome also appears to rearrange the exegesis of the Alexandrian.[16]

Psalms	Jerome, *Tractatus in Psalmos*	Origen, *Homilies on the Psalms* (CMG 314)	Jerome, *Ep.* 33
15	*In Ps. XV* (2nd ser.)	*H15Ps* I–II	3 homilies
36	—	*H36Ps* I–IV	5 homilies
67	*In Ps. LXVII* (1st ser.)	*H67Ps* I–II	7 homilies
73	—	*H73Ps* I–III	3 homilies
74	*In Ps. LXXIV* (1st ser.)	*H74Ps* I	1 homily
75	*In Ps. LXXV* (1st ser.)	*H75Ps* I	1 homily
76	*In Ps. LXXVI* (1st ser.)	*H76Ps* I–IV	3 homilies
77	*In Ps. LXXVII* (1st ser.)	*H77Ps* I–IX	9 homilies
78	*In Ps. LXXVIII* (1st ser.)	—	—
79	—	—	4 homilies
80	*In Ps. LXXX* (1st ser.)	*H80Ps* I–II	2 homilies
81	*In Ps. LXXXI* (1st ser.)	*H81Ps* I	1 homily
82	*In Ps. LXXXII* (1st and 2nd ser.)	—	3 homilies

14. Gilles Dorival, "Origen in the Catenae on Psalms: I. An Overall Outline," *Adamantius* 20 (2014): 8–13 and C. Bandt, "Origen in the Catenae on Psalms: II. The Rather Complicated Case of Psalms 51 to 76," *Adamantius* 20 (2014) 14–26.

15. Cf. *Tract. in Ps.* And V. Peri, "Omelie origeniane sui Psalmi," *Studi e Testi* 289 (Vatican City, 1980).

16. See, for instance, Alessandro Capone, "Folia vero in verbis sunt": parola divina e lingua umana nei Tractatus in psalmos attribuiti a Gerolamo." *Adamantius* 19 (2013): 437–56; Perrone, "Origenes rediuiuus," 63–65 (on the dependence of *Tr. in Ps. XV* upon *H15Ps*); Lorenzo Perrone, "Mysteria in Psalmis: Origen and Jerome as Interpreters of the Psalter," in *Studia Patristica, Vol. CIII: The Bible in the Patristic Period*, ed. M. Szram and M. Wysocki (Leuven: Peeters, 2021), 59–86.

If we add to our comparative evidence the catalogue of the *tomoi*, that is the commentaries on the Psalms in Jerome's *Letter 33*, it becomes even more clear that the physiognomy of the Munich collection, as far as its composition is concerned, mirrors the difficulties and hazards of the textual tradition of Origen's writings. Apart from Psalm 15, the list of forty-five *tomoi* does not comprise any of the psalms that Origen commented in the homilies. But we are allowed to presume that the catalogue is far from being complete, inasmuch as the Alexandrian occasionally refers to commentaries that do not figure in Jerome's list.[17] Therefore the difficulties for transmitting such a huge literary legacy must have begun quite early. Jerome witnesses that Pamphilus also could not find some commentaries on the Psalms when he tried to collect the works of the Alexandrian, as much as possible, for the library of Caesarea.[18] The Munich codex itself documents the loss of some pieces, that were already missing at the time the collection was assembled. This is, for instance, the case of the *5th Homily on Psalm* 36, accessible in Rufinus' translation but not attested by the *catenae*, which preserve instead excerpts from the first four homilies. Furthermore, of the seven *Homilies on Psalm 67* only two entered the collection. The survival of the first two sermons, with their lengthy treatment of only seven verses, certainly does not imply a selection on account of the presumably large size of this series, since the Munich manuscript has maintained the even larger one of the nine homilies on Psalm 77 in its entirety.

How were then the homilies copied, collected and transmitted? It is reasonable to suppose that initially they were copied singularly or perhaps they were put together when the sermons dealt with the same Psalm, provided that they did not form too large a collection. We have, at least, an interesting clue to support the latter assumption in the Munich manuscript. The series of the nine *Homilies on Psalm 77* is namely distinguished in two groups—more precisely in a first and a second *tomos*—, respectively comprising the first five sermons (*H77Ps* I–V) and the remaining four (*H77Ps* VI–IX), with a proportionate distribution of folia (59 vis-à-vis 56).[19] Actually, there was no reason for maintaining such distinction in the codex, inasmuch as the homilies follow one another with the indication of their respective number. Consequently, the

---

17. For instance, on Ps 47. See Nautin, *Origène*, 249–50; Marie Josèphe Rondeau, *Les commentaries patristiques du Psautier (IIIe-Ve siècles)* (Rome: Pontificium Institutum Studiorum Orientalium, 1982), 51.

18. Jerome, *Ep.* 34:1.

19. See respectively *H77Ps* V Subscr. (419,5): Εἰς τὸν οζ̈ <ψαλμὸν> [ms. τόμος] τόμος αʹ ("First volume on Ps 77") and *H77Ps* Inscr. (420) Τόμος βʹ εἰς τὸν οζʹ <ψαλμόν>, ὁμιλίας ʹ ("Second volume on Ps 77, Homily 6").

separation in two *tomoi* must go back to a previous stage of the manuscript tradition, in which the two groups were copied separately. Moreover, another 'archaic' feature, which points in the same way to an earlier stage in the preservation of the text, occurs in the *Homilies on Psalm 76*. The transcription of this particularly interesting series of sermons is accompanied by lemmas that surprisingly qualify them as "improvised speeches,"[20] though the homilies do not really differ from the others in terms of their literary characteristics. One of these sermons—the *2nd Homily on Psalm 76*—even exhibits in its prologue perhaps the most elaborate display of rhetoric within the entire collection.

On the other hand, we do not know to what extent the homilies happened to be, as a general rule, "improvised speeches," especially when they commented successively on the verses of a psalm in more than one sermon. Did Origen, for example, resort to *scholia*, whose tradition is still attested, serving perhaps as preparatory drafts for further treatment?[21] At all events, we should perhaps not generalize the case of the Jerusalem homily on the witch of Endor (1 Kingdoms 28), where bishop Alexander chose at the moment the text on which Origen was expected to preach, after the reading of several pericopes from the first book of *Reigns*.[22] According to Eusebius' witness in the *Ecclesiastical History*, when the Alexandrian dictated his writings, he had a host of shorthand-writers, copyists, and calligraphers at his disposal.[23] Furthermore, as far as the preaching is concerned, Origen allowed the tachigraphical transcription of the sermons only when he "was over sixty years of age, inasmuch as he had now acquired immense facility from long preparation."[24] Thus, the written texts of the homilies presumably went through the three following stages: a) stenographic record of the speech, b) its transcript into ordinary script, and c) "the first edited version prepared for copying by scribes and subsequent distribution."[25] It is difficult, however, to retrace this process inside

20. *H76Ps* I, Tit. (293): Εἰς τὸν ος′ ‹ψαλμὸν› ἐσχεδιασμέναι ὁμιλίαι. See also the end of *H76Ps* II (325,23): Σχέδιον β′ ψαλμοῦ ος′. For a similar case, compare the *Catecheses* of Cyril of Jerusalem, which are regularly introduced as σχεδιασθεῖσαι ("extemporary sermons"). Rufinus, in the preface to his translation of *HIos* (SCh 71, p. 92), points to their extemporary nature: *quas ex tempore in ecclesia perorauit Adamantius senex*, "(the homilies), that the Adamantius extemporarily held in the church in his old age."

21. F. X. Risch, "Zur lateinischen Rezeption der Scholia in Psalmos von Origenes," in *Origeniana Undecima: Origen and Origenism in the History of Western Thought* ed. A. C. Jacobsen (Leuven: Peeters, 2016), 277–301.

22. *HRg* V, 1.

23. Eusebius of Caesarea, *Hist. Eccl.* VI, 23.

24. Eusebius of Caesarea, *Hist. Eccl.* VI, 36: ἅτε δὴ μεγίστην ἤδη συλλέξαμενον ἐκ τῆς μακρᾶς παρασκευῆς ἕξιν (translation by J. E. L. Oulton).

25. Following the presumptive scheme of N. Lipatov-Chicherin, "Preaching as the Audience Heard it:

the texts of the Munich manuscript, also because the more explicit remnants of the oral delivery eventually could prove to be acceptable even for the written version. For instance, a slip occurring to the preacher in the quotation of a verse may serve after all in order to put an accent on a particular point, as we see with the erroneous rendering of Psalm 21:23 in the *1st Homily on Psalm 67*.[26] Or should we rather think that the mistake of Origen, recorded by the shorthand-writers, went through the transcript and the edited version without anybody noticing and correcting it?[27]

> Καὶ ὁ πατήρ σού ἐστιν ὁ θεὸς καὶ ἀδελφός σου ὁ κύριος ὁ λέγων· διηγήσομαι τὸ ὄνομά σου τοῖς ἀδελφοῖς σου, μᾶλλον δὲ τοῖς ἀδελφοῖς μου, ἐν μέσῳ ἐκκλησίας ὑμνήσω σε (Ps 21:23).

> And your Father is God and your brother is the Lord who says: "I will tell of your name to your brothers," or rather "my brothers, in the midst of the assembly I will sing a hymn to you" (Ps 21:23).

Another example from the same homily suggests likewise that we have rather to reckon with a feature typical of the rhetorical performance (as we shall observe in short in more detail). Among the manifold techniques available to the preacher, he made particular use of *Wortspiele*, playing with words, and to the connected art of *uariatio*, their 'variation,' as we see with the elaborate paraphrase of Luke 22:27 ("For who is greater, the one who is at the table or the one who serves? Is it not the one who is at the table? But I am among you as one who serves").[28] In this case Origen rephrases the contrast between διακονῶν ("one who serves") and ἀνακείμενος ("one who is recumbent") in the Gospel passage through the insertion of a play on words with the latter term: διακείμενος, in the sense of "one who is incumbent" (upon the service).

> Οὐ γάρ ἐστι μεῖζον τὸ προστάξαι τῷ θεῷ τοῦ κληρονόμον αὐτοῦ γενέσθαι· οὐκ ἔστι μεῖζον τὸ προστάξαι τῷ θεῷ τοῦ συγκληρονόμον αὐτῷ γενέσθαι τοῦ Χριστοῦ αὐτοῦ· οὐκ ἔστιν μεῖζον τὸ προστάξαι τῷ θεῷ τοῦ τὸν τηλικοῦτον υἱὸν τοῦ θεοῦ γεγονέναι ἐν μέσῳ ἀνθρώπων, οὐχ ὡς τὸν ἀνακείμενον ἀλλ' ὡς τὸν διακείμενον, τὸν διακονοῦντα (cf. Lk 22:27).

Unedited Transcripts of Patristic Homilies," *Studia Patristica* 64 (2013): 277–97 for patristic homiletics (see especially p. 278).

26. *H67Ps* I, 2 (179:6–8 [p. 143]).

27. As in the opinion of Metzler, "Tachygraphen-Fehler in den neu entdeckten Homilien des Origenes," *Adamantius* 19 (2013): 463–65. Yet the mistaken name of the father of James and John in *H74Ps* 2 (272:16: Ἰάκωβος ὁ τοῦ Ἀλφαίου καὶ Ἰωάννης ὁ ἀδελφὸς αὐτοῦ, "James the son of Alphaeus and John his brother") was not corrected.

28. *H67Ps* I, 2 (177:3–7 [p. 142 modif.]).

For commanding God is not a greater thing than becoming his heir. Commanding God is not a greater thing than becoming a joint heir with Christ himself. Commanding God is not a greater thing than the fact that such a son of God came to be in the midst of men not as one who is recumbent, but as one who is 'incumbent,' one who serves (cf. Lk 22:27).

Further study will hopefully help us to better grasp the literary 'stratigraphy' of the homilies in a tentatively 'diachronic' perspective and to establish with more precision the impact of their oral codes. For the moment, among the many questions raised by the collection as such, let us finally consider a further problem concerning the textual tradition of the homilies inside the exegetical *catenae*. I recalled before how they have contributed to the identification of Origen as the author of the homilies. Yet these fragments still demand a thorough investigation of the ways the compilers worked, inasmuch as they may derive their selections from an exemplar different from that of the Munich manuscript. Though their evidence is mostly rather limited, it can nevertheless help to improve the text of our manuscript.[29] At the same time the *catenae* shed light on the transmission of Origen's writings in the Byzantine world. Apparently, in the 11th century, Nicetas of Heraclea had access for the compilation of his *catena* to a manuscript of the *Homilies on the Psalms* that was not anonymous and was preserved in the Patriarchal Library of Constantinople.[30] In fact, Nicetas did not conceal the patristic sources from which he drew his excerpts, although he adds that he rejected most of Origen, because he was "more elaborate than necessary" (περιεργότερος τοῦ δέοντος).[31] This selective method may explain why the *catena* of Nicetas does not include fragments from nine sermons of the Munich codex. Or otherwise, since he completely ignores the important homilies on Psalm 15 and 73, the exemplar he had may not have included all the texts of our manuscript.

The commentator as preacher: the rhetorical performance of exegesis

If many questions about the composition of the collection will probably remain without answer, we have better chances for an inquiry into the new

---

29. We have excerpts in the following homilies: *H36Ps* I–IV; *H67Ps* I–II; *H74Ps*; *H75Ps*; *H76Ps* I; *H77Ps* I–IX; *H80Ps* I–II; *H81Ps*.

30. Bandt, "Origen in the Catenae on Psalms," 242.

31. Quoted by Bandt, "Origen in the Catenae on Psalms," 237 and n. 14.

homilies as far as their literary profile is concerned. There are indeed many aspects that deserve to be investigated: the more or less definite structure of the homilies with prologue, main body, and conclusion; the careful lemmatization of the verses that are gradually interpreted by the preacher; his lexical command or his stylistic devices; and also, the rhetorical techniques of which he tendentially makes use. Having in mind this ensemble of aspects, I became more and more aware that a commentator on the Bible like Origen, when preaching, could not avoid a certain application of rhetoric, in contrast with the common picture of his substantial disregard of it.[32] Now, to show in detail the rhetorical performance of exegesis that the Alexandrian unfolds would demand more time than the present occasion, since we have to do with a constitutive feature of the texts. Therefore, I shall restrict myself to an analysis of the prologues in the Munich homilies without further recalling here some of their most frequent rhetorical traits.[33]

As we know from his other writings, Origen pays attention to the prefaces both in the commentaries and in the treatises, inasmuch as they not only are often directed to particular addressees but also hint at the circumstances of the work or at the subject the author is going to treat[34]. Homilies, at first sight, present a different case, since they normally do not mention particular addressees, except those held in Jerusalem on the 1st Book of Kingdoms in the presence of bishop Alexander. Yet the audience attending the sermons demands in principle a more direct approach than in commentaries or treatises.[35] Therefore, we frequently observe the thoughtful mood through which Origen introduces his speech, though he does not follow the same pattern in every case and sometimes he even proceeds to comment without any preamble. Obviously, when he began to preach on a new psalm, there were, so to say, obligatory preliminaries as the explanation of the rubrics, with a short introduction on the author and the title. In spite of that, the Alexandrian does not always,

---

32. Apart from few important exceptions as Karen Jo Torjesen, *Hermeneutical Procedure and Theological Method in Origen's Exegesis.* (Berlin: Walter de Gruyter, 1986).

33. I present a preliminary overview in Lorenzo Perrone, "Origen's Interpretation of the Psalter Revisited: The Nine Homilies on Psalm 77(78) in the Munich Codex," *Annali di storia dell'esegesi* 36 (2019) 139–61. Reprinted in Perrone, «*Meine Zunge ist mein Ruhm,*» 199–219.

34. Adele Monaci-Castagno, "Origene e Ambrogio: l'indipendenza dell'intellettuale e le pretese del patronato," in *Origeniana Octava: Origen and the Alexandrian Tradition*, ed. Lorenzo Perrone, (Leuven: Peeters, 2003) 165–93, analyses the relations between some prefaces and their addressees.

35. See, for example, the prologue of *HIer* XIX,10 (165:11–12): Ταῦτά μοι ἐν προοιμίῳ εἴρηται, διεγείροντι καὶ ἐγείροντι καὶ ἐμαυτὸν καὶ τοὺς ἀκούοντας ἐπὶ τὸ προσέχειν τοῖς ἀναγνωσθεῖσιν, "I said this in the preamble awaking and exciting myself and the audience so that they be attentive to the texts that have been read."

or immediately, comply with such a task, as a 'grammarian of the Scripture' would be expected to do.[36] Nor does he generally take his point of departure from the most common habit of a teacher who starts to comment on a text either by connecting his speech to the psalm verses that have just been read or by recalling his preceding exposition. A unique occurrence of this kind figures in the *3rd Homily on Psalm 36*, where Origen—alluding initially to Psalm 36:14a-b—reminds his listeners that he "has spoken recently about the sword and the bow of the impious."[37] In this respect we notice some differences with the prologues of the *Homilies on Jeremiah*, where we can find formulations *in medias res*, pointing at once to "the beginning of the reading,"[38] or to "the lemma that has been read"[39].

Nonetheless, the typologies of the prefaces seem largely to converge in both series of the Greek sermons. Without tracing too rigid outlines among them, they may include prologues (a) with a doctrinal statement, b) of didascalic or historical nature, c) with a more circumstantial profile, d) of an apparently paradoxical character (in other words, implying an *aprosdoketon*). Apart from their length, which varies from one homily to another, a frequent feature consists in their opening with an axiomatic sentence that pregnantly condenses an important point of doctrine and proves useful as a prelude to the subject of the homily.[40] Such introductory statements more specifically address the doctrine of God or man, and also the hermeneutics required by the Scripture. In many cases they take their inspiration from a biblical quotation, be this connected or not with the psalm to be commented upon. For instance, the beginning of the *6th Homily on Psalm 77* insinuates with Psalm 77:38a ("Yet he is compassionate") the idea that God is "merciful" (οἰκτίρμων) by stressing his patience in the face of the many sins committed by men. So the initial sentence

---

36. Lorenzo Perrone, "Ne corrumpas (Sal 74, 1): l'omelia di Origene sul Salmo 74 nel codice di Monaco," in *Amicorum Munera: Studi in onore di Antonio V. Nazzaro*, ed. G. Luongo (Naples: Satura Editrice, 2016), 99–113.

37. *H36Ps* III, 1 (139:1–2): Προλαβόντες πρώην ἐλέγομεν περὶ τῆς ῥομφαίας καὶ τῶν τόξων τοῦ ἀσεβοῦς. It is not clear to what homily Origen is referring.

38. *HIer* III, 1 (20:13–14): Φησὶν ὁ Κύριος ἐν τῇ ἀρχῇ τῶν ἀναγνωσθέντων περὶ τοῦ Ἰσραήλ, ὅτι ἔρημος αὐτῷ οὐκ ἐγένετο οὐδὲ γῆ κεχερσωμένη (Jr 2:31), "The Lord, at the beginning of what has been read concerning Israel, says that 'he has not become a wilderness' to him or 'a dried-out land.'"

39. *HIer* IV, 1 (22:5–6): Αὐτὸ τὸ ῥητὸν τῆς ἀναγνωσθείσης λέξεως ἔχει τι ἀσαφές, ὅπερ πρότερον νοηθήτω, "The letter itself of the passage that has been read, has something obscure. We should first understand it." For an examination of the prologues in *HIer* see the analysis of Nautin (SC 232:123–25).

40. For the sake of commodity we can range into this group *H15Ps* I; *H36Ps* II; *H73Ps* III; *H74Ps*; *H75Ps*; *H76Ps* IV; *H77Ps* II; *H77Ps* III; *H77Ps* IV; *H77Ps* VI; *H77Ps* VII; *H77Ps* VIII; *H77Ps* IX; *H80Ps* I; *H80Ps*.

echoes a motive particularly dear to the Alexandrian and expressed, in a compelling way, also by the *1st Homily on Jeremiah* (and again by the *7th*).[41]

H77Ps VI,1 (420,1–6)

Τοῖς ἔργοις μᾶλλον ἢ τοῖς λόγοις φαίνεται ὅτι ὁ θεός ἐστιν ὁ *οἰκτίρμων* (Ps 77:38a).

Τίς γὰρ κατανοῶν τὸν κόσμον καὶ μάλιστα τὰ ἐπὶ γῆς πράγματα καὶ τὰς ἐν ἀνθρώποις τοσαύτας ἁμαρτίας οὐ θαυμάζει τὴν τοῦ θεοῦ μακροθυμίαν καὶ χρηστότητα, ἀνεχομένου τῶν τοσούτων καὶ τηλικούτων πταισμάτων καὶ μὴ χρωμένου τῇ ἐξουσίᾳ κατὰ τῶν ἀνθρώπων; *Κρίνων γὰρ κατὰ βραχὺ τόπον δίδωσι μετανοίας* (Wis 12:10; Hb 12:17).

God shows that he is the "merciful" (Ps 77:38a) one by deeds more than by words.

For who observes the world, especially the earthly affairs and the amount of sins among men, does not marvel at the patience and goodness of God, putting up with so many and such great offenses and not making full use of his authority against human beings? For "judging them little by little he gives them an opportunity to repent" (Wis 12:10; Hb 12:17).[42]

HIer I,1 (1,1–6)

Ὁ θεὸς εἰς ἀγαθοποιΐαν πρόχειρός ἐστι, εἰς δὲ τὸ κολάσαι τοὺς ἀξίους κολάσεως μελλητής.

Δυνάμενος γοῦν ἐπ-αγαγεῖν τὴν κόλασιν τοῖς ὑπ' αὐτοῦ καταδικαζομένοις μετὰ σιωπῆς, μετὰ τοῦ μὴ προδιαμαρτύρασθαι, οὐδαμῶς τοῦτο ποιεῖ· ἀλλὰ κἂν καταδικάζῃ λέγει, τοῦ λέγειν αὐτῷ προκειμένου ἐπὶ τὸ ἐπιστρέψαι ἀπὸ τῆς καταδίκης τὸν καταδικασθησόμενον.

God is ready to do good but hesitant to punish those who deserve punishment.

In fact, though he can inflict punishment on those whom he has sentenced without saying anything, without prior warning, he never does. For when he sentences, he says so, and the speaking is a way to turn the person to be condemned away from the sentencing.[43]

As for the approach required by the interpretation of the Holy Scriptures, the best example is provided by the prologue of the *1st Homily on Psalm 36*.

41. The theme figures also in *HIer* VII, 1 (51:18–21), with the quotation of Wis 12:10 (Hb 12:17) as in *H77Ps* VI, 1. For the English translation see Origen, *Homilies on Jeremiah. Homily on 1 Kings 28*, tr. J. Clark Smith, (Washington, DC: The Catholic University of America Press, 1998), 68.

Ὁ *κρίνων κατὰ βραχὺ* θεὸς τοὺς κολαζομένους *δίδωσι τόπον μετανοίας* (Wis 12:10; Hb 12:17), καὶ οὐκ ἅμα τῷ ἁμαρτῆσαι κολάζων φέρει τὴν συντέλειαν τῆς κολάσεως ἐπὶ τὸν ἡμαρτηκότα. Διὰ τοῦτο *κατὰ βραχὺ κρίνων* (Wis 12:10; Hb 12:17) κολάζει.

God, who judges "little by little" those punished, "gives a chance of repentance" (Wis 12:10; Hb 12:17), and, by not punishing all at once for the sinning, holds off for the sinner the consummation of the punishment. Because of this, by "judging little by little" (Wis 12:10; Hb 12:17) he punishes.

42. Transl. p. 352 (modif.).

43. Origen, *Homilies on Jeremiah*, 3.

Here Origen first exploits Hebrews 1:1 ("God spoke to our forefathers through the prophets at many times and in various ways") to assert the multiple senses of Scripture: the mystical, the prophetical or Christological, and the moral. Subsequently, the Alexandrian professes to comply with this hermeneutical criterion by attempting to catch from every scriptural passage its meaning as a text of prophetical, mystical (allegorical) or ethical character, before he proceeds to qualify Psalm 36 as "wholly moral" (δι' ὅλων.. ἠθικός).[44] Yet we may add other prefaces that aim at defining in advance the principles for a correct interpretation. In the *2nd Homily on Psalm 15* Origen evokes the apostolic authority for a Christological explanation of the Old Testament, on account of the quotation of Psalm 15:8–10 by the book of Acts (Acts 2:25–28).[45] In its turn, the prologue of the *2nd Homily on Ps 67* happily combines the request for a pneumatic exegesis worthy of God's commands with the recommendation of a searching attitude that should preserve us from a simplistic understanding of his words. This preface thus develops in a more elaborate form an idea that also appears in the shorter introduction to the *12th Homily on Jeremiah*.

H67Ps II, 1 (200,1–11)

Οὐκ ἔστιν δυνατὸν [τοῦ] ποιῆσαι τὰ προστάσσομενα ὑπὸ τοῦ θεοῦ ἐν ταῖς θείαις γραφαῖς ἢ τοῦ Χριστοῦ ἢ τοῦ ἁγίου πνεύματος μὴ πρότερον νενοηκότα τί ἐστι τὸ λεγόμενον.

Πολλαχοῦ δὲ δοκοῦμεν νοεῖν τινα, ἃ προσετάχθημεν· ἐξετάζοντες δὲ καὶ ἐρευνῶντες εἰ ἄξιόν ἐστι τὸ προστεταγμένον τοῦ προστάξαντος καὶ εἰ ἐμφαίνει τι μέγεθος ἄξιον τοῦ εἰπόντος θεοῦ, οὐ πάνυ τι αὐτὸ εὑρίσκομεν <ἐν> τῷ τοιούτῳ.

Εἶτα αὐτὸς ὁ λόγος ἡμᾶς παρακαλεῖ, κατὰ τὸ *ζητεῖτε καὶ εὑρήσετε* (Mt 7:7), καὶ ἐπὶ τὸ ζητῆσαι ὅπερ ἐδοκοῦμεν πρὶν ζητῆσαι νενοηκέναι, ἵνα ζητήσαντες εὕρωμεν οὖν ἐν τοῖς προστάγμασι τοῦ θεοῦ <τι> ἄξιον τοῦ προστάξαντος καὶ οὐχ ὑπὸ τῶν τυχόντων γινόμενον, ἀλλ' ὑπὸ τῶν τοιούτων καὶ τηλικούτων, οἳ ποιοῦσι καὶ τὰ ἄλλα μεγάλα καὶ θεῖα προστάγματα τοῦ θεοῦ.

It is not possible to do the things commanded by God or by Christ or the Holy Spirit in the divine Scriptures without first having perceived what is said.

Often, however, we seem to perceive things that we have been commanded; but when we examine and investigate whether or not what is commanded befits the one who commands and whether it unveils a greatness worthy of God as the speaker, we do not find that at all in such a command.

---

44. *H36Ps* I, 1 (113:1–7). See Perrone, «*Meine Zunge ist mein Ruhm*», 232–34.

45. *H15Ps* II, 1 (91:1–7). In this case the preacher mentions the preceding sermon (ll. 7–9): Εὕρομεν δέ τι ἐπὶ τούτου τοῦ ψαλμοῦ καινότερον, ὅτι οὐχ ὑπὸ δύο καὶ τριῶν μόνων μαρτύρων ἡρμηνεύθη τι τῶν ἀπὸ τοῦ ψαλμοῦ ἀναγνωσθέντων, "We have recently found something in the case of this psalm, for the things we have read from the Psalm have not been interpreted by two or three witnesses alone" (p. 58).

Then, the Logos himself, according to the words "Search and you will find" (Mt 7:7), exhorts us to search even concerning what we earlier seemed to have understood before searching, so that when searching we may find in the commands of God something worthy of the one who commands and that is brought about not just by any chance person, but only by such and such great persons who do the other great and divine commands of God.[46]

HIer XII, 1 (85,18–23)

Ὃ προστάσσεται ὁ προπφήτης λέγειν ὑπὸ θεοῦ, ὀφείλει ἄξιον εἶναι τοῦ θεοῦ, [οὐ] φαίνεται δὲ ὅτι οὐκ ἄξιόν ἐστι τοῦ θεοῦ, μενόντων ἡμῶν ἐπὶ τοῦ γράμματος, ὥστε εἰπεῖν ἄλλον τινὰ ἀκούσαντα τοῦ γράμματος· μωρία ἐστὶ ταῦτα τὰ γράμματα. Τοῦτο δὲ ἐρεῖ ψυχικός· ψυχικὸς γὰρ ἄνθρωπος οὐ δέχεται τὰ τοῦ πνεύματος τοῦ θεοῦ· μωρία γὰρ αὐτῷ ἐστιν (1 Cor 2:14).

What the prophet is appointed to say for God ought to be worthy of God, but it appears that it is not worthy of God when we rely on the letter, for someone might say when hearing the letter: these texts are foolish. But the unspiritual man will say this, for the "unspiritual man does not receive what is of the spirit of God. For it is folly to him" (1 Cor 2:14).[47]

The prologues of a historical or didascalic nature present preliminary information on biblical matters related to the text or illustrate situations and experiences that should serve as paradigms, as we see respectively in the *1st* and the *2nd Homily on Psalm 76*. The preface of the former, a brief paragraph on the explanation of the title ("Regarding completion. Over Idithoun. Pertaining to Asaph. A Psalm"), describes, among the priests holding services in the Temple, those who were in charge of the singing, both as composers of psalms and hymns and as their performers. The preacher, while delivering his concise instruction with a hint at the first book of *Chronicles*, does not omit to stress that "the Holy Spirit has written" this narrative "for the edification of those who pay attention."[48] In its turn, the prologue of the *2nd Homily on Psalm 76* expressly points to an 'example' (παράδειγμα). As I signaled earlier,[49] it is the most elaborate of the new homilies, inasmuch as the illustration of a series of learning experiences, both religious and mundane, that in truth do not yet represent a real apprenticeship, is artfully accompanied by the repetition, as a

---

46. Transl. p. 158 (modif.).

47. Origen, *Homilies on Jeremiah*, 110.

48. *H76Ps* I, 1 (293:1–11). See especially ll. 4–5: προσέχων ὅτι πάντα τὸ ἅγιον πνεῦμα ὑπὲρ οἰκοδομῆς τῶν προσεχόντων ἔγραψε. For another example of historical preface see *H77Ps* V, 1 (409:1–410,1) on Ps 77:30b-31a. In this case it preludes to a question on the two narratives of the quail (Ex 16:13; Nm 11:31–32; 21:5).

49. See above, p. 16.

refrain, of verse 11a: "Now I have begun" (*νῦν ἠρξάμην*). The first section of this long preface will suffice to prove its rhetorical qualities.[50]

Ὁ βιοὺς κατὰ θεὸν πολλάκις ἐν προοιμίοις ὢν τοῦ βίου τοῦ κατὰ θεὸν οἴεται τὴν ἀρχὴν πεποιῆσθαι τοῦ βιοῦν καθὸ χρὴ βιοῦν· ἐπὰν δὲ νοήσας τὴν διαφορὰν τοῦ προοιμίου τοῦ κατὰ θεὸν βίου γένηται μετὰ τὸ προοίμιον ἐπὶ τὴν ὁδὸν τοῦ κατὰ θεὸν βίου, ἐπιγινώσκων ὅτι πρότερον μὲν ἐδόκει ἄρχεσθαι, οὐκ ἦν δὲ ἀρξάμενος, ὕστερον δὲ ἔγνω τίς ἡ ἀρχή, φησὶ τὸ *νῦν ἠρξάμην* (Ps 76:11a).

Εἰ δὲ χρὴ ἀπὸ παραδείγματος καὶ τοῦτο σαφέστερον ποιῆσαι τοῖς ἀκούουσι, προσέχωμεν τοῖς λεχθησομένοις.

Πολλάκις ἐπιδούς τις ἑαυτὸν τῇ κατὰ Χριστὸν θεοσεβείᾳ κατὰ τὰς ἀρχὰς τοῦ ἐπιδεδωκέναι ἑαυτὸν ἤτοι αὐτὸς καθ᾽ αὑτὸν μὴ συνεὶς τὸν τρόπον καθ᾽ ὃν δεῖ θεοσεβεῖν, ἢ καὶ διδασκάλοις περιπεσὼν οὐ δεξιοῖς, δοκεῖ μὲν θεοσεβεῖν κατὰ Χριστόν, οὐδέπω δὲ ὃν δεῖ τρόπον θεοσεβῶν· ἐπὰν ὕστερον ζητήσας εὕρῃ, εὐεργετηθεὶς ὑπὸ τοῦ θεοῦ, λάβῃ ἢ εὐτυχήσῃ διδασκάλων ὁδηγούντων καλῶς, μετὰ τὸ πολὺν χρόνον πεποιηκέναι ἐν τῷ δοκεῖν εἶναι ἐν τῇ θεοσεβείᾳ, ἐλθὼν ἀληθῶς ἐπὶ τὴν θεοσέβειαν ἐρεῖ· *νῦν ἠρξάμην* (Ps 76:11a).

Often someone who lives according to God, at the beginning of his life according to God, thinks to have made the beginning of living as he ought to live, but when having understood the difference between the beginning and a life according to God, he comes to the way of the life according to God, recognizing that, at first, he seemed to be beginning when he was not actually beginning, but later he knew what the beginning was, he says: "Now I have begun" (Ps 76:11a).

But, if this should be made clearer to the listeners by an example, let us pay attention to what will be said.

Often someone, who has embraced the religion according to Christ—at the beginning of his embracing, because he is, on his own, unaware of how one should practice religion or because he has fallen among teachers who are unfit—, seems to practice the religion according to Christ, but is not actually doing so as he should. Yet, after he searched and benefited from God, if he finally finds, takes, or by happy chance meets teachers who guide him on the proper way, after spending much time thinking that he was already practicing the religion, once he has truly come to the religion of God, he says: "Now I have begun" (Ps 76:11a).

We would like to have more prologues likely to conjure the particular circumstances in which Origen preached (as it happens with the *1st* and the *5th Homilies on Kingdoms*). On the contrary, the new collection also demonstrates to what extent the mind of the Alexandrian is constantly centered on

---

50. *H76Ps* II, 1 (313:1–14 [p. 252 modif.]).

the Scriptures and his task as commentator. Actually, even the two cases which do carry some traces of a somehow recognizable situation—the *1st Homily on Psalm 67* and the *1st Homily on Psalm 73*—cannot but confirm the dominant picture of the exegetical or, to say it in etymological sense, "biblio-centric" horizon of Origen. Undoubtedly, the setting of the *1st Homily on Psalm 67* is far more perceptible, since it evokes the presence of a bishop who has just introduced the preacher to the audience with words of high esteem and praise. Given this presentation, it is natural to imagine that it was not the usual assembly of Caesarea. However, the Alexandrian turns the eulogy of the bishop first into a tribute to his modesty and then into a prayer for himself, by choosing to recite Psalm 69 (one of the psalms that had just been read) and asking those in attendance to do the same with him. Though prayer often accompanies the sermons, and not only at their beginning or conclusion,[51] the occurrence is rather unusual: certainly the repetition of Psalm 69 betrays in the preacher a concern for his impending duty, so that he needs to ask for the aid of God, on the one hand, to defeat his adversaries and, on the other, to rejoice the listeners with his words.[52] As a consequence, the personal aspect results once more in the assertion of Origen's spiritual hermeneutics. The same thing happens with the very brief preface to the *1st Homily on Psalm 73*, though it is more elusive as to its external circumstances. Notwithstanding that, we may infer that the community had just prayed for God's help in a period of drought, so that the Alexandrian is able to appropriate this prayer for the purpose of his pneumatic interpretation.[53]

> Δεηθῶμεν καὶ περὶ τοῦ πνευματικοῦ ὑετοῦ, ἵνα ταῖς πνευματικαῖς νεφέλαις ἐντείληται βρέξαι ἐπὶ τὰς ψυχὰς ἡμῶν ὑετὸν ὁ θεὸς καὶ μὴ τριβόλους βλαστήσωμεν, ἵνα μὴ [γῆ] ἀδόκιμος γένηται καὶ κατάρας ἐγγύς (Hbr 6:8), τίκτῃ δὲ βοτάνην εὔθετον (Hbr 6:7) καὶ γεννήσῃ καρπὸν ἑκατονταπλασίονα (Lk 8:8).

> Let us pray also for the spiritual rain: that God might command the spiritual clouds to shower rain upon our souls and that we might not sprout thorny plants, so that [the land] might not become "worthless and in danger of being cursed" (Hbr 6:8), but might bear "a useful crop" (Hbr 6:7) and bring forth a hundredfold fruit (Lk 8:8).

---

51. Lorenzo Perrone, *La preghiera secondo Origene. L'impossibilità donata* (Brescia: Morcelliana, 2011), 358–428.

52. *H67Ps* I, 1 (173:1–174,19).

53. *H73Ps* I, 1 (225:1–4 [p. 178 modif.]).

Finally, also in some prefaces of the homilies we can discern a 'surprise effect,' reminding the rhetorical figure of the ἀπροσδόκητον ("something unexpected"), as we observe it in other writings of Origen. It is an initial moment of apparent 'estrangement' or deliberate 'divagation,' that should move the readers and/or listeners—if not the author himself in their stead—to ask: "What does this preamble mean?" In the Greek *Homilies on the Psalms* we find such interrogative sentences at the end of the prologues to the *2nd Homily on Psalm 67* and the *2nd Homily on Psalm 80*. But they appear likewise in the Latin homilies, as shown by the prefaces of the *1st Homily on Psalm 37* and the *1st Homily on Psalm 38*.[54] A sample from the *2nd Homily on Psalm 80* can help us to understand the purpose of this kind of introductory 'digression': its intent is clearly to involve the audience by arousing its interest for what the preacher is going to say. In this way the simile of the musical instruments, apparently out of place, opens the way to the charming image of God as musician and of the prophets as the instruments of his heavenly music.[55]

Τῶν ὀργάνων ἃ μὲν ἔχει τὴν ἁρμονίαν τὴν μουσικήν, ἃ δέ ἐστιν ἀνάρμοστα. Ὁ οὖν γεγυμνασμένος ἐν τοῖς μουσικοῖς ἔργοις καὶ τὴν τέχνην ἐκείνην ἀνειληφὼς ἐπιλέγεται τὴν ἁρμόνιον λύραν ἢ κιθάραν ἢ ψαλτήριον, καὶ ἐπιλεξάμενος ἐπιδείκνυται δύναμιν τὴν ἐν αὐτῷ καὶ τέχνην τὴν μουσικήν· φεύγει δὲ προτροπάδην[56], μάλιστα ἐάν τις ἢ κιθάρα ἢ λύρα ἢ ψαλτήριον ἀνάρμοστον ᾖ, ἵνα μὴ ἀσχημονῇ διὰ τὸ ὄργανον ὡς οὐχ ὑπηρετοῦν τῇ τέχνῃ ὁ τεχνίτης.

Πρὸς τί μοι οὖν ταῦτα εἴρηται ἢ ὅτι πάντες ἄνθρωποι οἱονεὶ κιθάραι εἰσὶ καὶ ψαλτήρια καὶ λύραι;

Καὶ ζητεῖ ὁ τεχνίτης θεὸς λύραν μουσικῶς ἡρμοσμένην, κιθάραν καλῶς ἡρμοσμένην, ψαλτήριον ὃν δεῖ τρόπον τὰς χορδὰς ἔχον τετονωμένας· καὶ συγκρίνας ὅπου εὑρίσκοι τὰ τοιαῦτα ὁ θεός, δείκνυσι τὴν οὐράνιον μουσικήν. Ἐὰν δὲ ἀπορῇ τῶν ὀργάνων ἑαυτοῦ ὁ θεός, οὐ παρ' ἑαυτὸν ἀλλὰ παρὰ τὴν τῶν ὀργάνων ἀπορίαν, σιωπᾷ.

---

54. *H37PsL* I, 1 (246:7–8 Prinzivalli): *Quo nobis tendit ista praefatio?*, "What is the aim of this preface?"; *H38PsL* I, 2 (326:1–2): *Sed dicat aliquis fortassis auditorum: quid haec pertinent ad psalmum?*, "But perhaps someone in the audience could say: What has this to do with the Psalm?" For similar examples in other writings see *CIo* I, 2, 9 (5,9 Preuschen): Τί δὴ πάντα ταῦθ' ἡμῖν βούλεται, "Now, what is the meaning of all this?"; *Orat* II,1 (298:20–23): ὑμᾶς ἀπορεῖν τί δή ποτε, περὶ εὐχῆς προκειμένου ἡμῖν τοῦ λόγου, ταῦτα ἐν προοιμίοις περὶ τῶν ἀδυνάτων ἀνθρώποις δυνατῶν χάριτι θεοῦ γινομένων εἴρηται, "You will wonder why, having to deal with the discourse on prayer, I have spoken in the preamble about the things impossible to humankind, yet becoming possible through the grace of God?"; *HIos* I, 3 (100), as transitional formula for the allegorical interpretation: *Quo igitur nobis haec cuncta prospiciunt?*, "What does then all this suggest to us?"

55. *H80Ps* II,1 (496:1–13 [p. 425 modif.]).

56. The rare occurrence of the adverb προτροπάδην—used by Celsus and Origen also in *CC* VI,14—is probably a (ironical) reminiscence of Plato, *Symp.* 221b: σχεδὸν γάρ τι τῶν οὕτω διακειμένων ἐν τῷ πολέμῳ οὐδὲ ἅπτονται, ἀλλὰ τοὺς προτροπάδην φεύγοντας διώκουσι, "for those who behave so are not touched in war; those only are pursued who are running away headlong."

Among the instruments, some are endowed with the harmony of music, but others are devoid of it. Therefore, the one who is exerted in musical activities and has developed this art, chooses a lyre, a cithara, or a harp that are harmonious and after choosing them shows his ability and the art of music. Yet he "runs away headlong," especially if there is a cithara, a lyra, or a harp devoid of harmony, because such an instrument will embarrass him, giving the impression that the performing artist is lacking in skill.

To what purpose did I say this, if not because all human beings are, as it were, citharas, harps, and lyres?

And God, as a performing artist, seeks a lyre musically in tune, a cithara well-tuned, a harp that has well braced strings. God, after distinguishing where he can find such instruments, performs heavenly music. But if God lacks his (proper) instruments, not by his own fault, but on account of a lack of instruments, he is silent.

The Preacher of the *Homilies on the Psalms*: Neither a Grammarian nor a Philosopher, but the Teacher of the Logos

Was there anybody in the audience of Caesarea who could appreciate the eventual allusion to the *Symposion*, Plato's dialogue quoted by Origen in the *Against Celsus*,[57] or even the hidden reference to Homer's *Iliad* in the preface of the *5th Homily on Psalm 77*?[58] As a former grammarian and a reader of philosophers, the Alexandrian was well acquainted with the two classical authors. In both cases, his rephrasing of them betrays a mastery of language concurring in its turn with the rhetorical performance unfolded by the sermons. Moreover, the preacher displays his grammatical skills on other occasions: for instance, in the prefaces to the *1st* and the *4th Homily on Psalm 36*, by commenting in the former the verb παραζηλοῦν in Psalm 36:1b ("Do not fret among wicked people "),[59] in the latter the word διαβήματα in verse 23a ("A person's

---

57. *CC* IV, 39.

58. *H77Ps* V, 1 (409:12–13): Πάντων γὰρ κόρος ἐστίν, οὐχ ὕπνου μόνον, ἀλλὰ καὶ βρωμάτων κόρος ἐστίν, "For there is *satiety of all things*, not *sleep* alone, but there is also satiety of foods." Cf. Hom., *Il.* 13:636: πάντων μὲν κόρος ἐστί, καὶ ὕπνου, "There is satiety of all things, also of sleep."

59. *H36Ps* I, 1 (113:20–25): Τίς οὖν ἡ διαφορὰ τοῦ 'παραζηλοῦν' παρὰ τὸ 'ζηλοῦν' κατανοητέον. Οὐ πάνυ τίς ἐστιν ἡ λέξις Ἑλληνικὴ οὐδὲ τέτριπται ἐν τῇ συνηθείᾳ τῶν Ἑλλήνων οὔτε τῶν φιλολόγων οὔτε τῶν ἰδιωτικώτερον φραζόντων, ἀλλ' ἔοικε βεβιασμένη γενέσθαι ὑπὸ τῶν ἑρμηνευτῶν βουλομένων ἑρμηνεῦσαι τὸ Ἑβραϊκὸν ῥητὸν καὶ τὴν διαφορὰν παραστῆσαι κατὰ τὸ δυνατὸν ἀνθρωπίνῃ φύσει 'ζήλου' καὶ 'παραζηλώσεως', "One must comprehend, then, what distinguishes 'make jealous' from 'be jealous.' The Greek wording is not ordinarily employed either in literary or in colloquial Greek, but it seems to have been forced into service by translators wanting to translate the Hebrew statement and to set forth, as far as possible for human nature, the distinction between 'jealousy' and 'making jealous'" (pp. 76–77 modif.).

steps are directed by the Lord").[60] In both passages Origen notices that the Greek rendering of the Hebrew text, adopted by the Septuagint translators, is unusual among Greek-speakers, both uncultivated persons and those who care for the propriety of language or, to use the term of the *1st Homily on Psalm 36*, are "fond of words" (φιλόλογοι). The Alexandrian, in his solicitude about the correct semantics of the Greek Bible, goes once so far as to impart a lesson of grammar to the attendants. It is not a novel point, inasmuch as he formulates it also in the *Treatise on Prayer*, but this time his argument proves at first to be more 'pedantic.' So, in the *1st Homily on Psalm 67*, before explaining the verb ἀναστήτω in verse 2a ("Let God rise up"), he remarks that in the Bible the imperative mood is often used instead of the optative.[61] As in the *Peri euchês*, Origen exemplifies this peculiarity with the Lord's Prayer, but not content with that he rewrites in the optative mood all the verbs both in the "Our Father" and in Psalm 67:2a–4. That notwithstanding, after he has stressed the difference between a command to God and a prayer to him, with an interpretive turn he boldly returns to the imperative mood by asserting that one can use it even towards God, provided he does it with the liberty of the sons of God.[62] Grammar, then, like rhetoric, may prove a useful tool for a powerful exegesis.

In particular, the preacher relies on his philological skills when he has recourse to textual criticism.[63] Several passages of the sermons allow us to glimpse the immense work that Origen presumably was still doing for the

---

60. *H36Ps* IV, 1 (157:1–7): Παρὰ κυρίου φησὶ τὰ διαβήματα ἀνθρώπου κατευθύνεται (Ps 36:23a).Τὴν λέξιν τὴν διαβήματα, οὐ συνήθη οὖσαν παρὰ τοῖς ἑλληνίζουσιν οὔτε παρὰ τοῖς ἰδιωτεύουσιν οὔτε παρὰ τοῖς δοκοῦσιν ἀκριβῶσαι τὰ περὶ λέξεως, ὁμοίως ἐξέθεντο <οἱ> ἑρμηνεύσαντες, ἑνὸς μόνου ἰσοδυναμοῦντος τῇ λέξει τεθέντος, βουλόμενοι δουλεῦσαι ἐτυμολογίᾳ ἑβραϊκῇ <καὶ> ἐπιστῆσαι τὸν ἀναγινώσκοντα τὴν γραφὴν τί σημαίνεται ἐκ τοῦ ὀνόματος τοῦ διαβήματα, "*A person's steps*, it says, *are directed by the Lord* (Ps 36:23a). The word 'steps' is not customary among Greek-speakers, either among those who speak in simple language or among those who seem to care about their wording; likewise, the translators selected it, when it is the only word that has the same force as the (Hebrew) wording, intending to be faithful to the original Hebrew [and] that one reading the Scriptures should ascertain what is signified by the word 'steps'" (p. 120 modif.). There are apparently no hexaplaric readings for Ps 36:23a (see Field, 1875, II, 144).

61. *H67Ps* I, 2 (175:1–2): Πρῶτον εἰδέναι χρὴ ὅτι ἔθος ἐστὶ τῇ γραφῇ πολλαχοῦ τοῖς προστακτικοῖς ἀντὶ εὐκτικῶν χρῆσθαι, "It must be known first that it is custom in Scripture often to use imperatives in place of the optatives" (p. 140 modif.). In *Orat* XXIV, 5 (355:22–356, 6) the examples are taken from the Psalms.

62. *H67Ps* I, 2 (175:19–20): Εἴποι δ' ἄν τις ἐμοῦ τολμηρότερος ὅτι ταῦτα δύναται εἰρῆσθαι καὶ ἐπὶ τῶν προστακτικῶν, "Someone bolder than I am may say that these things may even be spoken as imperatives" (p. 141).

63. On Origen as philologist see Bernhard Neuschäfer, *Origenes als Philologe*, (Basel: Friedrich Reinhardt, 1987) and Peter W. Martens, *Origen and Scripture. The Contours of the Exegetical Life* (Oxford: Oxford University Press, 2012).

Hexapla. He indeed refers to his huge synopsis of the Old Testament more frequently than in the *Homilies on Jeremiah*, occasionally by bringing in the reference also to the Hebrew text together with the "editions" (ἐκδόσεις), even if he does not mention the name of the other translations next to the Septuagint. As we hear from his letter to Africanus or the one to some Alexandrian friends,[64] the philological activity for assuring a correct text of the Bible, including the New Testament, took him a lot of time. In the *1st Homily on Psalm 77*, while criticizing Marcion's arbitrary treatment of the Gospel text, he does not hesitate to claim his labors and merits as a philologist.[65]

> Καὶ ὅσα μὲν διὰ τὸν θεὸν καὶ τὴν χάριν αὐτοῦ ἐκάμομεν, συνεξετάζοντες καὶ τὰ Εβραϊκὰ καὶ τὰς ἐκδόσεις ὑπὲρ τοῦ ἰδεῖν τὴν διόρθωσιν τῶν σφαλμάτων, οἶδεν· ὅσα δὲ θέλομεν καὶ περὶ τὰ λείποντα ποιῆσαι, αὐτὸς εὐοδώσει.

> And as much as we labored through God and his grace, examining together both the Hebrew and the versions in order to see to the correction of errors, [God] knows. What we intend to do about the rest he will guide.

Yet, when we try to draw a profile of the preacher, we should not forget that grammar, after all, has an instrumental value for the Alexandrian and his self-awareness. Concerning this task we are, in a sense, luckier than with regard to some of the questions we examined before, since we have some remarkable clues to sketch, at least, a tentative portrait. As witnessed by his claim as a biblical philologist, our homilies make once again evident that Origen is much less reserved on his person, or his own experience, than one would think.[66] In the wake of such 'confessions,' the *2nd Homily on Psalm 77* unveils a crucial autobiographical frame by a passage that has already become famous. It is a short digression in the midst of what surely is the most elaborate and impressive exegesis in the new collection, as the Alexandrian quotes a large pericope from the book of Hosea (Hos 6:11–7:2) to support his interpretation of "Ephraim's sons" in Ps 77:9a as "the heretics," that is the Marcionites and the Gnostics.[67]

---

64. Lorenzo Perrone, "Origene a sua immagine: frammenti di autobiografia dalle lettere," in *Knowledge and Wisdom. Archaeological and Historical Essays in Honour of Leah Di Segni*, ed. G. C. Bottini, L. D. Chrupcala, J. Patrich (Milan: Edizioni Terra Santa, 2014), 311–27.

65. *H77Ps* I, 1 (351:24–352:2 [p. 288]).

66. Lorenzo Perrone, "Origen's 'Confessions': Recovering the Traces of a Self-Portrait," in *Studia Patristica. Vol. LVI/4*, ed. M. Vinzent (Leuven: Peeters, 2013), 3–27 and Perrone, "Origene a sua immagine."

67. *H77Ps* II,4 (371:15–372:6 [p. 307 modif.]). For other examples of textual criticism in the homilies, see Antonio Cacciari, "Nuova luce sull'officina origeniana. I LXX e gli 'altri'," *Adamantius* 20 (2014): 217–25; and Lorenzo Perrone, "The Find of the Munich Codex: A Collection of 29 Homilies on the Psalms," in *Origeniana Undecima. Origen and Origenism in the History of Western Thought*, ed. A-Ch. Jacobsen, (Leuven: Peeters, 2016), 209–20.

Καὶ τοῦτο τῇ πείρᾳ ἴσμεν· ἐν γὰρ τῇ πρώτῃ ἡμῶν ἡλικίᾳ πάνυ ἤνθουν αἱ αἱρέσεις καὶ ἐδόκουν πολλοὶ εἶναι οἱ ἐν αὐταῖς συναγόμενοι. Ὅσοι γὰρ ἦσαν λίχνοι περὶ τὰ μαθήματα τοῦ Χριστοῦ, μὴ εὐποροῦντες ἐν τῇ ἐκκλησίᾳ διδασκάλων ἱκανῶν, διὰ λιμὸν μιμούμενοι τοὺς ἐν λιμῷ ἐσθίοντας κρέα ἀνθρώπινα, ἀφιστάμενοι τοῦ ὑγιοῦς λόγου, προσεῖχον λόγοις ὁποιοισδήποτε, καὶ ἦν συγκροτούμενα αὐτῶν τὰ διδασκαλεῖα. Ὅτε δὲ ἡ χάρις τοῦ θεοῦ ἐπέλαμψε διδασκαλίαν πλείονα, ὁσημέραι αἱ αἱρέσεις κατελύοντο καὶ τὰ δοκοῦντα αὐτῶν ἀπόρρητα παραδειγματίζεται καὶ δείκνυται βλασφημίαι ὄντα καὶ λόγοι ἀσεβεῖς καὶ ἄθεοι.

We know this from personal experience, for when we were young the heresies were flourishing, and there seemed to be many gathered in them. Those who yearned for the teachings of Christ, lacking clever teachers in the Church, on account of such famine imitated those who eat human flesh during a famine. Thus, they separated from the sound doctrine and went after every possible teaching and united themselves in schools. But when the grace of God radiated a more abundant teaching, day after day the heresies broke up and their supposed secret doctrines were brought to light and denounced as being blasphemies and impious and godless words.

The personal confidence, by adding a note of authenticity and truthfulness to the preacher's anti-heretical discourse, seems to mirror the entire life span of the Alexandrian, from his youth to his old age (thus pointing, with other chronological evidence, to the final period of his life for the dating of the homilies).[68] In conformity with Eusebius' description in the *Ecclesiastical History*, Origen's Christian world, with the Alexandrian background of his beginnings, was characterized by the presence of schools (διδασκαλεῖα) and teachers, whereas the heretical masters initially appeared to be more successful than those of the Church. Things, however, changed in the course of time, as soon as clever teachers entered the stage on behalf of ecclesiastical orthodoxy and successfully fought against the heterodox doctrines. Who would not read this autobiographical description as a compendium of the life and work of Origen and his historical significance?

In the light of such recollection, we are led to say that teachers, for good or for bad, are the protagonists emerging now and then in the Munich homilies, more than other ecclesiastical figures, even those who, like the bishops, are at first sight more important. It is perhaps emblematic that the bishop who warmly commended the preacher in the *1st Homily on Psalm 67* totally disappears behind him in the course of his speech.[69] A curious passage in the

---

68. Adele Monaci-Castagno, "Contesto liturgico e cronologia della predicazione origeniana alla luce delle nuove Omelie sui Salmi," *Adamantius* 20 (2014): 238–54.

69. See above p. 25.

1st Homily on Psalm 76, meant to clear the relation between Asaph and Idithoun in the title, introduces the example of a newly appointed bishop who learns how to perform the Eucharist by following a more experienced colleague as his model.[70] The 'sacramental' activity seems as such to belong not so much to teaching as to experience, as shown likewise by the practice of private confession and penance. In the *3rd Homily on Psalm 73* Origen puts forth once more a personal reminiscence reporting an observation that he has made "in other churches" during one of his many journeys abroad: sinners, who were not known as such by the community, did not undergo the process of a public accusation and were treated privately by the bishop as their confessor and benevolent doctor.[71] The fatherly appearance of the bishop in this recollection contrasts with the less sympathetic picture of episcopal leaders whose harsh behavior may cause a schism inside their communities. In such eventuality, as witnessed by the *2nd Homily on Psalm 77*, Origen exhorts the faithful not to separate from the bishop and not to act in the same way as the schismatic tribes of Israel did when they broke with Rehoboam.[72]

70. *H76Ps* I,1 (294:6–10): Οἷον εἰ νεωστὶ κατασταθείς τις εἰς τὴν ἐπισκοπὴν ἀπὸ ἐπισκόπου ἤδη πλείονα ἔχοντος χρόνον ἐν τῇ λειτουργίᾳ καὶ μὴ μεμελετηκὼς ποιεῖν εὐχαριστίαν, λάβοι τὸν τύπον τῆς εὐχαριστίας, ἅτε αὐτὸς οὐδέπω δυνάμενος τῷ μὴ μεμελετηκέναι ποιεῖν εὐχαριστίαν, τοιοῦτόν τι νόει ἐπὶ τοῦ Ἀσάφ καὶ τοῦ Ἰδιθούμ, "For example, if someone has newly been instituted as a bishop, from a bishop who has spent a long time in worship service, and has not yet learnt to celebrate the Eucharist, he should receive the model of the Eucharist, inasmuch as he still is not able to learn how to celebrate the Eucharist; such may have been the case with Asaph and Jeduthun" (p. 239 modif.).

71. *H73Ps* III, 8 (265:8–14): Μετὰ τῶν ἄλλων θαυμασίων ὧν εἶδον ἐν ταῖς ἄλλαις ἐκκλησίαις καὶ τοῦτο ἑώρακα, ὃ καὶ ὑμῖν παραθήσομαι. Τινὲς τῶν ἁμαρτανόντων, μὴ ἔχοντες κατήγορον ἄνθρωπον, μηδὲ γινωσκόμενοι ἐφ' οἷς ἥμαρτον, εὔχονται καὶ παρατίθενται τῷ ἐπισκόπῳ τὰ ἁμαρτήματα· ὁ δὲ ὡς ἰατρὸς δακρύει καὶ οὐκ ἐξάγει οὐδὲ φέρει εἰς μέσον τὴν ἁμαρτίαν τοῦ ἡμαρτηκότος, ἀλλ' ὡς καλὸς πατὴρ θρηνήσας τὸν ἐξομολογούμενον, ἐμπλάστρους προσάγει λογικούς, ἐμβροχὰς πνευματικάς. Θεραπεύει καὶ ἐπιστρέφει ἑαυτοῦ τὸν υἱὸν κατὰ θεόν, "Along with the other marvels that I have seen in other churches, I have seen this one, which I present to you. Some of the sinners, not having a human accuser, nor being known for the sins they had committed, pray and present sins to the bishop; but he as a doctor weeps and does not call out or bring into the midst (of the Church) the sin of the person who has sinned, but as a good father lamenting what has been confessed, applies rational plasters, spiritual infusions. He treats and turns his own son back to God" (p. 216). Origen recognizes, after God, the role of the confessors, both bishops and priests, provided that they are really "good" as such. For a similar approach to the penitential practice of his time, see *H37PsL* II, 6 (312:14–26).

72. *H77Ps* II, 2 (368:9–15): ἔστω ἄνθρωπον ἐπίσκοπον τινὰ εἶναι σκληρότερον, ὥσπερ πάλαι ἀλλαχοῦ πατέρα τῶν ὑποτεταγμένων· ἐάν ποτε οὖν τύχῃ τοιοῦτον εἶναι, οἱ μὲν στασιώδεις μιμοῦνται τὰς δέκα φυλὰς καὶ αἱροῦνται τὸν Ἱεροβοὰμ υἱὸν Ναβάτ, ὃς ἐξήμαρτε τὸν Ἰσραήλ, οἱ δὲ εἰρηνικοὶ ἀνέχονται καὶ φέρουσι τὴν χαλεπότητα τοῦ Ῥοβοὰμ διὰ τὸν Δαυίδ, διὰ τὸ γένος, διὰ τὴν διαδοχὴν περιμένοντες, ἕως ἡ θεία πρόνοια ἢ τοῦτον θεραπεύσῃ ἢ ὃ βούλεται οἰκονομήσῃ, "Let us say that a certain human bishop is very harsh, as has occurred in former times and in other places, when a father is in charge of subordinates. If, then, such a thing should happen, troublemakers imitate the ten tribes and choose Jeroboam, son of Nabat, who caused Israel to sin, but the peaceable stay put and tolerate the harshness of Rehoboam, remaining where

The emphasis on the unity of the Christian community as the body of Christ, according to the Pauline ecclesiology (1 Cor 12:27), often accompanies the sermons, starting already with the initial one, the *1st Homily on Psalm 15*.[73] It becomes more insistent in the polemics of the preacher against the heretics, inasmuch as the disregard for the unity in the people of God is, in his opinion, the main cause of schisms and heresies. This concern finds its most notable expression in the exhortation to regularly attend the assemblies, instead of coming seldom or even only once a year, for the Easter festivities.[74] Unfortunately, Origen does not offer any further information on such celebrations, apart from what is always at stake for him as a teacher of the Church: the assembly essentially (if not exclusively, due to the unique explicit mention of the Eucharist that we saw above)[75] is a moment of spiritual nourishment and instruction focusing on the reading of the Scriptures and their interpretation. To abstain from the assembly means to be deprived of the Logos, the true "living bread," that has come down from heaven and "has been given to the saints" in the Church.[76] This would endanger our spiritual existence, as the Alexandrian elaborates especially in the *4th Homily on Psalm 77*. Therefore, no rational being is excluded from the need of receiving a spiritual feeding for his survival and growth, not even the angels or Christ. As Origen underlines in the *1st Homily on Psalm 15*, the Son himself is dependent upon the Father for his own "food" and "drink."[77]

Within this spiritual dynamism involving everybody's existence and leading it to God, the preacher has a fundamental role to play as the teacher of the Logos. He is the one who unveils the mysteries of God, by detecting the

they are on account of David, on account of the tribe, on account of the succession, until God's foresight should either cure him or arrange what it intends" (p. 304).

73. *H15Ps* I, 3 (77:14–22).

74. *H77Ps* IV, 4 (394:17–19): Ἤδη μέν τινες καταφρονοῦσι καὶ ὅλῳ τῷ ἐνιαυτῷ ἄτροφοι μένουσιν· ἔρχονται δὲ ἐπ᾽ ὀλίγας τὰς τοῦ πάσχα λεγομένας <ἡμέρας> ἐν αὐταῖς τραφησόμενοι. See also VI, 3 (429:16–18), "Already some are disdainful and stay without nourishment for a whole year, but they come on the few days of the so-called 'Passover'" (p. 329).

75. See n. 69.

76. *H77Ps* II, 5 (375:25–28): Ἡμεῖς δὲ εὐχώμεθα – ἀκούοντες τοῦ λέγοντος· ἐγώ εἰμι ὁ ἄρτος ὁ ζῶν ὁ ἐκ τοῦ οὐρανοῦ καταβάς· ὁ φαγὼν τοῦτον τὸν ἄρτον ζήσεται εἰς τὸν αἰῶνα (Jn 6:51) – μὴ ἐσθίειν ἄλλου ἄρτου ἢ τοῦ ἐκκλησιαστικοῦ τῆς ἀληθείας, ὃν ἔδωκεν ὁ θεὸς τοῖς ἁγίοις, "But let us pray—hearing the one who says, 'I am the living bread who came down from heaven; the one who eats this bread will live to the age' (Jn 6:51)—not to eat other bread than the bread of truth belonging to the Church, which God gave to the holy ones" (p. 311).

77. *H15Ps* I, 9 (87:14–15): οὕτως αὐτὸς τροφὴν ἔχει τὸν πατέρα καὶ ποτὸν ἔχει τὸν πατέρα, "In the same way he has the Father as his nourishment, and he has the Father as his cup" (p. 53).

hidden meanings of the Scripture and presenting their text as worthy of the divine Word, even if someone in attendance may not be happy about his pneumatic interpretation and demand from him "to stick to the letter."[78] In what represents the utmost challenge for him and his own task, the preacher is called to identify himself with Christ. As with the apostle Paul (2 Cor 13:3), the community should listen to the voice of Christ through him.[79] Origen's intense awareness of the unique role he should play clearly appears in a passage of the *Homily on Psalm 74*, where he contrasts the passing professions of the grammarian and the philosopher with the eternal activity of the Logos as master.[80] A *didaskalos*, of the kind Origen strove to be throughout his life (that is, always inspired by the model of the Logos himself), in contrast to the professions of the grammarian and the philosopher falling, after a while into an unavoidable repetition of their teachings, could only be engaged in an interpretation that constantly renewed itself. The Alexandrian does not appear too equitable with the two professions we are used to associating with his intellectual profile. But he could distance himself from them no less firmly and even harshly, as we see in the *3rd Homily on Psalm 36*. While dealing again with those who are "fond of words," he witnesses to know rhetors, grammarians, and philosophers, even those who teach dialectics, who lived a religiously and morally untenable life, described with the words of the Apostle in 1 Corinthians 6:9.[81] In this case Origen polemically opposes the ethically engaged conduct of the "simple faithful" (ἰδιώτης) to the immorality of "the wise of the world." Nonetheless, the homilies give enough evidence of his constitutive vocation as teacher, so that the anecdote reported by the preacher at the end of the long preface on

78. *H80Ps* I, 4 (485:11): Μὴ τροπολόγει καὶ μὴ ἀλληγόρει, φασίν, ἀλλὰ τήρει ἐπὶ τῆς λέξεως, "'Do not interpret figuratively and do not allegorize,' they say, 'but keep to the wording'" (p. 414).

79. *H15Ps* II, 1 (92:10–11); *H36Ps* III, 11 (154:21–24); *H67Ps* I, 1 (174:7–10); *H76Ps* II, 4 (318:6–9); III, 2 (333:22); *H80Ps* II, 3 (498:7).

80. *H74Ps* 6 (279:11–15): Ἐγὼ δὲ ἀπαγγελῶ εἰς τὸν αἰῶνα, ψαλῶ τῷ θεῷ Ιακώβ (Ps 74:10). Ὁ διδάσκαλος καὶ κύριος ἡμῶν τοσαῦτα ἔχει μαθήματα ὡς ἀπαγγέλλειν οὐκ ἐπὶ δέκα ἔτη, ὡς ἀπαγγέλλει γραμματικὸς καὶ οὐκ ἔχει τί διδάξει οὐδὲ ὡς φιλόσοφος ἀπαγγέλλει παραδιδοὺς καὶ οὐκέτι ἔχει καινότερόν τι εἴπῃ, ἀλλὰ τοσαῦτά ἐστι τὰ μαθήματα τοῦ Χριστοῦ ὥστε αὐτὸν ἀπαγγέλλειν εἰς ὅλον τὸν αἰῶνα, "'But I shall proclaim to the age, I shall make music to the God of Jacob' (Ps 74:10). Our Teacher and Lord has such lessons to proclaim not for ten years, as a grammarian proclaims before he runs out of things to teach, nor as a philosopher proclaims handing down what he knows until he has nothing new to say, but Christ's lessons are such that he proclaims for the entire age" (p. 227). See Perrone, "Ne corrumpas (Sal 74, 1)".

81. *H36Ps* III, 6 (146:16–19): Πολλάκις γοῦν οἶδα ῥήτορας καὶ γραμματικοὺς καὶ φιλόσοφα ἐπαγγελλομένους καὶ τὰ διαλεκτικά, οὐ μόνον εἰδωλολάτρας ἀλλὰ καὶ ἀρσενοκοίτας καὶ πόρνους καὶ μοιχούς, "In fact, I often know rhetors, grammarians and teachers of philosophy and dialectic who are not only idol-worshipers, but also persons who sleep with men, frequent prostitutes, and commit adultery" (p. 108 modif.).

apprenticeship and learning in the *2nd Homily on Psalm 76* cannot but convey again an autobiographical imprint, apt to resume the enriching contribution of the Munich homilies to our renewed image of Origen.[82]

Ἐγὼ πολλάκις ἤκουσα ὁμολογούντων πιστῶν πλείονα χρόνον ἐν τῇ πίστει πεποιηκότων καὶ μεμαθηκότων τὰ τῆς πίστεως μυστήρια, ἡνίκα ἐὰν περιτύχωσι διδασκάλῳ καλῶς τρανοῦντι, λεγόντων ὅτι "νῦν ἠρξάμην Χριστιανὸς γενέσθαι, νῦν μανθάνω πρῶτον τί ἐστι Χριστιανισμός." Ταῦτα δὲ λέγουσιν οὐχὶ τέλεον ἀθετοῦντες τὰ πρότερα, ἀλλ᾽ ὁρῶντες ὅτι πρότερον μὲν οὐ συνίεσαν τῶν μυστηρίων, ἀρχὴν δὲ ἔχουσι τοῦ νοεῖν ὅτε τετεύχασι διδασκαλίας ἀγαθῆς.

I have often heard believers testifying that they have been deemed to be in the faith for a long time and to have been taught the secrets of the faith, at some point finding a teacher who makes it clear, saying: "Now I have begun to become a Christian, now I am learning for the first time what Christianity is." They say these things not to take away from their earlier practice, but seeing that earlier they did not understand the mysteries, while they have begun to understand, when they enjoyed a good teaching.

82. *H76Ps* II, 1 (315:8–14 [p. 255 modif.]).

Joseph W. Trigg

2. WHAT CAN BE LEARNED BY TRANSLATING THE HOMILIES?

CMG 314 provides new and unexpected access to the mature work of a highly prolific and influential Christian thinker; its discovery is all the more welcome because the Psalms are vital to Christian thought and worship. Many contemporary Christians will welcome these newly discovered homilies because they unequivocally affirm the dignity of all human beings and the beauty and order of the cosmos and just as unequivocally deny any anger or vengefulness to God. Origen's stance toward Judaism, for which these homilies also provide new evidence, has a bearing on how adherents to living faith traditions relate to each other today. The newly discovered homilies bring us as close as we can get to Origen's living voice as he spoke his mind on these topics and many more. Those who do not read Greek should hear that voice, through translation, as clearly as possible.

The homilies show how Origen read the biblical text with close attention to nuances of vocabulary and expression. Nothing better illustrates the challenge of translation than the need to put accurately into English the sense of the terms he himself used when referring to language: the word for rational discourse itself, λόγος, and the two words for language as a sensible, bodily phenomenon, λέξις and ῥητόν. Domenico Pazzini demonstrated from Origen's *Commentary on John*, that Origen had a precise terminology informed by a Stoic understanding of language; Mark James has now demonstrated the same to be true in these homilies.[1] A saying attributed to Leo Strauss applies

---

1. Domenico Pazzini, *Lingua e teologia in Origene: Il Commento a Giovanni*, (Brescia: Paideia,

just as well to Origen: "to understand the way an author writes, one [has] to pay attention to the way he reads."[2] The precision of speech that he ascribed to the biblical authors and, perhaps mistakenly, to their Septuagint translators as well, was a precision that he sought in his own work. Origen found a bodily visitation (ἐπιδημία) of the divine Logos in the language of the Bible and sought for his own speech to be such a visitation as well. These homilies demonstrate that, as we might expect from someone so attuned to language, Origen was frustrated at reading the Psalms in translation. Although he trusted the competence of the Septuagint translators, he did not consider their translation a substitute for reading the Psalms in Hebrew.

Rufinus's Translation of Origen

Around 401, Rufinus translated nine of Origen's homilies on the Psalms, including four in CMG 314. In her essay in GCSO13 on Rufinus as translator, Emanuela Prinzivalli discusses Rufinus's translation of the homilies into Latin as illustrated by the four that we now are able to read in the original Greek. In doing so, she alerts the contemporary translator of Origen's homilies to issues that often still persist. Prinzivalli points out that the first challenge that confronted Rufinus was to render Origen's Greek into another language; Greek is more mobile and flexible, Latin more rigid and structured.[3] The challenge of translating Classical Greek into Latin pales before the challenge of translating Origen into English, which, to convey meaning, almost entirely depends on word order rather than inflections. The common assumption that translation into English calls for the short, direct sentences customary in journalistic prose enhances the difficulty of doing justice to Origen in English.[4] Biblical citations pose a second challenge. Rufinus evidently felt constrained to conform to the familiar Latin wording of the Psalms, even when that translation obscured philological distinctions Origen was making.[5] This

---

2009) and Mark Randall James, *Learning the Language of Scripture: Origen, Wisdom, and the Logic of Interpretation* (Leiden: Brill, 2021).

2. See Daniel Tanguay, *Leo Strauss: an Intellectual Biography*, tr. Christopher Nadon (New Haven, CT: Yale University Press, 2007), 2.

3. Emanuela Prinzivalli, GCSO13, p. 41.

4. In *The Art of Bible Translation* (Princeton, NJ: Princeton University Press, 2019), Richard Alter argues that such journalistic prose is neither appropriate or necessary for translating the Hebrew Bible, which poses similar issues. He urges "avoiding the impression that the Bible was written in the English of the day before yesterday" (p. 22).

5. Prinzivalli, GCSO13, p. 42–44.

issue immediately confronts anyone translating the homilies into English. If one uses the NRSV, for example, the first words of CMG 314, Ἔστι τινὰ γράμματα ἐν στήλαις ἐμψύχοις γραφόμενα,[6] "Some letters are written on animate monuments," and the subsequent discussion of memorials seems to come from nowhere. The NRSV has, for the inscription of Psalm 15/16, "A Miktam of David." This is in keeping with a tradition that goes back to the earliest English translations of the Psalms from Hebrew. Origen, however, bases his homily on the dubious LXX translation of the Hebrew word, *miktam*, as "monument inscription," στηλογραφία. In this particular case, the translator of the homilies could make do with the New English Translation of the Septuagint (NETS), which has "A stele inscription. Pertaining to David." Soon, on the verso of the fifth leaf of CMG 314, the translator finds a citation of 1 Cor 12:27 for which the NRSV reads, "Now you are the body of Christ, and individually members of it." The words translated "individually," ἐκ μέρους, are the same words translated a few verses later, as "only in part" in 1 Corinthians 13:9: "For we know only in part, and we prophesy only in part." In translating the phrase differently in these two nearby passages, the NRSV follows a tradition that, in this case, goes back, through Tyndale to Jerome.[7] It is clear from a reference to 1 Cor 12:9 elsewhere in CMG 314, though, that Origen believed that ἐκ μέρους has the same sense, "partially," in both passages.[8] To follow almost any existing English translation would misrepresent the way Origen read Paul. Not much farther into CMG 314, on the verso of the eighth leaf, Origen cites these words from Psalm 15, τοῖς ἁγίοις τοῖς ἐν τῇ γῇ αὐτοῦ ἐθαυμάτωσεν.[9] Here, even following NETS is impossible if we are to convey how Origen read the Psalm. NETS translates the verb ἐθαυμάτωσεν so that it governs the following phrase rather than the one before it, so that our verse 3 reads: "As for the holy ones who are in his land—he has made marvelous [ἐθαυμάτωσεν] all his wants among them." Origen, though, as his discussion shows, takes the words to mean, "He has made wonders [ἐθαυμάτωσεν] for the holy ones who are in his land, all of his things willed are in them." Thus, we find, eight leaves into the 371 leaves of CMG 314, that the translator of the homilies is obligated to

---

6. GCSO13.73.1.

7. GCSO13.77.20. Jerome translates ἐκ μέρους as "*ex parte*" in 1 Cor 13:9 and translates 1 Cor 12:27 as "*Vos autem estis corpus Christi et membra de membro.*"

8. See PS67H1.6, GCSO13.190.12–191.1: And then Christ comes in the rising up and will be in his own body, not partially [ἐκ μέρους], when Christ thus rises up god in the whole body when it has risen up ..." David Bentley Hart (in *The New Testament: A Translation* [New Haven, Connecticut: Yale University Press, 2017], 342–43) agrees with Origen.

9. GCSO13.

convey to the reader how Origen read the Bible, not how later biblical translators have read it.

Prinzivalli also shows how Rufinus had to deal with the oral character of the homilies, transcribed as Origen spoke them impromptu. Unlike treatises, which, even if dictated, were intended to be read by anyone at any time, these are homilies preached to particular people at a particular time. As a transcript, they cannot convey what is communicated through gesture or tone of voice. Prinzivalli shows how Rufinus translates them into literary prose.[10] This oral character is prominent throughout the homilies, giving them freshness and spontaneity. In the second homily on Psalm 15 Origen speaks of the "twelve" apostles who verify that our verses 8–10 are spoken in the persona of Christ. After apparently seeing some questioning looks, he verifies that it was indeed twelve, since Matthias had already replaced Judas.[11] At other times it is harder to understand why Origen feels compelled to speak as he does, as at the beginning of the first homily on Psalm 67; there Origen is reacting to something that a bishop has just said, but we can only guess what that was.[12] In another homily his tone of voice must have conveyed sarcasm when he invited those who objected to figurative interpretation to "trample on serpents" the next time they saw a cobra.[13] The same applies when he says that, without figurative interpretation, the angels must have been grinding grain, kneading dough and baking in order to prepare the "bread of angels" in Ps 77:25.[14] Origen shows his sense of humor when he discusses the figurative significance of Egyptian vegetables:

> Whenever we despise the spiritual nourishment and divine nourishment available to us, we scurry after wealth and want luxury. Do we not lust to eat stinking leeks; and onions that sting the eyes of the soul; and garlic, putrid sins, and do we not acquire for ourselves the stench of pleasures? Thus, also desiring the mushiness of the cosmos and the nature of bodies we desire gourds and, taking away what has been imparted for the wellbeing (ousia) of the soul, we want to substitute cucumbers.[15]

Like Nicola Pace in his work on Rufinus as a translator of the *Peri Archon*,[16] Prinzivalli considers Rufinus to have translated Origen in a good-faith attempt

---

10. GCSO13, p. 39.
11. PS15H2.1 (91.18–92.4).
12. PS67H1.1 (173.1–174.23).
13. PS73H3.7 (262.15–17).
14. PS77H4.5 (395.5–9).
15. PS77H4.11 (407.14–20).
16. Nicola Pace, *Ricerche sulla traduzione di Rufino del "De principiis" di Origene* (Florence: La Nuova Italia Editrice, 1990). Although not specifically related to Rufinus, the observations of Hermann

to make Origen's work accessible, not simply in a different language, but in a new cultural context:

> To understand Rufinus's *ratio interpretandi* one must touch briefly on the circumstances of composition. He, perhaps in 401 at Aquileia, translated five of Origen's homilies on Psalm 36, two on Psalm 37 and two on Psalm 38 for the Roman couple, Apronianus and Avita, his friends and protectors during the previous stay in Rome, recently consecrated to domestic asceticism. In the dedicatory preface Rufinus starts with the observation that these three psalms are of ethical content (*expositio tota moralis est*) and for that reason he has translated the corresponding homilies, specifying that he had wanted to construct a whole treatment, that could be kept on hand in one codex, suitable for making progress on the way of ethical perfection with the three moments of *conuersio* or *paenitentia*, *purgatio* and *profectus*. The work is addressed specifically to Avita and to all women who have embraced a religious life, so that the exposition is accomplished with clear phrases, in a simple manner, avoiding difficult issues; he makes it understood that Avita had in the past complained about the difficulty of his translations, he therefore reassures her with no little paternalism as to feminine limitations.[17]

Rufinus' translation is thus a work of "cultural mediation" aimed at transferring Origen's work into a new era and into a different cultural context in such a way that it would still "speak" to a new public. The works of Rufinus's friend, Evagrius Ponticus, entailed a similar cultural mediation aimed at making Origen's work accessible in new contexts: "If the West should acquire the spiritual depth and monastic spirit *ante litteram* of the Alexandrian, it was necessary to translate the sobriety and intellectual subtlety that characterize even these homilies into to more directly ethical impact."[18] This meant making

---

Josef Vogt on the anonymous Latin translation of Origen's Commentary on Matthew (*Origenes als Exeget* [Paderborn: Schöningh, 1999] 85–134) are also helpful.

17. GCSO13, 36: Per comprendere la *ratio interpretandi* di Rufino, bisogna brevemente accennare alle circostanze della composizione. Egli, forse nel 401 ad Aquileia, tradusse cinque omelie di Origene su Ps 36, due sul 37 e due sul 38 per i coniugi romani Aproniano e Avita, suoi amici e protettori durante il precedente soggiorno romano, da poco dedicatisi all'ascetismo domestico. Nella dedica prefatoria Rufino parte dalla costatazione che questi tre salmi sono di contenuto etico (*expositio tota moralis est*) e che per questa ragione ha tradotto le omelie corrispondenti, specificando di aver voluto costituire una trattazione organica, da tenere sottomano in un unico codice, adatta a far progredire sulla via del perfezionamento etico con i tre momenti della *conuersio* o *paenitentia*, della *purgatio* e del *profectus*. L'opera è rivolta in modo specifico ad Avita e alle donne che hanno abbracciato una vita religiosa perché l'esposizione è fatta con frasi chiare, in modo semplice, evitando problematiche difficili: egli fa capire che Avita si era in precedenza lamentata della difficoltà delle sue traduzioni e dunque la rassicura, con una punta di sufficienza paternalistica nei confronti della limitatezza femminile.

18. GCSO13.38: se l'occidente doveva acquisire l'altezza spirituale e lo spirito monastico *ante litteram* dell'Alessandrino, era necessario tradurre la sobrietà e la rarefazione intellettuale che caratterizza anche queste omelie in più immediata ricaduta etica.

explicit their implicit moral instruction. It also meant muting, if not altogether losing, what Prinzivalli calls their "tono zetetico," the tentative, inquisitive tone in which τάχα, "perhaps," has a vital function; Rufinus's Origen speaks as an authority to be respected, not as an inquirer searching for answers.[19] To be sure, the lost "tono zetetico" marked Origen as a philosopher in the Socratic tradition.

Rufinus translated his selection from the homilies in the wake of the Origenist controversy that had begun in 393 when Epiphanius of Salamis condemned John of Jerusalem for taking Origenist positions alleged to be heretical. By that time, Jerome, installed in Bethlehem, had already translated Origen's homilies on the Song of Songs, Isaiah, Jeremiah, Ezekiel and Luke, the earliest translations of Origen's work, as far as we know, into Latin. Nonetheless, he joined Epiphanius's repudiation of Origen as a heretic. Rufinus, then in Jerusalem, did not. Later, having left Jerusalem for Rome, he would seek to defend, preserve and transmit Origen's legacy. He sought to put concerns about Origen's orthodoxy to rest by translating the first book of the martyr Pamphilus's *Apology for Origen* and composing a tract *On the Adulteration of Origen's Books* that would explain how misconceptions arose. He also translated *Peri Archon*, implicitly inviting his readers to judge for themselves. These works only exacerbated the controversy around the reception of Origen. Remarks on Jerome's procedure in translating in the preface to that last work, published in 398, turned him into an implacable enemy. Some years later, recognizing that Origen was still respected in the West as a biblical interpreter even if suspect as a theologian, Rufinus turned to Origen's exegetical works. His translation of Origen's homilies on Psalms 36, 37 and 38, translated around 401, may have been the first of these. His preface indicated that his choice of a work to translate touched on none of the theological issues that had made Origen controversial: "everything would have regarded correction or advance of behavior."[20] In only one passage from the homilies had Origen ventured into what by Rufinus's time was dangerous theological territory: his discussion of Ps 36:7, "Be subordinate to the Lord" [ὑποτάγηθι τῷ κυρίῳ], raises the specter of subordinationism by linking that passage to 1 Cor 15:28, "then the Son himself will be subordinated to him who has subordinated all things to him" [τότε καὶ αὐτὸς ὁ υἱὸς ὑποταγήσεται τῳ ὑποτάξαντι αὐτῳ τὰ πάντα].

19. GCSO13.40. Any sentence containing τάχα is guaranteed to be interesting.

20. *Ad emendationem vel profectionem mora tota respiceret.* Rufinus, Preface to Origen, Homilies on Psalms 36, 37, and 38,

There we see how Rufinus transformed the discussion of 36.7. In the newly accessible Greek text Origen took pains to show that Christ is subordinate to the Father, even before all things are subjected to him. Rufinus, on the other hand, gives the impression that Origen taught that Christ is never subordinate to the Father, except in a special sense. He adds an entire paragraph, paraphrasing Origen from a different context in order to specify that Christ's subordination to the Father is a "mystical subjection" of all believers who constitute Christ's body. Prinzivalli's second contribution to GSC O13, an appendix in which the Greek text appears in parallel columns with Rufinus's Latin enables us to see at a glance what Rufinus did.

We translate in part

Origen's reading starts by attending to the exact wording of a text. This, he was convinced, reveals incongruities, often slight, that open up deeper meanings intended by the biblical authors through whom the divine logos spoke.[21] He takes this approach in Psalm homilies, inquiring, for example, why an imperative is used in a prayer instead of an optative[22] or why items are listed in a particular order.[23] Origen, believed, as we shall see, that the Septuagint translators did their best to convey the nuances of the original Hebrew, and gave them more credit than they deserved. However, he knew that reading the text of the Psalms in translation deprived him of the fuller insight he would have had were he able to read them in Hebrew. He understood that any translation, however competent, can never fully express all that is conveyed in the original language. As George Steiner explained,

> A 'perfect' act of translation would be one of total synonymity. It would presume an interpretation so precisely exhaustive as to leave no single unit of the source-text—phonetic, grammatical, semantic, contextual—out of complete account, and yet so calibrated as to have added nothing in the way of paraphrase, explication or variant.

Origen dealt with the limitations of translation from Hebrew to Greek in connection with two unusual prepositional compounds in Psalm 36.

---

21. See PA 4.2.8–9. Arthur M. Melzer's *Philosophy Between the Lines: The Lost History of Esoteric Writing* (Chicago: University of Chicago Press, 2014) explains how the search for hidden meaning necessarily entails such a close engagement with a text.

22. PS67H1.2 (175.1–177.2).

23. See especially PS77H1.5 (359.21–362.16), also PS74H.1 (270.3–12).

In the very first verse of the psalm, Origen, assuming that a distinction implies a difference, discussed the two verbs in the phrase μὴ παραζήλου ἐν πονηρευομένοις μηδὲ ζήλου τοὺς ποιοῦντας τὴν ἀνομίαν. The second verb, ζήλου, is the imperative form of a familiar verb that means "be envious" or "be jealous." The first verb, παραζήλου, is the same verb stem, but with a prefixed preposition that often means "beside." In Greek, such a compound must be treated as a word in its own right with a meaning that is not necessarily obvious and must be learned. Albert Piertesma in NETS translates παραζήλου as "fret" and ζήλου as "be envious" so that the passage reads, "Do not fret among wicked people, nor be envious of those who do lawlessness."[24] Origen seeks to discern the meaning of this unfamiliar word from other usages in the Septuagint. This would be an effective procedure as long as the translators were accurate and consistent. He finds παραζηλόω in the Song of Moses (Dt 31:21), cited in Rom 10:19 and in 1 Cor 10:22. He could also have found it in Ps 77:58, where he does not comment on the meaning, perhaps assuming that his hearers would have remembered this discussion. On the basis of those citations, he argues that Psalm 36:1 says "do not make jealous among those who do evil." Even so, it is not obvious what "make jealous" might mean in this context. To deal with that difficulty, Origen imagines a scenario that might have come from New Comedy or even neighborhood gossip: a loose woman flaunts her affair with a married man out of spite toward his wife. In this particular case, the procedure gives a plausible result; in Deuteronomy 31:21, as in Ps 77:58, παραζηλόω translates a *hiphil* (causative) formation of the verb קָנָא, "be jealous," a verbal formation that has no close parallel in Greek.

Origen points out that παραζηλοῦν (the infinitive equivalent to παραζήλου) occurs neither in literary nor in colloquial Greek.[25] He concludes that "it appears to have been brought into being by force by the translators who wanted to translate the Hebrew statement and present the distinction" (ἔοικε βεβιασμένη γενέσθαι ὑπὸ τῶν ἑρμηνευτῶν βουλομένων ἑρμηνεῦσαι τὸ Ἑβραϊκὸν ῥητὸν καὶ τὴν διαφορὰν παραστῆσαι). The translators, in other words, deliberately violated normal Greek usage by coining a new word. The translators, he concluded, wanted to differentiate (τὴν διαφορὰν παραστῆσαι) the two subtly different Hebrew verbs. (A search for the lemma παραζηλόω in

24. In Albert Piertesma and Benjamin Wright, editors, *A New English Translation of the Septuagint* (Oxford: Oxford University Press, 2009) 264.

25. Οὐ πάνυ τίς ἐστιν ἡ λέξις Ἑλληνικὴ οὐδὲ τέτριπται ἐν τῇ συνηθείᾳ τῶν Ἑλλήνων οὔτε τῶν φιλολόγων οὔτε τῶν ἰδιωτικώτερον φραζόντων (GCSO13.113.21–22).

the TLG confirms judgments Origen made on the basis of memory; the earliest attestations of the verb are those he cites in the LXX and its subsequent use is by authors such as Paul and Philo who knew the LXX.) One coins words when a language lacks a word that adequately expresses what one intends to say. Unlike Origen himself, whose coined words in the course of these homilies are easily understandable, the Septuagint translators presumably knew that when they used the coined word παραζήλου, that they were translating a clear Hebrew text into one that is obscure in Greek. Nonetheless, they considered themselves forced to do so in order to maintain, as best they could, a distinction intended by the Psalmist. Origen credits them with distinguishing the two Hebrew verbs "to the extent human nature could do so," κατὰ τὸ δυνατὸν ἀνθρωπίνῃ φύσει.[26]

In another homily on Psalm 36 he confronted a different compound word in verse 23. There he argues, referring to other passages, that the unusual compound διάβημα denotes a "step though" to a higher level of spiritual awareness. The noun, διάβημα, is tricky in a different way because, as Marguerite Harl observed, the translators of the Psalms in the Septuagint were mediocre and lacked any systematic procedure.[27] (Had he availed himself of the *Hexapla*, Origen could have determined this for himself.) Though διάβημα is an unfamiliar word, a familiar verbal compound with the same root means "step through" or "cross," clarifying the way the preposition modifies the meaning. Nonetheless, in three usages he cites from the Psalms, the Greek word translates three different Hebrew words. The crucial citation from Exodus 3:3, where he finds a compelling illustration of the word's use, is yet a fourth Hebrew stem and, in any event, Origen's memory had actually failed him, since it is a different word even in Greek.[28] In both cases Origen argues that the Septuagint translators would only have departed from ordinary Greek usage in order to convey a meaning that could not be conveyed otherwise.

Without CMG 314 we would not even know that Origen dealt with issues of translation in his homilies on the Psalms. Large gaps appear on the Latin side of Prinzivalli's column by column comparison of Rufinus's translation of the first four homilies on Psalm 36 with the Greek original.[29] In particular,

---

26. PS36H1.1 GSSO13.113.24–25.

27. See Marguerite Harl, Gilles Dorival and Olivier Munnich, *La Bible grecque des Septante: du Judaisme hellénistique au Christianisme ancien* (Paris: Cerf, 1994), 228–33.

28. The words are the nouns מִצְעָד in Ps 36:1, אֲשֶׁר in Ps 36:31, and רֶגֶל in Ps 72:1. In Ex 3:3 the verb סוּר is actually translated by παρέρχομαι, "turn aside,' not ἐπιβαίνω the verb corresponding to ἐπιβῆμα.

29. PS36H4.1 GCSO13.572–75.

it omits the entire discussions of παραζηλοῦν and διάβημα, maybe because, in Rufinus's judgment, such discussions could only distract from moral exhortation that he announced as the goal of his translation. Perhaps Rufinus also thought that Origen's demonstration of the inadequacy of translation to convey fully the sense of the Hebrew original would, if anything, lead simpler readers to doubt the reliability of their own biblical texts. (We have already seen how Rufinus also made strategic omissions that obscure Origen's teaching about the subordination of the Son to the Father.) Such omissions leave us to ponder how many others Rufinus made when translating the many homilies for which we lack the Greek original.

Another fascinating case where Origen dealt with the lack of any Greek word corresponding to a word in the original Hebrew comes in his discussion of a phrase in Ps 73:15, "You dried up *ētham* rivers,"[30] discussed in more detail below. It would not, in fact, have been difficult to render אֵיתָן, a word that designates an "ever-flowing" stream as opposed to one that only flowed seasonally, into Greek. Nonetheless, Origen notes that the Septuagint omits the phrase and the other five versions of the Psalms in the *Hexapla* each has a different rendering, one of which is simply to transliterate the Hebrew, meaningless as that might be. None can bear to transmit to the reader what the original plainly says; unimaginative translators must have thought that "dry up ever-flowing rivers" would constitute an absurd contradiction. This, as we have seen, is a common fault in Rufinus's translations of Origen (and, for that matter, in contemporary translations of the Bible). Origen, though, unable to read the original Hebrew and going only by the various renderings, took them all as good-faith attempts to make the best of what could not be fully expressed in Greek, an account of the prophets, which the *ētham* rivers signified figuratively.

Before the discovery of CMG 314, we knew that Origen considered Hebrew the original human language. In the *Homilies on Numbers,* he states that, in the story of the Tower of Babel when God addressed the angels, saying, "Come, let us confuse their tongues," [Gn 11:17] angels gave humans the full range of languages that now exist. Nonetheless, when God retained Israel as his own portion [Dt 32:7] he left to them the Hebrew language that he had originally given to Adam.[31] Before the discovery of the homilies, we knew that

---

30. PS73H3.1.
31. HomNum 11.4.4.

Origen interpreted Psalm 80:6 to indicate that the whole people "amazingly" resumed speaking Hebrew after their exodus from Egypt.[32] In the newly discovered Homily 1 on Psalm 80, Origen goes even farther:

> After this a secret [μυστήριον] said concerning the whole people that had not been written in Exodus but has been ventured [ἀποτετολμημένον] by the spirit in the prophet, for it is said, "When going out of the land of Egypt he heard a tongue that he did not know" [Ps 80:6]. When, it says, Israel was in Egypt they did not hear Hebrew, but when they went out of Egypt, "a tongue that he did not know"—for he did not know Hebrew— "he heard". And this secret is unspeakable [τοῦτο δὲ μυστήριον ἀπόρρητόν ἐστιν], for understand with me, the Hebrew tongue is announcing foreign things [τὰ περατικά], things above the cosmos [τὰ ὑπερκόσμια], so that "Hebrew" is interpreted "foreign" [περατικὸς] and the tongue "foreignese" [περατιστί][33].
>
> When then, we learn what is beyond bodies, what is beyond the cosmos, when we rationally discuss these things spiritually, we rationally discuss in Hebrew [Ὅταν οὖν τὰ περὶ τῶν πέρα τῶν σωμάτων, τὰ περὶ τῶν πέρα τοῦ κόσμου μανθάνωμεν, ὅταν ἐκεῖνα διαλεγώμεθα πνευματικῶς, Ἑβραϊστὶ διαλεγόμεθα].[34]

Hebrew is not just the original human language, which only the Jewish people conserved; inspired by the spirit, the prophet Asaph has dared to let it slip that Hebrew is also the language for discussing realities foreign to our bodily existence in this world. Hebrew is not just the primitive language of the human race, it is also the eschatological language.

Since no other language is so suited to the discussion of spiritual reality, the implication is that Hebrew can never be adequately translated into another human language. This means that the Septuagint could never, for Origen, be a substitute for or replacement of its Hebrew original. This is indirect evidence of an ongoing relationship with Jews, since as Nicholas de Lange has pointed out, he did not have a sufficient command of the Hebrew language to have worked with it without their assistance.[35] The newly discovered homilies give us no reason to modify de Lange's judgment. The only evidence in them that Origen knew any Hebrew is that he noted the omission of the definite article before *elohim* in Ps 67:2.[36] As de Lange puts it, "It was Origen's dilemma

---

32. See CC 3.7, cited in GCS13, 491, note a. From CC 3.8 Origen argues from the names the Hebrews gave their children in Egypt that Hebrew was their ancestral language.

33. This is a word Origen coined.

34. PS80H1.7 (491.10–20).

35. Nicholas de Lange, *Origen and the Jews: Studies in Jewish-Christian relations in third-century Palestine* (Cambridge: Cambridge University Press), 22, 58.

36. PS67H1.5 (185.17–20).

that as a theologian he must condemn the Jews while as a scholar and exegete he depended on them."[37]

As he undertook to interpret Psalm 77, Origen said that he was continuing to correct the Greek "versions," ἐκδόσεις, by comparing them with the Hebrew:

> In general, it must be said, that the devil plots against the living…. Because our salvation is through them, he contrives discord [διαφωνίαν][38] among the scriptures, so that by means of the discord readers might fall into a trap. What must be accepted, this or that? How much we toiled, through God and his grace, examining together [συνεξετάζοντες] both the Hebrew and the versions [ἐκδόσεις] in order to see to the correction of errors [τὴν διόρθωσιν τῶν σφαλμάτων], he [God] knows. What we intend to do about what remains he himself [God] will further [αὐτὸς εὐοδώσει].[39]

This poignant indication that Origen did not expect an imminent end of his life's work is consistent with the conclusions that Pierre Nautin drew from the two first-hand accounts accessible to him, those in Origen's Epistle to Julius Africanus and in his *Commentary on Matthew*, that testified to Origen's intentions in assembling the *Hexapla*. From these accounts and from his analysis of how Origen used the alternate versions, Nautin concluded that Origen did not simply use these versions to determine which reading was to be preferred when copies of the Septuagint differed. He also used them to rectify additions and omissions in the Septuagint when other versions indicated that it differed from the Hebrew original.[40] Nautin concluded that Origen devoted great effort and originality to construct a work that would enable him "to recover, as far as possible, the content of the original."[41]

Bernhardt Neuschäfer confirmed Nautin's conclusions in his own examination of Origen's use of the versions in the *Hexapla*. He suggested that the *Hexapla* was assembled to aid in the correction (διόρθωσις) of the text. The versions, on his interpretation, would initially have been a means for choosing between divergent readings in the Septuagint. The reading that could be corroborated by the versions, as independent translations from the same Hebrew

---

37. PS67H1.5 (185.17–20), 31.

38. The opposite of συμφωνία, see Sébastien Morlet, *Symphonia: La concorde des textes et des doctrines dans la littérature grecque jusquuà Origène* (Paris: Les Belles Lettres, 2019).

39. PS77H1.1 (351.24 - 352.2). In this, his last known work, Origen indicates that the *Hexapla* is a continuing project. Anthony Grafton and Megan Williams, *Christianity and the Transformation of the Book* (Cambridge, MA: Harvard University Press, 2006) make clear how original and innovative the *Hexapla* was.

40. See Pierre Nautin, *Origène: sa vie et son œuvre* (Paris: Beauchesne, 1977), 344–50.

41. "Pour retrouver, autant qu'il peut, la teneur de l'original," Nautin, *Origène*, 350.

source, would be preferred. Once Origen was using the versions in this way, though, it became obvious to him that there were places where the versions differed entirely from the Septuagint. The desire to find the best reading then led him into the laborious task of constructing the *Hexapla* to facilitate comparing the versions word-for-word with the Septuagint. This enabled Origen to supplement the Septuagint with other witnesses to the Hebrew original. Neuschäfer found no indication, though, that Origen used the versions to create a new, seemingly corrected version of the Septuagint by supplementing its omissions and deleting its additions on the basis of the versions.[42]

As Perrone notes in his introduction, he sometimes prefers readings in the versions.[43] Thus the newly-discovered homilies are consistent with what Nautin and Neuschäfer had observed before they were discovered: Origen does not treat the Septuagint as an authoritative replacement of that original Hebrew text.[44] In one of the most remarkable passages in the homilies the opening of his first homily on Psalm 77, Origen admits that the ascription of a statement in Psalm 77, an Asaph psalm, to the prophet Isaiah [Mt 13:35] is simply false and that he has no explanation for it other than mischief on the devil's part. Given that the text of the Bible is open to such tampering and, in any event, can easily be misinterpreted, he suggests that the order of the cosmos and the spread of the Christianity are a firmer basis for faith than the Bible itself. Indeed, he says, "much death comes in upon souls on the pretext of the letters [προφάσει τῶν γραμμάτων, the killing letters of scripture of 2 Cor 3:6]."[45] Nonetheless, mitigating such inconsistencies as much as possible is, as we have just seen, Origen's reason for using the *Hexapla,* which enables him to check the Septuagint against the Hebrew and other translations. We see him doing this in one case to uphold as the correct one a reading of Ps 77:63 found in only a few copies of the Septuagint, "their virgins were not commended [ἐπηνέθησαν]" rather than "their virgins were not bewailed [ἐπενθήθησαν]": "For so it must be read, as it holds in all the other versions [ἐν ταῖς λοιπαῖς ἐκδόσεσιν ἔχει πάσαις] and also in the Hebrew and in a few reliable copies [καὶ ἐν ὀλίγοις ἀντιγράφοις ἀσφαλέσιν]."[46] The versions and

---

42. Bernhard Neuschäfer, *Origenes als Philologe* (Basel: Friedrich Reinhardt Verlag, 1987), 86–103.

43. Briefly discussed on pp. 14–16 of Perrone's introduction to GCS O13.

44. R. P. C. Hanson came to the same conclusion and makes an argument for it in *Allegory and Event: A Study of the Sources and Significance of Origen's Interpretation of Scripture* (London: SDCM Press, 1959), 162–86.

45. PS77H1.1 (353.5).

46. PS77H8.9 (462.28–463.2).

the Hebrew text itself, which he indicates that he has examined on its own, determine which copies of the Septuagint are reliable. A little later, speaking of Psalm 77:68, Origen also refers to the versions:

> "And he built its sanctuary as of unicorns [ὡς μονοκερώτων]." The other versions have "and its sanctuary is high [ὕψη]," showing that "of unicorns" has been placed there instead of "lofty" [δηλοῦσαι ὅτι καὶ τὸ μονοκεράτων ἀντὶ τοῦ ὑψηλοῦ ἐτάχθη]. And perhaps [τάχα] "unicorns" is now figuratively [τροπικῶς] the name for those who are in God, goring enemies with one horn [ἐνὶ κέρατι κερατίζοντας τοὺς ἐχθροὺς] and saying, "In you we shall gore our enemies"[Ps 43.6] and "He has lifted the horn of his people"[Ps 148.14]; God lifts one "horn," not "the horns," of his people.[47]

Here Origen treats the Septuagint reading and that in the versions as complementary, together providing fuller access to an enigmatic Hebrew original than either could by itself, with the Septuagint revealing its implications for figurative interpretation. In PS77H9.6 the versions, while not having the same reading as the Septuagint, are consistent with it, so that Origen uses them as evidence that "his" in "in the innocence of his heart" refers to Christ.[48] Interestingly, in PS36H3.9 Origen substitutes τὰς ἡμέρας, "the days," a translation of the reading in our Hebrew text, for τὰς οδους, "the roads" in Ps 36:18, "The Lord knows the days of the blameless." Passing over the departure from what we have received as the Septuagint reading, a more obvious change than the correction of Psalm 78 that he was at pains to justify, Origen bases his interpretation on the corrected reading.

In the homilies, as in the rest of Origen's exegetical work, we observe Origen paying attention to strictly grammatical details such as whether the definite article is employed or not, where he sought out the Hebrew text to avoid, if possible, nuances that might not carry over in translation.[49] Nonetheless, Origen was not competent to evaluate Hebrew except in the most rudimentary way. Presumably he would have overcome this disability if he had known how to do so. The extraordinary creativity and immense labor and expense that went into the creation of the Hexapla was Origen's attempt, to compensate, in some measure, for his inability to read Hebrew.[50]

---

47. PS77H9.6 (476.3–8).
48. PS77H9.6 (478.2–7).
49. PS67H1.5 (185.17–20)
50. Anthony Grafton and Megan Williams, *Christianity and the Transformation of the Book* (Cambridge, MA: Harvard University Press, 2006) make clear how original and innovative conceiving the *Hexapla* was. See also Bernhard Neuschäfer, *Origenes als Philologe* (Basel: Friedrich Reinhardt Verlag, 1987) 86–103.

Origen's high estimate of the Hebrew language means that, at least for his purposes, the Septuagint could never replace the original Hebrew.[51] At the same time, it did not necessarily imply that he considered authoritative the Hebrew text used by his Jewish contemporaries. Nothing in CMG 314 indicates that he changed the view of the Septuagint that he had set forth in his response to a letter from Julius Africanus concerning the story of Susanna.[52] Africanus argued that the story did not belong in the Book of Daniel because, in the first place, it is missing in copies of that book accepted by Jews and because its style is incompatible with the rest of the book. Origen dismisses the second objection by saying that he does not share Africanus's estimate of the style. He responds that he is well aware that the story of Susanna is not in the Hebrew scriptures, providing a list of other passages in which the Septuagint includes passages not in the Hebrew texts accepted by the Jews or, occasionally, omits ones that are there. He argues that Christians should be aware of the Hebrew text accepted by the Jews but should not make it their sole standard; the Septuagint is the text divine providence has bestowed on those purchased at a great price [1 Cor 6:20, 7:23] for whom Christ died [Rom 14:5] and Christians should retain it.[53] On the basis of stories about the deaths of the prophets found in the New Testament but not in the Old, he argues that the text accepted by the Jews had been expurgated, so that stories like Susanna that reflected badly on the people and its leadership had been deleted. This has been taken to indicate that, for Origen, the Septuagint takes precedence over the Hebrew and the other versions. That, however, does not square with Origen's actual use of the *Hexapla*. It would seem, rather that Origen regarded the Septuagint, along with the Hebrew text received among Jews, as a witness to an original in Hebrew that is no longer fully recoverable. The irrecoverability of the original text would not be unduly disturbing, since Origen trusted the divine *oikonomia* to provide all that Christians actually needed from scripture. The same principle explains why Origen was not unduly concerned about divergences between manuscripts of the New Testament as well as different readings in the Hebrew Scriptures.[54]

---

51. This understanding of the LXX is often taken for granted, as by Naomi Seidman in *Faithful Renderings: Jewish-Christian Difference and the Politics of Translation* (Chicago: University of Chicago Press, 2006), 37–72.

52. See ed. by Nicholas de Lange in SC 302, Marguerite Harl and Nicholas de Lange, *Philocalie 1-20 et La Lettre à Africanus sur l'histoire de Susanne* (Paris: Cerf, 1983).

53. EpJA 8.

54. Hanson called his attitude to variants "disarmingly casual." Hanson, *Allegory and Event*, 175.

That the original Hebrew text could be irretrievably lost is the implication of Origen's attempt to refute Africanus's argument that two plays on words in Greek prove that the story of Susanna must have been composed in that language. The names of two varieties of tree, σχίνος (mastich) and πρίνος, (a kind of oak), are linked with the verbs σχίζω (cut) and πρίζω (saw) [Sus 54–55 and 58–59]. Arguing for the story's authenticity, Origen states that, as best he can determine from Jewish informants, the Hebrew words for the two trees have been lost. As a result, Africanus has not made his case because it cannot be proved that a pun in Hebrew was not actually translated word for word into a corresponding pun in Greek.[55] Furthermore:

> It is, then, nothing marvelous that some who were translating the Hebrew about Susanna, likely enough, deposited for a long time among things unspoken [ἐν ἀπορρήτοις] and preserved with those who were greater lovers of learning [φιλομαθεστέροις] and lovers of truth [φιλαληθεστέροις], had either accurately returned the contents of the wording [ἤτοι κυρίως ἐκδεδωκέναι τὰ τῆς λέξεως] or had found an analogy to the play on words in Hebrew [ἢ εὑρηκέναι τὸ ἀνάλογον τοῖς κατὰ τὸ Ἑβραϊκὸν παρωνύμοις] so that the Greeks might be enabled to follow them. And, indeed, in many other instances it is possible to find things returned in an accommodating manner [οἰκονομικῶς], which we have observed as we have investigated all the versions alongside each other [συνεξετάζοντες πάσας τὰς ἐκδόσεις ἀλλήλαις].[56]

Since plays on words are a common feature of Hebrew style, their presence in the story of Susanna could just as easily, Origen argued, be an argument for its authenticity. The story of Susanna, then, on this account, constitutes a witness to a lost Hebrew original. This does not mean, though, that the Jewish Hebrew texts or the other versions in Greek are not also witnesses to be taken into account. This is particularly true of Aquila, who made a practice of "being at the service of the Hebrew wording" [δουλεύων τῇ ἑβραικῇ λεξει] and is the translator "whom those who do not know the Hebrew language are most accustomed to use" [ᾧ μάλιστα εἰώθασιν οἱ ἀγνοοῦντες τὴν Ἑβραίων διάλεκτον χρῆσθαι].[57]

The homilies reinforce the conclusion reached by scholars such as Marguerite Harl and Peter Martens. Harl wrote that "the purpose of the *Hexapla* … was principally to exhibit a complete biblical text" where "Even if Origen's

55. Hanson, 10.
56. Hanson, 18.
57. Hanson, 4.

intention was not to propose modifications of the Septuagint, the lexical variants could in any event be found at the disposition of exegetes."[58] Martens wrote that "It is evident from a wider examination of Origen's corpus that no version of the Old Testament, the Hebrew text included, consistently served as an infallible criterion."[59] Nothing better illustrates this attitude to the Septuagint in relation to the Hebrew text accessible to him than Origen's discussion of Ps 73:16:[60]

> But it must be perceived more clearly about the things that happened among that people concerning whom it has been written, "You dried up the *ētham* rivers." [σὺ ἐξήρανας ποταμοὺς Ἐθάμ][61] This does not occur in the copies [ἐν τοῖς ἀντιγράφοις] of the Septuagint, but we find the line in the Hebrew and in the other versions [παρὰ τοῖς λοιποῖς]. And, not knowing what is "You dried up the *ētham* rivers," we read in one "old rivers" [ποταμοὺς ἀρχαίους]; in others the rivers running in the prophets are "old," "stiff" [στερροί],[62] "vigorous" [εὔτονοι] and "powerful" [δυνατοί], not because the prophets themselves have been dried up— far be it from us to say something slanderous—but because the Jewish prophets have stopped and there are no longer prophets among them.

According to Origen, his copy of the Septuagint did not have the line. One version transliterated the Hebrew without translating it. The rest gave four different translations. Translators may have sought to avoid an apparent contradiction; Hebrew אֵיתָן means "permanent" or "ever-flowing." According to Eusebius, who had access to the *Hexapla*, "stiff" was Aquila's reading and "old" was that of Symmachus.[63] Origen's treatment of the variant readings in the versions, simply setting them forth together and applying all of them to the Hebrew prophets, without making any judgment, bears out Marguerite Harl:

> The Fathers evidently did not practice a textual criticism of the books of the Old Testament in the sense of a method aimed at determining, among many forms of a text, that one that is considered the best, the closest to an original state, the only

---

58. Le but des *Hexaples* … était principalment de montrer un texte biblique complet.… Même si l'intention d'Origène n'était pas de proposer des modifications de la Septante, les variantes lexicales se trouvaient désormais à la disposition des exégètes. Marguerite Harl, *La langue de Japhet: Quinze études sur la Septante et le grec des Chrétiens* (Paris: Cerf, 1994), 259.

59. Peter W. Martens, *Origen and Scripture: The Contours of the Exegetical Life* (Oxford: Oxford University Press, 2012), 48n40.

60. Asaph was praying "with the mind" [see 1 Cor 14.15] in this prophetic psalm; he himself must have intended his words to refer to prophetic inspiration.

61. Ps 73:15b.

62. According to Eusebius [*Commentary on the Psalms*, 73.15], who had access to the *Hexapla*, "stiff" was Aquila's reading and "old" was that of Symmachus.

63. Eusebius, *Commentary on the Psalms*, 73.15.

one that will be canonical and will serve to exclude the other forms considered corrupt and secondary. They keep the Septuagint but can accept alongside it diverse forms that can be compared and juxtaposed, and that are meaningful, incapable of being arranged hierarchically.[64]

Confident in divine providence, Origen can live with an imperfect biblical text and an imperfect understanding of Hebrew, but he uses the versions to improve it as best he can. He assimilates his own struggle to learn Hebrew to the inevitability of human imperfection in this aeon, the extent of time before the eschaton. In this connection, throughout his works, he characteristically cites a Pauline text as a normative principle: 1 Cor 13:9, "we know in part and we prophesy in part."[65] In Homily 2, he extends this this norm to music, "we hymn in part, we sing in part."[66] He might just as easily have said, "we translate in part" and we have the original Hebrew text "in part."

Logos

Today translators often translate the same word with various words that an English speaker would ordinarily employ in any given context. Indeed, this is often seen as a hallmark of a sensitive translation. But words correspond to concepts, so that following this practice, can effectively make concepts of vital importance to the original author disappear. I think of a translation of *The Prince* in which Machiavelli's key concept, *virtù*, is dissipated into "strength," "importance," "ability," "skill," "cleverness," and "discipline."[67] In Origen's case, the preeminent example of such a concept, corresponding to no one English word, is λόγος. Λόγος, from the same verbal root as the verb λέγω, "say," originally meant "account" or "accounting," but came to have a wide variety of overlapping meanings and usages. Heraclitus was particularly influential in giving it the philosophical meaning "reason" or "rationality," both the

64. À l'évidence, les Pères n'ont pas pratiqué une critique textuelle des livres de l'Ancien Testament, au sens d'une méthode visant à fixer, parmi plusieurs formes d'un texte, celle qui est jugé la meilleure, la plus proche d'un état premier, la seule qui serait canonique et servirait à exclure les autres formes considérées comme corrompues ou secondaires. Ils gardent la Septante mais peuvent accepter à coté d'elle diverses formes, comparables, juxtaposables, porteuses de sens, non hiérarchisable. Harl, *La Langue de Japhet*, 265.

65. CMG 314 adds two additional explicit citations of 1 Cor 13:9, PS15H1.6 (84.8–16) and PS77H4.9 (401.10–402.2) to the 39 citations recorded in *Biblia Patristica*.

66. PS67H2.3 (207.12).

67. In *The Portable Machiavelli*, ed. and tr. By Peter Bondanella and Mark Musa (New York: Penguin, 1979),

reason that human beings use to make an argument and the immanent rational order that humans discover in the cosmos.

Translating λόγος brings us to the heart of Origen's teaching, with implications both for his "theology" in the patristic sense—his understanding of God—and for the way he conceived his own task as a pastor and teacher. Overseeing a translation of Clement of Alexandria, who shared Origen's concept of logos, led H.-I. Marrou to point out the difficulty this word presents:

> We must emphasize, right now, the ambiguity, constantly maintained and exploited by Clement, and keeping the translator at bay, concerning the word "Logos": this word will signify, from time to time, and often at the same time, the composed discourse, human reason and uncreated Reason, the divine Verb, Second Person of the Trinity, the Savior, the Christ, Jesus.[68]

Speaking of Origen, Rowan Williams refers to "a characteristic and significant ambiguity" in Origen's use of λόγος, which can refer "either to Origen's own rational spirit or the divine Logos."[69] Róbert Somos explains why translating λόγος is so difficult in his work on Origen's logic (published in 2013 and making use of the homilies):

> At the beginning of the fourth book of *First Principles*, Origen's aim is expressed in the following terms: "… we try also to conform our belief with reason" (λόγῳ τε πειρώμεθα κρατύνειν ἡμῶν τὴν πίστιν). This formula may be the motto of this book. Here the meaning of *logos* is not identical with the divine Word, but it is not independent of it either. *Logos*, as operation or argument capable of confirming a belief, may be "reason," "argument" or "ground" depending on the context.[70]

Divine Logos and human logos are intimately linked:

> According to Origen, although the *logos* used by us in our intellectual practice is a human capacity, the ultimate source of this rationality is the divine *Logos*, divine Wisdom, turned in the direction of created beings via creation, along with providence and the fulfillment of providence, the birth of Jesus Christ, his life and

68. Il nous faut souligner, dès maintenant, l'équivoque, constamment entretenue et exploitée par Clément ; et qui met le traducteur à abois, autour du mot Logos : celui-ci désignera tour à tour, et souvent à la fois, le discours rédigé, la raison humaine et la Raison incréée, le Verbe divin, Seconde Personne de la Trinité, le Sauveur, le Christ, Jésus. Introduction to *Clément d'Alexandrie, Le Pédagogue*, vol. 1, Cerf, 1960 (SC 70), p. 8. Marguerite Harl, in her remarks as translator of the volumes, makes much the same point (p. 104n2 from p. 103).

69. Rowan D. Williams, "Origen: Between Orthodoxy and Heresy" in Wolfgang A. Bienert and Uwe Kühneweg, eds., *Origeniana Septima: Origenes in den Auseinanderselzungen des 4. Jahrhunderts* (Leuven: Leuven University Press, 1999), 8.

70. Róbert Somos, *Logic and Argumentation in Origen* = Adamantiana 7 (Münster: Aschendorff Verlag, 2013), 1, citing PA 4.1.1.

teaching, his death and resurrection. According to the Alexandrian theologian, the organized structure of the world, our inner intellectual nature and the divine revelation crystallized in the divine texts constitute a uniform, organic but complex and perplexing message.[71]

All three agree that, while "logos" means different things in different contexts, it can be difficult or impossible, in some contexts, to distinguish one meaning from another.

This difficulty manifests itself in various ways. At the beginning of Homily 2 on Psalm 36 Origen says:

> When the logos is giving an order and saying [Προστάσσοντος τοῦ λόγου καὶ λέγοντος], "Be subordinate to the Lord"[72] it is necessary to unfold and present by the logos [ἀναγκαῖόν ἐστιν τὸ ἀναπτύξαι καὶ παραστῆσαι τῷ λόγῳ] who, on the one hand, is subordinate to the Lord, and who, on the other hand is not subordinated to him. [73]

Is the λόγος who gives an order the divine logos, or is it the Psalm itself conceived of as a human discourse? Is the logos by which we unfold the intention of the first logos the divine logos or human reason? Most likely, in both cases it is both, not because Origen is being deliberately ambiguous, but because distinguishing the two does not occur to him. Λόγος means many things, and those meanings often overlap. Origen's discussion of the plagues of flies and frogs is another instance of this amplitude of meaning:

> What was cause, then, for the Egyptians to find themselves beset with such scourges? Listen, judging by small increments, he gave them a place for change of mind. But perhaps, denigrating the Egyptians, the logos did not judge them to be human [Τάχα δὲ τοὺς Αἰγυπτίους ἐξευτελίζων ὁ λόγος οὐδὲ ἀνθρώπους αὐτοὺς ἔκρινεν εἶναι]. [74]

Is the logos here the message of the biblical text, the divine Logos working on the poor Egyptians, or both at once? The best way to capture this amplitude is by rendering λόγος, simply as "logos," a word that has become relatively familiar to English-speakers. A single word such as "reason" or "discourse" cannot fit into every usage, and seeking different words to fit different contexts entails narrowing the range of meaning that is always possible.

The considerations that lead to simply transcribing λόγος also militate against capitalizing it. Logos, Origen tells his congregation, in is the soul's food:

71. Somos, 2.
72. Ps 36:7a.
73. PS36H2.1 (126.1–3).
74. PS77H.7.3 (440.13–15).

And just as food and drink supply us—bodily food supplies as far as the body is concerned, remove this and we do not live; bodily drink supplies as far as the body is concerned, take away that and we do not live—in the same manner, change the subject to logos [μετάβα τῷ λόγῳ] and give the logos to the soul [καὶ ἐπὶ τὴν ψυχὴν δὸς τὸν λόγον]: for a human being will not live on bread alone, but a human being will live upon every utterance [ἀλλ' ἐπὶ παντὶ ῥήματι] coming out of God's mouth.[75]

In the logos that is given to the soul the divine Logos, the logos of scripture, or Origen's own logos? This is the ambiguity Williams pointed to, that where capitalizing "logos" when it denotes the second person of the Trinity precludes the possibility that it refers to Origen's own speech. In the passage above, his own speech seems likely to be included since, in almost the same breath, he identifies the logos that feeds the soul with his own "teaching logos":

> The teaching logos [λόγος διδασκαλικὸς] coming into the listener is a nourishment of the soul, the logos of wisdom and the logos of knowledge [λόγος σοφίας καὶ λόγος γνώσεως].[76] Just as, in the case of the body, logos has disposed [ὁ λόγος παρέστησεν] that, without nourishment and drink the body dies, so also a soul, if is not nourished and does not drink, it dies the soul's death.[77]

Origen is confident that the homily he is giving or the argument he is making thus genuinely incarnates, if only to some extent, the divine logos. When he discusses the logos as food, he does not suggest the presence of the logos in the eucharistic bread, but in the homily.[78] The divine logos is thus manifested in the teaching logos in many individual logoi, so that the ambiguity of the word even extends to the plural:

> To the extent that things come about well, they are God's. For example, good logoi are God's [οἷον οἱ λόγοι οἱ καλοὶ τοῦ θεοῦ εἰσιν], for someone does not speak his own things well, but speaks the things of God. But just as the logoi go out of my mouth [Ὥσπερ δὲ οἱ λόγοι κἂν ἐξίωσιν ἐκ στόματός μου], those that would be unassailable and divine, are not mine but God's, so that I am of good courage to say: "or do you seek proof of Christ who speaks in me".[79]

The question of capitalization also applies to words such as θεος , χριστος and πνευμα. How do we handle capitalization in a passage like this?

75. Dt 8:3, Mt 4:4, PS15H1.9 (88.1–6).
76. See 1 Cor 12:8.
77. PS77H7.3 (88.14–17).
78. On this subject see Fernando Soler, *Orígenes y los alimentos espirituales: El uso teológico de metáforas de comer y beber* (Leiden: Brill, 2021) and see the discussion below of the church "homilizing" the logos into the soul in PS81H.1.
79. 2 Cor 13:3, PS76H2.4 (318. 5–9).

But our teacher, Christ Jesus, is a god ['Εστιν δὲ ὁ διδάσκαλος ἡμῶν Χριστὸς Ἰησοῦς θεός] and if it is sufficient for the learner that he become like the teacher, the purpose of the learner is to become a christ from Christ and a god from a god [ἵνα γένηται ἀπὸ Χριστοῦ χριστός ἐστιν καὶ ἀπὸ θεοῦ θεός], and he learns from the light of the cosmos. [80]

In Origen's pre-Nicene theology God is infinitely transcendent, but, by virtue of divine condescension, there is continuity or, as Origen put it "kinship" συγγένεια between us and God, a concept that he references in Homily 2 on Psalm 73 as well as at the conclusion of *Peri Archon*.[81]

The Body of the Logos: Lexis and Rhēton

When God addresses our needs in the Bible, that speech is "logos," ultimately indistinguishable from the divine Logos, the second divine hypostasis. The divine Logos, though, becomes present or visits the realm of time and space by becoming flesh, not only in a human being, Jesus Christ, but in human speech, preeminently in the words of scripture. The Bible is thus, effectively, an animate being, as Origen puts it in *Peri Archon*:

> For just as the human being is composed of body and soul and spirit [ὥσπερ γάρ ὁ ἄωθρωπος συνέστηκεν ἐκ σώματος καὶ θυχῆς καὶ πνεύματος], in the same manner also the scripture arranged [οἰκονομηθεῖσα] by God for the salvation of human beings has been given.[82]

In *Peri Archon* the sensible "body" or "flesh" of scripture consists of its words, which provide the πρόχειρος ἐκδοχή, "at-hand take-away," from those words.[83]

Origen also speaks of scripture as a body animated by Christ in a text that belongs to a work that was, like the homilies in CMG 314, recovered in modern times, *On the Passover*:

> We participate in the flesh of Christ [μεταλαμβάνομεν τῶν σαρκῶν τοῦ Χριστοῦ], that is, of the divine scriptures [τῶν θείων γραφῶν] * * * of the genuine lamb,

80. PS80H1.1 (509.6–9).

81. PA 4,10.10, where συγγένεια lies behind Rufinus's *consanguinitas*, and in PS73H2.1 (238.1–11). On this concept, see Édouard des Places, *Suggeneia: La parenté de l'homme avec Dieu d'Homère à la patristique* (Paris: Klincksiek, 1965).

82. PA 4.2.4 (Koetschau 313.1–4).

83. Πρόχειρος εκδοχη is found in PA 4.2.6 (Koetschau 312.9–10) We also find this term in PA 4.3.4 CJ 5, CC 4.72, CC 5.16 and Fr. 2 on Eph and προχειροτέρα ἐκδοχή in CC 6.60. Κοινή ἐκδοχή, Πρώτη ἐκδοχή, "first take-away" occurs in PA 4.2.6, CC 4.48 and PS67H1.3. Elsewhere it is often referred to as κοινός or κοινοτέρα ἐκδοχή, "common" or "commoner take-away" (CC 7.43, CC 8.65 and PS67H1.3).

because the Apostle confesses that the lamb of our Passover is Christ, saying "For Christ, our Passover, has been sacrificed, whose flesh and bones and blood, as we have shown above, are the divine scriptures, which, whenever we eat them, we have Christ, when the wordings have become his bones [τῶν μὲν λέξεων τῶν ὀστῶν αὐτοῦ γενομένων], but the ideas from the wordings have become his flesh [τῶν δε σαρκῶν τῶν τῆς λέξεως νοημάτων], advancing on which, as is likely, we see the things after these things in a riddle and through a mirror, but the blood is the faith of the good news of the new covenant, as the Apostle witnesses, saying, "and they have profaned the blood of the new covenant," by which blood, anointed by faith, we escape the Destroyer.[84]

Here λέξις is Origen's term for the bones that hold the flesh together. These sensible words, as Origen puts it in Homily 2 on Psalm 67, constitute the indispensable "first step," or "foundation," from which the ascent to higher levels must begin:

> But so that the difference might be perceived between "sing" and "pluck" [Ἵνα δὲ νοηθῇ τοῦ ᾄδειν καὶ τοῦ ψάλλειν ἡ διαφορά],[85] we go back to the sensible [ἐπὶ τὸ αἰσθητόν], for sensible things become a ladder [ἐπιβάθρα γίνεται] towards understanding better things. For that very reason the whole scripture is spoken in sensible terms, so that we might step up on them into the spiritual things.[86]

In the translation that accompanied the edition of *On the Passover*, Pierre Nautin followed the common practice of translating the singular, λέξις, as "letter" or its equivalent. Translating λέξις as "letter," though, obscures Origen's careful choice of words. Although Origen often employed biblical terms, he usually avoids γράμμα, "letter," a term that as Manlio Simonetti has pointed out, normally negative connotations.[87] This is the case in the Psalm homilies as well. In Homily 1 on Psalm 80 he mocks the "lovers of the letter" [οἱ τοῦ γράμματος φίλοι]who suppose that the "sound of the trumpet" on the day of resurrection [1 Cor 52] implies that some angels constitute a heavenly "brass band," [χαλκεῖς]."[88] As we seen, in Homily 1 on Psalm 77, he blames much spiritual death on "the pretext of the letters," προφάσει τῶν γραμμάτων.[89]

---

84. *On the Passover*, 33–34 in Origène, *Sur la Pâque*, ed. Octave Guérand and Pierre Nautin (Paris: Beauchesne, 1979), 216–18.

85. In Ps 67:5.

86. PS67H2.4 (208.6–9).

87. See Manlio Simonetti, "Sul significato di alcuni termini tecnici nella letteratura esegetica greca," in Carmelo Curti, et al. edd., *La terminologia esegetica nell'antichità: Atti del Primo Seminario di antichità cristiane Bari, 25 ottobre 1984* (Bari: Edipuglia, 1987). 47n45.

88. PS80H1.5 (489.1–7).

89. PS77H1.1 (353.5). The use of the plural of γραμμα in a negative context is unusual. Γραμματα, "letters" is ordinarily used interchangeably with γραφη, "scripture."

Ordinarily, avoiding γράμμα, Origen uses two non-biblical terms, the above-mentioned, λέξις, and a second term, ῥητόν. Sometimes by themselves and sometimes together, these terms denote the bodily, sensible foundation of biblical interpretation. Λέξις, which can be translated as "wording," is a grammatical term for words themselves as visible or audible phenomena, as opposed to what those words signify, λόγος, "meaningful discourse."[90] In the usage of grammarians, "wording" might actually lack "logos"; Diogenes Laertius cites the non-sense word, "blityri" as an example of a "wording" that is ἄσημος, "without signification."[91] For Origen, though, it would seem that "wording" is always meaningful. In Homily 1 on Psalm 80, he declares that "crying out with the meaningless voice of a heart (ἀσήμῳ φωνῃ καρδίας)" occurs "through want of words (διὰ τὴν ἀπορίαν τῶν λέξεων)."[92] Ῥητόν, the neuter of the adjective ῥητός, used nominally, is a less common word. Ῥητός means "stated" or "stipulated" but, according to Pierre Chantraine, its original use, attested in Homer and the Tragedians, is to designate what can be said, what is can be spoken, as opposed to what is "unspeakable," ἄρρητος.[93] "Statement," seems the best translation, although the word, for Origen, probably retained also the sense of "what can be stated," as opposed to the ἄρρητα ῥήματα, "unspeakable utterances" of 2 Cor 12:4. Origen probably took the term from Philo and Clement, who used it much as he did.[94]

Origen chose words carefully and used them sparingly. As a grammarian himself, he saw a need for two separate words to designate the bodily level of scripture in order to distinguish, when necessary, the words themselves, λέξις, from the πρόχειρος ἐκδοχή, the "first take-away," the ῥητόν, "statement." We see this distinction in Homily 1 on 77, where Origen speaks of Matthew's gospel as paraphrasing a "statement," ῥητόν, the inscription of the Psalm, in "wordings," λέξεσι.[95] Because the "statement," ῥητόν, is meaningful, one can state it in other terms. Likewise, one can translate a "statement" into a wording; one does not translate a λέξις.[96] We see this in Homily 1 on Psalm 36:

<hr>

90. See Dionysius Thrax, *Ars grammatica* 1.1 and Diogenes Laertius, *Vitae philosophorum* 7.56–57

91. Diogenes, Ars grammatica, 7.57.

92. PS80H1.3 (484.1–7).

93. See Pierre Chantraine, *Dictionnaire étymologique de la langue grecque: Histoire des mots*, new edition (Paris: Klincksieck, 2009), 310.

94. See, for example, Philo, *De opificio mundi*, 126 and Clement, *Stromateis*, 3.2.7.2. Both authors use the term for a biblical "statement," and also contrast it with ἄρρητος.

95. PS77H1.1 (351.10–11).

96. In EPJA 18(12) Origen speaks of translating "the things accurately taken away from the wording" κυρίως ἐκδεδωκέναι τὰ τῆς λέξεως, not the λεξις itself.

One must come to understand, then, what distinguishes "make jealous" from "be jealous" [ἡ διαφορὰ τοῦ 'παραζηλοῦν' παρὰ τὸ 'ζηλοῦν']. The Greek wording [ἡ λέξις Ἑλληνικὴ] is not ordinarily employed at all either in literary or in colloquial Greek [Οὐ πάνυ τίς ἐστιν οὐδὲ τέτριπται ἐν τῇ συνηθείᾳ τῶν Ἑλλήνων οὔτε τῶν φιλολόγων οὔτε τῶν ἰδιωτικώτερον φραζόντων], but seems to have been drafted into service [βεβιασμένη γενέσθαι] by translators wanting to translate the Hebrew statement [τὸ Ἑβραϊκὸν ῥητὸν] and to set forth as far as humanly possible [παραστῆσαι κατὰ τὸ δυνατὸν ἀνθρωπίνῃ φύσει], the distinction between "making jealous" and "jealousy."[97]

The distinction between words themselves and their intelligible meaning that Origen makes between "wording" and "statement" thus resembles the distinction grammarians made between "wording" and "logos." Origen, however, refines the terminology. "Logos," the self-disclosure of God in the order of the cosmos, the message of the Bible, and the person of Jesus Christ, is not fully accessible when words assume meaning. The bodily level is, as we have seen, simply the first step in a long climb towards greater understanding. He uses ῥητόν rather than λόγος, because, as we have seen, the ultimate significance of biblical words is not disclosed by their immediate, intuitive sense, the "first take-away," πρώτη ἐκδοχή. There can be only one "statement" to the "wording," but there is not just one "logos." Thus, in his comments on Ps 73:3–4 in his first homily on that Psalm, Origen can say, "we see also some other logos in the statement" (βλέπομεν καὶ ἄλλον τινὰ λόγον ἐν τῷ ῥητῷ).[98] In the second homily on the same psalm he actually offers alternative logoi for the heads of the serpents [τὰς κεφαλὰς τῶν δρακόντων] in v. 13:

> According to one logos [καθ' ἕνα μὲν λόγον] I will say that all his rulers [ἄρχοντας] are his heads, but, according to another [καθ' ἕτερον δὲ], the rulers of the heresies; thus Basilides is a head of the devil, Valentinus is a head of the devil, Apelles another head and, in general, all the rulers among the heresies are heads of the one serpent.[99]

In that homily he also states that failing to understand the prophetic ῥητόν amounts to the same thing as rejecting their books altogether:

> And when you delete the prophets [ἀθετῇς τοὺς προφήτας], or you acknowledge their statement [ἢ ῥητὸν μὲν παραδέχῃ αὐτῶν], but do not fully receive their mind

---

97. PS36H1.1 (113.20–25).
98. PS73H1.9 (235.16–17).
99. PS73H2.6 (249.1–4).

60 Joseph W. Trigg

[τὸν δὲ ἐν αὐτοῖς νοῦν μὴ ἐκλαμβάνῃς] as you ought, there is no prophet for you; a prophet is for one who hears the prophetic logoi as the Holy Spirit intends.[100]

For Origen the ῥητόν, "statement," is simply what λέξις, "wording," actually says, not an interpretation of it to say something else. The intention of the original author, whose words embody the divine logos, is "logos." If, in Origen's image of the scripture as the body of the Passover lamb, the wording, which should never be broken, is the bones, then the statement is the flesh that feeds believers with the divine logos. Origen states in PA that in most cases the "statement" is a logos, although sometimes there is no logos at the bodily level of scripture.[101] We see the same thing in the homilies, for example, a statement is a logos in Ps 76:7:

> "At night I prattled with my heart and my spirit was dejected" [νυκτὸς μετὰ τῆς καρδίας μου ἠδολέσχουν καὶ ἐσκάλευον τὸ πνεῦμά μου] Learn from the statement [ἀπὸ τοῦ ῥητοῦ], if sleep abandons you and you are wakeful, do not waste the time of wakefulness in what you should not do, but, during the time you are awake, while sleep is abandoning you, take calculations of piety [διαλογισμοὺς λαμβάνειν θεοσεβείας].[102]

Since the statement is simply the what the wording says, it does not encompass ἀλληγορία, "allegory," or τροπολογία, "figurative language," where the words used stand for something else. Nonetheless, such interpretation may be necessary to avoid a statement unworthy of God:

> Next let us see what God commands us. For he speaks a wording [λέξιν], concerning which I beg him that I may understand why he says: *Widen your mouth and I will fill it.*[103] Let those who want us not to allegorize gain a deep understanding and not allegorize [θεωρήτωσαν οἱ βουλευόμενοι ἡμᾶς μὴ ἀλληγορεῖν καὶ μὴ ἀλληγορήτωσαν] , but let them put their minds to [ἐπινοείτωσαν] how God says, *Widen your mouth and I will fill it* and let them say how one must open the mouth. For does the logos actually want us to open it and make the lips wider? And how is it not shameful to reckon [αἰσχρὸν νομίζειν] that God said such things? How, then, is someone going to explain this passage without using figurative interpretation [πῶς οὖν ταῦτα τίς διηγήσεται μὴ τροπολογήσας τὸν τόπον]? How can what is said be suspected to befit God [πῶς ἀξίως τοῦ θεοῦ ὑπονοῆσαι τὰ εἰρημένα]?[104]

100. PS73H2.3 (243.5–8).
101. PA 4.2.4–5.
102. PS76H1.10 (309.9–13).
103. Ps 80:11c.
104. PS80H2.5 (501.25–502.7).

Attention to the wording can reveal that the statement is untenable, as in Ps 73:19:

> But I want at the same time to persuade the listener from the wording itself [ἐξ αὐτῆς τῆς λέξεως] that the clarification is not forced [ὅτι ἡ σαφήνεια αὕτη οὐκ ἔστιν βεβιασμένη] but handed over according to the intention of the scriptures. For it is not said, "Do not hand over to the beasts flesh confessing you" but "a soul confessing you." But it is evident that these "beasts" do not eat "souls," but "flesh," so other beasts eat souls.[105]

Origen's insistence that his "clarification" is not "forced" may be a defense against critics, but it is just as likely that he is pointing out to his own students how he has arrived at his position by engaging fully with the bodily level of scripture: beasts, in the normal sense of the word, eat flesh, not souls.

The important thing is to pay close attention to the wording. In one remarkable case, such attention can even reveal a secret about the cosmos in what the words say:

> Let us not pass over the statement even on its own [μὴ παρέλθωμεν δὲ μηδὲ τὸ ῥητὸν κατ'αὐτό] but let us see if it is possible that the wording [ἡ λέξις] that says, *"the waters have seen you and were afraid, the abysses are disturbed, multiple reverberation of waters"*[106] holds some understanding [ἔχειν τινα νοῦν]. It comes to me that it says that everything is animate and nothing in the cosmos is empty of soul [ὅτι πάντα ἐψύχωται καὶ οὐδέν ἐστιν ἐν τῷ κόσμῳ κενὸν ψυχῆς], but everything is animate in various bodies.[107] The heaven is animate, because to it, as to a living being, scripture says: "Give ear, earth, and I shall speak" and "hear, heaven."[108] The earth is animate: "utterances from my mouth and give ear, earth."[109] If indeed the heaven is animate and the earth also is animate, could the sea and rivers be inanimate? Or are they also animate? And we see, to be sure, that "the sea saw and fled, Jordan was turned backward."[110]

Origen presupposes the philosophical position, set forth in *Peri Archon* and *On Prayer,* that only animate beings have the capacity to move themselves.[111] When the wording itself contains commands to heaven earth, the sea, and a river to move themselves, it therefore implies that all of those addressed are animate beings capable of doing so:

---

105. PS73H3.7 (263.2–6).

106. Ps 76:17. It takes a soul to see, be afraid or be disturbed.

107. Philosophically, Origen holds the position that no body can initiate movement, unless it has a soul. See especially, OP 1.7.3 and PA 3.1.2.

108. Dt 32:1.

109. Is 1:2.

110. Ps 113:3. PS76H3.2 (329.18–330.6).

111. PA 3.1.1–2 and OP 6,1–2.

And that the logos is conversing as with animate beings [Καὶ ὅτι ὡς πρὸς ἐψυχωμένα ὁ λόγος διαλέγεται], I am now advocating by the wording [νῦν τῇ λέξει συναγορεύω]. I am proving this by the statement alone [τῷ ῥητῷ μόνῳ παρίσταμαι], wishing to show that we often fail to notice that even the wording, according to its statement, holds divine secrets and things not knowable by casual readers [θέλων παραστῆσαι ὅτι πολλάκις λανθάνει ἡμᾶς καὶ ἡ λέξις κατὰ τὸ ῥητὸν ἔχουσα μυστήρια θεῖα καὶ οὐ τοῖς τυχοῦσι γνωστά].[112]

Close attention is the key. To casual readers, those who simply happen upon the passage without any intention of interrogating it, this divine secret remains safely hidden in plain sight.

Visitations of the Logos

One is most aware that these homilies are transcripts of oral presentations at a particular time and place at the beginning of the first homily on Psalm 67. There Origen seems to be reacting to a prayer by a bishop who was present in which he was mentioned by name, putting him in a delicate position. Conceivably the bishop, as a show of support to Origen, prayed for or even thanked God in advance for a "heavenly discourse/logos" from him. Origen's response is to take a step back and to receive the bishop's seeming compliment as a prayer for a future outcome that could only happen through a visitation [ἐπιδημία] of Christ, the divine Logos:

Since I am persuaded that every logos [πάντα λόγον] without Christ's presence in the speaker [χωρὶς παρουσίας Χριστοῦ τῆς ἐν τῷ λέγοντι] is empty and from earth [κενὸν καὶ ἀπὸ γῆς εἶναι][113] but it is impossible for a heavenly logos to visit us [λόγον οὐράνιον ἐπιδημεῖν] apart from the Father God who sent him,[114]

As is often the case with Origen, this response is simultaneously humble, acknowledging the need for the divine presence, and bold, signaling that such a visitation is likely and that his congregation should look for it. Origen's homily would qualify as a "logos," in the sense of "discourse," about God or something heavenly, but "heavenly logos" is also an accepted term for the divine Logos.[115] Origen appears to be at pains to deny that such a result can be taken

---

112. PS76H3.2 (330.6–9).

113. See, possibly, 1 Cor 15:47 and 1 Sam 3:19.

114. PS67H1.1 (173.12–14). See John 17:18 and 20:21, 1 John 4:14.

115. See Clement of Alexandria, *Exhortation* 1.2.3 and 1.5.4; Acts of Thomas 80; Tatian, *Apology* 7.1, Hippolytus, *Refutation* 6.35.4.

for granted, even as he points out the implications of words the bishop may have used. Ἐπιδημεῖν is the verb Origen uses to speak of the earthly visitation of the incarnate divine Logos. The "sending Father God" who makes a heavenly logos possible recalls John 20:21, "as the Father has sent me, so I send you." By implication, Origen is one of those sent, whose λόγος in the sense of "discourse" has a prospect of incarnating in human words the divine λόγος.

The contrast between a λόγος "from earth" and a "heavenly" λόγος merits attention. The contrast recalls the Pauline distinction between Adam, the "dirty human being from the earth" [ἄνθρωπος ἐκ γῆς χοικός] and Christ, the "human being from heaven" ἄνθρωπος ἐξ οὐρανοῦ] of 1 Cor 15:47, suggesting that the "heavenly logos" does indeed incarnate Christ. The notion of a "logos from the earth" also recalls 1 Sam 3:19: "And Samuel became great, and the Lord was with him, and from all his discourses [ἀπὸ πάντων τῶν λόγων αὐτοῦ] it did not fall on the earth [ἐπὶ τὴν γῆν]." This suggests that the discourse Origen's hearers may hear will have a status comparable to Old Testament prophecy. Drawing on the fragments of Origen's homilies (or commentary) on 1 Corinthians, Gunnar af Hällström has shown that Origen found in Paul two kinds of Christian prophecy, an edifying prophecy in 1 Cor 12:8–10 that all believers are capable of exercising and a higher gift comparable to Old Testament prophecy, given only to some, in 1 Cor 1:28.[116] Since Origen taught that the divine Logos was indeed incarnate in the words of the prophets, it is easy to see how the ambiguity Rowan Williams noticed in the word λόγος might come about.

Taking seriously Origen's belief that his own speech was potentially a visitation of the divine Logos has implications, not just for capitalization, but for sentence structure in translation. Prinzivalli points out that Rufinus had to deal with the linguistic gap between the relatively loose structure of Greek and the more rigid structure of Latin.[117] Any translation into contemporary English faces a more challenging gap. Greek, like Latin, as a highly inflected language, exhibits a logical structure through a long, complex sentence. That is harder to do in English and militates against the journalistic style mentioned earlier. Nonetheless because he took full advantage of their structure, Origen's sentences resist being broken up. Thus, in one example out of many, we read in Homily on Psalm 81:

---

116. Gunnar af Hällström, *Charismatic Succession: A Study of Origen's Concept of Prophecy* (Helsinki: Publications of the Finnish Exegetical Society, 1985), 48–56.

117. GCSO 13, 41.

And here then it says well, "'I have said, "you are all gods and sons of the highest, but you"'—I see us practicing such things not worthy of divinity—it adds and says, "'see, in fact, you die as human beings and you fall as one of the rulers,'" and God's legacy coming to us, making us gods [καὶ ἐρχομένην δωρεὰν θεοῦ εἰς ἡμᾶς τὴν ποιοῦσαν ἡμᾶς θεούς], which ought to be received with the whole soul, we sinners do not accept, but tossing away and excising divinity, we accept the flesh's ways of thinking, accomplishing works of the flesh, not putting to death by spirit the deeds of the flesh, which we ought to do."[118]

One might be inclined to make this translation more acceptable by, at the very least, putting a period after "rulers," starting a new sentence at "and God's legacy," but this changes the effect of the sentence. A quotation from the Psalm (interrupted by explanatory comments) is followed its paraphrase. Both are in direct discourse following λέγει, "says." Breaking the sentence in two breaks the grammatical apposition linking the quotation and its paraphrase. Examining the implications of this seemingly trivial question of style reveals how bold Origen actually was: the second clause, in which Origen paraphrases the Psalm in his own words, is direct discourse because, in his own estimation, Origen, like the Psalmist, is a mouthpiece of the divine logos.

This sentence appears in Homily on Psalm 81, the final homily in CMG 314. Lorenzo Perrone, in this volume, addresses the obscurity of the process that determined which particular homilies it contains out of the much larger number that Origen preached and, for that matter, how it was that Origen himself preached on certain Psalms and not on others. Perrone's suggestion that a selection of the Asaph Psalms played a role in that process is convincing. Psalm 81 is the next-to-the-last Asaph Psalm, the last of which is Psalm 82, on which, according to Jerome,[119] Origen preached three homilies that do not survive. I would suggest that, at some point in the process that led to CMO 314, his Homily on Psalm 81 stood out as the fitting culmination of a selection of Origen's homilies on the first half of the Psalter, both because of the extraordinary language of the Psalm itself and because of the way Origen addressed it. Psalm 81, as received in John 10:34–35, legitimates the language of divinization. There Jesus asks a group of Jews why they are preparing to stone him, they respond, "We are not stoning you on account of a good work, but because of blasphemy and that, being a human being, you make yourself a

---

118. PS81H.1 (511.6–14), adapting Ps 81:7, Gal 5:19 and Rom 8:13.
119. In Jerome, Epistle 33, discussed in GCSO13.4–9.

god [ὅτι σὺ ἄνθρωπος ὢν ποιεῖς σεαυτὸν θεόν]." Jesus responds with a citation to Psalm 81: "Is it not written in your law that 'I have said, "You are gods"?' [Οὐκ ἔστιν γεγραμμένον ἐν τῷ νόμῳ ὑμῶν ὅτι Ἐγὼ εἶπα, Θεοί ἐστε;]. His response begins with the words, "If he called 'gods' those towards whom God's logos came to be" [πρὸς οὓς ὁ λόγος τοῦ θεοῦ ἐγένετο]. This is the process Origen expounds in his homily, He states that, in Jesus' parable of the yeast, the church is the woman who inserts yeast into three measures of dough, so that the whole is leavened [Mt 13:33, Lk 13:21], and the three measures of dough are the body, soul and spirit that, according to Paul, constitute the human person [1 Th 5:23]. The yeast itself is the god logos that divinizes the soul. Origen as preacher enables the divinization of the body as well by "homilizing this yeast into the three measures [ὁμιλήσασα ἡ ζύμη αὕτη τοῖς τρίσι σάτοις]" so that "it leavens this whole dough and has made the human being out of the whole to become a god [ἐζύμωσεν ὅλον τοῦτο τὸ φύραμα καὶ πεποτὸν ἄνθρωπον ἐξ ὅλων γενέσθαι θεόν]."[120]

As we have seen in the first homily on Psalm 67, Origen also holds out the possibility that, in his preaching, the divine logos will be present in his words and thus "visit" (ἐπιδημεῖν) the congregation. In another, the second homily on Psalm 15, he prays for divine guidance with a difficult issue of interpretation saying, "But come, Christ. Visit [ἐπιδήμει], God's logos. Explain to me and to those who genuinely want to listen …"[121] Here, implicitly, should Origen offer a convincing explanation, the hearer can infer that Christ is speaking through him. In the passage from the Homily on Psalm 81, such a visitation is what he expects. Just before that passage he has said:

> gathering [συναγωγὴ] then, if we genuinely are gathered, if we do not walk in a human manner, if we do not sow in the flesh what God says in "You harvest corruption,"[122] and we do not do the works of the flesh but the fruits of the spirit,[123] it is not a gathering of human beings, but a gathering of gods; the devil can do nothing, but God visits [ἐπιδημεῖ] standing in the midst of the gathering of gods. Therefore it is said "God stood in the gathering of gods."[124]

Origen's homily does not simply interpret the psalm, it reenacts it. The divine logos, making use of its prophetic author, "says" the Psalm and then, making

---

120. PS81H.1 (512.1–11).
121. PS15H2.6 (103.3).
122. See Gal 5:8.
123. See Gal 5:19 and 5:22.
124. PS81H.1 (510.1–6).

use of Origen, "says" the paraphrase that clarifies the addressee: the "you" of the Psalm becomes the "we" who have spurned our legacy and for whose sake the divine logos became one of us. Origen's words, apposed to the words of Psalm and paraphrasing them, are a visitation, an ἐπιδημία, of the divine logos. He then does the same thing with Apostle Paul:

> But what makes us human beings [ἀνθρώπους], so that, having fallen from divinity, we will destroy the legacy calling us to become gods? What makes human beings? Hear Paul speaking about very small sins, "for when there is among you jealousy and strife, are you not fleshly and do you not walk in a human manner?" And he adds, "Are you not human beings?"[125] Does he not all but cry out there and say: "The logos has called you [ὁ μὲν λόγος ὑμᾶς ἐκάλεσεν], so that you may be gods, but, for this reason and that, you are human beings"?[126]

The logos that has called is simultaneously the divine logos incarnated in Asaph's words in Psalm 81, the divine logos incarnated in Paul's words in of Paul 1 Cor 13:3, and in the discourse (λόγος) Origen himself is delivering. All are saying the same thing.

Origen explains how this is possible in the passage that concludes Homily on Psalm 77:

> Because it says, "*they did not have faith in God* [οὐκ ἐπίστευσαν ἐν τῷ θεῷ], *nor did they hope in his salvation.*"[127] It is well to believe, not just "God," but "in God" [οὐ μόνον τῷ θεῷ, ἀλλὰ καὶ ἐν τῷ θεῷ]. For I know that there is a distinction between believing God and believing in God: "Abraham believed God [τῷ θεῷ] and it was reckoned to him as justice."[128] But those whom the logos [of the Psalm] finds fault with "did not believe in God" [εν τῷ θεῷ]. How then shall we understand both to believe "God" and to believe "in God"? I call to mind the gospel statement [ῥητοῦ εὐαγγελικοῦ] that I have explained, when it becomes needful for me to say how believing "God" differs from believing "in God." The statement holds thus [Τὸ δὲ ῥητὸν οὕτως ἔχει], "Whoever will confess in me [ἐν ἐμοὶ] before human beings, I also will confess in him [κ'αγὼ ὁμολογήσω ἐν αὐτῷ] before my Father in heavens, but whoever will deny me [ὃς ἐὰν ἀρνήσεταί μοι]—not 'in me' [ἐν ἐμοὶ], for the one who denies is not 'in' Christ, but whoever will deny 'me'— I also will deny—he does not say 'in him' but I will deny—him."[129] In the logos ['Εν τῷ λόγῳ], then, if the confession occurs "in" the Savior, the Savior also confesses in the one confessing, but if denial occurs, it is not "in" the Savior, but the

---

125. See 1 Cor 3:3–4.
126. PS81H.1 (510.6–511.6).
127. Ps 77:22.
128. Gn 15:6, Rom 4:3.
129. Mt 10:32–33.

one denying is not in him; he denies him. And the Savior, not being "in" the one denying, denies him. According to this logos it is a better thing to believe "in God" than to believe "God." The beginning of progress is to believe God [ἀρχὴ δὲ προκοπῆς τὸ πιστεύειν θεῷ], so that after that, coming to be in God and standing [γενόμενοι ἐν τῷ θεῷ καὶ στάντες], we shall believe God himself through Jesus Christ our Savior, to whom is glory and power to the ages of ages. Amen.[130]

Origen speaks of the difference for that the preposition "in" [ἐν] makes in Ps 77:22; believing in "God" is not the same as simply believing "God." Believing "God" is what Abraham did when it was "reckoned to him in justice," but believing "in God' must mean something else. To determine what this difference is Origen turns to Mt 10:32–33, where Jesus uses the preposition following the verb "confess" [ὁμολογέω], but not following the verb "deny" [ἀρνέομαι]. When someone confesses "in" Christ, Christ within also confesses "in" that person. But when someone denies Christ, there is no Christ within. Thus, by analogy, the person who "believes God" is just at the beginning of a process that will eventuate in believing "in God." That is the one who believes "in God" is divinized to such an extent that there is little distinction between him and God. (Commenting on Rom 4:3 in his *Commentary on Romans* Origen also discusses degrees of faith.[131]) The mention of "standing" in connection with being "in God," an allusion to Eph 6:13, "and, having done all, to stand" [καὶ ἅπαντα κατεργασάμενοι στῆναι], refers to those who emerge victorious after a prolonged struggle.[132] As is so often the case in Origen's writings, this notion of inner unity with God has as much in common with Platonism as with Paul. Compare the idea of identification with God to Plotinus:[133]

> Everything that someone sees as a spectacle, he sees outside. But one must actually transfer into oneself and see as one [ἀλλὰ χρὴ εἰς αὐτὸν ἤδη μεταφέρειν καὶ βλέπειν ὡς ἕν], and see as oneself, just as one escorted by a god, taken by Phoebus or by some Muse, could make the vision of the god in himself [ἐν αὐτῷ ἂν ποιοῖτο τοῦ θεοῦ τὴν θέαν], if he should have power in himself [εἰ δύναμιν ἔχοι ἐν αὐτῷ] to see a god.

130. PS77H3.5 (388.24–389.11).

131. See Jean Schérer, *Le commentaire d'Origène sur Rom. III.5–V.7* (Cairo: L'Institut Français d'Archéologie Orientale, 1957), 182.

132. Origen returns again and again to the "spiritual wrestling" passage in Eph 6 in the homilies as in the rest of his work, perhaps nowhere to greater effect than in PS36H4.2 9 (162.19–165.3).

133. Plotinus, *Enn.* 5.8.10

The challenge of translation

In his still influential examination of Origen's method of scriptural interpretation, *Histoire et esprit*, Henri de Lubac suggests that Origen's concepts do not translate easily into ours: "sa terminologie est différent de la nôtre."[134] Not just Origen's terminology, but his way of conceiving language is rooted in a culture that is eighteen centuries distant from us and imperfectly known. Building on his Alexandrian predecessors, Philo and Clement, he developed his concept of a divine logos that can be embodied in human logos and of scripture as the embodiment of that logos. He also developed a way of articulating the distinction between the immediate sense of a biblical passage, its ῥητόν or "statement," in contrast to its deeper meaning. This distinguishes Origen's use of ῥητόν from what modern commentators, following a tradition that goes back at least to Augustine, usually mean by "literal sense," the sense intended by the original author.[135] In translating Origen into familiar terminology like "literal sense," we risk obscuring what is original to him. Origen showed himself aware of a similar challenge when he sought to gain access to the Bible by means of translations into Greek. He believed that translation poses challenges that can be overcome, if only "in part," by being attentive to them and signaling them to the reader. He commended the Septuagint translators for using unfamiliar words, as he believed that they did with παραζηλόω and διάβημα, in order to signal that the words in Hebrew had no precise equivalent in Greek; he understood why at least one of the versions, failing to find an adequate equivalent, left ηθάμ untranslated. Those linguistic challenges thus constitute what Origen called "stumbling blocks," passages providentially scattered throughout Scripture that, by resisting immediate interpretation, promote deeper insight into the text.[136]

We owe it to a man who cared about language, believing that it could be the means of God's presence, to attend to his own use of language and to

---

134. Henri de Lubac, *Histoire et esprit: L'intelligence de l'écriture d'après Origène* (Paris: Aubier, 1950), 113.

135. See, for example, Augustine, *De Genesi ad Litteram* 11.1.2: This is to be demanded from us: that what the person who wrote narrated as something that happened is defended at the specific meaning of the letter [*ut ad proprietatem litterae defendatur quod gestum narrat ipse qui scripsit*]. But if in the words of God, or of any person who has assumed the role of a prophet, something is said that cannot be understood to the letter without absurdity [*dicitur aliquid quod ad litteram nisi absurde non possit intellegi*], with hardly a doubt it should be received as have been said figuratively in order to signify something else [*procul dubio figurate dictum ob aliquam significationem accipi debet*].

136. See PA 4.2.9.

avoid, if we can, imposing our categories and terminology onto his. This applies especially to theological terminology that has acquired overtones that he could not have conceived, in the better part of two millennia that separate us from him. Thus, for example, "wonder" or "marvel" translates θαῦμα better than "miracle" and "lofty" is better for ὑψηλός than "transcendent." Origen's attitude to the Hebrew language, which, thanks to the discovery of CMG 314, we can now appreciate more fully, has implications for the vexed question of his relationship to Judaism. The homilies, like the rest of his writings, show that Origen believed that the Jews did not understand their own scripture and could not even carry out the prescriptions because they did not understand them. These homilies also show, nonetheless, that the Jews, as custodians of the Hebrew language, maintained a privileged—one might say "elect"— status: they alone spoke God's language. Origen's attitude to Hebrew thus reveals a mentality that today seems both naive and sophisticated. Reading about Adam's language makes us aware that we have actually learned a few things about language since Origen's time. Historical linguists, even though they can look back astonishingly far into the origins of modern languages, can only speculate about the first human speech.[137] One thing we can now be fairly certain of, though, is that our earliest recognizably human ancestors did not speak Hebrew. On the other hand, Origen's approach to the text of the Hebrew Scriptures has aged well. He did not naively accept the Septuagint as an adequate replacement for the Hebrew text. Because he valued the Septuagint, along with other early translations, as a witness to earlier Hebrew texts, he used the other versions to correct it only so as to judge between competing readings among Septuagint manuscripts. He did not think it necessary or even possible to reconstruct the divinely inspired original text. Origen believed that even an imperfectly known Scripture could help us, at a stage in our journey when we can, at best, know in part, to live our lives more fully by becoming more and more like God. More than, perhaps, any other work of his that has come down to us, Origen's *Homilies on the Psalms* makes us aware that Origen himself and his community believed that preaching could mediate a divine communication in the moment and that such an *epidēmia* would be recognizable if and when it came. In making Origen's logos available in translation, we should do our best to make it possible for the divine Logos to visit us, in some measure, as well.

137. See, for example, Steven Mithen, *The Singing Neanderthals: The Origins of Music, Language, Mind, and Body* (Cambridge, MA: Harvard University Press, 2006).

3. ORIGEN, CHRIST, THE LAW AND THE JEWISH PEOPLE
Some Important Arguments in the New Greek *Homilies on the Psalms*

In a well-crafted and nuanced entry on "Judaism" in the *Westminster Handbook to Origen*, Joseph S. O'Leary expresses what for many is a consensus view, about the deep ambiguities in Origen's extant writings on the Jewish people, the Law, and the divine plan. The entry begins on the most positive note:

> None of the Fathers knew and appreciated Judaism as well as Origen. His capacious theology resolved all apparent contradictions to affirm the unity of the Old and New Testaments, the old and new people of God, thus sealing the defeat of Marcionism. Christ's teaching cannot come from human wit but only from "the epiphany of God, with manifold wisdom and manifold powers first establishing Judaism (*Ioudaismos*), and after it Christianity (*Christianismos*)" (*CCels* 3.14). Origen's attention to the historical and theological bond between the two religions ensured that Christians would treasure their roots in ancient Israel and their spiritual unity with the patriarchs and prophets, who participate in their struggle and aid them with their prayers ... His study of Judaism ... gave Jewish learning a crucial place in Christian theology.[1]

Then, after cataloguing the impressive elements of Origen's learning of Hebrew, work on the Hexapla, private conversations and public debates with Jews, O'Leary turns to the ironic, tragic inverse side:

1. Joseph S. O'Leary, "Judaism," in *The Westminster Handbook to Origen*, ed. John Anthony McGuckin (Louisville: Westminster/John Knox, 2004), 135.

All this study served also to bolster Origen's theological claim that only in Christianity does Jewish tradition attain its proper fulfillment. Jews who fail to convert to Christ are in a tragic dead end, abandoned by God (though with a prospect of eschatological restoration). Thus, while Origen can correct the crude anti-Judaism of earlier and later theologians, the negative impact of his own account proved all the more dangerous for the future, in that it is so thoroughly argued, on a broad textual basis. A catena of his remarks seems to form an oppressive anti-Jewish vision, though it is questionable, perhaps, to take these out of their specific exegetical contexts so as to combine them in a system.[2]

After noting how important Paul is for Origen's arguments ("Paul often turns out to be a primary source of his anti-Judaistic apologetic"[3]), O'Leary pulls no punches about what is at stake in assessing Origen's legacy on this point:

> All of this is increasingly disturbing to [Origen's] contemporary readers, who with the hindsight of the traumatic events of the twentieth century are less and less able to share the serenity of those Christian scholars who have reported Origen's anti-Judaistic apologia without criticism, or even accentuated it, treating those views even as intrinsic to Christian orthodoxy.[4]

O'Leary's statement was written in 2004. In 2014, Alfons Fürst offered the first assessment of the contribution of the new Psalms homilies to this question. Proceeding from the assumption of prior research that there are these two sides of Origen's legacy vis à vis Jews and anti-Judaism,[5] Fürst concluded from a preliminary survey that "Die neu entdeckten Psalmenhomilien liefern neues Material für beides."[6] And yet in the course of his analysis he

---

2. O'Leary, "Judaism," 135.

3. O'Leary, "Judaism," 136.

4. O'Leary, "Judaism," 136. On p. 137 O'Leary proposes that "The increasingly hostile tone of the remarks in his later writings may also be contextualized in terms of attempted, and failed, exercises in interreligious dialogue at Caesarea." And yet he concludes the entry on the following (somewhat contradictorily) positive note: "In this sense, [Origen's retrieval of Paul's positive ideas about Israel's final destiny (Rom 11:26)] ... is something that distinguishes Origen from most of the Fathers and even makes him a precursor of contemporary Christian-Jewish dialogue" (p. 138).

5. Alfons Fürst, "Judentum, Judenchristentum und Antijudaismus in den neu entdeckten Psalmenhomilien des Origenes," *Adamantius* 20 (2014): 275–87. Fürst's opening, emphasizing the fundamental work of Nicholas de Lange, *Origen and the Jews. Studies in Jewish-Christian Relations in Third-century Palestine* (UCOP 25; Cambridge: Cambridge University Press, 1976), is in many ways a concise summation of the same position spelled out in more detail by O'Leary, quoted above: "Origenes wird gerne wahrgenommen und gelobt als christlicher Gelehrter, der mit jüdischen Gelehrten diskutiert, und als Exeget, der sich für jüdische Exegesen interessiert hat. Das ist auch richtig. Theologisch vertritt er jedoch gleichzeitig die antijudaistischen Überzeugungen, die für die gesamte altkirchliche Theologie charakteristisch sind" (275).

6. Fürst, "Judentum," 275.

observed, for instance, that the homilies contain little information about actual Jewish ritual practices in Palestine, even while talking directly about them,[7] and contain no traces of Origen's actual contacts with Jewish conversation partners.[8] By the end of the essay, one has seen more evidence of what Fürst refers to as Origen's "antijüdische Theologie" (p. 283), as well as his contestations against Judaizing Christians. Fürst accounts for this, and for the "sharper tone" of the Psalms homilies, by their genre as homilies and Origen's challenging role therein—as in the homilies on Jeremiah—as a preacher who had to deal with the difficult issues of Christian identity and practice on the ground in Caesarea. "Da konnte dann, wie die neu entdeckten Psalmenhomilien zeigen, auch der ansonsten eher moderate Origenes einen scharften Ton anschlagen, besonders wenn es um das Fehlverhalten von christlichen Frauen ging, und kompromisslos einen klar konturierten Antijudaismus vertreten" (p. 286).

Fürst's article is a valuable contribution to the question. He has brought forward some of the most important passages, and has also—in my view quite rightly—argued that the homilies on Jeremiah (also extant in Greek) deserve close comparison with the new finds.[9] At the same time, in addition to not more directly addressing why, if the balance still holds, the homilies appear to contain so little evidence of Origen's contacts with contemporary Jews, Jewish communities and Jewish life, one may contest whether one can separate, as Fürst does in his study, Origen's "theology" (and its place in relation to Christian "anti-Judaism") and his treatment of Jewish feasts, on the one hand, and Jewish and Judaizing Christians, on the other. How and where did Origen "do theology," and what most counts in that? This connects also with O'Leary's query about whether or how Origen's comments can or should be systematized, or, if they are, whether the "sharp tones" and denunciations are the aberration from the normally moderating voice of Origen, or if such statements are more the norm. And how should they be understood as acts of theologizing or disclosures of theological commitments?

John A. McGuckin has argued against the more "dual legacy" view, advocating a "more negative assessment of the significance of Jewish theology on

---

7. Fürst, "Judentum," 276–77.

8. "Auf der persönlichen Ebene sprechen die vielen Kontakte des Origenes—von denen in den Psalmenhomilien offenbar keine Spuren zu finden sind … " (Fürst, "Judentum," 285).

9. Fürst, "Judentum," 286. I would also agree with his contention that the Jeremiah homilies deserve more attention in scholarship, in general ("… wie auch schon die Jeremiahomilien, was nach meinem Eindruck allerdings wenig beachtet wird").

Origen."[10] His test case for this is Origen's use of the Pauline letters (and Acts), and the degree to which Origen's view of Jews and Judaism reflects in turn the genuinely dual legacy of Origen's beloved apostolic mentor, Paul, or a tendentiously selective one. McGuckin concluded from his study that "Origen has clearly been ready to alter the tenor of St. Paul himself, his master theologian, to firm up the apologetic at those instances the Apostle might be seen to have given too much away because of his love and respect for Judaism."[11] This leads McGuckin to contest the positive side of the consensus view:

> The conclusion that seems to arise from this is that Origen's personal attitude, as well as his professional theological approach to Judaism, might not be in reality as positive as has sometimes been suggested; and that his undoubted knowledge and use of rabbinical exegetical traditions may largely have come to him sporadically and without system, implying that the significance of such dependencies must be questioned. Indeed, the personal reshaping by Origen of the Pauline Jewish apologetic suggests someone whose dialogue with the Jewish tradition in Caesarea had been neither successful nor particularly happy.[12]

The purpose of the present essay is to examine closely some of the crucial arguments Origen makes about Christ, the Law and the Jewish people in the newly discovered homilies on the Psalms. In a previous study,[13] I analyzed Origen's first homily on Ps 77(78), and demonstrated that the entire homily, triggered by the word προβλήματα in the lemma, is cleverly focused by Origen on the philosophical and school form of προβλήματα/ζητήματα/ἀπορίαι καὶ λύσεις and the "zetetic method," which he sees prophetically foreshadowed in the first four verses of the Psalm itself, and in turn fulfilled in Matt 13:35, which cites the verse (if in a different form in verse 2b), and, for Origen, refers to a

10. "Origen on the Jews," *Studies in Church History* 29 (1992): 1–13; reprinted in Everett Ferguson, ed., *Christianity in Relation to Jews, Greeks, and Romans*, vol. 2 (Hamden, CT: Garland, 1999), 23–35. I cite the latter pagination.

11. "Origen on the Jews," 34–35.

12. "Origen on the Jews," 35. Contrast de Lange, *Origen and the Jews*, 76: "[Origen] does not completely whitewash the Jews, who had been repeatedly charged with having rejected Christ, been responsible for his death and persecuted his Church. Such sentiments were commonplace; it would be remarkable if Origen did not subscribe to them, but the fact that he does is not evidence of a negative attitude towards the Jews. His remarks about them are on the whole surprisingly free from the ill-informed rancour which pervades much of the literature on the subject which survives from the early Church." Note the tendency to dismiss Origen's more negative views on Jews and Judaism as less due to his own choices and more to the "commonplaces" of his own context.

13. Margaret M. Mitchell, "Problems and Solutions in Early Christian Biblical Interpretation: A Telling Case from Origen's Newly Discovered Greek Homilies on the Psalms (*codex Monacensis Graecus* 314)," *Adamantius* 22 (2016): 40–55.

didactic "Q and A" session that Christ held with his disciples at the end of the
parable discourse (Matt 13:36) on the mysteries of the origins of the universe,
as found in Genesis (i.e., προβλήματα ἀπ' ἀρχῆς). As his homily proceeds, I argued, Origen moves from one problem to another, as his ingenious solution
to one question occasions new problems, from a text-critical problem about
the true author of the Psalm (Ἀσάφ, so LXX, Ἠσαΐα, so Origen's mss of Matthew) solved first by scientific but then also by supernatural solutions (involving both the devil and God[14]), to the problem of the reliability of scripture, to
the problem of the speaker (which he identifies as Christ, with Matt 13:35, in
vv. 1–2, and as the disciples in vv. 3–4), to the problem of the rest of the referents of v. 1, if the first-person voice who speaks is Christ: Προσέχετε, λαός μου,
τὸν νόμον μου. In that earlier article, I was only able to devote a few brief paragraphs to the lengthy and complex argument about Christ, the Law, the Jewish people, and Judaizing that runs from §3–4 of the homily. In order to pursue the goal of the present paper, to see what contribution the new homilies
make to the question of Origen, the Law, and the Jewish people, we shall begin with a detailed analysis of these arguments and then provide a comparison
with some strikingly similar arguments made in the first and second homilies
on Ps 73(74). In each case, we can see Origen interacting with the Psalm text,
with some concrete issues involving his own congregants (women, men) and
neighboring Jews in Caesarea, with theological opponents, particularly Jews
and Marcionites, and with his own broader scriptural inheritance, including
in a significant way the letters of Paul, on God's chosen people(s), and the Law.

Homily One on Psalm 77(78)

The assumption behind this paper, and my study of patristic biblical interpretation in general, is that one cannot just dip into Origen's homilies and take
out and compare pieces of arguments on the Law, Jews, or Judaizing, but one
must examine them as rhetorical arguments with their own ἀκολουθία (logical and rhetorical progress) and σκοπός (goal), within what I term "the ago-
nistic paradigm of interpretation."[15] As I analyze the argument in *HPs77* I.3–4
(f. 219ᵛ–222ᵛ) 356, 13–359, 20, it is constructed in the following, interconnected

---

14. I.e., the devil tampers with the scriptures by interpolations, but also God allowed for variance
so that human faith would not rely primarily on the scriptures, but on the wonders of creation and the
power of Christ as known in the church, and only thereafter for it to be deepened and illuminated by a
properly informed reading of the scriptures.

15. Mitchell, *Paul, the Corinthians and the Birth of Christian Hermeneutics*, 25–26, and passim.

movements (I have included an asterisk at each place where I identify a Pauline quotation, reference, allusion, or discernible influence[16]):

A. Lawgiver/Recipients and Law in Ps 77:1—λύσις ἐκ προσώπου, Part I
  1. Intertext of Ps 9:21 prophesies Christ as coming τοῖς ἔθνεσιν νομοθέτης (as in Ps 77:1)
  2. *He brought not law of "a servant" (θεράπων/δοῦλος, Mal 3:24; cf. Heb 3:5–6)
  3. *If the Mosaic law were saving (Εἰ γὰρ ἔσωζεν …)
  4. *If Mosaic law were enough, τί ἔτι χρὴ τῆς Χριστοῦ ἐπιδημίας; (cf. Gal 3:21)

B. God Designated a Law Appropriate to Each Καιρός and People
  1. One God of creation and Father of the καιροί each of which has suitable requirements
    a. Law of Moses in time of Moses [for Jews, assumed but not stated]
    b. Law of Christ at time of Christ's ἐπιδημία, for Gentiles (τοῖς ἀπὸ τῶν ἐθνῶν)
  2. Same god enacted both the latter and the former (τοῦτο καὶ πρότερον ποιήσας)
  3. What about the καιρός pre-Moses?
    a. those before Moses (οἱ πρὸ Μωϋσέως) who did not read the Law were saved (Ἐσώθησαν)
    b. Enoch and Abel who did not do what is written in the Law [were saved, assumed, not stated]
  4. *Statement of general rule: ἦν καθ᾽ ἑκάστην γενεὰν τὰ ἁρμόζοντα τοῖς καιροῖς καὶ σώζοντα τοὺς βουλόμενους σώζεσθαι (interesting inversion of 1 Tim 2:4: ὃς πάντας ἀνθρώπους θέλει σωθῆναι)
  5. *Application of general rule to Gentiles in the past: God did not allow a law to be given (δοθῆναι) to the Gentiles that had already been given (τὸν δοθέντα, cf. Gal 3:21) to the Jews, who were living by it (πολιτεύεσθαι)

C. Jews in the Present Cannot Fulfill the Law Even if They Wish To, and So Are Cursed
  1. Charge: Even if the sons of Israel (υἱοὶ Ἰσραήλ) want to live according to the Law of Moses (πολιτεύεσθαι κατὰ τὸν Μωϋσέως νόμον), whatever they do, they cannot (οὐ δύνανται)
  2. Three examples, by way of taunt
    a. Celebrate the πάσχα in Jerusalem (cf. Deut 16:2, etc.)? They cannot (forbidden to enter Aelia Capitolina).
    b. Stone one caught in the act of adultery (cf. Lev 20:10; Deut 22:23)? They cannot (rulers have charge of stonings).
    c. Carry out ritual purifications (Lev 14:11, etc.)? They are ineffective.

---

16. Not all are of the same weight, obviously, given these different categories.

3. *Conclusion: rather than being purified (καθαρίζονται) by the law of Moses, they are ὑπὸ κατάραν (Gal 3:10, which Paul had justified by a citation of Deut 27:26)

D. New Covenant/Another Way/Another Heart to Fear God—λύσις ἐκ προσώπου, Part II

   1. Conclusion/Summation of Previous: Prophecies of Ps 77:1 and 9:21 show Christ is νομοθέτης τοῖς ἔθνεσιν

   2. Further Corroborating Evidence – Foretellings from the Prophet Jeremiah

      a. "New Covenant" (διαθήκη καινή) Prophecy (Jer 38:31–33)

      b. "Another heart to fear me" (Jer 39:39–40; cf. 38:)

      c. "Another way" (Jer 39:39)

   3. [*Christ brought New Covenant; Luke 22:20; 1 Cor 11:25—so obvious no need to state]

   4. Christ brought "Another Way" (i.e., New Covenant)

   5. But Did He Bring "Another heart 'to fear me'" (ἑτέρα καρδία τοῦ φοβεῖσθαι με)?

      a. Jews say "no, this is a reference to the age to come"

      b. Response—No, it refers to Christians now

         i. We have fear now about future perfectibility since it is based on fearlessness (1 John 4:18 both cited and alluded to)

         ii. Fear leads to punishment (1 John 4:18, cited)

         iii. Punishment is possible in the age to come

         iv. Fear then (in age to come) is not useful

         v. Love is at all times useful

         vi. *Proof that fear is for now, not the future—Rom 13:7 (Paul counseled to pay off your debt of fear in the present)

         vii. *Proof that love is for both now and then—Rom 13:8 (Paul counseled that this is a debt to be carried over and never repaid)

   6. [Conclusion (implied): Gentile Christians have received from their lawgiver, Christ, ἑτέρα καρδία τοῦ φοβεῖσθαι με]

E. General Significance of λύσις ἐκ προσώπου for Ps 77:1 Προσέχετε , λαός μου, τὸν νόμον μου as spoken by Christ

   1. Transition back to λύσις ἐκ προσώπου

      a. We have not forgotten the difference between the Old Testament and the New

      b. We have not lost our mind in invoking the letters of Paul, which are written to Christians, to Jews as a rebuttal (δυσώπησις)

   2. Attending to my law means *no longer attending* to the Law of Moses (μηκέτι τῷ Μωϋσέως)

   3. *No longer get circumcised (Gal 5:2–4)

   4. *No longer keep the Sabbath (Gal 4:10)

5. No longer walk (live) κατὰ τὰ πρῶτα καὶ κατὰ τὰ παλαιά

6. *Proof of incompatibility of old and new from Paul: 2 Cor 5:17, ἰδοὺ γέγονε καινά, τὰ ἀρχαῖα παρῆλθεν

F. Specific Significance of Christ's statement in Ps 77:1 for Feasts of ἄζυμα and ἡ ἡμέρα τοῦ ἱλασμοῦ

   1. *Invocation of audience as the "silly women" (γυναικάρια) of 2 Tim 3:6 to show the specific connection Christ has in mind in Ps 77:1 (τίνα τρόπον λέγει ὁ σωτήρ)

   2. Negative command: "Don't again celebrate the feast of unleavened bread" (μὴ πάλιν ἄζυμα ποιήσητε) (an inference taken from Ps 77:1, Προσέχετε , λαός μου, τὸν νόμον μου)

   3. *Positive command: ἀλλὰ ἄζυμα ποιήσατε εἰλικρινείας, ἄζυμα ποιήσατε ἀληθείας (taken from Paul in 1 Cor 5:8, which also provides hermeneutical key to next argument, G, about ἀληθιναί ἑορταί)

   4. Negative command: οὐ πάλιν τὴν Ἰουδαϊκὴν νηστείαν ποιήσετε (at Yom Kippur/Day of Atonement)

   5. Consequence for Christians who do this: καλῶς ἐκβάλλονται ἀπὸ τῆς Χριστοῦ ἐκκλησίας

   6. Reason: μὴ νοήσαντες τὴν ἡμέραν τοῦ ἱλασμοῦ

G. The Proper νοεῖν: True Feasts v. Prefigured Feasts

   1. *Old ἡμέρα τοῦ ἱλασμοῦ (cf. Lev 25:9) = τυπική (cf. 1 Cor 10:6, 11)

   2. *Day of Christ's crucifixion = ἀληθινή (ἡμέρα τοῦ ἱλασμοῦ) (cf. 1 John 2:2; Rom 3:25)

   3. Scriptural Proof: John 1:29, ὁ ἀμνὸς τοῦ θεοῦ, ὁ αἴρων τὴν ἁμαρτίαν τοῦ κόσμου

   4. Implication: since ἡ ἡμέρα τοῦ ἱλασμοῦ has taken place καὶ ἐν μοί (cf. Gal 2:19–20?) there is no need for νηστεία on the ("Jewish") Yom Kippur

   5. Rationale: Mark 2:19, οὐ δύνανται οἱ υἱοὶ τοῦ νυμφῶνος ὅσον μετ' αὐτῶν ἐστι ὁ νυμφίος νηστεύειν

   6. Consequences in conditionals: "if you wish to fast" (Εἰ θέλεις νηστεύειν)

     a. Ἰουδαϊκῶς? Then your bridegroom has been taken away (ἦρταί σου ὁ νυμφίος, with Mark 2:20)

     b. Fast the Christian fast (νήστευε νηστείαν Χριστιανήν)[17]

       i. As prescribed by ὁ νομοθέτης τῶν ἐθνῶν

       ii. Citation from his law about fasting: Matt 6:17–18, with inset from Matt 6:6

---

17. As is well known, *Didache* 8.1 instructs Christians to fast on Wednesday and Friday (rather than Mondays and Thursdays, as do Jews). While Origen is speaking here about the autumn feast of Yom Kippur, he is in some ways eliding it with the Passover, and hence he may have in mind the Paschal fast, as attested already in Irenaeus (apud Eusebius, *HE* 5.24.12–13), who indicates a variety of practices and times of fasting, and by Tertullian, *de oratione* 18.

H. Syllogistic Concluding Proof: ἡ νομοθεσία Χριστοῦ = νόμος θεοῦ, as he is
    God's Appointed νομοθέτης and υἱός
    1. Summation of argument from §3–4: in Ps 77:1 Christ is speaking about
       his νομοθεσία
    2. *Supporting proof from the holy apostle Paul
       a. *who knew the διαφορὰ νομίμων παλαιῶν καὶ καινῶν (cf. 2 Cor 5:17)
       b. *who showed that being ἔννομος Χριστοῦ ≠ ἄνομος θεοῦ
         (1 Cor 9:21, quoted)
    3. Reason: God appointed (κατέστησε) Christ as lawgiver (as prophecied in
       Ps 9:21, cited at start of the argument: κατάστησον νομοθέτην αὐτοῖς)
    4. *Inference: Christ as νομοθέτης = ἔννομος θεοῦ
    5. Renewed salvation-historical allusion about the καιροί: one who before
       ἡ ἐπιδημία Χριστου was inside the Law of Moses ≠ ἄνομος θεοῦ
    6. Reason: ἦν γὰρ νόμος ὁ Μωϋσέως θεοῦ νόμος
    7. Conclusion: Christ as the designated lawgiver for his own law (ὁ ἔννομος
       Χριστοῦ διατεταγμένος!) has been given by the Father to the Gentiles (ὑπὸ
       τοῦ πατρὸς δέδοται τοῖς ἔθνεσι)
    8. *Final proof uniting the καιροί, προφῆται and ὁ υἱός in the divine legislative
       plan (quotation of Heb 1:1–2; cf. Heb 3:5–6, alluded to in A.2., contrast
       of θεράπων/υἱός)

With this as an overview, let's look in more detail at the arguments.

A. Lawgiver/Recipients and Law in Ps 77:1—λύσις ἐκ προσώπου, Part I

After his identification of ὁ λέγων in Ps 77:1 as Christ, by λύσις ἐκ προσώπου,
Origen turns to the question of the referent of the other two nouns in the
sentence, λαός and νόμος. He deftly solves both by invoking a single intertext.

Προσέχετε, λαός μου, τὸν νόμον μου. Κατάστησον νομοθέτην αὐτοῖς,
γνώτωσαν ἔθνη ὅτι ἄνθρωποί εἰσιν· οὐκοῦν **εὔχεται τὸ ἐν τῷ προφήτῃ πνεῦμα**
<ἐν τῷ ἐνάτῳ ψαλμῷ>, νόμου ὄντος τοῦ κατὰ Μωϋσέα, ὅπως ἀναστήσῃ τοῖς
ἔθνεσι νομοθέτην. *Οὐ γὰρ ἔμελλεν ὁ σωτὴρ ἡμῶν ἐπιδημήσων ὑποτάσσειν ἡμᾶς*
τῷ νόμῳ τοῦ θεράποντος. Εἰ γὰρ ἔσωζεν[18] *ὁ νόμος τοῦ θεράποντος καὶ αὐτάρκης*
ἦν ἐκεῖνος, περὶ οὗ γέγραπται· μνήσθητε νόμου Μωϋσῆ τοῦ δούλου μου, τί ἔτι χρὴ
τῆς Χριστοῦ ἐπιδημίας; Ἔχω νομοθεσίαν, πολιτεύομαι κατ' αὐτήν, οὐ χρείαν
ἔχω ἄλλης νομοθεσίας (*H77Ps* I,3 [f. 219ᵛ], 356,13–20).

---

18. Adopting the reading of M, ἔσωζεν, rather than the emendation of Perrone, et al., ἐσώθην. This
represents a change from my text and translation in the Adamantius article, on further reflection and
working with the text, and especially noting Ἐσώθησαν two sentences later and σώζοντα/σώζεσθαι in the
following, with the sense of "being saved," or "saving." If one reads the passive here (presumably ἐσώθη,
not ἐσώθην), one must instead translate "has been preserved." As argued above, probably in Origen's mind
here is Gal 3:21, with ὁ δυνάμενος ζῳοποιῆσαι condensed to ἔσωζεν. The grammar supports this reading as
well; the sentence is an unreal conditional, with two imperfects in the protasis, and χρή without ἄν in
apodosis (cf. Smyth, *Greek Grammar*, §2313).

Attend, my people, to my law" (Ps 77:1a). "*Establish a lawgiver for them; let the nations know they are men*" (Ps 9:21). **So then, the spirit within the prophet prays in the ninth Psalm that even as there is a law of Moses, God might raise up a lawgiver for the Gentiles.**[19] For our savior wasn't going to come in order to subject us to the law of a servant. After all, if the servant's law were saving, and that law about which it was written, "*Remember the law of my servant Moses*" (Mal 3:24; cf. Heb 3:5–6), were sufficient, what need would there still have been of Christ's coming? [One might say then] "I have the law code, I live by it, I have no need of another law code."[20]

Interpreting scripture by scripture, Origen juxtaposes Ps 9:21 to Ps 77:1a to justify by another route that the πρόσωπον of "*Attend, my people, to my law*" is Christ, in his role as νομοθέτης. Then he ingeniously applies the second half of the verse to provide an answer to the question of the antecedent of the pronoun αὐτοῖς, for whom Christ serves as lawgiver—it is τὰ ἔθνη, the Gentiles.[21] The holy spirit within the prophet is presented as the voice speaking in Ps 9:21, imploring God to send a new lawgiver for the Gentiles to match the Law and lawgiver for the Jews, Moses. Then Origen makes a slightly denigrating allusion to Moses as only a θεράπων or δοῦλος (probably inspired by Heb 3:5 and supported by a quotation from Mal 3:24). But he does not dwell on the lower status of the lawgiver Moses (vis à vis Christ). Instead, he pivots in mid-sentence to an argument based on the quality of the Law itself, to the effect that, if the Law already given to Moses were already offering salvation (ἔσωζεν) and were sufficient (αὐτάρκης ἦν), why would Christ have had to come? To anchor that point Origen embarks without warning into a προσωποποΐα of an unnamed interlocutor, who, with shoulders shrugging, would say, if the Mosaic Law were sufficient, even once Christ had come "I don't need another Law." From the wider context, it is clear that Origen has in mind here people like Paul's Galatians converts, who (as Paul diagnoses them) think that the Law of Moses is in place for them and is all they need to know how to conduct themselves and to contribute to their salvation. One imagines that behind this argument in Origen's mind is Gal 3:21 (εἰ γὰρ ἐδόθη νόμος ὁ δυνάμενος ζῳοποιῆσαι [i.e., σῴζειν], ὄντως ἐκ νόμου ἂν ἦν ἡ δικαιοσύνη). As with Paul in Gal 3–4, Origen turns next to a salvation-historical argument that explains how God had a

---

19. Boldface, as in the Perrone edition, indicates overlaps with the Catenae fragments (ed. J. B. Pitra, *Analecta Sacra*, vol. III, Venice 1883, reprinted in J.-P. Migne, *PG* 17).

20. By προσωποποΐα Origen is giving voice to a position which he is about to refute.

21. Origen makes the same argument in *FrPs* 118,102, as cited by Perrone, et al., in the apparatus (*Origenes XIII*, 356).

plan in mind all along for *both* the Mosaic Law and the New Law after the arrival (ἐπιδημία) of Christ (or, for Paul, the arrival of πίστις by means of Christ [Gal 3:23, 25]).

B. God Designated a Law Appropriate to each καιρός (and people)

Νυνὶ δὲ ὁρῶν ὁ τῶν ὅλων θεὸς καὶ πατὴρ καιρῶν ἐπιτηδειότητας ἀπαιτούντων καταβολὰς νομοθεσιῶν καὶ πραγμάτων, ἤρξατο μὲν τῆς διὰ Μωϋσέως νομοθεσίας ἐπὶ Μωϋσέως,[22] ἔδειξε δὲ ἐπὶ τῆς Χριστοῦ ἐπιδημίας καὶ ἄλλους νόμους χρησιμωτέρους ἔθηκε τοῖς ἀπὸ τῶν ἐθνῶν, τοῦτο καὶ πρότερον ποιήσας (H77Ps I,3 [f. 219ᵛ–220ʳ], 356, 21–357, 3).

Now, the God of all creation and Father of the periods of time that require what is best suited to each, looking to found law codes and practices, made a beginning with legislation through Moses [357] at the time of Moses; but at the time of Christ's coming, he manifested[23] and laid down other, more useful laws, for the people from the Gentiles [220ʳ]. God enacted both the latter and the former.

Here Origen roots the two laws in the one God's[24] prerogative—and even responsibility—to do what is necessary according to what each καιρός requires (πατὴρ καιρῶν ἐπιτηδειότητας ἀπαιτούντων). A secondary argument made briefly, is that the later laws are "more useful" than those of the Mosaic Law.[25]

To establish the full temporal sequence of καιροί from creation to the present, Origen turns next to a question that we know occupied the rabbis, as well.[26] What about the patriarchs who lived before Sinai? Because Origen assumes, due to 1 Tim 2:4, that "God wished all people to be saved" (ὃς πάντας

---

22. I have altered the Perrone edition's punctuation to mark the grammatical contrast ἤρξατο μέν, ἔδειξε δέ (and hence putting the comma, not after νομοθεσίας, but after ἐπὶ Μωϋσέως). This does lead to some redundancy in the first clause, but I think Origen is repeating Moses twice to refer both to the Law he brought and to the time (καιρός) at which he brought it (ἐπὶ Μωϋσέως, which contrasts with the time of the coming of Christ, in the following clause: ἐπὶ τῆς Χριστοῦ ἐπιδημίας). Note also the same repetition, in the same sentence, a few lines later: Ἐσώθησαν γὰρ καὶ οἱ πρὸ Μωϋσέως οὐ τὸν νόμον ἀναγινώσκοντες Μωϋσέως.

23. Origen perhaps has in mind 1 Timothy 6:14–15 here: τηρῆσαί σε τὴν ἐντολὴν ἄσπιλον ἀνεπίλημπτον μέχρι τῆς ἐπιφανείας τοῦ κυρίου ἡμῶν Ἰησοῦ Χριστοῦ, ἣν καιροῖς ἰδίοις δείξει…. God reveals (δείξει, ἔδειξε) in his own times/seasons (καιροί, πατὴρ καιρῶν) the ἐπιφάνεια/ἐπιδημία of Christ, which includes the command to keep the requisite ἐντολή.

24. Presumably this august title for God is meant to forestall a Marcionite claim that the god of the Old Testament was a lower, inferior demiurge.

25. It depends upon how one takes the comparative χρησιμώτερους here. It is possible that it means that the laws for the Gentiles were more useful for them (i.e., an argument about appropriateness). But there are a number of these little negative punches throughout the argument, which leads me to take it as a dig at the Law (see also the next paragraph, where its laws about lustrations are pronounced ineffective).

26. For patriarchs following Torah, see, e.g., *b. Yoma* 28b; *Midr. Rabbah* (*Bereshith*) 95.3; *Tanhuma* 6.1; 8.9, etc.

ἀνθρώπους θέλει σωθῆναι), he goes on to say that "the people before Moses, who did not read the Law of Moses, were in fact saved" (Ἐσώθησαν γὰρ καὶ οἱ πρὸ Μωϋσέως οὐ τὸν νόμον ἀναγινώσκοντες Μωϋσέως).[27] With a polemical turn ("and if Jews press this point," Κἂν Ἰουδαῖοι βιάζωνται),[28] he agrees that "Enoch and Abel didn't do the things written in the Law and all the things recorded in Leviticus."[29] However, the divine rule held sway, such that "in every generation (γενεά) there were requirements that conformed with the times (τὰ ἁρμόζοντα τοῖς καιροῖς) and saved (σώζοντα) those who wished to be saved (σώζεσθαι)."[30] And surely the noble Enoch and Abel were among them.

As we have seen above, Origen's comparisons are complicated and criss-crossed, because they involve lawgivers (Moses, Christ), laws (Law of Moses, Law of Christ), law-recipients (Jews, Gentile Christians), and proper times (from Sinai forward, from Christ forward). From the appeal to periods of time he now moves back to recipients and says this is why "God didn't allow the Law that had been given (δοθέντα) to the children of Israel, who were living by it, to be given (δοθῆναι)[31] to the people from the Gentiles." The argument seems to imply both that the Gentiles didn't earlier receive the same Law as the Jews because they (the Gentiles) did not fit the criterion of wishing (βούλεσθαι) to be saved, and in turn, that this was because the Mosaic Law was in fact being carried out, already, by the children of Israel—and hence there was no need for it to be given to another people. Therefore, it was not the right time (καιρός) for that to take place.

C. Jews in the Present Cannot Fulfill the Law
Even if They Wish To, and So Are Cursed

The then-and-now commonplace *vis à vis* Jews and Gentiles leads Origen to a sudden and caustic castigation of Jews of his own time:

---

27. *H77Ps* I,3 (f. 220ʳ), 357, 4–5.

28. It is hard to know how to understand this since it is so laconic. Is Origen referring to Jews pressing the point with Christians in contemporary debate about the role of the Law before Sinai, or debating among themselves about it? Is there a reason a Jewish debater would bring the fates of noble Enoch and Abel, pre-Torah, against Origen? And does this aside provide evidence for the seriousness of Origen's dialogue with his contemporary Jews at Caesarea?

29. Note that Origen does not refer to them as Ἰουδαῖοι, which is consistent with Origen's customary terminological distinctions (as argued by de Lange, *Origen and the Jews*, 29–31).

30. *H77Ps* I,3 (f. 220ʳ), 357, 5–8.

31. *H77Ps* I,3 (f. 220ʳ), 357, 9). Again, here Origen may have in mind Gal 3:21: εἰ γὰρ ἐδόθη νόμος ὁ δυνάμενος ζῳοποιῆσαι....

Εἴτε γὰρ καὶ βούλονται πολιτεύεσθαι κατὰ τὸν Μωϋσέως νόμον <οἱ> υἱοὶ Ἰσραήλ,[32] ὅσα ἐὰν ποιήσωνται, οὐ δύνανται. Τὸ πάσχα ποιείτωσαν εἰς τὸν τόπον ὃν ἐξελέξατο <ὁ> κύριος, ἀλλ᾽ οὐκ ἔξεστιν αὐτοῖς. Τὸν μοιχεύοντα λιθοβολείτωσαν, ἀλλὰ ὑπὸ τὴν λιθοβολίαν εἰσὶ τῶν βασιλευόντων. Ἀλλὰ καὶ ἄλλα γέγραπται περὶ καθαρισμῶν, εἴ γε καθαρίζει ἐκεῖνα, οὐ γίνεται δέ· οὐ καθαρίζονται οἱ ὑπὸ τὸν Μωϋσέως νόμον, ἀλλ᾽ εἰσὶν *ὑπὸ κατάραν*[33] (*H77Ps* I,3 [f. 220ʳ], 357, 9–15).

Since whether the children of Israel even wish to live according to the law of Moses, whatever they do, they're not able. Let them celebrate the Passover in the place which the Lord has chosen (cf. Deut 16:2)? But they're not allowed to. Let them stone the adulterer? But the rulers have authority over stonings.[34] And there are also other things written about washings,[35] if indeed those commands do cleanse, but they don't. The people under the law of Moses are not [**220ᵛ**] cleansed, but they are *"under a curse"* (cf. Gal 3:10).

Although the second and third taunts may in some way be slight allusions to the Gospels,[36] the first resounds with historical particularity in Origen's time. It has in view the command in Deuteronomy to celebrate the Passover in the place God has chosen, the city where he had caused his name to dwell, Jerusalem. Jews of Origen's time are not allowed to carry out that command because the city is now Aelia Capitolina, founded by Hadrian, and under permanent guard of the Roman Tenth Legion and off-limits to them. Origen joins his barb about contemporary Jews not being able to fulfill the Law because of their present political-religious circumstances to Paul's statement in Gal 3:10,[37] in order to conclude that because of their inability to abide by all the things

32. This seems to contradict de Lange's claim that "Origen … uses 'Israel' only in biblical quotations and in arguments depending on such quotations, particularly when he is influenced by Pauline usage" (*Origen and the Jews*, 29). While there is much Pauline influence in the wider context in this homily, as we have shown, that does not account for the depiction of Jews who are Origen's contemporaries as οἱ υἱοὶ Ἰσραήλ.

33. This is not in italics in the Perrone edition, but I have put it in italics since it is a quote from Gal 3:10.

34. Origen probably has John 8:53–9:11 (the *pericope adulterae*), together with John 18:31, in mind. Or, perhaps, the Matthean Jesus' words about Jerusalem stoning the prophets (23:37)? Note that these sentences are punctuated as declarative in the Perrone edition, but I am taking them as interrogatives, with responses marked by ἀλλά.

35. Origen likely is thinking of passages like Matt 23:25–26; Mark 7:4.

36. But note that Origen combines the two examples in *comm. in Mt.* XIV, 19 (330, 3–14), as two signs of the "writ of divorce" (Matt 19:7) between God and his people, the Jews, as contrasted with the new marriage of the new covenant (this important passage is cited in full in Perrone's apparatus).

37. Which is part of an argument focused on why Gentile Jesus-believers do not need to keep the commandments of circumcision, etc. But Origen takes it as a blanket statement about all Jews not being able to fulfill the commandments of the Law, in general. Then he focalizes it on the particular injunction about celebrating the Passover in Jerusalem.

written in the book of the Law (according to the curse of Deut 27:26 that Paul quotes)—which, Origen adds, as a quick aside, aren't even effective[38]—"the children of Israel" are ὑπὸ κατάραν. Origen has deliberately chosen here one of the most scathing of Pauline statements on the Law. This by-product of Origen's "solution" to the problem of who are the λαός and what is the νόμος that Christ is said to bring in Ps 77:1 might cause its own problems for Origen's insistence that the one God of creation was responsible for both laws (that of Moses and that of Christ). But he will not take up that problem for several minutes. For now, he continues the salvation-historical argument, which leads him (as it had Paul before him[39]), to Jeremiah and the διαθήκη καινή.

D. New Covenant/Another Way/Another Heart to Fear God— λύσις ἐκ προσώπου, Part II

This is a complicated argument, which we shall treat in two parts, beginning with the transition:

> Φανερὸν τοίνυν ὅτι κατὰ τὰ εἰρημένα ὑπὸ τῶν προφητῶν ἦλθέ μου ὁ κύριος, νομοθέτης τοῖς ἔθνεσι, κατὰ τὰ εἰρημένα καὶ ὑπὸ Ἰερεμίου λέγοντος· *ἰδοὺ ἡμέραι ἔρχονται, λέγει κύριος, καὶ συντελέσω ἐπὶ τὸν οἶκον Ισραὴλ καὶ ἐπὶ τὸν οἶκον Ιούδα **διαθήκην καινήν**, οὐ κατὰ τὴν διαθήκην ἣν διεθέμην τοῖς πατράσιν αὐτῶν.* **Καὶ ἀλλαχόσε λέγεται· δώσω αὐτοῖς καρδίαν ἑτέραν τοῦ φοβεῖσθαί με καὶ ὁδὸν ἑτέραν** (*H77Ps* I,3 [f. 220ᵛ], 357, 16–21).

It is manifest, then, that in accordance with what was written by the prophets, my Lord[40] came as a lawgiver to the Gentiles, in accordance with what was spoken also by Jeremiah when he said, "*'Behold days are coming,' says the Lord, 'And I will complete with the house of Israel and the house of Judah **a new covenant**, not according to the covenant that I made with their ancestors*" (Jer 38:31–32). **And elsewhere it is said, "*I shall give to them another heart to fear me and another way*"** (Jer 39:39[41]).

As multiple attestation of his case that Christ came as lawgiver for the Gentiles, Origen adds the witness of Jeremiah to that of Ps 77:1 and Ps 9:21. The appeal to the new covenant, as found in Jeremiah and interpreted by Origen

---

38. This side comment may lead one to take the χρησιμώτερους above, in reference to the laws of the Gentiles, as a disparagement of the Mosaic Law.

39. Especially 2 Cor 3:1–18, but also 1 Cor 11:25.

40. I.e., Christ.

41. For the connection with his argument it is important to know the following verse, not quoted in the homily here, but clearly in Origen's mind: καὶ διαθήσομαι αὐτοῖς διαθήκνην αἰωνίαν, ἣν οὐ μὴ ἀποστρέψω ὄπισθεν αὐτῶν· καὶ τὸν φόβον μου δώσω εἰς τὴν καρδίαν αὐτῶν πρὸς τὸ μὴ ἀποστῆναι αὐτοὺς ἀπ᾽ ἐμοῦ.

(via Paul[42]), emphasizes both continuity and superiority to the "old" covenant established by Moses the lawgiver with the Jews. Although Origen does not spell out all the steps of his logic, it is important to know that within the context of Jeremiah 38, the mode of the new covenant lawgiving is as follows: Διδοὺς δώσω νόμους μου εἰς τὴν διάνοιαν αὐτῶν καὶ ἐπὶ καρδίας αὐτῶν γράψω αὐτούς ("I shall give my law right into their minds and upon their hearts I shall write them"). The promise of the law on the heart in the new and "eternal covenant" (διαθήκη αἰωνία) is repeated in the following chapter of Jeremiah LXX 39, from which Origen quotes next: δώσω αὐτοῖς καρδίαν ἑτέραν τοῦ φοβεῖσθαί με καὶ ὁδὸν ἑτέραν. So, what do the "other heart" and "other way"[43] have to do with Christ's law given to the Gentiles? The argument continues:

> Ἄρα ἔδωκεν ὁδὸν ἑτέραν καὶ καρδίαν ἑτέραν οὐκ ἔδωκεν; Ἀλλ᾽ εὑρησιλογοῦντες Ἰουδαῖοι λέγουσι ταῦτα εἰς τὸν μέλλοντα αἰῶνα λέγεσθαι. Ἀλλὰ φήσομεν πρὸς αὐτούς· τοῦ φοβεῖσθαί με, εἰ οὖν μέλλομεν καὶ εἰς τὸν μέλλοντα αἰῶνα λέγεσθαι, ὅτι φοβεῖσθαι νῦν, ἐὰν τελειωθῶμεν μὴ φοβούμενοι· ἡ γὰρ τελεία ἀγάπη ἔξω βάλλει τὸν φόβον. Εἰ ὁ φοβούμενος κόλασιν ἔχει,[44] μέλλομεν κἀκεῖ φοβεῖσθαι· δυνατὸν γὰρ ἡμᾶς μετὰ τὴν μακαριότητα καὶ κολάσει περιπεσεῖν. Οὐ δύναται οὖν ἐκεῖ φόβος εἶναι παιδαγωγὸς οὐδὲ χρήσιμος, πάντοτε ἀγάπη ἐστίν. Ὅτι δὲ οὐ δύναται χρήσιμον εἶναι τότε ὁ φόβος, ἄκουε Παύλου λέγοντος· ἀπόδοτε πᾶσι τὰς ὀφειλάς, τῷ τὸν φόρον τὸν φόρον, τῷ τὸν φόβον τὸν φόβον, τῷ τὸ τέλος τὸ τέλος, τῷ τὴν τιμὴν τὴν τιμήν. ὃ δὲ οὐ δέον[45] ἐστιν ἀποδοῦναι, τοῦτο κελεύει ἡμῖν ὀφείλειν λέγων· μηδενὶ μηδὲν ὀφείλετε, εἰ μὴ τὸ ἀλλήλους ἀγαπᾶν (H77Ps I,3 [f. 220ᵛ], 357, 21–358, 6).

42. 1 Cor 11:25; cf. 2 Cor 3:14.

43. Might Origen have in mind the use of ὁ ὁδός for the Christian movement in Acts (9:2; 19:23; 22:4; 24:14, 22)? In any case, he does not pursue with his Jewish interlocutor the question of whether or how the Christians fulfill the prophecy about "the other way" but instead turns as a point of controversy to the "other heart." We can only wonder if he has deflected the eye from a harder argument or charged right into it.

44. I have added italics to κόλασιν ἔχει, since it is a quotation from 1 John 4:18; Origen has conflated the last two clauses, substituting ὁ φοβούμενος for the subject, ὁ φόβος. The full verse, which Origen quotes twice and paraphrases once (ἐὰν τελειωθῶμεν μὴ φοβούμενοι), reads: φόβος οὐκ ἔστιν ἐν τῇ ἀγάπῃ, ἀλλ᾽ ἡ τελεία ἀγάπη ἔξω βάλλει τὸν φόβον, ὅτι ὁ φόβος κόλασιν ἔχει, ὁ δὲ φοβούμενος οὐ τετελείωται ἐν ἀγάπῃ.

45. Ὁ δὲ οὖν δέον is the reading of Perrone, et al., a conjectural emendation of οὖν for M's apparent reading, οὖ. Instead, I adopt the reading but not the diacritics, ὃ δὲ οὐ δέον and retain the punctuation of the Perrone edition, as they do, taking the ὃ … τοῦτο as the (common) resumptive use of the demonstrative after the relative: "But what it is not necessary to repay he commands us to owe, saying…." Alternatively, I toyed with the possibility of reading ὅδε οὐ δέον, which would nicely maintain the temporal contrasts of the previous verses: "In the present time it is not necessary to repay; he commands us to owe this when he says, 'Owe no one anything except to love one another.'" However, Origen does not appear to use the demonstrative with this locative usage in his extant Greek writings, but instead always as a personal pronoun.

So then, did he give[46] "another way"[47] and not give "another heart"? Now, Jews say by way of pretext[48] that these things are said about the age to come. But we shall ask them if it is our destiny for *"to fear me"* to be said about the age to come, as well, because we fear now whether we might be found[49] perfect if we are without fear![50] For *"perfect love casts out fear"* (1 John 4:18). If the one who fears *"has a punishment"* (1 John 4:18), then we are going to fear there, too.[51] For it is possible for us after [358/221ʳ] the blessing to also meet with punishment. Then fear cannot be either a guide or a useful help there,[52] as love always is.[53] As proof that fear cannot be useful in the future life, listen to Paul when he says, *"Repay to all people their due; to the one due tribute, tribute; to the one due fear, fear*[54]*; to the one due tax, tax; to the one due honor, honor"* (Rom 13:7). But what it is not necessary[55] to repay is what he commands us to owe, saying, *"owe nothing to anyone except to love one another"* (Rom 13:8).

This somewhat tortured argument is necessary in order for Origen to maintain that the new alternate heart "to fear God" has in fact been given to Christians now, in the present, and that it is not just a promise for the future as, he alleges, "Jews" understand it. But, via 1 John 4:18, Origen argues somewhat cheekily (if I have understood the somewhat awkward syntax) that, since perfect love is the key to future perfectibility, and perfect love casts out all fear, the Christians must have fear now about that future, in order to be fearless then and hence perfected.[56] Further, he argues, love is what remains (proba-

46. I.e., Christ gave the Gentiles.

47. Presumably, the law (for Gentiles). Behind this connection between the law and the way and fear for Origen (and perhaps, earlier, Jeremiah, but that is a long way back!) is a verse like Deut 8:6: καὶ φυλάξῃ τὰς ἐντολὰς κυρίου τοῦ θεοῦ σου πορεύεσθαι ἐν ταῖς ὁδοῖς αὐτοῦ καὶ φοβεῖσθαι αὐτόν.

48. Εὑρησιλογοῦντες may be more or less barbed. The verb can mean "invent ingenious arguments, explanations, or pretexts" (LSJ; cf. LPGL: "invent as ingenious explanations").

49. I.e., in the eschatological judgment.

50. I have puzzled at length over the syntax of this sentence (or sentences), finally deciding that the two conditional clauses (εἰ, ἐάν) are indirect questions, the first after the verb of speaking (φήσομεν) and the second after the verb of fearing, φοβεῖσθαι (with Smyth, §2234), and understanding the ὅτι clause as causal. Other construals are possible, but this seems both to unpack the grammar and to make some sense.

51. While he doesn't quote Romans 13 for another couple of lines, Origen seems to have v. 3 in mind in formulating this linkage between fear and punishment: οἱ γὰρ ἄρχοντες οὐκ εἰσὶν φόβος τῷ ἀγαθῷ ἔργῳ ἀλλὰ τῷ κακῷ. Θέλεις δὲ μὴ φοβεῖσθαι τὴν ἐξουσίαν· τὸ ἀγαθὸν ποίει, καὶ ἕξεις ἔπαινον ἐξ αὐτῆς.

52. I.e., in the age to come. The sense seems to be that fear cannot help because it is allied with punishment, not salvation.

53. Perhaps also an allusion to 1 Cor 13:8: ἡ ἀγάπη οὐδέποτε πίπτει.

54. Origen has reordered the clasuses, presumably to bring φόβος into more prominence (and its play with φόρος).

55. See textual note above.

56. Origen does not here name the problem—though he engages it elsewhere, as the wonderful collection of parallels in Perrone's apparatus at *HPs76* III.3 [199ᵛ–220ʳ] 335 shows—that often in the

bly he has in view 1 Cor 13:8–13) into the eternal age, whereas fear is one of the things characteristic of the present age, and of those who have good reason to fear future punishment. Like taxes, tribute, and honor, Origen argues, the apostle Paul taught that fear should be paid off before exiting this world because it cannot help in the age to come; by contrast, one should keep an accumulated debt of love, since it is the one thing that one is not commanded to pay off in the present life. All this is to refute the view of "the Jews" that the "other heart to fear me" refers to the afterlife, and not to the present. With a tangle of New Testament intertexts, Origen tries to refute it for both time zones: the Christian *does* fear already now in the present (indeed, is *obligated* to do so continually and without end) but *not* in the future.

E. General Significance of λύσις ἐκ προσώπου for Ps 77:1 Προσέχετε, λαός μου, τὸν νόμον μου as spoken by Christ

Aware that he's gone rather far afield, with a word-play Origen pulls up from this visit to Paul in Romans 13: "Now I do remember (μέμνημαι) that these things are said to Christians, whereas the earlier things were said to the Jews. "However, we've not lost our minds (μεμήναμεν)"! Why should we offer Paul's letters to them by way of rebuttal?" (ἵνα τί προσφέρωμεν αὐτοῖς εἰς δυσώπησιν τὰς Παύλου ἐπιστολάς;[57]). Having started to debate with Jews about the referent of the "alternate heart" of Jeremiah's new covenant and the bodies in which it resides, Origen has slipped into making claims from writings that, he realizes, are not addressed to Jews, but to Christians—i.e., the letter of Paul, his star witness, to the Romans. This concession to debate standards gives us some justification in thinking some real Ἰουδαῖοι and at least a possible real debate may lie behind this. In any case, Origen pulls himself back onto the track of his homily by using his lemma to link the Christian audiences of Paul's letter to the Romans with his claim that Ps 77:1 is a declaration by Christ to "his people" (λαός), the recipients of his Law. But, as we shall see, he has hardly left the apostle to the Gentiles aside.

Pentateuch and elsewhere God commands his people to fear him (e.g., Deut 4:10; 5:29; 6:24), precisely as part of their observance of the Law. It is of course not so easy to square that with 1 John 4:18.

57. Here I have altered Perrone's punctuation, placing a full stop after μεμήναμεν, and taking the following statement as an independent question (beginning ἵνα τί), with LSJ II.c. Alternately one could take it with II.d. as an "indignant exclamation": "to think I would offer Paul's letters to them by way of rebuttal!"

Ἐὰν οὖν λέγῃ μου ὁ σωτήρ· *προσέχετε, λαός μου, τὸν νόμον μου,* Χριστιανοῖς λαλεῖ· Χριστιανοὶ γὰρ λαός εἰσι Χριστοῦ. Καὶ λέγει· "**προσέχετε τῷ ἐμῷ νόμῳ,** μηκέτι τῷ Μωϋσέως, μηκέτι περιτέμνεσθε, **μηκέτι σαββατίζεσθε, μηκέτι κατὰ τὰ πρῶτα** καὶ κατὰ τὰ **παλαιὰ πορεύεσθε**"· *ἰδοὺ γέγονε καινά, τὰ ἀρχαῖα παρῆλθεν* (*H77Ps* I,3 [f. 221ʳ⁻ᵛ], 358, 9–13).

Well then, if my savior says, "*Attend, my people, to my law*" (Ps 77:1), he is speaking to Christians, for Christians are Christ's people. And he says, **"Attend to my law,"** i.e., no longer attend to the law of Moses. No longer practice circumcision, **no longer observe the Sabbath, no longer walk (live) in accordance with the first things and** in accordance with **the old things. "*Behold new things have come, the old have passed away*"** (2 Cor 5:17[58]).

The λύσις ἐκ προσώπου identifying Christ as the speaker in Ps 77:1 involves also a rejection of the counter-solution; just as Christ *and not Moses* speaks, so also he speaks to Christians *and not to Jews,* and he tells them to follow his (Christ's) law, which means in turn *not to observe the law of Moses* in terms of circumcision, Sabbath observance and any of the older and now obsolete things—the very things that Paul denounces in Galatians (Gal 2:3; 5:3; 5:10; 6:12–13). It is not clear here that Origen is worried about actual Christian circumcision so much as that he is echoing the historic argument by Paul in Galatians against it (and the way in which circumcision is a kind of metonymy for entering into the obligation for complete halachic observance, as Paul presents it in Gal 5:2). Then the Paul of 2 Cor 5:17 pronounces the hermeneutical key of non-compatible contraries (and in turn of supersessionism): if the new has arrived, the old has passed away.

F. Specific Significance of Christ's statement in Ps 77:1 for Feasts of ἄζυμα and ἡ ἡμέρα τοῦ ἱλασμοῦ

With a turn to yet another Pauline[59] text, Origen finally localizes his general concern about following the Law of Moses, with yet another Pauline inter-text:

---

58. Origen has reversed Paul's two clauses, which emphasis works better for his argument.

59. Of course, Origen regards all fourteen letters, including Hebrews (despite some famous conversation about its authorship) as available Pauline evidence for this argument.

Ἀλλὰ ἀκούετε καὶ τὰ[60] γυναικάρια, τὰ σεσωρευμένα ἁμαρτίαις ποικίλαις, καὶ ἴδετε τίνα τρόπον λέγει ὁ σωτήρ· προσέχετε, λαός μου, τὸν νόμον μου. Ἐὰν γὰρ προσέχητε τῷ νόμῳ ὡς λαὸς τοῦ Χριστοῦ, **μὴ πάλιν ἄζυμα ποιήσητε** καὶ ὅταν μὲν ἐνστῶσιν αἱ ἡμέραι τῶν ἀζύμων, ἀλλὰ ἄζυμα ποιήσατε εἰλικρινείας, ἄζυμα ποιήσατε ἀληθείας. Ἐὰν προσέχητε τῷ νόμῳ, οὐ πάλιν τὴν Ἰουδαϊκὴν νηστείαν ποιήσετε,[61] δι' ἧς καλῶς ἐκβάλλονται ἀπὸ τῆς Χριστοῦ ἐκκλησίας οἱ μὴ νοήσαντες τὴν ἡμέραν τοῦ ἱλασμοῦ (*H77Ps* I,4 [f. 221ᵛ], 358, 13–20).

But listen up, you[62] *"silly women, heaped up with manifold sins"* (2 Tim 3:6), and see in what way the savior says, *"Attend, my people, to my law."* If you attend to the law as Christ's people, **don't again perform the unleavening** even when the days of the feast of unleavened bread arrive,[63] but perform an unleavening of sincerity, perform an unleavening of truth (cf. 1 Cor 5:8). If you attend to the law, you will not again perform the Jewish fast, by which those who have not comprehended the day of atonement are rightly thrown out of the assembly of Christ.

Origen's concern is concrete, clear and now contemporized: Christians, Christ is speaking to you in Ps 77:1 and telling you *not* to perform the unleavening at the feast of unleavened bread, nor the fast on Yom Kippur. Origen's directing this at "silly women" involves a negative caricature about Judaizing as a special concern of women,[64] found elsewhere in his writings.[65] In this case it may also be rooted in social fact, a reference to the role of women in the domestic practices of removing leavening agents from the home and baking and eating unleavened bread.[66] But this reference to "silly women" can be used to

60. I have removed the italics from both instances of τά in the Perrone edition, because the article is not a part of the quotation (NA[28] lists no variant here; NA[26] lists as a variant τά before γυναικάρια but as poorly attested, in minuscule 2 [XII] and *pc*). Note that the noun and participle are indefinite also in Origen's citation of the lemma in Text K below (as also in *c. Cels.* 6.24).

61. I accept the reading of M, rather than Perrone's emendation, ποιήσητε.

62. I am understanding Origen to be taking the Paulinist text's Nominative case (τὰ γυναικάρια) as though Vocative here (though it has the definite article τά because of its original syntax). It is also possible that the lemma is the Accusative object of the imperative (though it lacks the quotation marker, τό).

63. From this we might be able to infer that this homily was delivered in or near spring. Cf. Fürst, "Judentum, Judenchristentum und Antijudaismus," 280–81. And yet Origen moves quickly from the Feast of the Unleavened Bread to the autumnal feast of the Day of Atonement.

64. In turn, within the context of the present homily on Psalm 77, it is possible, too, that there is an allusion to the Matthean text that quotes the Psalm, in 13:35, for it begins with the parable of the women and the leaven (13:33 ὁμοία ἐστὶν ἡ βασιλεία τῶν οὐρανῶν ζύμῃ, ἣν λαβοῦσα γυνὴ ἐνέκρυψεν εἰς ἀλεύρου σάτα τρία ἕως οὗ ἐζυμώθη ὅλον). With Origen, often more is more! (i.e., the more allusions are stitched together, the better).

65. Hom. in Jer. 12.13 [SC 238.46, ed. Pierre Nautin]; cf. John A. McGuckin, "Origen on the Jews," 26.

66. Fürst, "Judentum, Judenchristentum und Antijudaismus," 280, discusses some of the complexities involved in how we might understand of what these Christian women were doing in their own eyes, i.e., whether baking and eating unleaved bread might be considered self-conscious "Judaizing,"

stigmatize anyone who Judaizes as akin to such silly creatures (as the endlessly reusable diminutive noun γυναικάρια was intended by the Paulinist author of 2 Tim 3:6). After all, the full verse 2 Tim 3:6 stipulates that the problem of the γυναικάρια is that they are constantly learning but never coming εἰς ἐπίγνωσιν ἀληθείας. This inability to reach full knowledge, for Paul (and Origen) is what characterizes Jewish religious inferiority in the present (μαρτυρῶ γὰρ αὐτοῖς ὅτι ζῆλον θεοῦ ἔχουσιν ἀλλ' οὐ κατ' ἐπίγνωσιν[67] [Rom 10:2[68]]). In any case, as the argument proceeds it seems clear that Origen is not only addressing the women, because he switches to the masculine (referring to men and mixed groups) in line 20: οἱ μὴ νοήσαντες. So, this characterization of his audience as γυναικάρια is part real and part analogy, to set up for Origen's explanation of what Christ is saying in Ps 77:1: when the days of the feast of unleavened bread arrive, they should hear their lawgiver, Christ, in this verse telling them *not* to adhere to the Mosaic Law. Without warning Origen shifts from the spring Feast of the Unleavened Bread to the autumn feast of Yom Kippur, the Day of Atonement. By way of a blunt reminder of what appears to be recognizable, actual precedent, the preacher presages a threat of the same for the future: by observing the Jewish feasts they will be thrown out of the Χριστοῦ ἐκκλησία as others rightly have been. We can of course see this as further evidence of "a slight blurring of the line at a popular level between Church and Synagogue practices of worship"[69] in Caesarea, and Origen's vehemence certainly discloses his own view of this as a grave threat.[70] At the same time it also seems to reflect some concrete action by some churches (even if a kind of

____

or an act of associating with neighboring Jews, or more as a private household custom without the kind of public or "religious" or "theological" associations Origen assumes.

67. Cf. also 1 Tim 2:4, mentioned previously as a piece of Origen's logic: ὃς [θεός] πάντας ἀνθρώπους θέλει σωθῆναι καὶ εἰς ἐπίγνωσιν ἀληθείας ἐλθεῖν.

68. Origen does not cite some of the more positive statements about Jews in Romans 9–11 here, such as 9:4–5.

69. McGuckin, "Origen on the Jews," 26.

70. The stark contrast de Lange, *Origen and the Jews*, 87, draws between Origen and, later, Chrysostom, seems hard to sustain: "Possibly the problem was not as grave as that which later confronted John Chrysostom in Antioch, but it is still informative to contrast Origen's mild reasonableness with Chrysostom's hellfire and thunder" (p. 87; but see also p. 135: "[Origen] could be severe in his condemnation of those who 'fawned on the Jews', and who introduced Jewish teaching and practices into the Church. He lost no opportunity, in his sermons, to attack Jewish literalism, and his powerful invective no doubt made its contribution to the later tragic persecution of Jews by Christians. Yet Origen was not by nature a persecutor: his weapon was reason, not force … His attitude owes much to that of Paul, and like Paul his concern is less to condemn the Jews than to persuade them of the need to reform Judaism in the light of the Christian teaching."). To that final point, it is striking that in none of the passages we are investigating in the new homilies does Origen call for Jews to reform, or even to accept Christ.

reverse allusion to John 9:22). But Origen's concern is not just with the status of unleavened bread in itself or the eating of it, or of the fast on the Day of Atonement, but with the proper understanding (νοεῖν) of scripture and of divine truth (ἀλήθεια).

G. True Feasts v. Prefigured Feasts (the proper νοεῖν)

Ἡμέρα γὰρ ἱλασμοῦ πάλαι, ὅτε ἐνήστευον, ἡ τυπικὴ δὲ ἡμέρα τοῦ ἱλασμοῦ· ἡ ἀληθινή, ὅτε ὁ κύριός μου Χριστὸς Ἰησοῦς ὑπὲρ τοῦ κόσμου ἐσταύρωται,[71] ὁ ἀμνὸς τοῦ θεοῦ, ὁ αἴρων τὴν ἁμαρτίαν τοῦ κόσμου. Γέγονεν οὖν καὶ ἐν ἐμοὶ ἡ ἡμέρα τοῦ ἱλασμοῦ, οὐκέτι χρείαν ἔχω νηστείας· οὐ δύνανται οἱ υἱοὶ τοῦ νυμφῶνος ὅσον μετ᾽ αὐτῶν ἐστι ὁ νυμφίος νηστεύειν. Εἰ θέλεις νηστεύειν Ἰουδαϊκῶς, ἦρταί σου ὁ νυμφίος κατὰ τὰ εἰρημένα· ὅταν ἀρθῇ ἀπ᾽ αὐτῶν ὁ νυμφίος, τότε νηστεύουσιν ἐν ἐκείναις ταῖς ἡμέραις. Εἰ θέλεις νηστεύειν, νήστευε νηστείαν Χριστιανήν. Ἐδίδαξεν ὁ νομοθέτης τῶν ἐθνῶν εἰπών· ὅταν νηστεύῃς, ἄλειψαί σου τὴν κεφαλὴν καὶ τὸ πρόσωπόν σου νίψαι καὶ πρόσευξαι τῷ πατρί σου τῷ ἐν κρυπτῷ, ἵνα μὴ φανῇς νηστεύων τοῖς ἀνθρώποις (H77Ps I,4 [f. 221ᵛ], 358, 20–359, 8).

There was a day of atonement of old when they used to fast, but it was a figurative day of atonement; the true one was when my Lord Christ Jesus has been crucified on behalf of the world, *"the lamb of God who takes away* [**359**] *the sin of the world"* (John 1:29). So then, this day of atonement has taken place also in me[72]; I no longer have need of fasting. *"The sons of the bridegroom are not able to fast as long as the bridegroom is with them"* (Mark 2:19). If you wish to fast [**222ʳ**] in a Jewish fashion, then the bridegroom has been taken away from you according to what was said, *"When the bridegroom is taken away from them, then they fast[73] in those days"* (Mark 2:20). If you wish to fast, fast the Christian fast. The lawgiver of the Gentiles taught in these words, *"When you fast, anoint your head and wash your face and pray to your Father who is in secret* (Matt 6:6), *so that you might not appear to people to be fasting"* (Matt 6:17–18).

Previously, the apostle of 1 Cor 5:8 joined the lawgiver of Ps 77:1 to spiritualize the spring feast of unleavened bread at Passover—a feast of sincerity and truth—which at Origen's hands is cleverly both an ethical requirement and, all the more, a hermeneutical key to all the feasts. Origen then shifts focus to the second case mentioned above, the autumnal festival of the day of atonement (ἡ ἡμέρα τοῦ ἱλασμοῦ)[74] and its fast (νηστεία). Perhaps the connection is made easier by the fact that Origen seems—like his favored apostle and the

---

71. Cf. Gal 6:14, somewhat inverted.
72. Cf. Paul on being co-crucified with Christ, who "lives in me" (ζῇ δὲ ἐν ἐμοὶ Χριστός) in Gal 2:19–20.
73. Origen (according to M) reads the present tense, νηστεύουσιν for Mark's future, νηστεύσουσιν.
74. Cf. Lev 23:27–28, ἡμέρα ἐξιλασμοῦ.

evangelist John in 1:29[75]—to be conflating in some sense the Day of Atonement with Passover,[76] because he sees in both a figurative rendering ("type") of the death of Christ.[77] From his muse, Paul, Origen gets the language and logic of "figurative" (τυπικός) Old Testament events,[78] and their counterparts, which alone are "true" (ἀληθινός). The "Day of Atonement" has already taken place in the past, and so there is no need for a yearly commemoration, no need for the fast. The logia about the bridegroom from Mark's Gospel support this sense that this is a festival that is no longer needed; indeed, to celebrate it Ἰουδαϊκῶς would be to send Christ, the bridegroom away.[79] This logic allows Origen also to return his focus to Christ as lawgiver, and to his injunctions in the Sermon on the Mount about proper fasting, Christian fasting (νηστεία Χριστιανή), which also, on this telling, supersedes the traditional fast at the Day of Atonement with new teaching. With this invocation of a νόμος found in the Gospels and brought by ὁ νομοθέτης τῶν ἐθνῶν, the preacher turns once again to an explanation of how that νόμος and its νομοθέτης are to be understood within the divine plan.[80]

H. Syllogistic Concluding Proof: ἡ νομοθεσία Χριστοῦ = νόμος θεοῦ, as he is God's Appointed νομοθέτης and υἱός

The final movement of this argument in *H77Ps* 1 that we shall examine here[81] brings many of the elements in what has proceeded to a resounding

75. As Raymond E. Brown documents well for the history of interpretation, John 1:29, which Origen cites here, was itself taken to refer both to the suffering servant of Isaiah and the Passover lamb (*The Gospel according to John, I–XX*, AB 29 [New York: Doubleday, 1966], 60–63).

76. 1 Cor 5:7: καὶ γὰρ τὸ πάσχα ἡμῶν ἐτύθη Χριστός; Rom 3:24: ὃν προέθετο ὁ θεὸς ἱλαστήριον διὰ τῆς πίστεως ἐν τῷ αὐτοῦ αἵματι; cf. Heb 2:17: ἵνα ἐλεήμων γένηται καὶ πιστὸς ἀρχιερεὺς τὰ πρὸς τὸν θεὸν εἰς τὸ ἱλάσκεσθαι τὰς ἁμαρτίας τοῦ λαοῦ. Origen conflates the two again in hom. in *H77Ps* 6.2 ([f. 278ᵛ], 425, 23–24): Διὸ οὗτός ἐστιν ὁ ἀμνὸς τοῦ θεοῦ, ὡς ἱλαστήριον αἴρων τὴν ἁμαρτίαν τοῦ κόσμου (with assistance also from 1 John 2:1–2).

77. Origen links hidden meaning (when read κεκρυμμένως) of ἡ τοῦ ἱλασμοῦ ἡμέρα with the death of Christ, via Rom 3:25 and 1 John 2:2, also at *hom. in Jer.* 12.13 [SC 238, ed. Pierre Nautin, p. 48], an argument with various similarities to this one.

78. For τυπική cf. 1 Cor 10:6 (τύποι) and 11 (τυπικῶς). For this as part of Origen's standard vocabulary for allegorical or figurative interpretations, see Peter W. Martens, "Revisiting the Allegory/Typology Distinction: The Case of Origen," *Journal of Early Christian Studies* 16 (2008): 283–317.

79. The logic here is similar to Gal 5:4: κατηργήθητε ἀπὸ Χριστοῦ, οἵτινες ἐν νόμῳ δικαιοῦσθε.

80. Within this homily, while we do find that Christ brought a new, superior law to the Gentiles, and that he represents the true meaning of the biblical feasts, Origen does not say that the festivals have been taken away from the Jews and given to the Gentile Christians. That argument is found in the homilies on Psalm 73, to which we shall turn next.

81. In what follows Origen maps the νόμος and ῥήματα/λόγος of Ps 77:1a and b onto the Gospel according to Matthew's Sermon on the Mount (ch. 5–7) and Parable Discourse (ch. 13), respectively.

conclusion. Origen returns to the λύσις ἐκ προσώπου and to the referent of νόμον μοῦ in Ps 77:1:

> Ἔστιν οὖν νομοθεσία Χριστοῦ, περὶ ἧς λέγει Χριστός· προσέχετε, λαός
> μου, τὸν νόμον μου, τὸν κατὰ τὸ εὐαγγέλιον. Ταῦτα ἐπιστάμενος καὶ διαφορὰν
> εἰδὼς νομίμων παλαιῶν καὶ καινῶν ὁ ἱερὸς ἀπόστολος Χριστοῦ Ἰησοῦ φησι·
> γέγονα τοῖς ἀνόμοις ὡς ἄνομος, μὴ ὢν ἄνομος θεοῦ, ἀλλ᾽ ἔννομος Χριστοῦ, ἵνα
> κερδήσω τοὺς ἀνόμους. Οὐ γὰρ ἐάν τις γένηται ἔννομος Χριστοῦ, ἄνομος
> γίνεται θεοῦ ἀλλ᾽ ἔννομος Χριστοῦ, ἐπεὶ θεὸς κατέστησε τοῦτον· νομοθέτης
> ἔννομός ἐστι θεοῦ. Ὡς γὰρ ὁ ἐν νόμῳ Μωϋσέως, πρὶν ἔλθη ἡ Χριστοῦ ἐπιδημία,
> οὐκ ἦν ἄνομος θεοῦ, εἰ καὶ τῷ Μωϋσέως νόμῳ πείθεσθαι ἐδόκει—ἦν γὰρ
> νόμος ὁ Μωϋσέως θεοῦ νόμος—, οὕτω τοίνυν ὁ ἔννομος Χριστοῦ διατεταγμένος
> ὑπὸ τοῦ πατρὸς δέδοται τοῖς ἔθνεσι· πολυμερῶς οὖν καὶ πολυτρόπως πάλαι ὁ
> θεὸς λαλήσας τοῖς πατράσιν ἐν τοῖς προφήταις, ἐπ᾽ ἐσχάτου τῶν ἡμερῶν
> τούτων ἐλάλησεν ἡμῖν ἐν υἱῷ (H77Ps I,4 [f. 222ʳ⁻ᵛ], 359, 9–20).

So then, it is concerning the legislation of Christ that Christ says, "*Attend, my people, to my law,*" i.e., the law that is in accordance with the gospel. Because the holy apostle of Christ Jesus knew these things and recognized the distinction between the old laws and the new, he says, I have been "*to those outside the law as one outside the law, although I am not outside God's law, but inside Christ's law, so that I might gain those outside the law*" (1 Cor 9:21).[82] For it is not the case that if someone is "*inside Christ's law*" he is "*outside God's law,*" but rather he is "*inside Christ's law*" since God appointed him (sc. Christ). The lawgiver is "*inside God's law.*" For just as he who was inside the law of Moses before the arrival of Christ was not "*outside God's law*" even if he seemed to be obeying Moses's law[83] [222ᵛ]—for Moses's law was in fact God's law—so now the one who has been appointed "*inside Christ's law*" has been given by the Father to the Gentiles. For "*in many ways and by many turns God, having spoken in ancient times to the ancestors in the prophets, in these the end of days has spoken to us in a son*" (Heb 1:1–2).

As we have seen, Origen's λύσις ἐκ προσώπου involves proper alignment of Lawgiver (Christ, not Moses), recipients (Gentiles/Christians, not Jews) and Law (new, not old). Now for the first time, having just quoted from three of the four Gospels in the previous paragraph, Origen draws the connection that Christ's law was the νόμος (ὁ) κατὰ εὐαγγέλιον. Drawing yet again on the apostle Paul as one who "knew these things" (i.e., the true meaning of the festivals)

---

82. Note that Origen has sidestepped the prior verse, 9:20, and the question of whether or not Paul was ὑπὸ νόμον.

83. In my prior article, I translated the εἰ καί clause, "if indeed he appeared to comply with the law of Moses" (taking the καί as intensive). That is possible, but the real concession ("even if he seemed to be obeying Moses' law") may be closer to the grammar and the sense of the passage.

"and recognized the distinction (διαφορά) between the old laws and the new" (cf. 2 Cor 5:17, just recently quoted), Origen makes use of Paul's brief disclaimer in 1 Cor 9:21 that the person who is ἔννομος Χριστοῦ is ἄνομος θεοῦ. However, Origen's interest seems to be less about the status of the *recipients* of the law (which is Paul's concern[84]) than about the status of the *lawgiver* himself. Christ, he avers, was not and could not have been ἄνομος θεοῦ. Instead, Christ was himself ἔννομος Χριστοῦ, because God appointed him as lawgiver, and νομοθέτης ἔννομός ἐστι θεοῦ. Returning implicitly here to the argument about the καιροί, Origen argues that those from the time of Moses to that of Christ may have looked like they were following Moses' law, but actually they were following God's law, since "the Law of Moses was God's law" (ἦν γὰρ νόμος ὁ Μωϋσέως θεοῦ νόμος). In the earlier study of προβλήματα καὶ λύσεις, I took this to be a kind of self-correction by Origen against the extreme position earlier, that contemporary Jews in obedience to the law are ὑπὸ κατάραν, in order to protect against a possible Marcionite reading. In view of the present investigation, I might modulate that view somewhat. Surely, the statement that the law of Moses was God's law is there; but it is made *en passant*, and is not quite the focus of the passage, so much as the insistence that Christ was appointed as lawgiver by God, which reverberates back to the quotation of Ps 9:21 at the start of this wider argument at which our analysis began (Κατάστησον νομόθετην αὐτοῖς; θεὸς κατέστησε τοῦτον). Now Origen wants to claim that, since Christ was himself ἔννομος θεοῦ, and, appointed to bring and be[85] ἔννομος Χριστοῦ, his law, as God's law, is to be obeyed—and that means that the law of Moses is *not to be obeyed*, as Origen has reworded it above. Even if there is a hint of concern here to insist once more that the law of Moses was from the one God, the emphasis on the temporal limit of that law up until the time of Χριστοῦ ἐπιδημία remains consistent with the argument in §3, that the law was

---

84. And in Origen's in *frag. in 1 Cor.* on this verse: φημὶ δὲ ὅτι εἰ καὶ μὴ τηρῶ τὸν νόμον κατὰ τὸ ῥητὸν οὐκ εἰμὶ ἄνομος τοῦ θεοῦ ἀλλ' ἔννομός εἰμι τοῦ Χριστοῦ τηρῶν τὴν πολιτείαν τὴν κατὰ τὸ εὐαγγέλιον, ἵνα κερδή σω τοὺς ἀνόμους, or in *H67Ps* I.3 [fol. 88^(v−r)] 181, 12 – 182, 12.

85. In some ways, this argument seems to be logically problematic, and I wonder if there might not be some textual corruption. It isn't clear why Christ as lawgiver is parallel to the person who was ἐν νόμῳ Μωϋσέως πρὶν ἔλθῃ ἡ Χριστοῦ ἐπιδημία, or exactly what it means that Christ, appointed as νομοθέτης by the Father, is "appointed as 'inside the law of Christ'" (ὁ ἔννομος Χριστοῦ διατεταγμένος). None of the other four places where Origen quotes and treats 1 Cor 9:21 (*comm. in Joh.* 10.7.29; *comm. in Matt.* 17.32; *frag. in 1 Cor.*, 2x) turns the argument toward Christ being ἔννομος Χριστοῦ, as in this homily. Perhaps the phrase ὁ δὲ νομοθέτης ὁ has dropped out before διατεταγμένος? Thus, one would translate, "so also is the person 'inside Christ's law' [not outside God's law]. And the lawgiver who has been appointed by the Father has been given to the Gentiles."

given as appropriate to the καιροί, with the advent of Christ as the dividing line. The final quotation from Heb 1:1–2 that Origen knits into his argument is meant to reestablish both that God has been responsible for both laws (because he spoke earlier to the ancestors via the prophets), and that Christ has been appointed lawgiver "in these the end of days" (the final καιρός) for the Gentiles.

The Pauline passages Origen has used throughout this argument have consistently emphasized a break between the "old" and the "new"—whether "things" [καινά/ἀρχαῖα], covenants [διαθῆκαι], or laws [νόμιμα]—and the "figurative" [τυπική] and the "true" [ἀληθινή], in regard to festivals. The Pauline muse has led Origen to assume that if Christ is commanding his people to attend to his law, by the antithetical rhetoric of a text like Gal 2:16 (cf. Gal 6:2), Christ is really saying *do not attend to the law of Moses*, which means do not circumcise, keep the Sabbath, or celebrate the pilgrimage festivals. He has also found in Paul a source for very negative characterizations, either of Judaizing women (from 2 Tim 3:6) or of contemporary Jews as ὑπὸ κατάραν (Gal 3:10). The latter argument involves both the Pauline logic applying the Deuteronomic covenantal curse of 27:26, and something Origen himself adds: the taunt that the Jews of his own day are not allowed to carry out the pilgrimage that the law requires for fulfilling the commandments about the Passover. Origen does not adduce such passages as Rom 7:14, on how the law is πνευματικός, or place much emphasis on the special role of Israel in God's plan and her election (Rom 9:4–5), nor an "end of days" hope for all Israel to be saved (Rom 11:26).[86] Along the way are a few swipes at the Mosaic law, as coming from a servant (θεράπων, δοῦλος), which might, via Heb 3:5–6, be reverberating in the final quotation from that same letter (Heb 1:2) that emphasizes that Christ as lawgiver comes as υἱός (καὶ Μωϋσέως μὲν πιστὸς ἐν ὅλῳ τῷ οἴκῳ αὐτοῦ ὡς θεράπων … Χριστὸς δὲ ὡς υἱός ἐπὶ τὸν οἶκον αὐτοῦ). The argument is theologically consistent, rooted in these antitheses between Christians and Jews as people, their laws, and their lawgivers, and a salvation-historical schema that, while it emphasizes the continuity of the one God's hand and purpose in the full history, including the Sinai covenant and Mosaic law, is unambiguous about the superiority of the new covenant over the old.

---

86. Following here the methodological lead of McGuckin, as introduced at the outset of this paper. As the notes show, some of the Pauline invocations and echoes here are even stronger when one takes into account the readings of M, and various choices about syntax.

Homilies One and Two on Ps 73(74)

In pursuing our topic, it is useful to compare two other arguments in the new homilies that show significant overlap, but also differences, from the arguments in *H77Ps* I.3–4. On balance they continue, and in some respects, amplify further, the more negative sides of Origen's engagement with and about Christ, the Law and the Jewish people we have seen in *H77Ps*. I.

First, here is a compositional analysis of *H73Ps* I.8–9 (f. 125ʳ–126ᵛ) 234, 13–235, 22 before we examine it in more detail.[87]

A. It was at the Feast of Passover that "The Jews" Killed Christ, the Passover Sacrifice (as foretold by both the Psalmist and Isaiah, and confirmed by Paul)
   1. The lemma Ps 73:4a: Καὶ ἐνεκαυχήσαντο οἱ μισοῦντές σε ἐν μέσῳ τῆς ἑορτῆς σου
   2. Focusing mechanism to find the historical referent: Κατὰ τὸ ῥητόν
   3. Imperative: ἐλθέ μοι ἐπὶ τὸν χρόνον τῆς ἑορτῆς ἐκείνης, ὅτε ὁ Ἰησοῦς μου, πάσχα ὄντος, παραδίδοται εἰς τὸ σταυρωθῆναι (Matt 26:2)
   4. Identification of historical protagonists: οἱ μισοῦντές σε ἐν μέσῳ τῆς ἑορτῆς σου = οἱ Ἰουδαῖοι, οἱ πολέμιοι τῷ Χριστῷ, καὶ ἐνεργοῦντες τοὺς Ἰουδαίους ἐν μέσῳ τῆς ἑορτῆς (cf. Mark 14:1–2 and pars.)
   5. Identification of Christ as Passover sacrifice in the past event: ἑορτὴ γὰρ ἦν, ὅτε παρεδόθη καὶ ἀντὶ προβάτου ἀπέκτειναν τὸν σωτῆρα
   6. *Scriptural Proof: Isaiah 53:7, quoted (ὡς πρόβατον ἐπὶ σφαγὴν ἤχθη …)
     a. No longer read as a statement made ἁπλούστερον
     b. Must be read as a statement made μυστικῶς
     c. *Reason: the prophet said Isaiah 53:7 because he knew what Paul was later to say: τὸ πάσχα ἡμῶν ὑπὲρ ἡμῶν ἐτύθη Χριστός (1 Cor 5:7)
   7. *Identification of the two pascal sacrifices: Ὡς ἐν τῷ πάσχα τὰ πρόβατα, οὕτως ἐν τῷ ἀληθινῷ πάσχα ὁ Χριστὸς ἄγεται ("led away in ceremony")
   8. Lemma repeated (reworded with third person pronoun) to seal the point

B. Because "the Jews" Killed Christ at the Passover, They Can No Longer Celebrate the Passover
   1. Past result of that Fateful Passover: μετ᾽ ἐκείνην ἑορτὴν οὐκέτι ἑορτάζουσιν[88]
   2. Reason: ἐμόλυναν τὴν ἑορτήν, ἐμόλυναν τὰ ἅγια
   3. Present result: Κἂν θέλωσιν ἑορτάζειν Ἰουδαῖοι, οὐκέτι δύνανται

---

87. I continue the practice of marking Pauline influence with *.

88. These judgments are always difficult, but in demarcating the argument, I would place a paragraph break after the lemma and before Διὰ τοῦτο (rather than after οὐκέτι δύνανται [Perrone, 234, 25]). Origen's argument proceeds first historically, and then to the contemporary situation, with this line as the transitus.

4. Scriptural requirement: the Passover feast must be celebrated in "this place deemed holy" (ἐν τῷ τόπῳ τούτῳ τῷ νομιζομένῳ ἁγίῳ) (cf. Deut 16:2, etc.)

5. Current situation: they are not allowed to do so, because they have "been expelled from Jerusalem" (ὅθεν ἐκβέβληνται)

6. No longer can they ἑορτάζειν any of the three pilgrimage festivals (Exod 23:17): πάσχα, πεντηκοστή, σκηνοπηγία

7. Transferal: αἱ ἑορταὶ αὐτῶν ἤρθησαν ἀπ' αὐτῶν καὶ ἐδόθησαν ἡμῖν [to be developed in next sub-argument, C]

8. Scriptural prophecy fulfilled: Amos 8:10, quoted: στραφέτωσαν αἱ ἑορταὶ ὑμῶν εἰς πένθος καὶ αἱ ᾠδαι ὑμῶν εἰς θρήνους

C. It is "We" Christians Who Have Received the Feasts, and in a Different Mode (ἑτέρως) than "the Jews"

1. Transition to Supersessionist argument mentioned above (καὶ ἐδόθησαν ἡμῖν): Ἡμεῖς οὖν ἐλάβομεν τὰς ἑορτάς

2. New Theme—A New Mode of Feasts: καὶ ἑτέρως ἢ ὡς ἐκεῖνοι ἔλαβον

3. *Temporal and qualitative contrast: Ἔλαβον γὰρ ἐκεῖνοι τυπικῶς (cf. 1 Cor 10:11), ἕως ἔλθῃ ἡ ἀλήθεια

4. *Pauline temporal transition: ἐλθούσης δὲ τῆς ἀληθείας (cf. Gal 3:25: ἐλθούσης δὲ τῆς πίστεως)

5. Christian claim (ἡμεῖς λέγομεν): ἐλάβομεν τὸ πάσχα τὸ ἀληθινόν

6. *Identification by scriptural adaptation, joining 1 Cor 5:7 and 8: τὸ πάσχα τὸ ἀληθινόν ἐτύθη Χριστός

7. *Paul in 1 Cor 5:8 recasts ἄζυμα (καινά) as ἐν ἀζύμοις εἰλικρινείας καὶ ἀληθείας

8. Application of "true" feast hermeneutic to the other two pilgrimage feasts for Christians
   a. πεντηκοστή of spiritual fruits (οἱ καρποὶ οἱ πνευματικοί)
   b. σκηνοπηγία of truly temporary dwellings for "aliens and sojourners" (1 Pet 2:11)

D. The Signs of the Sin of Those Who Harmed Christ: the καθαίρεσις Ἰσραήλ and Χριστοῦ μετάβασις

1. The extended lemma Ps 77:4b-5: ἔθεντο τὰ σημεῖα αὐτῶν σημεῖα καὶ οὐκ ἔγνωσαν, ὡς εἰς τὴν εἴσοδον ὑπεράνω

2. First interpretation: signs about those who opposed the savior
   a. Subject of verb ἔθεντο identified: αἱ δυνάμεις ἀντικείμεναι καὶ οἱ πονηρευσάμενοι κατὰ τοῦ σωτῆρος (the adversaries of Christ)
   b. Identification of the "signs" as "the signs of their sin" (τὰ σημεῖα τῆς ἁμαρτίας) and "the desolation of Israel" (ἡ καθαίρεσις Ἰσραήλ)
   c. Τίνα τὰ σημεῖα τῆς ἁμαρτίας αὐτῶν;

   d. Answers:
      i. ἡ Χριστοῦ μετάβασις ("Christ left them and came to 'us'")
     ii. Explanation: since they threw him out, he went to those who
        accepted him
    iii. Rationale from Ps 77:4b-5: the Gentiles "knew that Christ was really
        an entryway into the higher sphere" (ἔγνωσαν ὡς εἰς τὴν εἴσοδον ὑπεράνω)
  3. A different, heresiological interpretation: unreal ὡς explains the dangers
    of the "heterodox":
    a. they set up false signs (κατὰ τῆς ἀληθείας σημεῖα) that contain a
      promise of an entryway into the higher sphere
    b. But instead their words are false (ψευδεῖς) and contrary to the truth
      (ἐναντία τῇ ἀληθείᾳ)
    c. They do not lead where they promise to lead
    d. Conclusion: recite this verse against the "heterodox" when you
      see them coming your way

A. It was at the Feast of Passover that "The Jews" Killed Christ, the Passover Sacrifice

In *H73Ps* I.8, where Origen is engaging a Psalm that will go on to describe in painful detail the destruction of the temple, he confronts the verse that reads: καὶ ἐνεκαυχήσαντο οἱ μισοῦντές σε ἐν μέσῳ τῆς ἑορτῆς σου ("And those who hate you boasted over you in the midst of your feast" [73:4a]). Origen's first move is to identify these "hating" figures with the role played by those whom he characterizes as "the Jews" (οἱ Ἰουδαῖοι), against Jesus at the ἑορτή of Passover (πάσχα), at which feast, according to the gospel passion narratives, he was arrested and crucified: "Attending to the letter of the text, come with me to the time of that feast when my Jesus, when it was Passover, *'is handed over in order to be crucified.'*"[89] Next comes a complex historical fusion of that past event as narrated in the gospels, and as foretold by Isaiah in the suffering servant song of Isa 53 (understood μυστικῶς), and as later explained by Paul in 1 Cor 5:7:

> *Ἐνεκαυχήσαντο* οὖν οἱ Ἰουδαῖοι, οἱ πολέμιοι τῷ Χριστῷ, καὶ ἐνεργοῦντες τοὺς
> Ἰουδαίους *ἐν μέσῳ τῆς ἑορτῆς.* ἑορτὴ γὰρ ἦν, ὅτε *παρεδόθη*[90] καὶ ἀντὶ προβάτου
> ἀπέκτειναν τὸν σωτῆρα, ὅστις ὡς πρόβατον ἐπὶ σφαγὴν ἤχθη καὶ ὡς ἀμνὸς ἐνώπιον τοῦ

---

89. Κατὰ τὸ ῥητόν, ἐλθέ μοι ἐπὶ τὸν χρόνον τῆς ἑορτῆς ἐκείνης, ὅτε ὁ Ἰησοῦς μου, *πάσχα ὄντος, παραδίδοται εἰς σταυρωθῆναι* (*H73Ps* I.8 [f. 125ʳ] 234, 13–15; I have added italics to παραδίδοται εἰς σταυρωθῆναι, as it is a quotation from Matt 26:2; note that that verse begins μετὰ δύο ἡμέρας τὸ πάσχα γίνεται).

90. Given the key role of the exact word παρεδόθη in cementing the prophecy (Isa 53:12; Rom 4:25), as Origen well knows, I have added italics here to treat it as a quotation.

κείροντος αὐτὸν ἄφωνος. Οὐκέτι οὖν ἀκούω τοῦ προφήτου ἁπλούστερον λέγοντος
ὡς πρόβατον ἐπὶ σφαγὴν ἤχθη· μυστικῶς γὰρ εἶπεν ὁ προφήτης εἰδὼς ὅτι τὸ πάσχα
ἡμῶν[91] ὑπὲρ ἡμῶν ἐτύθη Χριστός, ὅτι ὡς πρόβατον ἐπὶ σφαγὴν ἤχθη. Ὡς ἐν τῷ πάσχα
τὰ πρόβατα, οὕτως ἐν τῷ ἀληθινῷ πάσχα ὁ Χριστὸς ἄγεται. καὶ ἐνεκαυχήσαντο οἱ
μισοῦντές αὐτὸν ἐν μέσῳ τῆς ἑορτῆς (H73Ps I.8 [f. 125ʳ⁻ᵛ] 234, 15–23).

The Jews, the enemies of Christ, boasted,[92] and incited the Jews to action
"in the midst of the feast." For it was at the feast when he *"was handed over"*
(Isa 53:12; Rom 4:25; Mark 14:12–21 and pars.) and they killed the Savoir in
place of a sheep, *"who, like a sheep was led to the slaughter and like a lamb before
the one shearering him, he made no sound."* Hence no longer do I hear the
prophet saying *"like a sheep he was led to the slaughter"* in the more literal sense
(ἁπλούστερον[93]), since the prophet said *"like a sheep he was led to the slaughter"*
in mystical sense (μυστικῶς), because he knew that *"our Passover has been
sacrificed on our behalf, Christ"* (1 Cor 5:7). As in the Passover it is sheep that
are ceremoniously led away,[94] so in the true Passover it is Christ. *"And those
who hate* him *have boasted over him in the midst of the feast."*

Origen argues that "the Jews" killed Christ, in place of the Passover lamb at
that Passover. The passion narratives in fact do not overtly say "the Jews" killed
Christ,[95] but that inference from them is made, for instance, by Luke in Acts 3:15

---

91. The Perrone edition reads ἦν here (followed by a comma), but on my reading of the digital
image of f. 125ᵛ, the scribe at the end of the line has written ἡ, with μ above it, and a circumflex marking
the abbreviation for the pronoun, ἡμῶν. This is also the reading of the continuous lemma of 1 Cor 5:7
(no need for a comma mid-verse, either), according to ℵ² C³ L P Ψ Maj: τὸ πάσχα ἡμῶν ὑπὲρ ἡμῶν ἐτύθη
Χριστός. Once again, the new homily shows a different reading by Origen of a biblical text than in the
previously extant corpus. The Nestle-Aland²⁸ apparatus lists Origen for the reading without ὑπὲρ ἡμῶν,
presumably having in view, e.g., c. Cels. 8.22; comm. in Joh. 10.14.82 (bis); 10.15.87; De pascha 90.17; 90.21;
102.20; 124.12). However, in two places in the catenae Origen is said to witness to this longer reading,
with ὑπὲρ ἡμῶν (frag. in 1 Cor., the lemma at 1 Cor 5:7–8; Selecta in Exod. [PG 12.296]). Given that in
all the other places in his works Origen cites the short reading, however, one must reckon with the
possibility that there has been assimilation to the reading of Maj in the scribal tradition of this homily,
in a way that helps along the very argument that Origen is making here about Christ's Passover sacrifice.
Note that Origen cites the lemma later in this paragraph without ὑπὲρ ἡμῶν (H73Ps I.8 [f. 126ʳ] 235, 4),
which could support either hypothesis.

92. In his interpretation here Origen doesn't do much with this idea of their "boasting."

93. Translation with LPGL B.3., which cites other instances of the antithesis ἁπλούστερος/μυστικός
in Origen's writings.

94. The Greek has a play that is hard to capture in English, because ἄγειν can mean to carry away
or to conduct, as in "keep" or "observe" or "celebrate" a feast (see LSJ s.v. IV), a usage common in Origen
when speaking about ἑορταί.

95. Within the canonical passion narratives, the phrase οἱ Ἰουδαῖοι ironically appears almost entirely
in the title for Christ as ὁ βασιλεὺς τῶν Ἰουδαίων in questioning by Pilate, in the mocking by the Roman
soldiers, and on the titulus (e.g., Mark 15:2; 15:26, and pars.). Exceptions are in Jn 19:21, where in the
Genitive it modifies the high priests (and links them ironically with the titulus), and, just after the
passion narrative, in relation to the burial in Matt 28:15. From verses such as these, and others, Origen has
harmonized "the Jews" into the texts of the passion narratives.

(τὸν δὲ ἀρχηγὸν τῆς ζωῆς ἀπεκτείνατε)[96] and 4:10, which fits also his theme of Jerusalem as the slayer of the prophets (Luke 13:34//Matt 23:37; cf. 1 Thess 2:15). Origen tacitly acknowledges this in the somewhat illogically phrased claim that "the Jews incited the Jews to action," likely in reference to the Jewish leaders inciting of the crowds in Matt 27:20–23 (and parallels) to ask for Barabbas and call for Jesus to be crucified. On Origen's telling all these actors are collapsed into a single character, οἱ Ἰουδαῖοι, who are the enemies (πολέμιοι) of Christ. While the gospels, and John in particular, indicate that Christ is a Passover lamb (John 1:29; cf. 19:36), none claims that "the Jews" killed Christ as the Passover lamb. As in the first homily we examined, it is the Paul of 1 Cor 5:7–8 who supplies a hermeneutical key for Origen, but Paul's passive voice verb ἐτύθη is ambiguous,[97] though it is perhaps a divine passive.[98] Different from the first homily on Psalm 77, here Origen focuses not on the Feast of the Unleavened Bread (or Day of Atonement), but on Christ as the πάσχα that has been sacrificed. And yet in the designation of the ἀληθινὸν πάσχα we can glimpse the same distinction derived from 1 Cor 5:8 about the "true" feasts (ἐν ἀζύμοις ... ἀληθείας). Probably the reason the full antithesis, with τυπικόν, is not in this argument, is because Origen is not referring back to the Exodus and the originating occasion for the cultic celebration that later took place during the time of Jesus. He ends the first sub-argument with a restatement of the lemma, Origen now replacing the second person pronouns of the Psalm (σέ, σου) with αὐτόν, for Christ to finalize his historical claim that this was the moment where the prophecy of Ps 73:4a met its fulfillment.

B. Because "the Jews" Killed Christ at the Passover, They Can No Longer Celebrate the Passover

With διὰ τοῦτο Origen makes a transition into the implications of this past event, thus interpreted, for what comes next.

> Διὰ τοῦτο μετ' ἐκείνην ἑορτὴν οὐκέτι ἑορτάζουσιν· ἐμόλυναν τὴν ἑορτήν, ἐμόλυναν τὰ ἅγια. Κἂν θέλωσιν ἑορτάζειν Ἰουδαῖοι, οὐκέτι δύνανται. Οὐ γὰρ ἔξεστιν, ὅσον ἐπὶ τῇ γραφῇ, ἑορτάζειν τὸ πάσχα, εἰ μὴ ἐν τῷ τόπῳ τούτῳ τῷ νομιζομένῳ ἁγίῳ, ὅθεν ἐκβέβληνται. Οὐκέτι οὖν ἑορτάζουσιν, ἀλλ' οὐδὲ τὴν ἑορτὴν τὴν πεντηκοστήν, οὐδὲ τὴν ἑορτὴν τῆς σκηνοπηγίας. Ἀλλὰ αἱ

---

96. Unaccountably, de Lange understands this verse as "Luke [seeming] to go out of his way to absolve the Jews from blame" (*Origen and the Jews*, 77, with n. 12 on p. 185).

97. Earlier in the same letter, at 1 Cor 2:8, Paul says that οἱ ἄρχοντες τοῦ αἰῶνος τούτου crucified Christ.

98. In reference either to God handing him over for the sacrifice, or handing himself over (cf., e.g., Gal 1:4; 2:20).

ἑορταὶ αὐτῶν ἤρθησαν ἀπ᾽ αὐτῶν καὶ ἐδόθησαν ἡμῖν καὶ πεπλήρωται ἐπ᾽
αὐτῶν τὸ ὑπὸ τοῦ Ἀμῶς εἰρημένον· στραφέτωσαν αἱ ἑορταὶ ὑμῶν εἰς πένθος
καὶ αἱ ᾠδαὶ ὑμῶν εἰς θρήνους (*H73Ps* I.8 [f. 125ᵛ–126ʳ] 234, 23–235, 1).

That is why after that feast they no longer observe the feast. They defiled the
feast; they defiled the holy rites.[99] Even if Jews wish to observe the feast, they're
no longer able. For it is not Lawful, as is much attested in Scripture, to observe
the feast of Passover except in this place that is deemed holy, from which they
have been cast out (cf. Deut16:2, etc.). Then no longer do they observe the feast
(of Passover), nor the feast of Pentecost, nor the feast of Booths.[100] Instead,
their feasts were taken away from them[101] and they were given to us. And the
statement made by Amos, "*Let your feasts be turned into mourning and your
odes into dirges*" (Amos 8:10) has been fulfilled in them.

Origen's initial statement is that after the death of Jesus Jews no longer celebrate Passover, which is of course not empirically true. His main point in
marking the time from the Passover at which Christ died is to insist that the
punishment fit the crime; the Passover, he alleges, was taken away from Jews
because it was at Passover that they polluted the feast and the holy city. Like
others before him, beginning with the evangelist Mark, Origen regards the destruction of the temple in CE 70 as punishment for the death of Christ. Now
in mid-third century, the expulsion of Jews from the holy city under Hadrian
adds the further irony that they can no longer fulfill the requirement to celebrate the feast of Passover in the city from which they have been expelled. We
note here the same argument we saw in *H77Ps* I.3 and its barbed expression:
"even if they wish to celebrate the feast, they are no longer able to." Origen
then extends this special claim about Passover to the other two pilgrimage festivals (Exod 23:17[102]) that are now also forbidden due to Jews' exile from the
city. This allows him to employ with bitter irony the plural ἑορταί of Amos'
solemn foreboding (8:10): for Jews festivals have been turned into mourning,
joyful odes into dirges.

99. Or "the holy place" (both meanings fit in this context).

100. The three main pilgrimage festivals prescribed in the Torah (Exod 23:17: τρεῖς καιροὺς τοῦ
ἐνιαυτοῦ ὀφθήσεται πᾶν ἀρσενικόν σου ἐνώπιον κυρίου τοῦ θεοῦ σου).

101. Psalm 73, as mentioned, gives a graphic description of the destruction of the temple. In this
first homily Origen has already from the action of the hateful boasters (now applied to "the Jews" of the
passion narrative and those later on whom Origen maps that destiny, with Matt 27:25) and drawn an
implication of what that means for the future of Passover as a Jewish feast. But likely he already has in
mind verse 8 of this very Psalm, Δεῦτε καὶ κατακαύσωμεν πάσας τὰς ἑορτὰς τοῦ θεοῦ ἀπὸ τῆς γῆς ("Come,
let's put a stop to all the feasts of God from upon the earth!"). He will return to this theme in the following homily (*H73Ps* II.2) when he arrives at this verse.

102. τρεῖς καιροὺς τοῦ ἐνιαυτοῦ ὀφθήσεται πᾶν ἀρσενικόν σου ἐνώπιον κυρίου τοῦ θεοῦ σου.

C. "We" Christians Have Received the Feasts, and
in a Different Mode (ἑτέρως) than "the Jews"

But this argument is not solely about the lamentable fate of the Jews. Origen has already declared that the festivals of the Jews have been taken from them and given "to us," the Christians. What follows next is a full, supersessionist explanation about the "true Passover" introduced above, that spells out the full antithetical framework he has crafted from Paul:

Ἡμεῖς οὖν ἐλάβομεν τὰς ἑορτὰς καὶ ἑτέρως ἢ ὡς ἐκεῖνοι ἔλαβον. Ἔλαβον γὰρ ἐκεῖνοι τυπικῶς, ἕως ἔλθῃ ἡ ἀλήθεια· ἐλθούσης δὲ τῆς ἀληθείας, ἡμεῖς λέγομεν ὅτι ἐλάβομεν τὸ πάσχα τὸ ἀληθινόν· τὸ γὰρ πάσχα ἡμῶν[103] τὸ ἀληθινὸν ἐτύθη Χριστός καὶ ἑορτάζομεν οὐ ζύμῃ παλαιᾷ, οὐδὲ ζύμῃ κακίας καὶ πονηρίας, ἀλλ' ἐν ἀζύμοις εἰλικρινείας καὶ ἀληθείας. Οὕτω δὲ ἄγομεν καὶ πεντηκοστήν, καὶ ἔτι ἀπὸ τῶν καρπῶν τῶν πνευματικῶν, οὕτως καὶ σκηνοπηγοῦμεν οἰκίας, κατοικοῦμεν <δὲ>[104] οὐκ ἐν οἰκίαις πάροικοι καὶ παρεπίδημοι ὄντες ἐπὶ τῆς γῆς (*H73Ps* I.8 [f. 126ʳ] 235, 1–8).

So then, it is we who have received the feasts, and in a different form than they received them. For they received[105] them by way of prefiguration,[106] until the truth might arrive. But after the truth arrived,[107] we call the Passover we received "the true Passover." "*For our Passover—the true one—has been sacrificed, Christ,*" *and we feast not in old leaven, nor in the leaven of wickness and evil, but in the unleavenings of sincerity and truth*" (1 Cor 5:7–8[108]). And in the same way, too, we conduct the feast of Pentecost, and yet from fruits that are spiritual. And in the same way also we erect booths as dwellings (i.e., at the feast of Sukkoth),

---

103. ἡμῶν is not in italics in Perrone edition, but I have added it, since it is part of the quotation.

104. σκηνοπηγοῦμεν οἰκίας, κατοικοῦμεν <δὲ> is my reconstruction. Perrone reads σκηνοπηγοῦμεν, οἰκίας <οὐ> κατοικοῦμεν (M lacks οὐ). Instead, I am taking οἰκίας as the object of σκηνοπηγοῦμεν (and thus would place the comma after), which means there is no need for the conjectural emendation οὐ before κατοικοῦμεν. The verb σκηνοπηγεῖν is rare, but in the few attestations of it in Greek literature it is found in at least one place with an object, as in Athenaeus, *Deipnosophistae* 10:59: διὸ καὶ πολεμουμένων ποτὲ αὐτῶν καὶ οὐ προσκαρτερούντων τοῖς τείχεσι Λεωνίδης ὁ στρατηγὸς ἐκέλευσε τὰ καπηλεῖα ἐπὶ τῶν τειχῶν σκηνοπηγεῖν καὶ μόλις ποτὲ ἐπαύσαντο λιποτακτοῦντες ("Therefore, one time once when they were embattled and not watching the walls, Leonides the general commanded them to set up taverns in tents on the walls, and hardly then did they stop deserting"). I have added a conjectural emendation of δέ κατοικοῦμεν, instead, trying to restore some balance between the two sentences (as signaled by the repeated οὕτως).

105. λαμβάνειν here has a dual sense, both of having "received" the feasts from God, and of their way of "taking," as in "understanding" or "interpreting" them.

106. Or, perhaps, "exemplary," or "as a type." Origen of course gets this language from Paul (1 Cor 10:11; cf. v. 6), and it is a frequently used piece of his hermeneutical vocabulary (as argued by Martens, "Revisiting the Allegory/Typology Distinction: The Case of Origen").

107. Note the parallel phrasing to Gal 3:25: ἐλθούσης δὲ τῆς πίστεως.

108. Origen has rephrased Paul's exhortative ὥστε ἑορτάζωμεν into an indicative (καὶ ἑορτάζομεν); other minor variations include οὐ for μή, and minus ἐν before ζύμῃ (both twice).

(but) it is not in dwellings that we abide, since we are *"aliens and sojourners"* (1 Pet 2:11) on the earth.

On this argument, the feasts commanded in the Torah and conducted by Hebrews in biblical times and Jews later on up until the arrival of Christ, were "pre-figurations" of the "true" feasts that would thenceforth be given to the (Gentile) Christians. Origen inherits from Paul (1 Cor 10:6, 11; 1 Cor 5:8) both the language of prefigured and truthful. Origen insists that the feasts have had both on a change of hands and a change of modes, in the latter case, both ethical and ritual: the Christian Passover, Pentecost, and Booths are not false, but "true," carried out, as the Apostle put it, "with unleavenings of sincerity and truth" (ἐν ἀζύμοις εἰλικρινείας καὶ ἀληθείας [1 Cor 5:8]). At the same time, they have a higher meaning beyond the material: a harvest festival of spiritual fruits (not hard wheat kernels) and a tent dwelling erected but not really dwelt in, for the Christians who build them are wayfarers on earth (with an assist from 1 Pet 2:11).

D. The Signs of the Sin of those who harmed Christ:
καθαίρεσις Ἰσραήλ and Χριστοῦ μετάβασις

Continuing his homiletic treatment of Psalm 73, Origen quotes again the initial verse of this argument about the feasts and then adds to it the next part of the lemma: ἔθεντο τὰ σημεῖα αὐτῶν σημεῖα καὶ οὐκ ἔγνωσαν, ὡς εἰς τὴν εἴσοδον ὑπεράνω ("They set up their signs as signs, as though for an entryway into a higher sphere, and they did not recognize it"). In the curious sentence structure in the Greek[109] Origen sees two possible useful interpretations, the first of which continues the theme of Jewish rejection of Jesus and the punishment it has brought upon them:

> *Καὶ ἐνεκαυχήσαντο οἱ μισοῦντες με ἐν μέσῳ τῆς ἑορτῆς σου. Ἔθεντο*
> *τὰ σημεῖα αὐτῶν σημεῖα καὶ οὐκ ἔγνωσαν, ὡς εἰς τὴν εἴσοδον ὑπεράνω.*
> *Ἔθεντο σημεῖα* καὶ <αἱ> δυνάμεις αἱ ἀντικείμεναι καὶ οἱ πονηρευσάμενοι κατὰ
> τοῦ σωτῆρος·[110] ἔθεντο καὶ μέχρι σήμερον κεῖνται τὰ σημεῖα τῆς ἁμαρτίας
> αὐτῶν, ἡ καθαίρεσις Ἰσραήλ. Τίνα τὰ σημεῖα τῆς ἁμαρτίας αὐτῶν; Ἡ Χριστοῦ
> μετάβασις· μετέβη ἀπ᾽ ἐκείνων, ἦλθε πρὸς ἡμᾶς. *Ἐξέβαλον*[111] ἐκεῖνοι τὸν

---

109. For MT שמו אותתם אתות ידע כמביא למעלה. NETS translation (Albert Pietersma) reads "They set up their emblems as emblems and did not know. As though into the entrance above...." Origen appears to read this as a single grammatical sentence.

110. Who these two groups are will be developed in the following homily.

111. Italics added to Perrone edition, on the grounds that this is a quotation of Matt 21:39.

Χριστόν, ἦλθε πρὸς τοὺς μὴ ἐκβάλλοντας αὐτὸν[112] ἀλλὰ τοὺς παραδεχομένους αὐτόν, κἀκεῖνοι ἔγνωσαν ὡς εἰς τὴν εἴσοδον ὑπεράνω· βλέπομεν καὶ ἄλλον τινὰ λόγον ἐν τῷ ῥητῷ, ὅτι πολλάκις οἱ πονηρευόμενοι κατὰ τῆς ἀληθείας σημεῖά τινα τίθενται καὶ σημεῖα ὡς εἰς τὴν εἴσοδον. Οἷον ἐὰν ἴδῃς ἐν τοῖς ἑτεροδόξοις ἐπαγγελίαν μὲν εἰσόδου, λόγους δὲ ψευδεῖς καὶ ἐναντίους τῇ ἀληθείᾳ, οὐκ εἰσάγοντας δὲ κατὰ τὴν ἐπαγγελίαν αὐτῶν εἰς εἴσοδον· ἐὰν ἴδῃς αὐτοὺς ἐπαγγελλομένους ὑψηλὰ καὶ οὐρανίων διήγησιν, λέγε· ἔθεντο τὰ σημεῖα αὐτῶν, σημεῖα δὲ ὡς εἰς τὴν εἴσοδον ὑπεράνωθεν (*H73Ps* I.9 [f. 126[r–v]] 235, 9–22).

"And those who hate me[113] *boasted over me in the midst of your feast"* (Ps 73:4a). *They set up their signs as signs, as though for an entryway to a higher sphere, and they did not recognize* it (Ps 73:4b-5). The opposing powers and those who did acted with evil intent against the savior *"set up signs."* *"They set them up"* and until this very day the signs of their sin stand there, the destruction of Israel.[114] What are the signs of their sin? The transferal of the Christ. For he transferred away from them; he came to us. *They cast out* the Christ (Matt 21:39); he came to those who don't cast him out but welcome him (cf. John 1:10–12), and the latter were the ones who *"recognized him as an entryway to a higher sphere."* We see another sense in this statement, as well, to the effect that many who act with evil intent against the truth set up some signs, and those signs are *"as though*[115] an entryway."* This is what you see among the heterodox: a promise of an entryway, but actually words that are false and contradict the truth, that don't lead not into an entryway, as they promise! If you see them promising lofty teachings and an explanation of heavenly matters, say, *"They set up their signs,* but[116] *they are signs 'as though*[117] *for an entryway* to a *higher sphere."*

The continuation of the Psalm verse allows Origen to reemphasize the significance of the destruction of Jerusalem as one of the "signs of the sin" of Israel. The other sign, he maintains, is the Χριστοῦ μετάβασις, Christ having left the people who did not recognize him (cf. John 1:10–12) and cast him out (cf. Matt 21:39), and he has gone over to the Christians ("us"). He finds in Ps 73:5 the

112. Typo in printed edition, αὐτὸον (235, 15), corrected (as it has been already in TLG).

113. Having identified this person earlier as Christ, Origen now rewords the lemma with με for σε.

114. Probably an allusion to the destruction of Jerusalem, with reference to Matt 23:38//Luke 13:35, though without verbal parallel.

115. If I am following this argument correctly, Origen in the first interpretation took the ὡς as real, stating the hopes of those who accepted Christ, but in this second he takes it as unreal, the basis of deception by the heterodox.

116. Origen has subtly reworded the text, removing καὶ οὐκ ἔγνωσαν and inserting a δέ after the second σημεῖα to effect the contrast he is making (δέ should not be in italics). He has also changed ὑπεράνω to ὑπεράνωθεν. There may not be much of a difference, but possibly the locative is meant to emphasize the falsehood—that what these heretics teach does not come from above at all, but from them below.

117. I.e., "ersatz signs."

reason for Christ's acceptance by the Christians: they, unlike "the Jews," recognized that he really did offer them "an entryway to a higher sphere."[118] But Origen knows that the conjunction ὡς can have real and unreal senses. His alternate explanation switches (as Origen often does) from the anti-Judaistic rhetoric to inner-Christian heresiological rhetoric that inveighs against the "heterodox"[119] for promising—but not delivering on—"an entryway to a higher sphere."

Within this argument, we can see Origen aligning αἱ δυνάμεις αἱ ἀντικείμεναι ("the opposing powers") καὶ οἱ πονηρευσάμενοι κατὰ τοῦ σωτῆρος ("those who acted with evil intent against the savior"). Who are these figures, and how do they relate to one another? Origen does not spell this out in full here but will in the following homily (*HPs 73* II.2), to which we now turn. The linkage is provided by the Psalm itself, which in v. 8 reads: εἶπαν ἐν τῇ καρδίᾳ αὐτῶν ἡ συγγένεια αὐτῶν ἐπὶ τὸ αὐτό | Δεῦτε καὶ καταπαύσωμεν πάσας τὰς ἑορτὰς τοῦ θεοῦ ἀπὸ τῆς γῆς ("the close kinship of men in their heart said together, 'Come and let's cause all the feasts of God to cease from off the land.'"[120]).

Once again, we begin with a compositional analysis and overview of the argument:

HPs73 II.2–3 (f. 129ᵛ–133ʳ) 239, 5–243, 12

A. The συγγένεια ("close kinship") of the enemies of the people of God
(τῶν ἐχθρῶν τῷ λαῷ)
   1. Quotation of the lemma: Ps 73:81-b, connecting the συγγένεια and
     the speech
   2. Application: Christ's death was at the hand of a "kinship" of two
     enemy forces
     a. αἱ ἀόρατοι δυνάμεις – in accordance with Ps 2:2, as quoted in Acts 4:26
     b. οἱ ἐνεργούμενοι ὑπ' αὐτῶν Ἰουδαῖοι – in accordance with Acts 22:22 (sic);
       John 19:15; Matt 27:25
   3. Characterization of the collusion: ἐπιβουεύεσθαι
   4. Goal of the collusion: to cause the αἱ ἑορταὶ τοῦ θεοῦ to cease ἀπὸ τῆς γῆς

---

118. Perhaps Origen has in mind Eph 1:20–21 and 4:10, which associate Christ with the region ὑπεράνω.

119. Presumably he has in mind "gnostics" like Heracleon here.

120. Compare the translation by Albert Pietersma in NETS: "They said in their heart—the clan of them together—'Come, and let us burn all the feasts of God from off the land.'" Note that some mss (according to Rahlfs) read καταπαύσωμεν (as does Origen, "let us cause to cease") instead of κατακαύσωμεν, the reading of the text Pietersma adopts.

B. The Enactment of the Plot, and its Result
  1. Plot at Passion against Christ led to the end of Passover and all feasts
    a. as foretold by Amos (8:10)
    b. Restatement of argument in A about the συγγένεια
  2. Result: what the enemies said came to pass for οἱ Ἰουδαῖοι—an end
    to the feasts
  3. Further results for ὁ λαός: Ps 73:9a and b cited· τὰ σημεῖα ἡμῶν οὐκ εἴδομεν,
    οὐκ ἔστιν ἔτι προφήτης
    a. End of σημεῖα
      i. ὁ λαός themselves said this
      ii. Signs ended for them at Christ's death
      iii. Signs had been there before his death
        α. Angelic vision to Zachariah in the temple (Luke 1:11)
        β. Signs at the moment of Christ's death (Matt 27:45, 51–53)
      iv. There were signs after Christ's death, but not for Ἰουδαῖοι
    b. Reason: signs transferred (μετέβη) from "the people" to "the Gentiles"
      (τὰ ἔθνη)
    c. Confirmation in the words themselves
      i) the people say Ps 73:9b
      ii. the people still say it now
    d. Supporting Proof: law and prophets prophesy up until JBap
      (conflation of Luke 16:16 and Matt 11:13)
  4. Consequences
    a. Holy Spirit left them
    b. Divine benefaction (εὐεργεσία) transferred (μετέβη) to the Gentiles
    c. Qualification: that is, if "we" don't lose God's grace poured out in
      prophecy upon us (Acts 2:17, 18, 33)
    d. Threatened Result: we would be the ones saying we have no sign
      and no prophet

C. *Vehement Exhortation against Forsaking Grace by Judaizing
  1. Direct address: Χριστιανέ
  2. Identity: λαὸς ὁ χάριτι θεοῦ κεκλημένος
  3. *Don't go backwards! (παλινδρομεῖν) (cf. Gal 4:9)
  4. Why flee to go join a people forsaken
    a. of χάρις
    b. of the Holy Spirit
  5. Isaiah offers proof that the daughter of Zion has been forsaken (Isa 1:8)
  6. *Counter-invitation: ἧκε
    a. to the ἐκκλησία θεοῦ
    b. to where τὸ ἅγιον πνεῦμα is
    c. *where ἡ δύναμις τοῦ Ἰησοῦ is gathered together, according to
      1 Cor 5:4, quoted

D. Does God Know οἱ Ἰουδαῖοι Now? Will He Ever?
   1. Quotation of the lemma: ἡμᾶς οὐ γνώσεται ἔτι (Ps 73:9b)
   2. Prophecy fulfilled now, and into the future, in οἱ ἐγκαταλελειμμένοι Ἰουδαῖοι
      (contrast presumed with Gal 4:9?)
   3. Until the συντέλεια (cf. Matt 28:20) he will not know ἐκεῖνος ὁ λαός
      (does this hold a promise for restoration then, with, e.g., Rom 11:26?)
   4. Reason: the γνῶσις has been transferred (μεταβεβηκυῖα) ἐπὶ τὸν ἐξ ἐθνῶν
      λαόν (Acts 15:14)

E. *An Alternative Interpretation with a Warning for You, Christians:
  "The Close Kinship of Evil" (συγγένεια τοῦ πονηροῦ) Could Be Said
  About You if You Don't Watch Out
   1. Warning, with repeat citation of Ps 73:8
   2. *Reminder: Christians called not to feast ἐν ζύμῃ παλαιᾷ, but ἐν ἀζύμοις
      εἰλικρινείας καὶ ἀληθείας (1 Cor 5:8)
   3. Lack of understanding (νοεῖν) of this can lead to a deadly plot to end
      your feasts, as well
   4. Proper understanding of τὰ ἄζυμα
     a. not about grain or leaven
     b. *about εἰλικρινεία καὶ ἀλήθεια
   5. *A Recipe for Disaster: How to "Fall Away" (cf. Gal 5:4) from the real feast
      of truth and sincerity, and instead become a badly kneaded (φυρᾶται)
      lump of dough
     a. *lose τὸ εἰλικρινές and take up τὸ δόλιον
     b. *lose τὸ ἀληθές and take up τὸ ψεῦδος
   6. Result: You will have brought the prophecy about ending the feasts
      (Ps 73:8b) down on yourselves by your conduct

F. The Christian Feast of ἄζυμα
   1. *Not for the wicked (cf. 1 Cor 5:8: μηδὲ ἐν ζύμῃ κακίας καὶ πονηρίας)
   2. *Concerning those who wish (οἱ θέλοντες; cf. Gal 4:21) to keep the old feast
      after Χριστιανισμός has come
   3. *τὰ θεῖα μαθήματα, as given by Paul in 1 Cor 5:7–8, teach about how ἄζυμα
      is to be celebrated
   4. *Christ abolished the feast dealing with αἰσθητά by fulfilling the law
      (cf. Gal 5:4) via πνευματικά
   5. *Those who try to do the former have clearly ἐκπεσόντες τῆς χάριτος τοῦ θεοῦ
      (Gal 5:4)
   6. Actually, they are not even celebrating a feast. Why?
     a. a physical feast is not a feast
     b. Christ isn't in it
     c. Holy Spirit isn't in it
   7. *Trying to Do Both is Even Worse!

    a. *Example: the γυναικάρια of 2 Tim 3:6

    b. *Trying to walk on both paths—καὶ Ἰουδαΐζειν καὶ Χριστιανίζειν (cf. Gal 2:14)

    c. Imperative: μετανοήσατε, μεταβάλεσθε

    d. You must choose: ἢ Ἰουδαία ἢ Χριστιανὴ γένεσθε

  8. Supporting exhortation from Elijah (3 Kgdms 18:21)

G. Christians Do Have Signs Now (so, contradicting Ps 73:9a)— But Could Lose Them in Future

  1. Proposition: There are Plenty of Christian signs today

    a. Demons cast out

    b. Means used: prayer

    c. Means not used: craft, amulets, potions, odes, invocations of Solomon

    d. Means: τὸ ὄνομα Ἰησοῦ

    e. Means and mode: εὐαγγελικῶς

    f. Result: a more subtle sign (ἀμαυρότερον)

  2. Supporting proof: Matt 11:5 (signs of the messiah, with Isa 29:18; 35:5; 42:18; 26:19), still true today

  3. Superior signs, of spiritual realities

    a. Not about physical matters (αἰσθητά)

    b. About spiritual ones (πνευματικά)

    c. Example: better to regain sight in one's ψυχῆς ὀφθαλμός than in σώματος ὀφθαλμός

  4. The Christian Threat is potentially worse: to lose not physical (σωματικῶς) signs, as οἱ Ἰουδαῖοι did, but spiritual ones (πνευματικά)

    a. threat found in Ps 73:9a if spoken by/about Christians

    b. Cause: ἁμαρτία

  5. Christian Threatened that they could lose prophets, too

    a. threat found in Ps 73:9b if spoken by/about Christians

    b. Cause: either rejecting prophets or misinterpreting them

    c. Rule of right reading: hearing the prophets as the Holy Spirit wishes

  6. Counterexample: Marcionites, who have neither prophets nor God

  7. *Authoritative rule from the apostle Paul: do not extinguish the Spirit or despise prophecies (1 Thess 5:19–20)

  8. Final Warning: if you reject signs and prophecy, Ps 73:9b-c will redound upon your head!

A. The συγγένεια ("close kinship") of the enemies of the people of God (τῶν ἐχθρῶν τῷ λαῷ)

Ἐνθάδε οὖν εἶπεν ἡ συγγένεια αὐτῶν ἐπὶ τὸ αὐτό, τῶν ἐχθρῶν τῷ λαῷ τοῦ θεοῦ, δεῦτε καὶ καταπαύσωμεν αὐτοὺς ἐξ ὄρους τοῦ θεοῦ ἀπὸ τῆς γῆς.

Ἡνίκα γὰρ ὁ σωτὴρ καὶ κύριος ἡμῶν ἐπεβουλεύετο ὑπὸ τῶν ἀοράτων δυνάμεων
καὶ ὑπὸ τῶν ἐνεργουμένων ὑπ' αὐτῶν Ἰουδαίων· ἀοράτων μὲν δυνάμεων κατὰ
τὸ παρέστησαν οἱ βασιλεῖς τῆς γῆς καὶ οἱ ἄρχοντες συνήχθησαν ἐπὶ τὸ
αὐτὸ κατὰ τοῦ κυρίου, κατὰ τοῦ Χριστοῦ αὐτοῦ, Ἰουδαίων δὲ κατὰ τὸ
ὁμονοήσαντας πάντας εἰρηκέναι· αἶρε, αἶρε ἀπὸ τῆς γῆς τὸν τοιοῦτον,[121]
σταύρωσον σταύρωσον αὐτόν,[122] τὸ αἷμα αὐτοῦ ἐφ' ἡμᾶς καὶ ἐπὶ τὰ τέκνα
ἡμῶν. Κατὰ τὸν καιρὸν τοῦ πάθους τοῦ σωτῆρος, πᾶσαι αἱ δυνάμεις αἱ
ἀντικείμεναι, ἐπιβουλεύουσαι τῷ σωτῆρι, ἐνήργουν τοὺς πονηρευομένους
κατ' αὐτοῦ καὶ ἔλεγον αἱ συγγένειαι αἱ πονηραί· δεῦτε καὶ καταπαύσωμεν
πάσας τὰς ἑορτὰς τοῦ θεοῦ ἀπὸ τῆς γῆς (*H73Ps* II.2 [f. 129ᵛ–130ʳ] 239, 5–16).

Here, then, "*the close kinship* (συγγένεια) *of them*"—i.e., of the enemies of the
people of God—"*said together, 'Come and let's cause* them (i.e., persons[123])
to cease from God's mountain, *from off the land*'" (Ps 73:8). For when our savior
and lord was plotted against by the unseen powers and by the Jews who were
incited to action by them, the unseen powers were in accord with the statement,
"*The kings of the earth stood side by side and the leaders were gathered together
against the lord, against his Christ*" (Ps 2:2; Acts 4:26), and "Jews" in accordance
with the fact that they all said in unison, "Take him away, *take this man away
from the land*" (Acts 22:22; cf. Luke 23:18[124]), "crucify him, *crucify him*"
(John 19:15[125]), "*his blood be upon us and upon our children*" (Matt 27:25).
At the time of the savior's passion all the opposing powers, plotting against
the savior, incited to action those who acted against him with evil intent.
And these close kinships of the wicked said, "*Come and let's cause all the feasts
of God to cease from off the land*" (Ps 73:8).

In this argument, which has much in common with *HPs73* I.9, Origen identifies the two parties of the συγγένεια mentioned by the Psalm with the two
corporate groups involved in the death of Christ as he understands it: the "unseen powers" (αἱ ἀόρατοι δυνάμεις) and οἱ Ἰουδαῖοι, who, in collusion to kill
him, had in mind as the ultimate result what is placed on their own lips in
the continuation of the psalm verse: the end of all the feasts of God. In each

121. I have put this in italics rather than quotation marks; it is a quotation of Acts 22:22 (sic!) and
not Luke 23:18. Origen has doubled the initial imperative for emphasis, probably under the influence of
John 19:15 (which he is about to cite next).

122. I have put this in italics, as a quotation from John 19:15 (as Perrone edition indicates), but have
removed the quotation marks, and the italics from one of the imperatives.

123. Origen has changed the lemma from referring to the feasts (πάσας τὰς ἑορτάς) to people
(αὐτούς). He quotes the verse correctly at the end of this paragraph.

124. Origen has retrojected onto the passion narrative of Jesus, Luke's expansion of Luke 23:18
(αἶρε) in Acts 22:21, to refer to Paul (and has added a repeated αἶρε for emphasis, probably under the
influence of John 19:15, ἆρον, ἆρον, σταύρωσον αὐτόν, which he is about to cite next).

125. As indicated in the prior note, Origen has doubled the wrong imperative in his rendering of
John 19:15.

case Origen quotes other biblical passages that support the identification. For the powers, it is Ps 2:2, as quoted by Luke in Acts 4:26 (and deftly linked with Ps 73:8a by the phrase ἐπὶ τὸ αὐτό). And in the case of "the Jews," Origen has created a composite portrait by harmonizing and conflating passages from several sources in the Gospels (Luke 23:18; John 19:15; Matt 27:25) to show their speech in unison calling for Christ's death, and even reaching forward to the Acts account of Paul (22:22) because the wording fits the repetitive amplification of this unified crowd voice.

B. The Enactment of the Plot, and its Result

Beginning with a reprise of several themes from the previous homily—that the Passover plot against Christ led to the end of the feasts for ὁ λαός, and the fulfillment of the prophecy of Amos 8:10 that feasts are turned to mourning—Origen continues to build the case that Psalm 73 foretold what happened to οἱ Ἰουδαῖοι after Christ's death. Having recapitulated these points, he moves to further consequences of that fateful act, as he sees them foretold in Psalm 73:9.

Διὰ γὰρ τοῦ ἐν ἑορτῇ τοῦ πάσχα ἐπιβουλεύεσθαι τὸν σωτῆρα, πᾶσα ἑορτὴ κατήργηται ἀπὸ τοῦ λαοῦ καὶ ἐστράφησαν αἱ ἑορταὶ αὐτῶν εἰς πένθος καὶ αἱ ᾠδαὶ αὐτῶν εἰς θρῆνον. Εἶπαν οὖν ἡ συγγένεια αὐτῶν ἐπὶ τὸ αὐτό· δεῦτε καὶ καταπαύσωμεν πάσας τὰς ἑορτὰς τοῦ θεοῦ ἀπὸ τῆς γῆς. Ταῦτα μὲν ἐκεῖνοι λέγουσι, γέγονε δὲ ὃ εἰρήκασιν ἐκεῖνοι τοῖς Ἰουδαίοις. Διὸ φησιν ὁ λαός·τὰ σημεῖα ἡμῶν οὐκ εἴδομεν. Ἐξ οὗ ὁ σωτὴρ ἡμῶν πέπονθεν ἐπαύσατο τὰ σημεῖα ἐπὶ τὸν λαόν. Οὐκέτι σημεῖα καὶ τέρατα, καίτοι γέγονε μέχρι τότε ἐπ' αὐτῇ <τῇ> γενέσει τοῦ σωτῆρος, οἷα γέγονε σημεῖα πρὸ βραχέος· ὀπτασία ἀγγέλου ἐφάνη τῷ Ζαχαρίᾳ· οἷα ἦν σημεῖα ἐπὶ τὸ πάθει τοῦ σωτῆρος. Μετ' ἐκεῖνα τὰ σημεῖα, γέγονε μὲν σημεῖα, οὐκ Ἰουδαίοις δὲ οὐδὲ ἀπὸ Ἰουδαίων, ἀλλὰ τὰ σημεῖα μετέβη ἀπὸ τοῦ λαοῦ ἐπὶ τὰ ἔθνη. Διὸ λέγει ὁ λαός·τὰ σημεῖα ἡμῶν οὐκ εἴδομεν, οὐκ ἔστιν ἔτι προφήτης. Ὁ λαὸς ἐκεῖνος λέγει καὶ μέχρι τοῦ δεῦρο· οὐκ ἔστιν ἡμῖν προφήτης. Πέπαυται γὰρ ἡ προφητεία, ἐπεὶ ὁ νόμος καὶ οἱ προφῆται ἄχρις Ἰωάννου προεφήτευσαν. Καὶ πεπαυμένης τῆς προφητείας ἀκολούθως πέπαυται τὸ πνεῦμα τὸ ἅγιον ἀπ' ἐκείνων καὶ μετέβη ἡ εὐεργεσία ἐπὶ τὰ ἔθνη, ἐὰν μὴ καὶ ἡμεῖς στρηνιάσωμεν, ἐὰν μὴ ἐξυδαρωθῶμεν, ἐὰν μὴ χυδαῖοι γενώμεθα καὶ ἀπολέσωμεν τὴν χάριν τὴν ἐκχυθεῖσαν ἐκ θεοῦ εἰς ἡμᾶς, λέγων αὖ ὁ λαὸς εἰς οἰκονομίαν ἡμῶν, ὃ ἀληθὲς περὶ αὐτοῦ· τὰ σημεῖα ἡμῶν οὐκ εἴδομεν, οὐκ ἔστιν ἔτι προφήτης (*H73Ps* II.2 [f. 130ʳ-131ʳ] 239, 17–240, 15).

For because the savior was plotted against on the feast of Passover, every feast has been abolished from the people, and "*their feasts have been turned into mourning and their odes into dirges*" (Amos 8:10). Therefore, "*the close kinship* (συγγένεια) *of them*" (i.e., of the enemies of the people of God) "*said together, 'Come and let's cause all the feasts of God to cease from off the land'*" (Ps 73:8). These are the things they [240] said, and what they had said is what happened to the Jews. That is why the people says, *"Our signs we did not see"* (Ps 73:9a). From the time our savior met his passion, the signs ceased so far as the people were concerned. There were no longer signs and wonders,[126] although the kinds of signs that had taken place shortly before his birth, such as the vision of the angel that appeared to Zachariah (Luke 1:11), occurred up until the very point of the birth. Such signs as these were present at the passion of the savior (cf. Matt 27:51–53). After those signs signs did occur, but not to the Jews nor from the Jews, but the signs transferred from the people to the Gentiles. That is why the people says, *"Our signs we did not see, there is no longer a prophet"* (Ps 73:9b). That people says even until the very present day, *"there is no prophet* for us.[127]" For the prophecy has ceased, since *"the Law and the prophets prophesied until John"* (Luke 16:16; Matt 11:13). And since the prophecy has ceased, it follows that the Holy Spirit has ceased from them and the divine benefaction transferred to the Gentiles. That is, if we, too, don't wantonly stray, if we don't go wishy-washy, don't get drained away and lose the gift of grace from God that has been poured into us" (cf. Acts 2:17, 18, 33), and in turn the people say[128] in regard to our stewardship what was truly said about theirs: *"Our signs we did not see, there is no longer a prophet"* (Ps 73:9b).

Read as the voice of Jews living in the time after Christ, the Psalm has them declare in the first person that they have lost not only the feasts, but also the σημεῖα and προφητεία. Origen briefly includes a salvation-historical sequence about signs and prophecy, such that they were still present up until the time of Christ's birth, and there were also signs that accompanied the death of Christ (Matt 27:45, 51–53). Signs, he insists, were another thing that "transferred" (μετέβη) from the Jews to the Gentile Christians, joining Christ himself who was said to have made such a μετάβασις in *HPs73* I.9. Origen then uses the same pattern with prophecy, first declaring that it has "ceased" (πέπαυται, as with the feasts, καταπαύσωμεν) from the Jews, and then invoking an historical shift (via the logion of Luke 16:16 which he conflates with its parallel in Matt 11:13[129]) to support his case that there was a time for prophecy, but for the Jewish people it came to an end with John. Then follows the conclusion that what is really at stake in prophecy is the presence of the Holy Spirit. If

---

126. Cf. John 4:48, also in a context of Jewish unbelief (but probably not a quotation here, in context; Perrone rightly puts it in roman type and includes this verse in the apparatus; I think Mark 13:22 and Matt 24:25 do not quite fit, since, though they contain the phrase, they refer to future signs).

127. Origen has added the ἡμῖν to the lemma.

128. The syntactical connection of this participial phrase with what precedes is not clear.

129. Origen has combined the two versions of this saying, because he wants both the compound subject and the verb (Matt 11:13 should be added to the apparatus).

the Jews do not have prophecy, Origen reasons, that means the Holy Spirit
has ceased attending to them, and the divine benefaction has transferred from
them to the Gentiles (μετέβη ἡ εὐεργεσία ἐπὶ τὰ ἔθνη). The supersessionistic
argument here is unmistakable. But in the same breath Origen also issues a
warning from what has befallen the Jews to his own congregation (from one
λαός to another): if they wax wanton they could lose the gift of the spirit that
has been "poured out" (ἐκχυθῆναι) to us from God—a reference to the Pentecost narrative in Acts 2 (vv. 17, 18, 33) about the genesis of Christian prophecy
in fulfillment of Joel 3:1–5.[130] Should Christians lose that grace, then truly the
same thing could be said of and about them: that they lost, correspondingly,
the gifts of grace, i.e., σημεῖα καὶ προφητεία.

C. Vehement Exhortation against Forsaking Grace by Judaizing

The previous argument now comes to a more direct indication of just
how Christians could lose those precious gifts of grace and the Spirit that they
have received after these benisons left οἱ Ἰουδαῖοι.

> Εἰ τοίνυν, Χριστιανὲ κεκλημένε ἐπὶ τηλικαύτην χάριν, παλινδρομεῖς πάλιν καὶ
> καταλείπεις λαὸν τὸν χάριτι θεοῦ κεκλημένον, ἵνα ἀπέλθῃς ἐπὶ λαὸν ἐστερημένον
> χάριτος θεοῦ καὶ καταλείπεις λαὸν ἔχοντα πνεῦμα ἅγιον, ἵνα ἀπέλθῃς πρὸς λαὸν οὐκ
> ἔχοντα πνεῦμα ἅγιον—ἐγκατελείφθη ἡ θυγάτηρ Σιὼν ὡς σκηνὴ ἐν ἀμπελῶνι καὶ ὡς
> ὀπωροφυλάκιον ἐν σικυηλάτῳ —, τί φεύγεις καὶ αὐτομολεῖς πρὸς τοὺς
> ἐγκαταλειφθέντας; Ἧκε ὅπου ἡ ἐκκλησία τοῦ θεοῦ, ἧκε ὅπου τὸ ἅγιον πνεῦμα, ὅπου
> συνάγεται ἡ δύναμις τοῦ Ἰησοῦ κατὰ τὸ συναχθέντων ὑμῶν καὶ τοῦ ἐμοῦ πνεύματος
> σὺν τῇ δυνάμει τοῦ Κυρίου ἡμῶν Ἰησοῦ Χριστοῦ (H73Ps II.2 [f. 131ʳ] 240, 16–24).

So then, if you, O Christian called to such enormous grace, run back again, and
forsake a people that has been called by the grace of God so you might go off to a
people that is bereft of the grace of God, and forsake a people that has the Holy
Spirit so you might go off to a people that doesn't have the Holy Spirit—*for the
daughter of Zion has been forsaken like a lean-to in a vineyard and like a gardener's
shed in a cucumber patch*" (Isa 1:8)—why do you run away of your own accord to
those who have been forsaken? Come where the church of God is, come where
the Holy Spirit is, where the power of Jesus is gathered together, according to the
statement, "*when you and my spirit have been gathered together with the power of
our Lord Jesus Christ*" (1 Cor 5:4).

With forceful rhetorical questions that call to mind the Paul of Galatians, Origen argues that for Christians to go away to the Jewish people is to "relapse"

---

130. Perrone's apparatus now lists Ps 44:3, but the Acts 2 passages are more pertinent.

(παλινδρομεῖν πάλιν; compare πῶς ἐπιστρέφετε πάλιν in Gal 4:9). Playing on the term καταλείπειν, Origen argues that Christians who "forsake" their own people, who have been called by the grace of God (λαὸς ὁ χάριτι θεοῦ κελημένος) and have received the Holy Spirit, to go away to a people who lack both that grace and the spirit, is to forsake and flee to the forsaken. To anchor that point Origen quotes Isa 1:8 about the forsakenness of the daughter of Zion. The excoriation is then followed by an invitation: ἧκε. Origen completes the σύγκρισις he sets up between the two λαοί in exacting fashion: come to the church (ἐκκλησία/κεκλημένοι) of God; come to where the Holy Spirit is. The other λαός had those two things and had forsaken them. On Origen's argument, it is the third, the δύναμις τοῦ Ἰησοῦ, the special province of the Christians, that completes the transfer of benefits from the "forsaken" people. Naturally it is Paul, one more time from 1 Corinthians 5, who provides the witness Origen seeks. Origen is not specific here about what "going away to the other people" would entail. Possibly the final reference to the power (δύναμις) of Jesus hints at healing and exorcistic needs. But in the context of the wider argument about the ἑορταί, we shall not be surprised when Origen turns, just a bit later in this homily, once more to participation in the feast of unleavened bread as at issue. But first Origen wishes to engage the final clause of Ps 73:9c that he has not yet mentioned: καὶ ἡμᾶς οὐ γνώσεται ἔτι.

D. Does God Know οἱ Ἰουδαῖοι Now? Will He Ever?

Ἔτι δὲ λέγουσι μετὰ τὸ *οὐκ ἔστιν ἡμῖν προφήτης* καὶ τὸ *ἡμᾶς οὐ γνώσεται ἔτι*, οἷον προφητεύουσι περὶ αὐτῶν[131] οἱ ἐγκαταλελειμμένοι Ἰουδαῖοι λέγοντες ὅτι οὐ μόνον οὐκ οἶδεν ἡμᾶς ἄρτι, ἀλλ᾽ οὐκέτι *ἡμᾶς γνώσεται*. Μέχρι γὰρ τῆς συντελείας οὐκέτι γνώσεται ἐκεῖνον τὸν λαόν, μεταβεβηκυίας τῆς γνώσεως ἐπὶ τὸν ἐξ ἐθνῶν λαόν. Ταῦτα μὲν κατὰ μίαν ἑρμηνείαν ὡς περὶ τοῦ λαοῦ ἐκείνου (*H73Ps* II.2 [f. 131ʳ – 131ᵛ] 240, 1–6).

And after "*there is no prophet* for us," they go on to say, "*he will no longer know us*" (Ps 73:9b). This is the kind of thing the forsaken Jews prophesy about themselves, saying, "not only does he not know us now, but no longer '*will he know us.*'" For until the completion of this age no longer will he know that people, since "knowing"[132] has transferred to "*the people from the Gentiles*" (Acts 15:14). Now these things are the case according to one interpretation, taking the statement as having to do with that people.

---

131. Correcting for Perrone's αὐτῶν after checking the digital ms, fol. 131ʳ line 22, which has a rough breathing mark.

132. I.e., the state of being known by God.

Whereas with the previous argument about signs and prophecy Origen insisted that the voice of the Psalm referred to "the Jews" as ὁ λαός both past and present who lost these endowments, in the case of divine knowledge, the future tense verb in the Psalm itself at 73:9c causes him to think about the relationship between the people who at this moment are (in his view) οἱ ἐγκαταλελειμμένοι Ἰουδαῖοι, whom God does not "know," and their fate in the future. Likely for Origen, being known by God is a definition of a Christian, as it is for Paul in Gal 4:9, which I suggested he may be thinking of in castigating Christians for "reverting" to the forsaken people in the previous argument. In that same verse, Paul stipulates why for Gentile converts to Christ adopting circumcision or calendrical observances (Sabbath, feasts) is going backwards: νῦν δὲ γνόντες θεόν, μᾶλλον δὲ γνωσθέντες ὑπὸ θεοῦ. This, in Origen's eyes, is precisely what οἱ ἐγκαταλελειμμένοι Ἰουδαῖοι do not presently have, because, presumably, it is the transferal of election that this knowledge or recognition by God entails, as he adds yet another μετάβασις of a property from οἱ Ἰουδαῖοι to a new λαός, a λαὸς ἐξ ἐθνῶν. A part of the bitter power of this reading is that Origen takes the Psalm as a self-prophecy of doom by "the Jews."

And yet in this argument there is possibly a hint that Origen may expect the restoration of οἱ Ἰουδαῖοι at the end time, for he says that God will no longer know that people μέχρι … τῆς συντελείας, i.e., until the eschaton (cf. Matt 13:39; 24:3; 28:20). Behind this may well be an influence of Rom 11:26,[133] such that πᾶς Ἰσραὴλ σωθήσεται, or, more broadly, his view of the ἀποκατάστσις of all (with strong influence of 1 Cor 15:28).[134] If this is correct, it is one of the most positive statements in the homilies we have been considering. But it is admittedly allied with the supersessionist motif of the μετάβασις of God's knowledge and recognition away from Jews and onto Christians and is, at least in this context, undeveloped. Origen has now concluded the line of interpretation in arguments A through D, as characterized by the assumption that the words of the Psalm were spoken ὡς περὶ τοῦ λαοῦ ἐκείνου. The μέν signals a transition to a new set of arguments to follow, on the interpretive possibility that these words are spoken instead περὶ σοῦ, i.e., the Χριστιανός whom Origen directly addressed in argument C.

133. Origen interpreted that famous crux in several different ways in his writings (three different options are surveyed in Joseph A. Fitmyer, *Romans*, AB 33 (New York: Doubleday, 1993), 624: all Israel are ethnic Israel [*CRom* 8.13]; all Israel is the "spiritual Israel" of believers [*CMt* 17.5]; all Israel is the remnant of Israel [*Hom. in Jer.* 5.4]). This is obviously an important point requiring further analysis.

134. As championed vigorously by Ilaria Ramelli, *The Christian Doctrine of Apokatastasis: A Critical Assessment from the New Testament to Eriugena*, VCSup 120 (Leiden: Brill, 2013).

E. An Alternative Interpretation with a Warning for You, Christians: "The Close Kinship of Evil" (συγγένεια τοῦ πονηροῦ) Could Be Said About You if You Don't Watch Out

Ὅρα δὲ μήποτε καὶ περὶ σοῦ εἴπῃ ἡ συγγένεια τοῦ πονηροῦ· δεῦτε καὶ καταπαύσωμεν πάσας τὰς ἑορτὰς τοῦ θεοῦ ἀπὸ τῆς γῆς. Καὶ σὺ γὰρ ἐκλήθης ἐπὶ ἑορτὰς ἁγίας, καθὰ λέλεκται· ὥστε ἑορτάζωμεν μὴ <ἐν> ζύμῃ παλαιᾷ, μηδὲ ἐν ζύμῃ κακίας καὶ πονηρίας, ἀλλ᾽ ἐν ἀζύμοις εἰλικρινείας καὶ ἀληθείας. Εἰ νοεῖς πάσας ἑορτὰς καὶ τὰ ἄζυμα, ὅρα μήποτε καὶ σὺ ἐπιβουλευθῇς ὑπὸ τῶν ἐχθρῶν πρὸς τὸ καταπαῦσαι τὰς ἑορτὰς τοῦ θεοῦ ἀπὸ σοῦ. Πότε δὲ καταπαύουσιν αἱ ἑορταὶ τοῦ θεοῦ ἀπὸ σοῦ; Ἐὰν τὰ ἄζυμα τῆς εἰλικρινείας καὶ ἀληθείας[135] μὴ ἔχῃς—ὡς γὰρ καθ᾽ ὑπόθεσιν, ἐὰν μὴ ᾖ σῖτος τότε μηδὲ τὸ ζυμοῦν, οὐκ ἦν ἡ ὕλη τῶν ἀζύμων—, οὕτω εἴπερ τὰ ἄζυμά σου ἀπὸ ἀληθείας καὶ εἰλικρινείας, ἵν᾽ οὕτως ὀνομάσω, πεσεῖται καὶ οὕτω φυρᾶται, ἐὰν ἀπολέσῃς τὸ εἰλικρινὲς καὶ ἀναλάβῃς τὸ δόλιον, ἐὰν ἀπολέσῃς τὸ ἀληθὲς καὶ ἀναλάβῃς τὸ ψεῦδος, τῆς συγγενείας τοῦ πονηροῦ εἰπούσης δεῦτε καὶ καταπαύσωμεν τὰς ἑορτὰς τοῦ θεοῦ ἀπὸ τῆς γῆς, ὅσον ἐπὶ σοὶ κατέπαυσας τὰς ἑορτὰς τοῦ θεοῦ (*H73Ps* II.3 [f. 131ᵛ – 132ʳ] 241, 7–20).

But watch out lest *"the close kinship"* of evil be said about you, too: *"Come and let's cause all the feasts of God to cease from off the land"* (Ps 73:8). For indeed it is the case that you (Christian) were called to a holy feast, as has been said, *"therefore let us feast not in old leaven, nor in the leaven of wickness and evil, but in the unleavenings of sincerity and truth"* (1 Cor 5:8). If you comprehend all the feasts and the feast of the unleavened bread, watch out lest you, too, be plotted against by the enemies toward the goal of having *"the feasts of God"* cease from you (cf. Ps 73:8b). And when do the feasts of God cease from you? If you do not hold to the unleavenings *"of sincerity and truth,"* in the supposition that if there isn't grain nor leaven present, then the substance of the feast wouldn't be there. In that way, if your feast of the unleavened bread will fall away (if I might put it this way) from truth and sincerity, and is kneaded together in this fashion: if you lose sincerity and take up deceit; if you lose the truth and take up the falsehood. This is as *"the close kinship"* of evil has said, *"Come and let's cause the feasts of God to cease from off the land"* (Ps 73:8), in as much as by your own power you have caused the feasts of God to cease.

As he had earlier with the gifts of grace, after pronouncing their transference to the Gentile Christians, Origen issues a warning that these gifts are not to be taken for granted by their new recipients. Ironically, the threat that Christians could "lose *their* feasts" in accordance with the prophecy about "the close kinship" of evil powers, is actually due to Christians attending or otherwise participating in the feast of ἄζυμα as it is customarily practiced among

---

135. Italics added, as a quotation from 1 Cor 5:8, repeated.

their contemporary Jewish neighbors. Yet again it is Paul who provides, via
1 Cor 5:8, the feast hermeneutic and ethic, the concepts and the language, of
εἰλικρινεία and ἀλήθεια. As we have observed in *HPs77* I.4, Origen predictably
sees the problem not just of action, but of improper νοεῖν which mistakes the
material for the spiritual. With Paul at his side and quoted in full for emphasis, Origen argues for practicing a feast that is true in the sense that it is characterized by ethical purity, rather than its opposite (guilefulness and falsehood),
and by metaphysical priority, rather than the material practices of grain and
and leavening agent. Mixing those things into the recipe leads to a badly
kneaded lump.[136] And if this happens, then the Psalm prophecy will have been
fulfilled in Christians who have "caused the feasts of God to cease" rejecting
the Pauline mandates for the holy feast.

F. The Christian Feast of ἄζυμα

Origen now directs his ire at those who celebrate the *Christian* feast of
ἄζυμα improperly, and once again (as in HPs77 I.4), he targets women.

> Οὐδεὶς γὰρ ἔχων πονηρίαν ἑορτάζει τὴν ἑορτὴν τῶν ἀζύμων, τῶν Χριστιανῶν ἀζύμων.
> Οἱ δὲ θέλοντες μετὰ Χριστιανισμὸν καὶ τὰ θεῖα μαθήματα, δέον ἑορτάζειν *ἀζύμοις*
> *εἰλικρινείας καὶ ἀληθείας,*[137] ἑορτάζουσιν ἀζύμοις τοῖς ἀπὸ σίτου καὶ ἀζύμοις τοῖς ἀπὸ
> τῶν αἰσθητῶν πραγμάτων, ἃ κατήργησε Χριστὸς πληρῶν τὸν νόμον ἐν τοῖς
> πνευματικοῖς, δηλονότι ἐκπεσόντες τῆς χάριτος τοῦ θεοῦ οὔτε ταύτην ἑορτάζουσι τὴν
> ἑορτὴν οὔτε ἐκείνην. Οὐκ ἔστι γὰρ ἐκείνη ἑορτή· Χριστοῦ μὴ ὄντος ἐν αὐτῇ, ἁγίου
> πνεύματος οὐκ ὄντος, οὐ δύναται εἶναι ἑορτή. Παρακαλῶ, εἴ τινά ἐστι *γυναικάρια*
> *σεσωρευμένα ἁμαρτίαις, ἀγόμενα ἐπιθυμίαις ποικίλαις,* ἐπιθυμοῦντα ἐπ' ἀμφότερα
> βαίνειν τοὺς πόδας, καὶ Ἰουδαΐζειν καὶ Χριστιανίζειν, μετανοήσατε, μεταβάλεσθε·
> ἢ Ἰουδαία ἢ Χριστιανὴ γένεσθε. Ἐρῶ γὰρ πρὸς ὑμᾶς λόγον Ἡλίου τοῦ προφήτου,
> ὃν ἐλάλησέ ποτε πρὸς τοὺς διψύχους· *ἕως πότε ὑμεῖς χωλαίνετε ἐπ' ἀμφοτέραις ταῖς*
> *ἰγνύαις ὑμῶν;* (*H73Ps* II.3 [f. 132ʳ – 132ᵛ] 241, 21–242, 12).

No one who is wicked[138] feasts the feast of the unleavened bread, that is,
the Christian feast of the unleavened bread. Those who wish to do so, after
Christianity and the divine teachings, should celebrate the feast with the
"unleavened bread of sincerity and truth" [1 Cor 5:8].[139] They celebrate the feast

---

136. One might have expected Origen to quote or allude to Gal 5:9 here: μικρὰ ζύμη ὅλον τὸ φύραμα
ζυμοῖ.

137. I have added italics to these four words to Perrone, 242, line 2, as they are a quotation from
1 Cor 5:8.

138. Cf. 1 Cor 5:8: μηδὲ ἐν ζύμῃ κακίας καὶ πονηρίας.

139. I would put a full stop here and take ἑορτάζουσιν as beginning a new (asyndetic) sentence,
because I have construed the sentence structure differently than Perrone (but I have retained his in

with an unleavening from grain and an unleavening from physical realities which Christ has abolished by fulfilling the law in spiritual realities. It is clear that, having fallen out of grace (cf. Gal 5:4), they celebrate neither the latter feast nor the former. But the former isn't actually a feast; since Christ isn't in it, the Holy Spirit isn't in it, so it cannot be a feast. I beg you, if some are *"silly women heaped up with sins, led by*[140] *manifold desires"* (2 Tim 3:6) desiring to set their feet on both paths—that is, both to live as Jews and live as Christians (cf. Gal 2:14)—repent, turn back! Be either a Jew or a Christian, women! For I will direct at you the statement of Elijah the prophet, which he spoke to the divided souls[141] of his own day: *"How long will you walk lamely on both your legs?"* (3 Kgdms 18:21).

No one "who is wicked" (ἔχων πονηρίαν)[142] is able to celebrate the Christian feast of ἄζυμα. The feast has changed after the arrival of Χριστιανισμός. Origen casts the statement of Paul in 1 Corinthians 5:8 as a prescription among the Christian μαθήματα for how τὰ ἄζυμα is to be celebrated, with εἰλικρινεία and ἀλήθεια. He sets against that the admonition of the Paul of Galatians in 5:4, that those who choose a different way to celebrate the feast have "fallen out of grace" (ἐκπεσόντες τῆς χάριτος; cf. Gal 5:4[143]). Now the εἰλικρινεία and ἀλήθεια extend beyond ethical dispositions to metaphysical ones. Celebrating a feast concerned with physical realities (αἰσθητά),[144] after Christ has fulfilled the law (cf. Matt 5:17[145]) with spiritual realities (πνευματικά), such that he has abolished (καταργεῖν[146]) the physical ones (αἰσθητά), is fundamentally to misapprehend the true feast, the preacher insists. Then Origen tries a bit of inverted logic: in fact, celebrating ἄζυμα in a material way (with grain, with leaven) doesn't actually constitute a feast, because it fails to meet the criteria of a true feast: neither Christ nor the Holy Spirit are in it. Now the caricature of the "silly women" is reintroduced,[147] and the problem of practicing the "materi-

---

the Greek above). Admittedly one would expect a stronger adversative before ἑορτάζουσιν (rather than asyndeton), but the sense seems to require a change in subject to "Jews" or "Judaizers."

140. One wonders if in this context Origen is taking ἀγόμενα as a reference to "celebrating the feast" (though it is Middle or Passive, not the usual Active for this sense).

141. With δίψυχος Origen may have in mind Jas 1:8; 4:8, or possibly Hermas, Mandates 9.6; 10.2, etc.

142. Probably an allusion to 1 Cor 5:8: ἑορτάζωμεν … μηδὲ ἐν ζύμῃ κακίας καὶ πονηρίας, as just quoted in full in the previous paragraph.

143. Τῆς χάριτος ἐξεπέσατε. Although it is not a quotation, perhaps a note should be added to the apparatus for this strong allusion.

144. Such as grain and leaven.

145. Μὴ νομίσητε ὅτι ἦλθον καταλῦσαι τὸν νόμον ἢ τοὺς προφήτας· οὐκ ἦλθον καταλῦσαι ἀλλὰ πληρῶσαι.

146. Cf. Eph 2:15: [Χριστὸς] τὸν νόμον τῶν ἐντολῶν ἐν δόγμασιν καταργήσας; Rom 7:6: νυνὶ δὲ κατηργήθημεν ἀπὸ τοῦ νόμου.

147. As argued above, for Origen this image from 2 Tim 3:6 suits "Judaizers" because, like Jews, according to Rom 10:2, they are always learning, but not able to come to ἐπίγνωσις ἀληθείας. These women, according to 2 Tim 3:8, are like Jannes and Jambres (whom later Jewish tradition includes among

al" feast is renamed as the quest to live as a Jew and as a Christian at the same time (καὶ Ἰουδαΐζειν καὶ Χριστιανίζειν[148]). Origen issues a double imperative: "Repent, turn back!" (μετανοήσατε, μεταβάλεσθε)[149] and insists they choose: "Be either a Jew or a Christian, women!" (ἢ Ἰουδαία ἢ Χριστιανὴ γένεσθε). Likely we can learn from this that women were more involved in the feast of the unleavened bread, but caution is required, since turning to the invective of 2 Tim 3:6 allows Origen to join misogyny with his argument, such that men who are conjoining ritual observances are tarred as "silly women" who don't know if they are Jews or Christians. Once again, a prophetic voice heaps on the disdain, this time from Elijah (3 Kgdms 18:21), about walking clumsily on two legs. But the overall *topoi* on which the argument depends are unmistakably Pauline.

G. Christians Do Have Signs Now (so, contradicting Ps 73:9a)— But Could Lose Them in Future

Origen's final argument against the dangers of Christian "Judaizing" involves a return to the earlier discussion about σημεῖα and προφητεία, now with the philosophical material/spiritual (αἰσθητά/πνευματικά) distinction in full force.

> Ἀλλὰ καὶ σημεῖα ἔχει ὁ Χριστιανὸς λαός, ἀμαυρῶν μὲν τοὺς ἐξελαυνομένους δαίμονας διὰ τῶν εὐχῶν ἀπεριέργως, οὐ μετὰ περιαμμάτων, οὐ μετὰ φαρμάκων, οὐ μετὰ μεμελετημένων ἐπῳδῶν, οὐ μετὰ Σολομωντείων, ὡς μηδὲν ἰσχύοντος τοῦ ὀνόματος Ἰησοῦ, ἀλλὰ εὐαγγελικῶς, καὶ τοῦτο ἀμαυρότερονσημεῖον. Καθ' ἡμέραν δὲ σημεῖα γίνεται ἐν Χριστιανοῖς· *τυφλοὶ ἀναβλέπουσι, χωλοὶ περιπατοῦσι, λεπροὶ καθαρίζονται, πτωχοὶ εὐαγγελίζονται.* Τί γὰρ σημεῖον γίνεται νῦν καὶ γίνεται κρεῖττον ἢ ὡς ἐγίνετο ἐπὶ τῶν αἰσθητῶν; Θέλω γὰρ ψυχῆς ἀναβλέποντα ὀφθαλμὸν ἢ σώματος, ἐὰν οὖν καὶ σὺ ἀμαρτάνῃς, ἐρεῖς οὐ σωματικῶς ὡς Ἰουδαῖοι ἔλεγον, ἀλλὰ περὶ πνευματικῶν σημείων· *τὰ σημεῖα ἡμῶν οὐκ εἴδομεν.* Καὶ ὅταν μὲν ἀθετῇς τοὺς προφήτας ἢ ῥητὸν μὲν παραδέχῃ αὐτῶν, τὸν δὲ ἐν αὐτοῖς νοῦν μὴ ἐκλαμβάνῃς ὡς χρή, *οὐκ ἔστι σοι προφήτης·* προφήτης γὰρ ἔστι τῷ ἀκούοντι τῶν προφητικῶν λόγων, ὡς θέλει τὸ ἅγιον πνεῦμα. Καὶ ὥσπερ Μαρκιωνισταὶ ἀναγινώσκοντες τοὺς προφήτας οὐκ ἔχουσι τοὺς προφήτας (οὐ γὰρ ἔχουσι τὸν θεὸν τὸν δημιουργὸν τὸν δεδωκότα τὰς προφητείας), οὕτως καὶ σύ, ἐὰν λέγῃς κακῶς τοὺς προφήτας — λέγοντος τοῦ ἀποστόλου *τὸ πνεῦμα μὴ σβέννυτε, προφητείας μὴ ἐξουθενεῖτε*

---

the Egyptian magicians in Exod 7:10–12) "opposed to the truth" (ἀνθίστανται τῇ ἀληθείᾳ) and mentally corrupted (ἄνθρωποι κατεφθαρμένοι τὸν νοῦν).

148. Cf. Gal 2:14: εἰ σὺ Ἰουδαῖος ὑπάρχων ἐθνικῶς καὶ οὐχὶ Ἰουδαϊκῶς ζῇς, πῶς τὰ ἔθνη ἀναγκάζεις ἰουδαΐζειν;

149. Cf. Acts 3:19: μετανοήσατε οὖν καὶ ἐπιστρέψατε (cf. 26:20).

—ἐρεῖς[150]· οὐκ ἔστιν ἔτι προφήτης καὶ ἡμᾶς οὐ γνώσεται ἔτι (*H73Ps* II.3 [f. 132ᵛ–133ʳ] 242, 13–243, 12).

> However, the Christian people also have signs. They send into obscurity demons who are driven out by prayer not craft, without amulets, without potions, without carefully practiced odes, nor with invocations of Solomon, as though the name of Jesus had no power. No, instead this is done by means of the gospel, and this is a more obscure sign. Signs take place among Christians on a daily basis: *"the blind see, the lame walk, lepers are cleansed, the poor have the gospel preached to them"* (Matt 11:5). Why is a sign taking place now, and one that is greater than those that took place in the past with material realities? I wish the eye of your soul[151]—rather than that of your body—would look up![152] So, then, if indeed you, too, sin, you will say *"Our signs we did not see"* (Ps 73:9a)—saying this concerning bodily matters, as the Jews did, but about spiritual signs. And when you reject the prophets, or when you accept one of their statements but don't take the meaning of them as you should, *"there is no prophet"* for you (Ps 73:9b). For the one who has a prophet is the person who hears the prophetic words as the Holy Spirit wishes. When Marcionites read the prophets, they don't have the prophets, for they don't have the creator God who has given the prophesies. In the same way, if you speak badly of the prophets—as the apostle says, *"Don't extinguish the Spirit, don't reject prophecies!"* (1 Thess 5:19–20), you will say, *"There is no longer a prophet, he will no longer know us"* (Ps 73:9b-c).

The Psalm verse, 73:9a, does not seem to fit Christians now, for they in fact do see signs: exorcisms of demons carried out, not by magical craft (an impressive list of techniques *not used* follows) but by prayer and by the τὸ ὄνομα Ἰησοῦ (not incantations of the magician-monarch Solomon). And the list of the signs of the messiah, Christ, in Matt 11:5, Origen insists, reflects also the reality today (sight restored to the blind, lame walking, etc.). But there are even greater signs than these that take place on the material level (αἰσθητά). The order of this list, with blindness coming first, suits Origen's argument very well, because he can aver his preference for restored sight in the ψυχῆς ὀφθαλμός (that good Platonic concept) than in σώματος ὀφθαλμός. Now comes a devastating comparison for Christians: not only can you suffer the same fate as "the Jews" of losing the divine favor of signs and prophecy, but if you do that, your fault will be in some sense even worse, because you will have lost the ability to see the superior, spiritual signs (τὰ πνευματικὰ σημεῖα). This brings Origen to the role of hermeneutics, and the proper understanding of the prophetic

---

150. I have removed the comma before ἐρεῖς as unnecessary after the em-dash.

151. A Platonic concept, of course, often τὸ τῆς ψυχῆς ὄμμα.

152. ἀναβλέπειν here in all its senses, of "look up," "see again," and "regain one's sight."

words, which, on his telling, is reading them in accord with the wishes of the Holy Spirit, the animator of prophecy. Marcionites of course are textbook examples of this, since they don't even accept the prophetic books, or the God who sent those prophets. But the warning is stern for Christians, and, as so often, it comes from the apostle Paul in 1 Thess 5:19–20. That injunction is taken as a guard to ensure that Ps 73:9 in the future not be said about the Christians.

Summary Conclusions

The lengthy and developed arguments on the Law, the feasts, Jews and Judaizing in these three homilies (*HPs73* I and II; *HPs 77* I) each have their own progression of thought and distinctive moments, as can be appreciated only through close reading and attention to the logic and the intertextual allusions Origen constantly makes. But they also share quite a few elements. They each toggle between the more abstract considerations about the divine plan and very sharp complaints about Christian participating—yet exactly *how* still remains surprisingly vague—in the feasts. The prominence of ἄζυμα in these arguments probably reflects some actual practice on the ground, and yet in Origen's hands it has been chosen because the analogical argument made by Paul in 1 Cor 5:7–8 has become for him a θεῖον μάθημα about all the feasts, indeed, the entire law and its "true" meaning (ἐν ἀζύμοις … ἀληθείας). The feasts of Passover, Pentacost and Yom Kippur each in some sense serves within this metonymy of ἑορταί, even as festival observance is itself a metonymy for Law observance and for community alignment and identification.

Another interpretive element for Origen is history: the exile of Jews from Jerusalem is for Origen a divine proof that the Jews have been punished for killing Christ at the Passover, from which they have now been utterly excluded (hence prohibiting their ability to celebrate the pilgrimage festivals in the holy city). Within these arguments there is some concern about the "third rail" of Marcionism (which Origen of course regards as a real threat), but it receives far less alarm than he expresses about Judaizing, i.e., about confusing one's place, one's identity, one's λαός. The repeated language of μετάβασις (of the Christ, of the Holy Spirit, of the feasts, of divine benefaction, of signs, of prophecy, of divine acknowledgement) is unmistakably supersessionist. One cannot separate the theological from the practical or rhetorical here. And yet at times Origen emphasizes these attainments he thinks Christians have taken over—in an improved form—from Jews, in order to heighten what is at stake for them in turn: these gifts can be lost if they are not careful, either in their ethical conduct or noetic acuity. But never in these homilies does this lead him to say overtly that these gifts might redound back to Jews.

Origen draws heavily and repeatedly on Paul within these arguments, both by name, by quotation, and by allusion and imitation. Within the Pauline corpus, in addition to the frequent invocation of 1 Cor 5:7–8, Origen draws repeatedly on 2 Tim 3:6 to characterize the Judaizing problem as the noetic failure of τὰ γυναικάρια, and often one can see distinct white-caps of the influence of Paul's most insistent letter on the question, Galatians, as I have sought to highlight here. Origen reads—and reiterates in his context—Paul's letter to the Galatians as uncompromising; one must either Χριστιανίζειν *or* Ἰουδαΐζειν (cf. 2:14), and he applies that unwaveringly here. There is surprisingly little influence of Romans, or of the more moderating voice of Ephesians, emphasizing the unification of the two peoples, either in common sin (Rom 3:22; 10:12) or the Christ mission to the estranged Gentiles (Eph 2:11–22). There is no call for Jews to join the Christian λαός, or emphasis on common ground now or into the foreseeable future. There may be one hint of a reading of Rom 11:26 as allowing for "all Israel to be saved" at the συντέλεια, but that is not developed at all. Overall, one must conclude that the present analysis of the new homilies corroborates McGuckin's more tempered view of Origen's embrace of Jews and Judaism, based upon his selective use of the Pauline epistles toward invective and repudiation of Jews and Judaism. Whether one can sustain the argument of Fürst that the homilies represent a more intemperate Origenic voice than is customarily found elsewhere would require a different kind of study, to determine how these new sources relate to Origen's entire extant oeuvre. At the least we can say that definitively on the basis of the newly discovered texts that the kind of sermonic argumentation against Judaizing that we find in the Greek twelfth Homily on Jeremiah[153] was by no means unique in Origen's preaching at Caesarea.[154]

153. Fürst, "Judentum, Judenchristentum und Antijudaismus," 278, neatly notes that in the 17th century these twenty Greek homilies by Origen were the new discovery (at Rome in 1623 and Madrid in 1648)!

154. *Hom. in Jer.* 12.13 (SC 238, ed. Pierre Nautin, 1977, 44–50) has much in common with the arguments in the new homilies, especially the prominence of 1 Cor 5:7; the insistence that the Jews killed Jesus; concern about the fast and ἡ τοῦ ἱλασμοῦ ἡμέρα, as well as πάσχα and ἄζυμα; an invective against women following the law (focusing on the case of Sabbath observance, not ἄζυμα), and no citation of 2 Tim 3:6; an explicit citation of Gal 4:9 (rather than an allusion, as here) to urge not returning to those observances, and a concern throughout with the hermeneutical underpinnings—and repercussions—of the whole discussion (in this case, incited by Jer 13:12 and hearing the text κεκρυμμένως, i.e., according to its hidden meaning). There are also differences: invocation of the manifest and secret Jew and περιτομή of Rom 2:28–29; the movement of the mission from Jews to Gentiles in Acts 13:46; and a selective invocation of Rom 11:17, 24 on the "wild olive tree" (ἀγριέλαιος), among other things.

Elizabeth Ann Dively Lauro

4. THE INADEQUACY OF THE TERM "SUBORDINATION" FOR ORIGEN'S THEOLOGY AND MINISTRY

A Study of Origen's Homilies on Psalm 15

Introduction

Throughout the history of Origen studies, scholars have disagreed about the similarity of Origen's Trinitarian theology to the Arian view of the Son's subordination to the Father. While some scholars argue that Origen steers clear of any bitheism,[1] others maintain that Origen's comments about the Father and Son suggest non-monotheistic sentiments.[2] A study of newly discovered homi-

---

1. See the following brief selection of recent scholarly works that perceive in Origen's works an equality of nature between the Father and Son in Origen: Henri Crouzel, *Origen: The Life and Thought of the First Great Theologian,* Tr. A. S. Worrall (San Francisco: Harper & Row Publishers, 1989) 181–205; Robert M. Berchman, *From Philo to Origen: Middle Platonism in Transition*, Brown Judaic Studies 69 (Chico, CA: Scholars Press, 1984) 117–56; Elizabeth Ann Dively Lauro, "The Meaning and Significance of Scripture's Sacramental Nature within Origen's Thought," *Studia Patristica* (prospectively Vol. 92) (Leuven: Peeters, 2017), 2–8. See also Christoph Markschies, "Trinitarianism," *The Westminster Handbook to Origen,* Ed. John Anthony McGuckin (Louisville: Westminster John Knox Press, 2004) 207–9: Markschies focuses on Origen's lack of a clear use of the term *homoousios,* and he also emphasizes that Origen presents a hierarchy of taxonomy within a consubstantial Trinity. This he suggests is a "legitimate subordination," arguably similar to Crouzel's view that "the Son is both subordinate and equal to the Father." See Crouzel, *Origen,* 188, and Dively Lauro, "The Meaning and Significance," 5n15. This paper addresses this topic below in the discussion of degrees or forces or reach of power within the Trinity.

2. See the following brief selection of recent scholarly works that perceive in Origen's theology separate natures between the Son and Father or at least a true inferiority of the Son to the Father: Jean Daniélou, *Origen,* Tr. Walter Mitchell (London and New York: Sheed and Ward, 1955) esp. 261; Joseph

121

lies on Psalm 15[3] reveals the inadequacy of the term "subordination" for Origen's description of the Son-Father relationship. These homilies are especially useful for their insights since they were preserved in the Greek and date well after *De Principiis*.[4] This paper argues that, for Origen, the Son is "in need of" the Father causally for his existence, but the Son remains equal to the Father in nature and power. This insight is crucial to understanding how Origen views the Son's, and, by identity, Scripture's,[5] salvific power for the believer.

To demonstrate how the term "subordination" is not adequate for Origen's understanding of the Father-Son relationship, and, in turn, how their equality in nature and power are integral to the believer's salvific *telos,* this paper demonstrates the following: First, Origen understands Christ to be the *prosopon,*[6] or person, speaking the prayerful words of Psalm 15 to the Father. Second, Origen explains how Christ, as the Son of the Trinity, is equal to the

<hr />

Wilson Trigg, *Origen: The Bible and Philosophy in the Third-century Church* (Atlanta: John Knox Press, 1983) esp. 98–99.

3. I thank Robin Darling Young, Philip Rousseau, Joseph Trigg, and Lorenzo Perrone for the invitation to prepare this paper for inclusion in the proceedings to the colloquium on the newly discovered homilies on the Psalms by Origen held in May of 2017 at The Catholic University of America, in Washington, D.C. I also thank Joseph Trigg for generously sharing drafts of his forthcoming translation of the newly discovered homilies with the *Fathers of the Church* series. While in this paper I provide my own translation of passages cited, I owe a great deal to the influence of Joseph Trigg's working draft. On one particular point, in a few instances I translate λόγος as Logos rather than Word as a more appropriate way to capture Origen's complex view of the Son or Christ, but I wish to acknowledge Joseph Trigg's brilliant and precedent insight (which he announced at the May 2017 colloquium) to translate the word as logos generally within his translation of the newly discovered homilies on the Psalms.

4. For the likely dates and order of chronology of Origen's works (and their supporting documentation and scholarship), see Dively Lauro, *The Soul and Spirit of Scripture within Origen's Exegesis*, The Bible in Ancient Christianity 3 (Boston and Leiden: Brill, 2005) 7–11, esp. 10. Origen likely produced *De Principiis* in Alexandria between 229 and 230 (likely ages 44–45), and likely delivered the homilies later in Caesarea in a three-year cycle between 239 and 242 (likely ages 54–57). He likely produced C. John over time, but finished C. Jn. 32, as well as produced C. Cant., C. Matt., C. Rom. and *Contra Celsum* between 245 and 249 (likely ages 60–64). (His likely death was in 254 around the age of 69.)

5. See the following scholarly works for the idea in Origen that Scripture is Christ: Dively Lauro, "The Meaning and Significance," *Studia Patristica,* prospectively Vol. 92 (2017); Dively Lauro, "The Eschatological Significance of Scripture According to Origen, *Studia Patristica* 56.4 (2013): 83–102; Dively Lauro, *The Soul and Spirit of Scripture,* esp. 26–31 and 43–44; Karen Jo Torjesen, *Hermeneutical Procedure and Theological Method in Origen's Exegesis* (Berlin and New York: [Publisher?],1986), 108–47, esp. 119–20; Henri Crouzel, *Origen,* esp. 70; Henri de Lubac, *History and Spirit: The Understanding of Scripture according to Origen,* Tr. Anne Englund Nash (San Francisco: Ignatius, 2007) 385–426; and Jean Daniélou, *Origen,* 160, 172, 265 and 314.

6. Prosopological exegesis is the practice of designating a particular person as the speaker of the Scriptural text, often Christ as the speaker of a psalm, for the spiritual edification of the hearer or reader of Scripture. This approach is discussed in detail below. For a brief description of the scholarly history on this approach, see note 7 below.

Father but still can appropriately speak the submissive language of the psalm. Third, Christ, as the human Jesus, also appropriately prays the submissive words to the Father, because in his humanity he represents all humans as actual parts of his body. Finally, Origen calls his audience to speak the words of the psalm in imitation of its *prosopon,* Christ. By so doing, the believer unites with Christ through the shared words of Scripture, and this union is the gateway for the believer ultimately to enter into the Trinitarian union of the Son and Father in heaven.

Christ as the Prosopon (πρόσωπον) of Psalm 15

Early in both homilies, Origen stresses that "the psalm is spoken by the person (*prosopon*) of our Lord Jesus Christ."[7] *Prosopon* (πρόσωπον) means "character" or "person."[8] Origen wants his audience to hear the words of the

7. Hom. Ps. 15.1.2. (ὅτι ὁ ψαλμὸς ἐκ προσώπου λέγεται τοῦ κυρίου ἡμῶν Ἰησοῦ Χριστοῦ). (GCS NF 19:76) See also Hom. Ps. 15.2.1. (περὶ τοῦ τὸν ψαλμὸν τοῦτον ἐκ προσώπου εἰρῆσθαι τοῦ Χριστοῦ). (GCS NF 19:91–92) This paper relies on the following Greek edition of the Psalm homilies: *Origenes XIII: Die neuen Psalmenhomilien eine kritische Edition des Codex Monacensis Graecus 314,* Ed. Lorenzo Perrone (GCS NF 19) (Berlin: Walter de Gruyter, 2015), esp. 73–112. I thank Miriam DeCock for her insightful presentation at the May 2017 colloquium on the newly discovered homilies on the Psalms by Origen, in which she discusses Origen's use of the prosopological method of interpretation by which he directs his audience to understand the speaker of the psalm to be Christ. As she points out, in some circumstances, Origen uses the word "*prosopon,*" but not always. Here, in Hom. Ps. 15.1 and 15.2 Origen does use the term "*prosopon*" when announcing that the Savior as the speaker of this psalm. I wish to point out that Miriam DeCock, in her contributory presentation, also elucidates well the contributions to this aspect of Origen's hermeneutics by Marie-Josèphe Rondeau (*Les commentateurs patristiques du Psautier (IIIe-Ve siècles)* 1: *Les travaux des Pères grecs et latins sur le Psautier, Recherches et bilan*; 2: *Exégèse prosopologique et théologie* (Rome: Oriental Institute, 1982 and 1985). For more on the study of prosopological exegesis, see Carl Andresen, "Zur Entstehung und Geschichte des trinitarischen Personbegriffes," *Zeitschrift für die neutestamentliche Wissenschaft* 52 (1961): 1–39, and Michael Slusser, "The Exegetical Roots of Trinitarian Theology," *Theological Studies* 49 (1988), as well as Karen Jo Torjesen's application of this concept of prosopological exegesis to Origen's works in *Hermeneutical Procedure*. Also, Ronald E. Heine wrote a detailed commentary on excerpts of Origen's commentaries or homilies on the Psalms available before the recent discovery of homilies on the Psalms, wherein Origen stresses that Christ is the speaker of the psalm. See R. E. Heine, *Reading the Old Testament with the Ancient Church: Exploring the Formation of Early Christian Thought* (Evangelical Ressourcement: Ancient Sources for the Church's Future, Ed. D. H. Williams) (Grand Rapids, MI: Baker Academic, 2007) 154–63. Also, note Lorenzo Perrone's consideration of how Origen stresses the mystery of Christ's union of Divinity and humanity by employing a prosopological exegesis (to Ps 44:7–8 in Comm. Jn. 1:29) in "'Four Gospels, Four Councils' – One Lord Jesus Christ: The Patristic Developments of Christology within the Church of Palestine," *LA* 49 (1999) 357–96, esp. 362–63.

8. *Prosopon* (πρόσωπον) means (1) "face, countenance" or "outward appearance," (2) "mask" or "dramatic part or character," or (3) "person" or more specifically, "legal personality" or "feature of a person." For Greek definitions, refer to Liddell and Scott, *Greek-English Lexicon* (Oxford), including all versions (large, medium, and smaller).

psalm coming from the lips of Christ. For intertextual support, Origen points out that verse 10 ("you will not leave behind my soul in Hades, nor allow your devout one to see death")[9] reveals Christ as the speaker of this psalm, since Acts 2:25–31 makes the same reference to Christ.[10] Also, Origen explains, when David composed the psalm, he foresaw Christ's resurrection, knowing he "would not be left behind in Hades nor would his flesh see death."[11] Thus, Origen urges his audience to hear with assurance the words of Psalm 15 as Christ's own words.

The Savior's Relation to the Father (ἐνδέω)

Origen immediately acknowledges the difficulty with identifying Christ as the speaker of Psalm 15, for its words are of a submissive nature before God the Father. The first words of the psalm, for example, express a need for God's protection: "Guard me, Lord, for I have hoped in you…."[12] Origen explains how it is appropriate for Christ, the Savior and Son of God, to speak submissively to—therefore expressing need for—God the Father. To establish the relationship between the Savior, or Son, and the Father, he uses the verb ἐνδέω, which means "to be in need of or lack."[13] A second definition of this same word means "to bind in, on or to" or "to be bound fast to" something or to "bind oneself to" another.[14] Note the logical connection between these two separate meanings: one may bind oneself to another because the first is somehow in need of the latter. This paper shows that it would be misleading to translate ἐνδέω as "to be subordinate to," and that the dictionary definitions "to be in need of" and "to be bound to" are more useful (and less prejudicial) to determining Origen's understanding of *how* the Savior relates to the Father.

---

9. Hom. Ps. 15.1.2, quoting Ps. 15:10 (*οὐκ ἐγκαταλείψεις τὴν ψυχήν μου εἰς τὸν ᾅδην, οὐδὲ δώσεις τὸν ὅσιόν σου ἰδεῖν διαφθοράν*). (GCS NF 19:75) This quotation of Ps 15:10 in Hom. Ps. 15.1.2 matches the Greek in LXX. Note that the term διαφθορά, translated here as "death, can also mean "destruction, ruin," or "corruption."

10. See Hom. Ps. 15.1.2. (GCS NF 19:76)

11. Hom. Ps. 15.1.2, referring to Acts 2:25–31. (The fuller Greek text reads as follows: *Δαυὶδ … Προφήτης οὖν ὑπάρχων καὶ εἰδὼς ὅτι ὅρκῳ ὤμοσεν αὐτῷ ὁ θεὸς ἐκ καρποῦ τῆς ὀσφύος αὐτοῦ καθίσαι ἐπὶ τοῦ θρόνου αὐτοῦ, προϊδὼν ἐλάλησε περὶ τῆς ἀναστάσεως τοῦ Χριστοῦ ὅτι οὔτε ἐγκατελείφθη εἰς ᾅδην οὔτε ἡ σὰρξ αὐτοῦ εἶδεν διαφθοράν*). (GCS NF 19:76)

12. Hom. Ps. 15.1.3, quoting Ps 15:1 (*Φύλαξόν με, κύριε, ὅτι ἐπὶ σοὶ ἤλπισα …*). (GCS NF 19:76) Note that the verb φυλάσσω (presented as the first aorist imperative active, 2nd person singular—φύλαξόν) as a transitive verb means "to watch, guard, defend."

13. ἐνδέω can also mean "to fall short of" or "be in a deficiency." See Liddell and Scott, large, new edition, (Oxford: Oxford University Press, 1992) 559a–b.

14. Liddell and Scott, 559a–b.

Origen explains that the Father has an *"exceptional* property,"[15] in that he has no need for "the good things that those who are under him bring before him" or for any of the "good things"[16] that they can give to him.[17] Origen understands Christ to acknowledge the Father's complete lack of need, when he states verse 2: "You are my Lord, because you have no need of my good things."[18]

The Savior also possesses an *"exceptional* property,"[19] for he is in need of no one except the Father:

> [T]he Savior is in need of the Father, and only the God of the Universe is in need of nothing and has need of no one. But the Savior, even if he is in need, possesses something *exceptional,* for he is in need *only* of the God of the Universe.[20]

The Savior, or Son, is different from all others because he needs the Father but does not need anyone else. Using Moses as an example, Origen points out that humans (like Moses) are "in need of God, of Christ, of the Holy Spirit, and of

15. Hom. Ps. 15.1.3 and 15.1.5 (… ἐξαίρετόν τι ἔχει …). (GCS NF 19:76 and 81) Note that ἐξαιρέω can mean "special, singular, remarkable," and in the adverbial form "exclusively" or "characteristically."

16. Hom. Ps. 15.1.5, quoting Ps 15.2b (… τῶν ἀγαθῶν …). (GCS NF 19:81) Note a rhetorical progression in the first homily on Ps 15 regarding the concept of good things or offerings. In Hom. Ps. 15.1.1, Origen calls his audience to make themselves "monuments" of things that God "loves." Yet, later, in Hom. Ps. 15.1.5, Origen stresses that the Father and Son each have no need for the "good things" we may offer up to God. Finally, in Hom Ps. 15.1.6, Origen exhorts his audience to try to see God's "good things," God's many wonders, that are to be found in the "holy land." For only someone who has made himself holy can enter the holy land and see God's good things or wonders. Origen, then, understands that we need to offer ourselves with virtues and virtuous acts to God and we need the great wonders God has waiting for us as rewards for becoming holy, but we must always keep in mind that, in contrast, God needs nothing from us. At most, the Father takes pleasure in our spiritual progress and good deeds, but he does not need them, since he needs nothing at all. (GCS NF 19:73–75 and 81–84)

17. Hom. Ps. 15.1.5 (Ὄντων δὲ πολλῶν κυρίων, ὁ εἷς οὗτος κύριος, ὃν κύριον καὶ ὁ σωτὴρ ὀνομάζει, τὸν πατέρα οὕτω καλῶν, ἐξαίρετόν <τι> ἔχει παρὰ τοὺς πολλοὺς κυρίους· οἱ μὲν γὰρ ἄλλοι κύριοι χρείαν ἔχουσι τῶν ἀγαθῶν, ὧν προσάγουσιν αὐτοῖς οἱ ὑπ’ αὐτούς, οὗτος δὲ μόνος ὁ κύριος τῶν ἀγαθῶν χρείαν οὐκ ἔκει οὐδενὸς τούτων ὧν ἐστι κύριος. Διὸ λέγει ὡς ἐξαίρετόν τι ἀναφέρων ἐπὶ κύριον τὸν πατέρα αὐτοῦ ὁ σωτήρ· "εἶπα τῷ κυρίῳ μου· κύριός μου εἶ σύ, ὅτι τῶν ἀγαθῶν μου οὐ χρείαν ἔχεις.… οὐ γὰρ ἐνδεὴς αὐτῶν τυγχάνεις). (GCS NF 19:81) Note that here the words for "to have no need" are not a form of ἐνδέω but, rather, … χρείαν οὐκ ἔκει. The term χρεία means "need" and is related to χρεῖος or χρέος, which means "obligation or debt, what is owing." These all come from the verb χρεώ, which means "to need." Origen seems to use this word here synonymously with ἐνδέω, since, as we explore, Origen understands the Son to be in need of, or in debt to, the Father for his existence, while the Father is not in need of and owes no debt to anyone for his existence.

18. Hom. Ps. 15.1.5, quoting Ps 15:2 (*Κύριός μου εἶ σύ, ὅτι τῶν ἀγαθῶν μου οὐ χρείαν ἔχεις*). (GCS NF 19:81)

19. Hom. Ps. 15.1.3 (… ἐξαίρετόν τι ἔχει …). (GCS NF 19:76) Note that the same phrase is used here to indicate that the Son has a unique property as is used in Hom. Ps. 15.1.5 (GCS NF 19:81) to indicate that the Father has a unique property, both regarding their respective needs for others.

20. Hom. Ps. 15.1.3 (ὁ σωτὴρ ἐνδεὴς τοῦ πατρὸς καὶ μόνος ὁ θεὸς τῶν ὅλων ἀνενδεὴς καὶ οὐδενὸς χρείαν ἔχει. Ὁ δὲ σωτήρ, κἂν ἐνδεὴς ᾖ, ἐξαίρετόν τι ἔχει· μόνου γὰρ τοῦ θεοῦ τῶν ὅλων ἐνδεής ἐστι). (GCS NF 19:76)

the angels coming to aid, and standing by, him."[21] Human also are in need of each other.[22] Unlike the Savior, we are "not capable of receiving help from only God."[23] The Son, though, is uniquely "bound" to the Father, since he alone is in need only of the Father.

Origen's Narrow Ontological Distinction Between the Son and Father

Yet, this "need" of the Savior for the Father, when read in conjunction with his view of the Father-Son relationship in other works, should not be construed to mean that Origen views the Son as subordinate, or inferior, to the Father in substance or power. The Savior's exclusive need for the Father, not reciprocated by the Father, is consistent with other works in which Origen clarifies that the Son is distinct from the Father only in the ontological category of cause. Simply put, the Father *exists per se,* while the Son *exists per accidens.* Robert Berchman, in his 1980s work, has demonstrated that Origen employed these Aristotelian causal categories to stress that the Father and Son are equal in substance and power.[24] The distinction that the Father *caused the Son's existence* while no one caused the Father's does not suggest separate natures or degrees of power.

The context for Origen's view of the Father-Son relationship is his understanding that the Father eternally generates or begets the Son or Word of God, who also is Christ.[25] The Son's "eternal and everlasting begetting" means that the Son is not "adopted" but is "Son by nature."[26] This view spans Origen's works from his earlier theological treatises to his later homilies.[27] Henri

---

21. Hom. Ps. 15.1.3 (The fuller passage: Μωϋσῆς δέ, ἐὰν ᾖ ἐνδεής, καὶ τοῦ θεοῦ ἐνδεής ἐστι καὶ τοῦ Χριστοῦ καὶ τοῦ ἁγίου πνεύματος καὶ ἀγγέλων τῶν βοηθούντων καὶ παρισταμένων αὐτῷ). (GCS NF 19:76)

22. See Hom. Ps. 15.1.5. (GCS NF 19:81)

23. Hom. Ps. 15.1.3 (… οὐ χωροῦντος οὐδενὸς ἀπὸ μόνου ὠφελεῖσθαι τοῦ θεοῦ). (GCS NF 19:76). See also later in Hom. Ps. 15.1.3 (GCS NF 19:77), where Origen points out that our prayers reach God the Father only through Jesus Christ.

24. See Berchman, *From Philo to Origen,* esp. 141–56. See also the analysis of this matter in Dively Lauro, "The Meaning and Significance," 6–7, nn 18 and 21.

25. While I treat this in a prior work, I will briefly set forth the main points here. See Dively Lauro, "The Meaning and Significance," 2–8.

26. *De Principiis* (DP) 1.2.4, referring to Wis 7:26, Heb 1:3 and Rom 8:15. For the English text, see *Origen: On First Prinicples,* Tr. G. W. Butterworth (Gloucester, Mass., 1973) 18 (*Est namque ita aeterna ac sempiterna generatio, sicut splendor generator ex luce. Non enim per adoptionem spiritus filius fit extrinsecus, sed natura filius est); Origène: Traité des Principes, Tomes I et II, Tr. et Ed. Henri Crouzel et Manlio Simonetti,* SC 252 et 253 (Paris, 1978), 252:118.

27. See DP 1.2.1–4 and Hom. Jer. 9.4.4. For a more detailed treatment of these relevant passages, see Dively Lauro, "The Meaning and Significance," 2–8 (and nn 15, 16, 18 and 21).

Crouzel recognizes that this is not only an "[e]ternal generation but also continual generation."[28] The Father's eternal begetting is reciprocated by the Son, who, as Wisdom, is "the reflection of everlasting light," and gives a "reflection" of the "glory" or "light" of the Father,[29] by "continu[ing] in unceasing contemplation of the depth of the Father."[30]

Crouzel explains that Origen's thought "does not bring into question either identity of nature or equality of power" between the Father and Son, but, rather, the Son is "subordinate" (or lesser than) only in that (1) he receives his existence from the Father, (2) he is an agent of the Father in his "divine mission," and (3) he holds many titles as the mediator between the Father and creation.[31] Regarding the first difference, Berchman shows that for Origen the Son is not "subordinate" to the Father in nature but exists *contingently,* as οὐσία *per accidens* from the Father, while the Father exists *necessarily,* as οὐσία *per* se.[32] The latter differences point to a distinction in the *reach* (*though not degree or force*) *of power,* reflecting simply the respective tasks of the persons of the Trinity: the Father brings existence to all creatures, the Son brings wisdom and knowledge to all rational creatures, and the Holy Spirit brings God's goodness to all believers seeking holiness.[33]

Origen's notion of eternal generation, then, is not grounded in a distinction of substance or power but, rather, points to an active relationship within the Godhead. This active relationship encompasses not just the Father and Son, but also the Trinity as a whole, since Origen includes the Holy Spirit in this internal unity and inter-relationship. He stresses the unchangeability of the Father, Son and Holy Spirit, logically suggesting that they are all God,

---

28. Crouzel, *Origen,* 187, referring to Hom. Jer. 9.4, Comm. Jn. 2:18 and Comm. Jn. 13.219.

29. See Hom. Jer. 9.4.5, referring to Heb 1:3, Wis 7:26, 1 Jn. 1:5, 1 Cor 1:24, Wis 7:26. *Origen: Homilies on Jeremiah,* Tr. John Clark Smith, FOTC 97 (Washington, DC: The Catholic University of America Press, 1998), 93 (Ἴδωμεν δὲ τίς ἡμῶν ἐστιν ὁ σωτήρ ʽἈπαύγασμα δόξης.ʼ Τὸ ἀπαύγασμα τῆς δόξης οὐχὶ ἅπαξ γεγέννηται καὶ οὐχὶ γεννᾶται ἀλλά ὅσον ἐστὶν τὸ ʽφὼςʼ ποιητικὸν τοῦ ἀπαυγάσματος, ἐπὶ τοσοῦτον γεννᾶται τὸ ἀπαύγασμα τῆς δόξης τοῦ θεοῦ. Ὁ σωτὴρ ἡμῶν ʽσοφίαʼ ἐστὶν ʽτοῦ θεοῦʼ ἔστιν δὲ ἡ σοφία <<ἀπαύγασμα φωτὸς ἀιδίου>>) (*Origène: Homélies sur Jérémie* (Tome I), Trs. Pierre Husson et Pierre Nautin, SC 232 (Paris: Cerf, 1976) 392.)

30. Comm. Jn. 2:18. *Origen: Commentary on the Gospel According to John, Books 1–10,* Tr. Ronald E. Heine, FOTC 80 (Washington, DC: The Catholic University of America Press, 1989), 99 (… παρέμενε τῇ ἀδιαλείπτῳ θέᾳ τοῦ πατρικοῦ βάθους). (*Origène: Commentaire sur Saint Jean Tome* I (Livres I–V), Tr. Cécile Blanc, SC 120 (Paris: Cerf, 1966) 218.)

31. Crouzel, *Origen,* 187–94, esp. 188.

32. See Berchman, *From Philo to Origen,* 141–56.

33. See DP 1.3.5–8; Dively Lauro, *"The Meaning and Significance,"* 7n21; Crouzel, *Origen,* 187–88 and 191–92; and Berchman, *From Philo to Origen,* 123.

sharing in the "unity" of the Divine nature.[34] The relationship of eternal generation by the Father and reflection of glory or light back by the Son is one of love, and Origen refers to each within the Trinity—Father, Son and Holy Spirit—as "love," making each Person "one and the same in every respect."[35] The Trinity, then, enjoys an eternal activity of love within one nature and equal force of power, in stark contrast to any suggestion that the relationship is "subordinate."[36] The Son is not subordinate, but is "in need of" and "bound to" the Father for his existence, and so it is not offensive for the Divine Son to speak humbly toward the Father.

Christ Unites His Humanity to His Divinity

The equality of substance and power between the Father and Son is significant, indeed, crucial, to understanding Origen's unfolding homiletic message. Believers are invited ultimately, as their salvific *telos,* to unite with Christ, and, in turn, to join in the Trinity's eternal activity of generation and reflection. This can happen only if humanity has a path to enter into the Divine nature. To this end, Origen explains that Christ, in his union of Divinity and humanity, introduces humanity into the Father-Son relationship.

In his homilies on Psalm 15, Origen explains the union of Christ's Divinity and humanity as follows:

> The spirit of wisdom rests upon the one from the root of Jesse, begotten from the seed of David according to the flesh. For "the first born of all creation," "the spirit of counsel and might" has become one with the Savior understood according to the humanity, born from the seed of David according to the flesh. And he says this, taking part in the union, "I will praise the Lord who makes me understand."[37]

34. For the Son's unchangeability, see Comm. Jn. 2: 9–10, Comm. Jn. 2:18, and Comm. Jn. 13:219, as well as Crouzel, *Origen,* 187, and Dively Lauro, *"The Meaning and Significance,"* 2–6. For the Holy Spirit's unchangeability, see DP 1.3.4 and Hom. Num. 11.8, as well as Dively Lauro, *"The Meaning and Significance,"* 6–8.

35. For naming the Father and Son "love" and as "one and the same," see Comm. Cant. Prol. 2 (*Quod si Deus Pater caritas est et Filius caritas est, caritas autem et caritas unum est et in nullo differt, consequenter ergo Pater et Filius unum est et in nullo differt*) (Tr. R. P. Lawson, ACW 26:32; Eds. Henri Crouzel et Marcel Borret, SC 375:110), as well as Dively Lauro, *"The Meaning and Significance,"* 7. For naming the Holy Spirit "love" and including him in the "oneness" of the Father and the Son, see Comm. Cant. Prol. 2 (Tr. Lawson, ACW 26:39; Eds. Crouzel et Borret, SC 375:124).

36. The following additional texts in Origen's works support an equality of nature and power between the Son and Father: DP 1.2.9, 1.3.5 (and especially for equal forces of power), 1.6.2, and 4.4.1 (Greek); Comm. Jn. 2.16–18, 2.37–41, 2.75; and Cont. Cels. 5.39.

37. Hom. Ps. 15.2.2, quoting Is 11:10 and Rom 15:12a, Rom 1:3, Ps 15:7a, Col 1:15 and Is 11:1–2 (... ἀναπέπαυται τὸ πνεῦμα τῆς συνέσεως ἐπὶ τὸν ἐκ ῥίζης Ιεσσαί, γενόμενον ἐκ σπέρματος Δαυὶδ κατὰ σάρκα....

Thus, Jesus, the Divine "spirit of counsel and might," possesses a human body of flesh. Origen points out that Jesus also possesses a "human soul."[38] He stresses that not only was "'the first born of all creation' … always present with it … but … rather *united*, so that the man is no longer one thing and the first born of all creation something else."[39] The Divine Son of the Trinity, as Christ the Savior, unites with a full human nature, body and soul.[40] Origen stresses that this union preserves the original integrity of its parts, for the Savior "remains the complete Logos."[41] Therefore, Christ the Savior enjoys within himself a union of Divinity and humanity that does not change these respective natures.

Christ Brings this Union of Divinity
and Humanity into Heaven

Origen explains that Christ the Savior enjoyed this union of Divinity and humanity not only on earth but also has brought this union up into heaven:

> "My flesh will rest in hope." My Lord Jesus says this. His flesh first rested in hope, for he was crucified and raised on the third day, having become the first born of the dead, and once raised, he was taken up into heaven and brought up from earth an earthly body, … flesh ascending into heaven.… Before my Lord Jesus Christ no one ascended into heaven.… [B]ecause he is the first born of the dead, so *he also is the first flesh brought up into heaven*.[42]

Ἡνώθη γὰρ ὁ πρωτότοκος πάσης κτίσεως, τὸ πνεῦμα τῆς βουλῆς καὶ ἰσχύος, τῷ σωτῆρι τῷ νοουμένῳ κατὰ τὸ ἀνθρώπινον, γεννωμένῳ ἐκ σπέρματος Δαυὶδ κατὰ σάρκα. Καὶ οὕτως λέγει, τῆς ἑνώσεως ἀντιλαμβανόμενος, τὸ εὐλογήσω τὸν κύριον τὸν συνετίσαντά με.) (GCS NF 19:93–94) Note that the word for "wisdom" here, σύνεσις, first means "coming together, uniting, union," and can also mean "comprehension, intelligence, sagacity," or "conscience."

38. Origen points out that it is the human soul of Jesus that prays the words of Ps 15:8a. Hom. Ps. 15.2.3, quoting Ps 15.8a (Ἡ ἀνθρωπίνη λέγει ψυχὴ Ἰησοῦ …). (GCS NF 19:97)

39. Hom. Ps. 15.2.3, quoting Col 1:15 (ἆρά γε τὸν πατέρα λέγει ἢ τὸν πρωτότοκον πάσης τῆς κτίσεως ἀεὶ αὐτῇ παρόντα; Τί δὲ λέγω "παρόντα"; ἡνωμένον, ἵνα μηκέτι ἄλλος ἢ ἄνθρωπος καὶ ἄλλος ὁ πρωτότοκος πάσης κτίσεως). (GCS NF 19:97)

40. Albeit the human soul of Jesus is "the soul that does not sin, the one that voluntarily came down, the one that did not think equality with God a prize, to have become one spirit and to have become one with the first born of all creation." Hom. Ps. 15.2.3, referring to Phil 2:6 and quoting Col. 1:15 (… οὐ θέλεις δὲ τὴν μὴ ἁμαρτάνουσαν ψυχήν, τὴν ἑκουσίως καταβᾶσαν, τὴν μὴ ἁρπαγμὸν ἡγησαμένην τὸ εἶναι ἴσα θεῷ, ἓν πνεῦμα γεγονέναι καὶ ἓν γεγονέναι πρὸς τὸν πρωτότοκον πάσης κτίσεως). (GCS NF 19:97) Origen continues the import of this theme in Hom. Ps. 15.2.4. (GCS NF 19:98)

41. See Hom. Ps. 15.1.9 and the discussion and Greek language at and around note 47 below.

42. Hom. Ps. 15.2.8, quoting Ps 15:9b and referring to Col 1:18 and Rev 1:5 and quoting Jn 3:13, emphasis added (Ἔτι δὲ καὶ ἡ σάρξ μου κατασκηνώσει ἐπ' ἐλπίδι. Ὁ κύριός μου Ἰησοῦς ταῦτα λέγει, οὗ πρώτου ἡ σὰρξ κατεσκήνωσεν ἐπ' ἐλπίδι· ἐσταύρωται γὰρ καὶ τῇ τρίτῃ ἡμέρᾳ ἐγήγερται γενόμενος πρωτότοκος ἐκ τῶν νεκρῶν καὶ ἐγερθεὶς ἀνελήφθη εἰς οὐρανὸν καὶ ἀνήγαγεν ἀπὸ γῆς γήϊνον σῶμα.… σάρκα ἀναβαίνουσαν εἰς τὸν

Origen does not say that Christ is the *only* one to bring flesh into heaven but that he is the *first*. As Christ is the *first* to be resurrected from the dead, he is the first to bring *flesh* into heaven. He is the promise that brings our humanity into heaven as well. Logically, when "the Savior is always nourished by the Father"[43] in *eternal* generation, his whole nature, as a union of Divinity and humanity, is so nourished. He becomes the *first* to have his humanity directly nourished by the Father within heaven. Christ, through his Divinity and humanity, becomes the pathfinder, the first of humanity to be directly nourished by the Father for eternity. He becomes the hope that we humans will be invited into heaven's union and directly nourished by the Father as well.

Christ Unites the Humanity of Believers within his own Humanity

Humans can share in Christ's union of his Divinity and humanity, because he holds humans within his body as its "actual" parts. This is possible because Christ's humanity, like ours, is a composite of body, soul and spirit:

> [When] "the Savior says, Guard me, Lord, for I have hoped in you,' ... he says this to his Lord and Father about those who are his actual limbs.... [S]ince you are the limbs of Christ and limbs from the parts, you indeed are the body of Christ. When he prays and says, 'Guard me, Lord,' *he is praying about you and speaking about himself.* For you are his body, you are a limb of him, if you are not willing to be cast away from him.[44]

The Savior not only intercedes with the Father for those who "do not want to be withdrawn from him," that is, believers, but he also holds them in himself before the Father. He gives not only an example of prayer, but he prays for believers as he prays for himself; he stands in for them before the Father, praying for himself while he holds believers in himself.[45] Indeed, Origen stresses,

----

οὐρανόν.... Πρὸ τοῦ κυρίου μου Ἰησοῦ Χριστοῦ *οὐδεὶς εἰς οὐρανὸν ἀναβέβηκεν.... ὡς πρωτότοκός ἐστιν ἐκ τῶν νεκρῶν, οὕτως καὶ πρῶτος σάρκα ἀνήγαγεν εἰς οὐρανόν*). (GCS NF 19:104–105).

43. See Ps 15.1.9 (GCS NF 19:89) and n. 50 below for the Greek text.

44. Hom. Ps. 15.1.3, quoting Ps 15.1 and referring to 1 Cor 12:27, emphasis added (... πῶς ὁ σωτὴρ λέγει τὸ φύλαξόν με, κύριε, ὅτι ἐπὶ σοὶ ἤλπισα. Λέγω γὰρ ὅτι τοῦτο εἶπε τῷ κυρίῳ καὶ πατρὶ αὐτοῦ περὶ τῶν ὄντων μελῶν ἑαυτοῦ ... ἐπεὶ ὑμεῖς δέ ἐστε μέλη Χριστοῦ καὶ μέλη ἐκ μέρους καὶ ὑμεῖς δέ ἐστε σῶμα Χριστοῦ— εὐχόμενον καὶ λέγοντα: φύλαξόν με, κύριε, εὐχόμενον περὶ σοῦ λέγειν περὶ ἑαυτοῦ. Σῶμα γὰρ εἶ αὐτοῦ, μέλος εἶ αὐτοῦ, εἰ μὴ θέλεις ἐκκεχωρίσθαι αὐτοῦ). (GCS NF 19:77) Note that the word "actual" for "actual limbs" (ὄντων μελῶν) is ὄντα, which comes from εἰμι (sum) and also means "the things that really exist," "the present," "reality, truth," "actual object," or "that which one has or property."

45. He stresses that our prayers only reach the Father if and because they go through "Jesus Christ"

Christ became human for our sake, for the sake of the church, for all the faithful, so that he could hold them in himself before the Father.

> The Savior is composite *for your sake.* You [humans] are composite, having a body inferior to the substance of your soul and to the nature of your spirit. And my Savior and Lord is composite *for the sake of the church*, insofar as it is his body, about which, when he prays, as one needing safeguarding, he says: 'Guard me, Lord.' ... *including everyone in his body ...*[46]

If believers are the "actual" parts of Christ's body, then, when he brings his own humanity into union with the Father, he brings also the humans who are believers into that same union, a union that exists because the Son is not subordinate in nature to the Father.

Christ is the Nourishment of Humans as the Father is the Nourishment of the Son

The question then arises: how is a believer to ensure that he will be one whom Christ holds in himself and therefore brings to the Father? Origen

---

who both represents us and holds us within his body. Christ is both our example and our vessel of prayer. Origen explains that our prayers are "effectual" only if we direct them to the Father with the mediation of Jesus Christ. Origen explains: "My prayer, if it is sent up to God, is to be sent up through Jesus Christ, the high priest and protector of our souls. For the Father will not receive the prayer favorably, if I bring it without employing the high priest, since it cannot come first to him [the Father] apart from it being offered by Jesus Christ." Hom. Ps. 15.1.3 and referring to Ps 109:4 and Heb 5:6 (The fuller text: Ἐὰν δέ ποτε ἐγὼ θέλω, ὡς ἐνδεὴς μόνου τοῦ θεοῦ, ὁμοίως τῷ σωτῆρι εὔξασθαι τῷ θεῷ καὶ χωρὶς τοῦ σωτῆρος προσαγάγω τὴν προσευχήν μου, ἀτελῆ εὐχὴν εὔχομαι. Δεῖ γάρ μου τὴν εὐχήν, κἂν ἀναπέμπηται τῷ θεῷ, διὰ Ἰησοῦ Χριστοῦ ἀναπέμπεσθαι, τοῦ ἀρχιερέως καὶ προστάτου τῶν ψυχῶν ἡμῶν. Οὐ γὰρ προσδέξεται ὁ πατὴρ τὴν εὐχήν, ἐὰν ἐγὼ αὐτὴν προσαγάγω μὴ χρησάμενος τῷ ἀρχιερεῖ, μὴ δυναμένην φθάσαι πρὸς αὐτὸν χωρὶς τοῦ προσφέροντος αὐτὴν Ἰησοῦ Χριστοῦ). (GCS NF 19:77)

46. Hom. Ps. 15.1.3, quoting Ps 15:1 (Σύνθετός ἐστιν ὁ σωτὴρ διὰ σέ· σὺ μὲν σύνθετος εἶ, ἔχων σῶμα ἔλαττον τῆς οὐσίας τῆς ψυχῆς σου καὶ τῆς φύσεως τοῦ πνεύματός σου. Ὁ δὲ σωτήρ μου καὶ κύριος σύνθετός ἐστι διὰ τὴν ἐκκλησίαν οὖσαν αὐτοῦ σῶμα, περὶ ἧς εὐχόμενος δεομένης φυλακῆς λέγει, *φύλαξόν με, κύριε.* Διὰ τοῦτο καὶ ἐπὶ τὸ σῶμα αὐτοῦ φέρων ὡσαύτως πάντα λέγει). (GCS NF 19:77–78) Note that Origen clarifies that "everyone" held within the Savior's body includes only those within the "church," which is, by definition, "the body of Christ." Christ prays only "on behalf" of those within his body. See Origen's further discussion in Hom. Ps. 15.1.3 (GCS NF 19:78). Note that the word translated here as "composite" is σύνθετός, which also means "compound" or "put together." Also note that the word translated here as "inferior" is ἐλάσσων and can also mean "smaller, less," or "of less account," or "worse off." Note Origen's reference here to his understanding of the tripartite nature of humans, with a body, soul, and spirit, wherein the soul holds the free will to choose to follow the body or the spirit and becomes like God if it chooses the spirit and falls into sin if it lets the impulses of the body lead decisions. For a fuller discussion of Origen's tripartite anthropology, see Dively Lauro, "The Anthropological Context of Origen's Two Higher Senses of Scriptural Meaning," *Origeniana Octava* I (2003) 613–24, esp. 614–15, and Dively Lauro, *The Soul and Spirit of Scripture*, 86–91.

explains that the believer should seek Christ as his nourishment in the same way that Christ finds the Father to be his nourishment.

> [T]he Savior has something done to himself because of us. Yet, *he remains the complete logos* even when we eat him … his flesh … and he remains complete even when we drink him … his blood. Therefore, just as *he is himself our nourishment* and he is our drink, … *in the same way he has the Father as his nourishment* and he has the Father as his cup.[47]

As our bodies need proper "nourishment" (τροφή), so do our souls: "The body is nourished and, without nourishment, it dies. [So also] the soul is nourished with its own proper food … Christ himself, … the Logos … , and without nourishment, it dies … the soul's death."[48] Origen admits that he himself often "has neglected [his] proper nourishment," and, as a result, "in proportion to the neglect," he "has become sick or died."[49] On the contrary, "the Savior never neglects his own nourishment, but always is awake and is nourished by the Father."[50] Logically, when the believer partakes of the nourishment of Christ, they too will share in the nourishment the Savior receives from the Father.[51]

The Savior is indeed the pathway between humans and the Father. Origen

47. Hom. Ps. 15.1.9, referring to Jn 6:51, Jn 15:1, and Jn 6:53 and quoting Matt 26:28–29, emphasis added (the fuller text: πάσχει τι ὁ σωτὴρ ἀφ' ἡμῶν. Μένει γὰρ ὁλόκληρος λόγος κἂν ἐσθίωμεν αὐτὸν … καὶ τὰς σάρκας αὐτοῦ … καὶ μένει ὁλόκληρος κἂν πίνωμεν αὐτόν … καὶ ἐπεὶ πίνομεν αὐτοῦ τὸ αἷμα.… Ὥσπερ οὖν αὐτὸς τροφὴ ἡμῶν ἐστι καὶ ποτὸν ἡμῶν ἐστι—καὶ τοῦτό ἐστί μου τὸ αἷμα τῆς καινῆς διαθήκῆς—, καὶ περὶ ἑαυτοῦ ἐπαγγέλλεται λέγων: οὐ μὴ αὐτὸ πίω, ἕως αὐτὸ πίνω μεθ' ὑμῶν καινὸν ἐν τῇ βασιλείᾳ τοῦ θεοῦ, οὕτως αὐτὸς τροφὴν ἔχει τὸν πατέρα καὶ ποτὸν ἔχει τὸν πατέρα) (GCS NF 19:87). Note that πάσχω, translated here as "has something done," can also mean "suffers": the Savior suffers something for us yet remains the complete Word of God. Also note that the word for "complete" here, ὁλόκληρος, means "complete in all its parts, entire, perfect": the Savior remains perfectly the Word of God even though he unites with human nature. Finally, also note that the word here for nourishment, τροφή, also means "food" or "means of maintenance": the Savior is the food that maintains us or keeps us alive spiritually.

48. Hom. Ps. 15.1.9 (σῶμα τρέφεται καὶ χωρὶς τροφῆς ἀποθνήσκει: ψυχὴ τρέφεται οἰκείᾳ τροφῇ, τρέφεται αὐτῷ τῷ Χριστῷ … τῷ λόγῳ … καὶ χωρὶς τροφῆς ἀποθνήσκει.… τὸν τῆς ψυχῆς θάνατον …) (GCS NF 19:89, 88). Note that the word τρέφω means not only "to feed or maintain" but also "to grow or raise."

49. Hom. Ps. 15.1.9 (the fuller text: Ἀλλ' ἐγὼ μὲν πολλάκις ἠμέλησα τῆς ἐμῆς τροφῆς καὶ ὁσάκις ἠμέλησα, κατὰ τὴν ἀναλογίαν τῆς ἀμελείας, ἤτοι ἐνόσησα ἢ ἀποτέθνηκα) (GCS NF 19:89).

50. Hom. Ps. 15.1.9 (Ὁ δὲ σωτήρ μου οὐδέποτε ἀμελεῖ τῆς ἑαυτοῦ τροφῆς, ἀλλὰ ἀεὶ ἐγρήγορε καὶ τρέφεται ἀπὸ τοῦ πατρός) (GCS NF 19:89).

51. I have argued in earlier works that Origen understands this nourishment—or consumption—of Christ, and here ultimately the nourishment of the Father, to continue into eternity. As Origen here states that the Son is always nourished by the Father, indeed, eternally generated, so also will the believer invited into union with the Son and Father enjoy continued nourishment, or consumption of Christ, for eternity. Indeed, it will be the eternal eucharistic, heavenly feast, the wedding banquet, to which we are invited. See Dively Lauro, "The Meaning and Significance," ms. pgs. 28–30; Dively Lauro "The Eschatological Significance," 95–101. For a full discussion of Origen's general analysis of the eternal wedding feast in *Comm. Cant.* I, see Dively Lauro, *The Soul and Spirit of Scripture*, 195–237.

even stresses that Christ, "the one saying, 'I am the way,' leads to the God and Father of the Universe."[52] Christ is for humans the perfect gate to the Father, because he, as a union of the composite human nature and Divine nature, holds everyone in himself. When believers are nourished by Christ, they are "bound to" him. As a result, when Christ shares his inheritance from the Father with believers, he is making himself their inheritance. Christ speaks the words of Ps 15:5, "The Lord is the portion of my inheritance and of my cup; you are the one who restores my inheritance to me,"[53] because

> [t]he Savior has *two inheritances,* one in the higher place and one in the lower place. God is the one in the higher place, so that he [God] may be served by him [Christ] and benefited by the Father. His holy ones are in the lower place, so that the things most beneficial, which he takes from the Father, he [Christ] may give to those who are being helped.[54]

So "[t]he Lord [Father] is the portion of the Savior's inheritance and of his 'cup,'"[55] but the Savior, Christ, delivers himself to be the inheritance of humans so that they may share in his inheritance from the Father. By being "bound to" Christ as Christ is "bound to" the Father, the believer also enjoys the nourishment that the Father gives, and so may "become perfect, just as [the] Father in heaven is perfect."[56]

The Believer is Called to Unite with Christ through Imitation, by Speaking the Psalm

Origen offers specific ways that the believer can receive nourishment from Christ and therefore share in his inheritance with the Father, all of which begin by imitating the speaker (*prosopon*) of the psalm, Christ, by praying the

---

52. When commenting on the words of Ps 15:11a ("You have made me know roads of life") in Hom. Ps. 15.2.10 (*Ἐγνώρισάς μοι ὁδοὺς ζωῆς*) (GCS NF 19:111), Origen draws the connection to Christ as the "road" or "way" (same word, ὁδός) in John 14:6 and states here specifically that Christ is the way that leads to the Father. Hom. Ps. 15.2.10, quoting Jn 14:6 (Ὁ δὲ εἰπών: ἐγώ εἰμι ἡ ὁδός, φέρει πρὸς τὸν θεὸν καὶ πατέρα τῶν ὅλων) (GCS NF 19:112).

53. Hom. Ps. 15.1.8, quoting Ps 15:5 (*Κύριος ἡ μερὶς τῆς κληρονομίας μου καὶ τοῦ ποτηρίου μου: σὺ εἶ ὁ ἀποκαθιστῶν τὴν κληρονομίαν μου ἐμοί*). (GCS NF 19:86)

54. Hom. Ps. 15.1.8 (Δύο κληρονομίας ἔχει ὁ σωτήρ, τὴν μὲν ἐπὶ τῷ ἀνωτέρῳ, τὴν δὲ ἐπὶ τῷ κατωτέρῳ: ἐπὶ τῷ ἀνωτέρῳ τὸν θεόν, ἵνα ἀπ᾽ αὐτοῦ ὠφελῆται καὶ εὐεργετῆται ἀπὸ τοῦ πατρός: ἐπὶ τῷ κατωτέρῳ τοὺς ἁγίους αὐτοῦ, ἵνα τὰ ὠφελιμώτατα, ἃ λαμβάνει ἀπὸ τοῦ πατρός, διδῷ τοῖς ὠφελουμένοις). (GCS NF 19:86)

55. Hom. Ps. 15.1.9, quoting Ps 15:5a (*Κύριος ἡ μερὶς τῆς κληρονομίας ἐστὶ τοῦ σωτῆρος καὶ τοῦ ποτηρίου αὐτοῦ*) (GCS NF 19:87).

56. Hom. Ps. 15.2.4, quoting Matt 5:48 ("γίνεσθε γὰρ, φησί, τέλειοι καθὼς ὁ πατὴρ ὑμῶν ὁ ἐν οὐρανοῖς τέλειός ἐστι …"). (GCS NF 19:99)

psalm themselves. This imitation is easy, because Christ speaks the words of Psalm 15 from his humanity:

> [Here] Christ [as *prosopon*] is understood according to his humanity. For, in the Scriptures, you separate when the Lord speaks, understood according to the Divinity, and when Christ speaks, understood according to his humanity."[57]

Origen stresses that the Savior speaks the humble words of Psalm 15 as "the man" Jesus,[58] and so provides an example of how humans should address the Father.[59] When the believer speaks the words of the psalm, he specifically imitates the human Jesus in his stance of humble prayer to the Father.

> When you hear Jesus saying these things, hear Paul also, ordering this to you: "Be imitators of me, just as I also am of Christ." Whose imitator must I become? Is it the firstborn of all creation? Wisdom? Logos? Truth? Or am I, as a human being, ordered to become the imitator of the human Jesus, so that I may imitate his humanity? I do not say that it is impossible to imitate his Divinity, for ascending I progress and by the grace of God I am able to overcome and imitate the Divinity of Christ; and if it is actually possible to imitate the Divinity of Christ, then I am also able to imitate the God of the Universe: for, he says, "become perfect, just as your Father in heaven is perfect." ... Then, having also become imitators of Christ, let us strive to say as much as the humanity of Christ says. For that is why he says these things, so that we may have some model.[60]

57. Hom. Ps.15.2.2, quoting Ps 15:7a (The fuller passage: Ἦν δὲ ἡ ἀρχὴ τοῦ σήμερον ἀναγνώσματος: εὐλογήσω τὸν κύριον τὸν συνετίσαντά με, Χριστὸς ὁ κατὰ τὸ ἀνθρώπινον νοούμενος. Ἐν γὰρ ταῖς γραφαῖς διαστέλλεις πότε λέγει κύριος, ὁ κατὰ τὴν θεότητα νοούμενος, καὶ πότε λέγει Χριστός, ὁ κατὰ τὸ ἀνθρώπινον νοούμενος. Τὰ δὴ ἐν τῷ ψαλμῷ νῦν ἀπὸ Χριστοῦ προσώπου λέγεται τοῦ νοουμένου κατὰ τὸ ἀνθρώπινον). (GCS NF 19:92)

58. Hom. Ps. 15.2.3, later quoting 1 Pt 2:22 (Ἀλλὰ ὁ ἔπαινος περὶ τοῦ μὴ ἁμαρτάνειν τὸν Ἰησοῦν ἐπὶ τὸν ἄνθρωπον ἀναφέρεται …). (GCS NF 19:95)

59. Origen explains that not only the Divine Logos, but also the human Jesus, though sinless, needs the Father. See Hom. Ps. 15.1.3–4 and Hom. Ps. 15.2.2–3, esp. 15.1.3 (GCS NF 19:77). Thus, Origen can say of the Savior, "he is not without need." Hom. Ps. 15.1.9 (… οὐ γάρ ἐστιν ἀνενδεής …). (GCS NF 19:87) The human Jesus displays that he "is in need of the one God and Father, to whom he also prayed even through the prophets as now, and in the gospels when he withdrew into solitary places and offered prayers to him as one in need of God." Hom. Ps. 15.1.3, referring to Mark 1:35, Luke 5:16, Luke 6:12, Luke 9.18, and Luke 11:1 (Οὐχ ὁμοίως αὐτὸν λέγω εἶναι ἐνδεῆ σοι ἤ τινι τῶν δεομένων βοηθείας τῆς ἀπὸ τῶν ὑπὸ τὸν θεόν, ἀλλὰ λέγω ἐνδεῆ αὐτὸν εἶναι ἑνὸς τοῦ θεοῦ καὶ πατρός, ᾧ καὶ ηὔχετο καὶ διὰ τῶν προφητῶν ὡς νῦν: καὶ ἐν τοῖς εὐαγγελίοις δὲ ἦν ἀναχωρῶν ἐν ταῖς ἐρήμοις καὶ ὡς ἐνδεὴς τοῦ θεοῦ προσευχόμενος αὐτῷ). (GCSS NF 19:76–77) For example, he went alone to Gethsemane to pray and asked the Father to "take this cup" from him. Yet, Origen contrasts Jesus to Moses, who, as an example of other humans, needs the assistance of God, Christ, the Holy Spirit, and angels. See Hom. Ps. 15.1.3. Origen also points out that even human lords, or masters, need the help of those humans who serve him, to help complete the tasks that they oversee. See Hom. Ps. 15.1.5. However, Origen maintains that the Savior, even as he walks the earth as a human, is only in need of the Father.

60. Hom. Ps. 15.2.4, quoting 1 Cor 11:1, Col 1:15, and Matt 5:48 (Ταῦτα δὲ ἐπὰν ἀκούῃς λέγοντος

When the believer prays the words of Christ in Psalm 15, he follows Christ's example of how humans should pray humbly to the Father. Indeed, arguably, not only are Paul and Origen calling the believer to imitate Christ by speaking Christ's words in the psalm, but Christ, by the very act of modelling, is the one calling believers to imitate him. As Origen points out here, this will lead ultimately, as a result of spiritual progress, to an imitation of Christ's Divine nature as well.

When imitating the *prosopon* by speaking words of Scripture, the believer engages in multiple activities that nourish him and help him to become like Christ and ready for union with the Father. Speaking the words of the psalm constitutes prayer, which "is nourishment for the soul, especially when it [the soul] offers prayers with the mind also (καὶ τῷ νοΐ)."[61] This prayerful engagement with Scripture joins the believer to "the teaching Logos," or "the Logos of wisdom and the Logos of knowledge," that is, Scripture itself, who "enter[s] into the hearer" and "is nourishment for the soul."[62] This engagement with Scripture, God's wisdom, leads the believer to understand spiritual things[63] through "more deeply hearing what is said" in Scripture.[64] In turn, by being "enlightened by the Word,"[65] the believer "hope[s] in God,'"[66] and keeps God's law.[67] He becomes like Christ, who is the virtues,[68] and, ultimately, like the Father, who is "perfect."[69]

τοῦ Ἰησοῦ, ἄκουε καὶ Παύλου προστάσσοντός σοι τὸ *μιμηταί μου γίνεσθε καθὼς κἀγὼ Χριστοῦ.* Τίνος μιμητὴν με δεῖ γενέσθαι; Ἆρα τοῦ *πρωτοτόκου πάσης κτίσεως,* τῆς σοφίας, τοῦ λόγου, τῆς ἀληθείας ἢ μιμητὴς προστάσσομαι γενέσθαι, ἄνθρωπος ὤν, τοῦ ἀνθρώπου Ἰησοῦ, ἵνα μιμήσωμαι τὸ ἀνθρώπινον αὐτοῦ; Οὐ λέγω ὅτι ἀμήχανόν ἐστι μιμήσασθαι τὴν θεότητα αὐτοῦ· ἀναβαίνων γὰρ προκόπτω καὶ χάριτι θεοῦ φθάσαι δύναμαι ἐπὶ καὶ τὸ μιμήσασθαι τὴν θεότητα τοῦ Χριστοῦ, εἴ γε πρόκειται μιμήσασθαι τὴν θεότητα τοῦ Χριστοῦ καὶ <τοῦ> θεοῦ τῶν ὅλων· γίνεσθε γάρ, φησί, *τέλειοι καθὼς ὁ πατὴρ ὑμῶν ὁ ἐν οὐρανοῖς τέλειός ἐστι.* … Μιμηταὶ οὖν τοῦ Χριστοῦ γινόμενοι καὶ ἡμεῖς, ὅσα λέγει τὸ ἀνθρώπινον τοῦ Χριστοῦ φιλοτιμούμεθα εἰπεῖν. Διὰ τοῦτο γὰρ ταῦτα λέγει, ἵν' ἔχωμεν ὑπογραμμὸν). (GCS NF 19:99–100)

61. See the next footnote for the relevant Greek text.

62. Hom. Ps. 15.1.9, referring to 1 Cor 14:15 and 1 Cor 12:8 (Εὐχὴ τροφὴ ψυχῆς ἐστι καὶ μάλιστα ὅτε προσεύχεται καὶ τῷ νοΐ· λόγος διδασκαλικὸς εἰσερχόμενος εἰς τὸν ἀκούοντα τροφὴ ψυχῆς ἐστι, λόγος σοφίας καὶ λόγος γνώσεως) (GCS NF 19:88). Origen scolds his audience for "neglect[ing] [to] keep[] the soul always nourished," for they do not pray enough or take in the Scriptures enough. See Hom. Ps. 15.1.9 (Προσέχετε οἱ ἀμελοῦντες τοῦ τρέφειν τὴν ψυχὴν ἀεί) (GCS NF 19:88)

63. See Hom. Ps. 15.2.4–5, quoting Ps 15:7a and referring to 1 Cor 2:13 (Τοιαῦτά τινα νοήσεις, ἐὰν δυνηθῇς ἀκούειν καὶ συγκρίνειν πνευματικὰ πνευματικοῖς). (GCS NF 19:100)

64. Hom. Ps. 15.2.6 (Ἐρεῖ γὰρ ὁ βαθύτερον ἀκούειν τῶν λεγομένων δυνάμενος). (GCS NF 19:102)

65. Hom. Ps. 15.2.1 (φωτιζόμενοι ὑπὸ τοῦ λόγου). (GCS NF 19:92)

66. Hom. Ps. 15.1.4, quoting Ps. 15:1b (*ὅτι ἐπὶ σοί, φησίν, ἤλπισα*). (GCS NF 19:79)

67. Hom. Ps. 15.2.5 (ὅτε τηρῶ τὸν νόμον τὸν τοῦ θεοῦ). (GCS NF 19:102)

68. Origen discusses at length his view that each virtue equals Christ and that all virtues together equal Christ in *Comm. Cant.* I.5. For analysis, see Dively Lauro, *The Soul and Spirit of Scripture,* 230.

69. Matt 5:48, quoted in Hom. Ps. 15.2.4.

By praying the words of Christ when speaking the words of Scripture, the believer invites Christ to dwell in him and allows him not only to speak *for* us, but he also "speaks *in* us."[70] If the believer "[b]ecome[s] [Christ's] imitator like Paul, … [he] will find that the Lord is always *in* [him]."[71] By beginning with imitation of the human Jesus, the believer progresses to imitating Christ in his Divinity and ultimately entering into the Father-Son relationship.[72] Through oneness with the Logos, the believer shares in the Savior's "inheritance"[73] of "immortality,"[74] and so in the Savior's union with the Father. The inheritance of Christ into which believers are ultimately invited is the relationship of eternal generation and reflected adoration between the Father and Son.[75]

Conclusion

Origen's homilies on Psalm 15 show that the term "subordination" is not only inadequate to explain his understanding of the Father-Son relationship, but also that their equality in substance and power is critical to the *telos* for humans that Origen envisions: union with Christ in his union with the Father. The notion of "subordination" misses the larger picture of Origen's theology and misconstrues the intent of his homilies: we are in "need of" and "bound to" Christ, as Christ is "in need of" and "bound to" the Father, so that we can be joined to the Father and participate in the union, indeed relationship, of the Trinity. Origen does not direct his hearers on an "eternal ascent" toward

70. Hom. Ps. 15.2.1, referring to II Cor. 13.3, emphasis added (The fuller passage: … ὅλον δὲ τὸν ψαλμὸν σαφηνίσαι καὶ πρὸς λέξιν ἐφαρμόσαι ἑαυτῷ, ἀποδεικνύντα ὅτι τοῦ σωτῆρός ἐστι τὸ πρόσωπον, καὶ διδάξαι ἀξίως τοῦ σωτῆρος τὰ λεγόμενα, δοκεῖ μοι αὐτοῦ τοῦ σωτῆρος χρείαν ἔχειν, ἵνα δυνηθῶμεν εἰπεῖν, <u>λαλοῦντος ἐν ἡμῖν</u> αὐτοῦ τοῦ κυρίου.…). (GCS NF 19:92)

71. Hom. Ps. 15.2.5, referring to Ps 15:7–8 and Gal 2:20, emphasis added (The fuller text: Καὶ γάρ σοι ἐνοικεῖ ὁ κύριος, ἐὰν θέλῃς, διὰ παντός. Γενοῦ ὡς Παῦλος ἐκείνου μιμητὴς καὶ εὑρήσεις ὅτι ἐν σοί ἐστιν ἀεὶ ὁ κύριος). (GCS NF 19:102)

72. This spiritual progress is arguably a divinization, then, and how this works within Origen's theology is a fruitful subject for a future study.

73. Hom. Ps. 15.1.8, quoting Ps 15:5 (*Κύριος ἡ μερὶς τῆς κληρονομίας μου καὶ τοῦ ποτηρίου μου: σὺ εἶ ὁ ἀποκαθιστῶν τὴν κληρονομίαν μου ἐμοί*). (GCS NF 19:86) See notes 53–55 and the discussion above.

74. While for the Father "immortality is not something acquired by him, but it is so according to his nature," "the Savior is immortal, immortality being provided to him" by the Father," for "he himself shares it from the Father." See Hom. Ps. 15.1.9, referring to 1 Tim 6:16 and Ps 15:5 (*ἄρα μόνος ἔχει ἀθανασίαν ὁ πατήρ.… οὐ γὰρ ἐπίκτητος ἐκείνου ἡ ἀθανασία, ἀλλὰ φύσει πέφυκεν αὐτῷ.… ὁ δὲ σωτὴρ ἀθάνατος, ἐπισκευαζομένης αὐτῷ τῆς ἀθανασίας … μεταλαμβάνειν ἑαυτὸν τοῦ πατρὸς*). (GCS NF 19:89)

75. In an earlier work, I consider how Origen may understand the mystery of *how* a human nature, or, more specifically, a resurrected body, can unite with the Trinity's Divine nature in heaven (be it Christ's or another's resurrected body), but a fuller analysis of his works on this subject are merited. See Dively Lauro, "The Meaning and Significance,". 9–16.

God,[76] wherein one becomes infinitely closer to God but never reaches God, nor does he suggest that the greatest hope is to stand somehow beside God for all eternity. Rather, in these homilies Origen encourages a goal of divinization, wherein believers become more and more like Christ and therefore more and more united with Christ and so on the path to sharing in his union with the Father. Origen urges his homiletic audience to imitate Christ as the *prosopon* of the psalm and stresses that this interaction with Christ in Scripture will make the believer like Christ, united with Christ and, in turn, on the pathway to union with the Father. The promise is participation in the Trinity's eternal, relational activity of love, constituted by the Father's eternal generation of a Son who has taken on humanity and that Son's continual reflection back of the Father's light and glory. This is the *telos* or fulfillment that God intends for humans, and Origen will settle for nothing less for those to whom he ministers.

76. Gregory of Nyssa explains his famous notion of eternal ascent in *The Life of Moses,* 2.233–43. See *Gregory of Nyssa: The Life of Moses* (The Classics of Western Spirituality) Trs. Abraham J. Malherbe and Everett Ferguson (New York: Paulist Press, 1978) 115–17.

Alex Poulos

5. CONTINUITY AND DEVELOPMENT IN ORIGEN'S UNDERSTANDING OF THE SOUL

Introduction[1]

The soul is a key middle term in the philosophical system of Origen of Alexandria. As Benjamin Blosser states, "The soul ... constitutes the very heart of the human person. It is the soul that defines the person, both morally and ontologically, and the soul that determines his destiny."[2] Indeed for Origen, the questions, and problems, associated with psychology[3] extend beyond the human person to all rational natures (angels and demons), and are thus of cosmic significance. The happy discovery of the 29 new *Homilies on the Psalms* has provided students of Origen with a wealth of new material through which to sort and sift. Perrone has shown that they most likely date to near the end of the Alexandrian's long career;[4] they thus constitute an invaluable resource

---

1. In addition to the editors and contributors to this volume, who have provided invaluable criticism, I would like to thank Ryan Clevenger, Benjamin Blosser of Benedictine College, along with William McCarthy and Matthias Vorwerk of Catholic University of America for their generous comments on drafts of this article. References to the Psalms follow the numbering of the Septuagint; translations throughout are my own unless otherwise noted.

2. Blosser, *Become Like the Angels: Origen's Doctrine of the Soul* (Washington DC: The Catholic University of America Press, 2012), 3. Blosser's work is the fullest and most recent treatment of Origen's psychology.

3. I use the term throughout in to refer, *stricto sensu*, to teaching about the *pysché*, that is, the soul.

4. Origen, *Die neuen Psalmenhomilien: Eine kritische Edition des* Codex Monacensis Graecus 314, ed. Lorenzo Perrone, Emanuela Prinzivalli, and Antonio Cacciari. Origenes Werke 13 (Berlin, New York: Walter de Gruyter, 2015), 17–25.

for charting both the continuities and the developments in Origen's theological and philosophical system. We shall see that the homilies supplement and occasionally correct our understanding of this most influential philosopher and theologian.

Non-Human Souls

Origen's *HPs76.3* is most striking for his endorsement of panpsychism, the notion that, "everything is ensouled." This notion was not uncommon for either Stoics or Platonists, though the two schools would explain it rather differently. It is puzzling for Origen, however, because in *princ.* 3.1.2 he limits souls only to animals, people, and higher forms of life. As Lorenzo Perrone has recently noted, this panpsychism is a *unicum* in Origen's corpus.[5] I wish here to consider in more detail the philosophical issues at play in the homily. I argue that Origen's panpsychism should be understood as an expansion of angelic guardianship from humans to the rest of the natural world. Thus, though the developments from *princ.* and other earlier works are real, Origen's framework has changed less than it seems at first glance.

> The waters beheld you, O God; The waters beheld you and were afraid. The depths were terrified, the multitude of a sound of waters. (Ps 76:17)

The nature of these waters that behold God furnish the opening question in *HPs76.3*. Origen is obliged to explain how waters can be said to see and fear, and how abysses may be terrified. Origen first offers a spiritual interpretation but is not content to offer only this. Perhaps because his audience often complains about his allegorizing,[6] he continues to the literal sense of the passage: "Let's not pass over even the bare meaning of the passage, but see if the lemma has some sense."[7] Recourse to a middle platonic notion provides Origen a means to preserve the literal sense of scripture: "In fact, it occurs to me to say, 'everything possesses soul and nothing in the cosmos is without soul.'"[8] Origen marshals several passages from the Old Testament to show that Heaven, the Earth, the seas, and rivers are all addressed as living creatures (ὡς πρὸς

---

5. Perrone, " Origen's Interpretation of the Psalter Revisited: The Nine Homilies on Psalm 77(78) in the Munich Codex." Lecture at the NAPS Conference, Chicago 2017, 59.

6. e.g. *HPs80.2* sec. 4: "Μὴ τροπολόγει καὶ μὴ ἀλληγόρει, φασίν, ἀλλὰ τήρει ἐπὶ τῆς λέξεως"!

7. Μὴ παρέλθωμεν δὲ μηδὲ τὸ ῥητὸν κατ' αὐτό, ἀλλ' ἴδωμεν εἰ δύναται ἔχειν τινὰ νοῦν ἡ λέξις ἡ λέγουσα· εἴδοσάν σε ὕδατα καὶ ἐφοβήθησαν, ἐταράχθησαν ἄβυσσοι, πλῆθος ἤχους ὑδάτων. *HPs76.3* sec. 2.

8. ἐπέρχεται δή μοι λέγειν, ὅτι πάντα ἐψύχωται καὶ οὐδέν ἐστιν ἐν τῷ κόσμῳ κενὸν ψυχῆς. *HPs76.3* sec. 2.

ζῷον),[9] and concludes that since the Scripture addresses these all as living creatures, they must be ensouled beings.

Origen then elaborates his observation. He explains that everything is administered by angels or powers. Some angelic powers are given control over "maritime affairs" and so take on the body of the sea, others of particular rivers, and others of the air.[10] Angelic governance has physical consequences: he explains that the air is sometimes governed by "higher powers" and is healthy but is at other times turned over to "lower powers" because of human sin. This regime-change causes the air to carry disease. Origen reckons it entirely natural that these angelic beings should be called the same thing as the features of the natural world over which they preside. So "waters" in our psalm here refers to the "powers" that preside over the waters.

Origen then explains this development in his thinking. He tells us that he used to flee to allegory when confronted with Ps 148.[11] After all, how could snakes, abysses, fire, hail, etc. be told to praise the Lord?

> So then, as I was reading, I was trying to figure out what this could mean; I quickly ran to allegory because I saw the lemma was preposterous. But later at some point I thought to myself, "perhaps administering powers are addressed by the same name as what they administer."[12]

Origen then discusses the hierarchy of these governing spirits: some spirits are only given control over snakes, others preside over the trees of the field, farming, as it were, alongside men.

This new scheme raises a number of questions, both about the development of Origen's thinking on the question and about Origen's position within the broader tradition of middle Platonism. In *princ.* 3.1.2–3, Origen had adopted a different scheme that is Stoic in origin. According to this schema, inanimate objects cohere by a principle of *hexis* ('coherence-principle'), plants by a principle of *physis* (not nature, here, but 'growth-principle'), animals

9. e.g. Dt 32:1, "Hearken O Heaven, and heed the words of my lips, O Earth."

10. Ζητῶ οὖν, εἰ δύναμίς τις ἐνδέδυται τὸ σῶμα τὸ <τῆς> θαλάσσης καὶ ἄλλη δύναμις ἐνδέδυται σῶμα ποταμοῦ τοῦ Ἰορδάνου καὶ ἄλλου ποταμοῦ, φέρ᾽ εἰπεῖν τοῦ Γηών, ἄλλη δύναμις, καὶ οὕτως ἐπὶ πάντων.

11. Origen cites Ps 148:1–2 and 7–9. The difficult part is the latter, which reads, "Praise the Lord from the earth, snakes and all the depths, fire, hail, snow, crystal, wind of the storm, all you who do carry out his word; mountains and all the hills, fruit-bearing trees and all the cedars." (αἰνεῖτε τὸν κύριον ἐκ τῆς γῆς, δράκοντες καὶ πᾶσαι ἄβυσσοι· (8) πῦρ, χάλαζα, χιών, κρύσταλλος, πνεῦμα καταιγίδος, τὰ ποιοῦντα τὸν λόγον αὐτοῦ· (9) τὰ ὄρη καὶ πάντες οἱ βουνοί, ξύλα καρποφόρα καὶ πᾶσαι κέδροι).

12. Ἀναγινώσκων οὖν ἐζήτουν τί βούλεται ταῦτα καὶ εὐχερῶς μὲν κατέφευγον ἐπὶ τὴν τροπολογίαν βλέπων τὴν ἀπέμφασιν τῆς λέξεως, ὕστερον δέ ποτε ἐσκόπουν κατ᾽ ἐμαυτὸν μήποτε ὁμωνύμως τοῖς οἰκονομουμένοις αἱ οἰκονομοῦσαι δυνάμεις ὀνομάζωνται. *HPs76.3* sec. 2.

by *psyché* (souls), and humans have in addition *logos* (reason).[13] In the Stoic scheme, therefore, soul is limited only to entities capable of sensation, chiefly, animals and humans. This follows neatly from Origen's definition of soul in *princ.* 2.8: soul (*psyché*) is a substance capable of movement and sensation (φανταστική καὶ ὁρμητική). In *orat.* 6.1, Origen shows some ambivalence with this scheme, but mostly reproduces it. He entertains the idea that plants might also possess movement because of a soul (*psyché*) instead of a growth-principle (*physis*).[14] In this homily, by contrast, he seems to have abandoned the entire Stoic paradigm in favor of something more Platonic. His statement that "everything possesses soul" is an adaptation of a line from Plato's *Phaedrus*, which then became popular for later Platonists.[15]

Origen's "expansion" of soul occurs through a broadening of angelic administration. In *princ.* 1.8.1, angels preside only over other rational creatures.[16] Origen's hierarchy is similar in *HPs76.3*, but angels are responsible for a broader array of phenomena: trees, snow, hail, springs, snakes, and a host of other things. Indeed, one should point here to *HPs80.2* sec. 2, where Origen reminds us that even if no other person sees our sin, the angels will bear witness at the consummation, for everything is full of angels.[17] How tightly bound are these powers to the natural phenomena they govern? Origen speaks primarily of "administering angels" or "presiding powers." These angelic powers are said,

13. *De princ.* 3.1.2–3. ἐν ἑαυτοῖς δὲ ἔχει τὴν αἰτίαν τοῦ κινεῖσθαι ζῷα καὶ φυτὰ καὶ ἁπαξαπλῶς ὅσα ὑπὸ φύσεως καὶ ψυχῆς συνέχεται· ἐξ ὧν φασιν εἶναι καὶ τὰ μέταλλα, πρὸς δὲ τούτοις καὶ τὸ πῦρ αὐτοκίνητόν ἐστι, τάχα δὲ καὶ αἱ πηγαί. τῶν δὲ ἐν ἑαυτοῖς τὴν αἰτίαν τοῦ κινεῖσθαι ἐχόντων τὰ μέν φασιν ἐξ ἑαυτῶν κινεῖσθαι, τὰ δὲ ἀφ᾽ ἑαυτῶν· **ἐξ ἑαυτῶν μὲν τὰ ἄψυχα, ἀφ᾽ ἑαυτῶν δὲ τὰ ἔμψυχα**. καὶ ἀφ᾽ ἑαυτῶν κινεῖται τὰ ἔμψυχα φαντασίας ἐγγινομένης ὁρμὴν προκαλουμένης.

For Stoic comparanda, see for example *SVF* 2.715 and 718.

14. *orat.* 6.1 Τῶν κινουμένων τὰ μέν τινα τὸ κινοῦν ἔξωθεν ἔχει ὥσπερ τὰ ἄψυχα καὶ ὑπὸ ἕξεως μόνης συνεχόμενα καὶ τὰ ὑπὸ φύσεως καὶ ψυχῆς κινούμενα, ... δεύτερα δὲ παρὰ ταῦτά ἐστι κινούμενα τὰ ὑπὸ τῆς ἐνυπαρχούσης **φύσεως ἢ ψυχῆς** κινούμενα (s.c. τὰ φῦτα), ἃ καὶ ἐξ αὐτῶν κινεῖσθαι λέγεται παρὰ τοῖς κυριώτερον χρωμένοις τοῖς ὀνόμασι.

Clement of Alexandria reproduces the same scheme in *Strom.* 2.20.110–11 and also expresses ambivalence over whether plants have souls.

15. "All soul exerts care over all that is without soul" (ψυχὴ πᾶσα παντὸς ἐπιμελεῖται τοῦ ἀψύχου. *Phdr.* 246b). Alcinous states that *daemones* are instituted "so that no part of the cosmos should be without a share of soul" (ὡς μηδὲν κόσμου μέρος ψυχῆς ἄμοιρον εἶναι). Plotinus uses the image of a net in water to describe the cosmos being held by soul: Κεῖται γὰρ ἐν τῆι ψυχῆ ἀνεχούσῃ αὐτὸν καὶ **οὐδὲν ἄμοιρόν ἐστιν αὐτῆς**, ὡς ἂν ἐν ὕδασι δίκτυον τεγγόμενον ζώη, οὐ δυνάμενον δὲ αὐτοῦ ποιεῖσθαι ἐν ὧι ἐστιν· ἀλλὰ τὸ μὲν δίκτυον ἐκτεινομένης ἤδη τῆς θαλάσσης συνεκτέταται, ὅσον αὐτὸ δύναται· οὐ γὰρ δύναται ἀλλαχόθι ἕκαστον τῶν μορίων ἢ ὅπου κεῖται εἶναι. (*Enn.* 4.3.9).

16. This is not explicitly stated, but the only examples Origen gives for angelic charges pertain to human beings, whether singularly or corporately.

17. παντὰ πεπλήρωται ἀγγέλων. *cf. HEz* 1.7, *omnia angelis plena sunt.*

e.g., "to be over the waters" (αἱ ἐπὶ τῆς θαλάσσης δυνάμεις), "to preside over" (αἱ ἐπιστασοῦσαι δυνάμεις), and "to administer" (αἱ διοικοῦσαι δυνάμεις) various natural phenomena. Origen speaks also, however, of souls that take on the body of that which they administer. So, the power responsible for the sea is said to "put on the body" of the sea.[18] The section on "snake powers" illustrates the tension the best:

> Those who are assigned care over the snakes are called snakes, for does not an administering power preside over each kind of living creature? For reasons God knows, one particular power is not worthy of being entrusted with one of the greater tasks, but only of overseeing the snakes; another power, by contrast, is worthy of, as it were, farming alongside men, so that he oversees the trees of the field. One power administers in accordance with what is said by the farmer, while another administers based on what is thought by the angel or angels who administer such things.[19]

Earlier we are told that an angelic power resides "within the body of the sea," and here in fact we are told that there are multiple angelic powers that have charge over snakes. But we are also told that a single angel is given charge over a species (snakes), and that another is given charge not over a single tree, but over wood. Origen does not explain how these angelic souls interact with the irrational or vital souls present in the individual animals and trees, though we do have enough clues to reconstruct a likely account. We are probably meant to imagine a hierarchy, with the lowliest angels given charge over individual life-forms in a manner analogous to the guardian angels of human beings, while more exalted angels preside over regions or species in their entirety. This would explain nicely what Origen says about one power taking its cue from the thought of a higher angel or angels. The guardian angel analogy would also account for how these angelic powers are present within the bodies of individual life-forms. For Origen, a guardian angel forms a unit with the soul over which it exerts care. For a person, this bond is separable in the case of moral change or death, but it is nevertheless intimate enough that the resulting angel-human pair can be called a unit (Rufinus' *unum* presumably renders ἕν).[20]

18. *HPs76.3* sec. 2. ζητῶ οὖν εἰ δύναμίς τις ἐνδέδυται τὸ σῶμα τὸ τῆς θαλάσσης.

19. *HPs76.3* sec. 2. —αἱ μὲν τεταγμέναι ἐπὶ τῶν δρακόντων δράκοντες—ᾧ γὰρ ἑκάστου εἴδους ζῴου ἐπιστατεῖ τις δύναμις ἡ διοικοῦσα. Δι' οὓς οἶδεν ὁ θεὸς λόγους ὅτι ἥδε μὲν ἠξίωται οὐχὶ πιστευθῆναί τινα τῶν κρειττόνων ἀλλὰ δράκοντας οἰκονομεῖν, ἥδε δέ τις δύναμις ἠξίωται οἱονεὶ συγγεωργεῖν τοῖς ἀνθρώποις, ἵνα τὰ ξύλα τοῦ ἀγροῦ οἰκονομῇ· ἡ μὲν κατὰ τὸ λεγόμενον ὑπὸ τοῦ γεωργοῦ [παντὸς] ἀνθρώπου, ἡ δὲ κατὰ τὸ νοούμενον ὑπὸ τοῦ διοικοῦντος τὰ τοιαῦτα ἀγγέλου ἢ ἀγγέλων πλειόνων.

I have secluded παντός.

20. In *princ.* 2.10.7 Origen considers various ways to explain the evil servant who is "cut in two"

Origen thus has likely not jettisoned the Stoic framework of *princ.* 3.1.2–3. Features of the natural world like trees and snakes still cohere within themselves through *physis* or an irrational *psyché*.[21] Now, however, they also possess, or rather, are possessed by an angelic power who holds them as charge. Origen has thus filled his *cosmos* with angelic powers intimately involved with every aspect of natural life. His is very much a haunted world.

Human Souls

Soul and Body

Let us now turn to human souls and begin with the relationship of the soul to the body. I wish here to enter but one debate: for Origen, can the soul exist without a body? Origen was infamously condemned in the sixth century in part because he was held to believe in the preexistence of souls without bodies (γυμναί ψυχαί).[22] This contradicts *princ.* 2.1.1–2, where rational natures are joined necessarily to bodies, and only the Trinity can be said to be completely incorporeal.[23] Scholars are divided over how to resolve the issue. Most maintain that Origen did, in fact, allow for a disincarnate soul.[24] Others give more weight to the passage in *princ.* 2.1.1–2 and argue that rational natures must be embodied in some form.[25] I argue here that Origen changed his

---

in Lk 12:46. The third option he offers describes the separation of the guardian angel from the soul in its charge:

> *Potest autem etiam tertio sensu illud intellegi de divisione ista, ut quoniam unicuique fidelium, etiamsi 'minimus sit in ecclesia', adesse angelus dicitur, qui et 'semper videre faciem dei patris' a salvatore perhibetur, et hic, **qui utique unum erat cum eo, cui praeerat, si is per inoboedientiam efficiatur indignus, auferri ab eo dei angelus dicatur,** et tunc 'pars eius', id est humanae naturae pars, avulsa a dei parte 'cum infidelibus' deputetur, quoniam commonitiones appositi sibi a deo angeli non fideliter custodivit.*

For further analysis of Origen's understanding of guardian angels, see Joseph W. Trigg, "The Angel of Great Counsel: Christ and the Angelic Hierarchy in Origen's Theology," *The Journal of Theological Studies* 42 no. 1 (1991): 35–51.

21. Origen reprises the same framework in *cels.* 4.87, where he says that a φυσικὴ κατασκευή is responsible for the life in plants and animals.

22. Canon 2 condemns the opinion that bodiless and immaterial minds preexisted and fell by satiety of the good. Canon 9 concerns the proposition that Christ descended as a mind (*nous*) to Hades, and 14 the proposition that people will become bare minds (γυμνοί νόες) at the consummation of all things.

23. *solius namque trinitatis incorporea uita existere recte putabitur.*

24. See, *e.g.*, Peter W. Martens, "Embodiment, Heresy, and the Hellenization of Christianity: The Descent of the Soul in Plato and Origen," *Harvard Theological Review* 108, no. 4 (2015): 611, Henri Crouzel, *Théologie de l'image de Dieu chez Origène* (Paris: Aubier, 1956), 148–53.

25. Most recently, Blosser, *Become Like the Angels*, 176–80 and Ilaria Ramelli, "Evagrius and Gregory: Nazianzen or Nyssen? A Remarkable Issue that Bears on the Cappadocian (and Origenian) Influence on Evagrius." *Greek, Roman and Byzantine Studies* 53 (2013): 117–37. See also Lambert Lies,

mind. Several passages demonstrate that in his later work, "bare souls" are in fact possible.

Most of the scholarly debate has centered on Origen's protology: the status of rational souls before their descent into various bodies. As we shall see later, Origen does once employ the doctrine of preexistence in the new homilies to solve an exegetical difficulty;[26] that passage, however, does not directly address the problem of "bare souls." For this, we must consider another piece of salvation history: the harrowing of Hades.

In *HPs15.2* sec. 8, Origen comments on Ps 15:9c, "and even my flesh will dwell in hope." Origen explains that Christ's ascension to heaven was quite unlike what happened to Elijah and Enoch, because Christ ascended into heaven with his flesh intact. In a passage full of lovely rhetorical flourishes, he imagines the astonishment of the angelic host as they behold the Christ ascending, still bearing his body with its scars and wounds. Origen then discusses Christ's prior descent into hell:

> Only his soul descended to Hades, a place where there were only souls. If it were the case that here too there were only souls and that living creatures here were not composite beings, then he would not have come here as a composite being. This is why those people are wrong who say that the Savior did not come as a composite, but that he took on a body like (ὅμοιον) his essence that surpasses Logos, or better still, a body the same as the nature of the Logos, and that his soul was the same in essence as the Logos. These people reject the loving-kindness of the one who after clothing himself as a composite human said, "My flesh will dwell in hope, you will not forsake my soul to Hades." So then, where there were bare souls, he went as a soul alone, and where the living creatures were composite, he went as a composite creature with soul.[27]

___

"Origenes Und Reinkarnation," *Zeitschrift Für Katholische Theologie* 121, no. 2 (1999): 139–58. In private correspondence, Blosser has stated that his position should be taken to refer to *princ.* only, and that he is open to the idea that Origen subsequently changed his mind.

26. See Ramelli, "Preexistence and Recollection," 117–37.

27. *HPs15.2* sec. 8. Μόνη ἡ ψυχὴ εἰς ᾅδου καταβέβηκεν, ὅπου μόνον ψυχαὶ ἦσαν. Εἰ καὶ ἐνθάδε ψυχαὶ μόνον ἦσαν καὶ μὴ ἦν τὸ ζῷον σύνθετον, οὐκ ἂν ἐληλύθει ἐνθάδε σύνθετος. Ὅθεν πλανῶνται οἱ λέγοντες ὅτι οὐ σύνθετος ὁ σωτὴρ ἐπιδεδήμηκεν, ἀλλὰ ἀναλαβὼν σῶμα ὅμοιον τῇ ὑπερεχούσῃ τοῦ αὐτοῦ λόγου οὐσίᾳ, μᾶλλον δὲ ταὐτὸν τῇ οὐσίᾳ τοῦ λόγου, καὶ ὅτι ἡ ψυχὴ ταὐτὴ τῇ οὐσίᾳ τοῦ λόγου ἦν. Οὗτοι δὴ ἀθετοῦσι τὴν χρηστότητα αὐτοῦ ἐνδυσαμένου τὸν σύνθετον ἄνθρωπον * λέγοντος· ἡ σάρξ μου κατασκηνώσει ἐπ᾽ ἐλπίδι, οὐκ ἐγκαταλείψεις τὴν ψυχήν μου εἰς τὸν ᾅδην. Ὅπου οὖν **γυμναὶ ψυχαὶ ἦσαν, ψυχὴ μόνη καταβέβηκεν·** ὅπου οὖν σύνθετον τὸ ζῷον ἦν, ὁ σύνθετος ἦλθε μετὰ ψυχῆς.

*I have removed a καί supplied by Perrone, and I suspect that the final clause should read, ὁ σύνθετος ἦλθε μετὰ ψυχῆς <καὶ σώματος>.

The distinction is clear: souls in Hades are "bare" because they lack a body, while human beings on earth are composite, since they have both a body and soul. Jesus descended as a bare soul to Hades because Hades is a place where souls exist in a bodiless manner. This position is consistent with other later works of Origen. The Alexandrian notes in *dial.* 7 that at Jesus' death, his spirit is deposited with the Father, his body stays in the tomb, and his soul descends to Hades. In *Cels.* 2.43, Jesus becomes a bare soul after his death and converses with bare souls in Hades.[28]

How do we adjudicate the disjunction between the "bare souls" of Origen's later work and *princ.* 2.1.1–2, where only the trinity is fully incorporeal? There are two possibilities: either Rufinus indulged in substantial doctrinal redaction, or Origen changed his mind. The first is rather unlikely. Rufinus did make small additions in his translation and would sometimes skip over passages he deemed interpolated.[29] For example, in *HPs 36.4* sec. 1, he takes what is in Greek an implicitly trinitarian statement and makes it explicit in the Latin.[30] As such, he may well be responsible for the line in *princ.* that states, "the only truly incorporeal life is that of the Trinity."[31] And yet, even if Rufinus has inserted a line about the trinity, he has only made explicit what is implied by the rest of the argument, namely that created souls must be joined to bodies of some type. Rufinus, so far as we can tell, may amplify, modify, or excise bits of Origen to serve the needs of his audience, but he does not create complicated philosophical arguments and foist them back onto Origen.[32] The simplest explanation is that Origen held to the necessity of the body for created souls when he was writing *princ.*, but had abandoned this position by the time

28. It is noteworthy that *Cels.* 2.43 has suffered intentional scribal editing. The portion of text that explains how Christ descended to Hades as a bare soul is absent from the primary manuscript of *Cels.*, *Vat.gr.* 386. It has been restored from the Tura Papyrus (Cairo N° 88747). For the edition of the papyrus, see Origen, *Extraits des Livres I et II du Contre Celse d'Origène, d'après la papyrus no 88747 du Musée du Caire, par Jean Scherer*, ed. Jean Scherer (Cairo : Imprimerie de l'Institut français d'archéologie orientale, 1956). For the relationship of the papyrus to the mss tradition, see Origen, *Contra Celsum: Libri VIII*, ed. Miroslav Marcovich (Leiden: Brill, 2001), XII–XIII. I suspect that something similar occurred at in *HPs* 73 sec. 1.

29. See his discussion in his preface to *Princ.*, sec. 3.

30. *HPs 36.4*, 1. Compare Origen's Greek and Rufinus' Latin: Τί δ' ἂν εἴη τὸ μέγα ὅραμα ἢ ὁ καθαρᾷ καρδίᾳ βλεπόμενος θεός; Τί δ' ἂν εἴη τὸ μέγα ὅραμα ἢ ἡ σοφία καὶ ὁ λόγος τοῦ θεοῦ, ὁ Χριστὸς αὐτοῦ, ὃν οὐδεὶς δύναται γινώσκειν, ἐὰν μὴ ὁ πατὴρ αὐτῷ ἀποκαλύψῃ; Τί δ' ἂν εἴη τὸ μέγα ὅραμα ἢ τὸ πνεῦμα τὸ ἅγιον;

Magna ergo est uisio, cum puro corde Deus uidetur. Magna est uisio cum puro corde uerbum Dei et sapientia Dei qui est Christus eius agnoscitur. Magna uisio est agnoscere et credere in Spiritum sanctum. **Magna ergo haec uisio scientia Trinitatis est.**

31. *solius namque trinitatis incorporea uita existere recte putabitur. princ.* 2.1.2.

32. See Prinzivalli's sage analysis on Rufinus as translator, Origen, *Die neuen Psalmenhomilien*, 35–57.

he wrote *dial.*, *Cels.*, and the *HPs*. That Origen would change his mind on certain points of detail should not be surprising, for Crouzel is right to characterize his work *théologie en recherche*. Origen sets forth a number of philosophical positions in *princ.* that he thinks true, but repeatedly acknowledges they are only hypotheses. This is true even of positions like the preexistence of the soul, which he maintains continuously over the course of his career.

Teasing out the implications for protology and eschatology is rather more difficult. In his later work, does he think that the soul is disembodied before birth in this world? Origen refers in passing to preexisting souls in *HPs15.2*. He argues that exalted statements in scripture that refer to Christ may be taken as referring either to the *Logos*, or to his "soul before the body."[33] Conceivably Origen could still think that preexistent souls have an ethereal body of some sort. We would then imagine "before the body" is shorthand for "before his earthly body." To adopt such a position, however, would take Origen rather close to Platonic metempsychosis, which he eschews repeatedly.[34] The most straightforward reading is again the likeliest: prior to birth, the soul is not yet embodied.

The key passages for eschatology are *HPs15.2* sec. 8 and *HPs80.2* sec. 2. In the former, Origen describes the ascension of Christ to heaven. Origen explains how the angelic host are utterly astonished at the sight of Christ rising to heaven, for he comes still bearing his flesh, with wounds and scars still visible. The angels have never before seen flesh ascending to heaven[35] and are astonished at this new development in history.[36] In *HPs81.1* sec. 1, Origen comments on Ps. 81:1, "God stands in the assembly of the gods, in their midst he judges the gods."[37] He explains that the perfected human being is divinized by God's gift. This divinization is not simply of the soul or the spirit, but of the entire human being:

---

33. *HPs15.2* sec. 2. νόει αὐτοῦ τὴν θεότητα, εἴτε κατὰ τὸν πρωτότοκον πάσης κτίσεως, εἴτε κατὰ τὴν πρὸ τοῦ σώματος ψυχὴν αὐτοῦ.

34. See Blosser, *Become*, 159. Lothar Lies argues that though Origen rejects metempsychosis, the Alexandrian nevertheless holds to a certain transformation of the body that is in some way analogous: see Lies, "Origenes," 256–57. Yet this does not offer a satisfying interpretation of crucifixion, descent, resurrection, and ascension. We would then have to suppose that the body Christ leaves in the tomb becomes "not his body."

35. *HPs15.2* sec. 8. ὥστε ξενίζεσθαι τοὺς οὐρανίους δυνάμεις μηδέποτε ἑωρακυίας τοῦτο τὸ θέαμα· σάρκα ἀναβαίνουσαν εἰς τὸν οὐρανόν.

36. *HPs15.2* sec. 8. Ξενίζονται γοῦν αἱ δυνάμεις ἐπὶ τῇ καινῇ ἱστορίᾳ, ὅτι βλέπουσι σάρκα ἀναβεβηκυῖαν εἰς οὐρανόν.

37. *HPs81.1* sec. 1. Ὁ θεὸς ἔστη ἐν συναγωγῇ θεῶν, / ἐν μέσῳ δὲ θεοὺς διακρίνει.

It is no great marvel that he divinizes our spirit, since it has a certain familial relationship with God, and since "the imperishable spirit resides in all." It is, however, remarkable that the soul is divinized in such a way that it no longer sins and perishes, for 'the soul that sins, this one will die.' What is most astonishing of all is that he also divinizes the body in such a way that it is no longer flesh and blood, but becomes 'conformed to the glorious body of Christ Jesus.' Once it is divinized, it is taken up in glory to heaven in accordance with the passage, "we shall be snatched up in the clouds to meet the Lord in the air and will be so with the Lord for ever." Having become Gods, we will in this manner dwell forever with Jesus Christ our God standing in the assembly of the gods.[38]

These passages suggest that Origen's eschatological vision has changed somewhat since *princ.* There Origen holds to the principle that the end must resemble the beginning.[39] This, in fact, seems to be the major reason for why in *princ.* Origen supposes that souls must be necessarily embodied throughout their existence, because the resurrection of the body is a key component of the rule of faith. Though Origen nowhere explicitly rejects this principle, there are indications that his views have changed somewhat. It is plain that at the eschaton he foresees the glorification of the entire human, body, soul, and spirit. These divinized human bodies will resemble Jesus' glorified body, and like his, they will be taken up into heaven. There, divinized humanity will reside forever with Christ. There is no suggestion here of a subsequent obliteration of materiality, when God becomes "all in all." Instead, Origen states in *HPs81.1* sec. 1 that glorified humanity will dwell forever (πάντοτε) in a divinized embodied state alongside Christ.

On the other hand, one should not exaggerate the discontinuity with *princ.* As in *princ.* 3.6.6, the entire person is divinized and resides with Christ in heaven, in a deified "spiritual" body. I see no reason to suppose, in *princ.* or later, that Origen imagines a complete assumption of the human being into the divine nature such that the personality is obliterated. It is reasonably clear in both *princ.* 3.6.6 and in *HPs81.1* sec. 1 that the divinized human body, soul,

38. *HPs81.1* sec. 1. Καὶ οὐ θαῦμα μὲν εἰ τὸ ἐν ἡμῖν πνεῦμα ἐθεοποίησεν, συγγένειαν ἔχον πρὸς θεόν, ἐπεὶ καὶ τὸ ἄφθαρτον πνεῦμά ἐστιν ἐν πᾶσι· θαῦμα δὲ τὸ τὴν ψυχὴν τεθεοποιεῖσθαι, ἵνα μηκέτι ἁμαρτάνῃ, μηκέτι ἀποθνήσκουσα· ψυχὴ γὰρ ἡ ἁμαρτάνουσα αὕτη ἀποθανεῖται. Τὸ δὲ τούτων πάντων θαυμασιώτερον, ὅτι καὶ τὸ σῶμα ἐθεοποίησεν, ἵνα μηκέτι σὰρξ καὶ αἷμα ᾖ, ἀλλὰ γένηται σύμμορφον τῷ σώματι τῆς δόξης Χριστοῦ Ἰησοῦ καὶ θεοποιηθὲν ἀναληφθῇ ἐν δόξῃ εἰς οὐρανόν, κατὰ τὸ εἰρημένον ἁρπαγησόμεθα ἐν νεφέλαις εἰς ἀπάντησιν τοῦ κυρίου εἰς ἀέρα καὶ οὕτω πάντοτε σὺν κυρίῳ ἐσόμεθα, γενόμενοι θεοί, μετὰ ἱσταμένου θεοῦ ἐν μέσῳ τῆς συναγωγῆς ἡμῶν, Ἰησοῦ Χριστοῦ.

39. *princ.* 1.5.2. *Semper enim similis est finis initiis.* For lucid description of this principle, see Joseph W. Trigg, *Origen of Alexandria* (Abingdon: Routledge, 1998), 27–30.

and spirit are the final destiny of the human person.[40] Union with Christ is not narrated by Origen as an obliteration of the personality, but as a complete alignment of the mind, soul, and body with God.[41] Christology provides a clue for the ultimate human destiny. In *HPs15.2* sec. 3, Origen explains that the human soul of Jesus has been so united to the *Logos* that one may no longer speak of two subjects:

> The human soul of Jesus says the phrase, "I would behold the Lord before me." What is the nature of this Lord? Does he mean the Father, or the Firstborn of All Creation, who was always present to his soul? And what do I mean by "present"? I mean "united," such that the human being and the Firstborn of All Creation were no longer separate subjects.[42]

Origen anticipates the controversy that will arise and continues,

> If you take offense at this union, heed the apostle's words, which will console you and heal your offense: "The one who is joined to the Lord is no longer two, but one spirit." (1 Cor 6:17) Since "the one who is joined to the Lord is one spirit," surely you are willing to grant that Jesus' sinless soul, which willingly descended and did not consider equality with God as something to be exploited, has become one spirit and been made one with the Firstborn of All Creation?[43]

This union does not obliterate Christ's human soul, but it does result in a unified subject. Origen likely has something similar in mind for humanity more broadly, since humans are, after all, the body of Christ.[44]

---

40. *Princ.* 3.6.6. "Moreover, we are obliged to hold that we will abide forever and unchangeably in this state (sc. a glorified human body) by the will of the Creator. (*In quo statu etiam permanere semper et immutabiliter creatoris voluntate credendum est.*

41. See for example *princ.* 3.6.3, where being one with God means that one thinks of nothing but God.

42. *HPs15.2* sec. 3. Ἡ ἀνθρωπίνη λέγει ψυχὴ Ἰησοῦ τὸ *προωρώμην τὸν κύριον ἐνώπιόν μου*. Ποῖον κύριον; ἀρά γε τὸν πατέρα λέγει ἢ τὸν πρωτότοκον πάσης τῆς κτίσεως ἀεὶ αὐτῇ παρόντα; **Τί δὲ λέγω "παρόντα"; ἡνωμένον, ἵνα μηκέτι ἄλλος ἢ ἄνθρωπος καὶ ἄλλος ὁ πρωτότοκος πάσης κτίσεως.**

43. *HPs15.2* sec. 3. Ἐὰν προσκόψῃς περὶ τοῦ ἡνωμένου, ἄκουε παραμυθίαν θεραπεύουσάν σου τὴν προσκοπὴν καὶ παραμυθίαν ἀποστολικήν· ὁ κολλώμενος τῷ κυρίῳ οὐκέτι ἐστὶ δύο, ἀλλὰ ἓν πνεῦμά ἐστιν. Εἶτα ὁ μὲν κολλώμενος τῷ κυρίῳ ἓν πνεῦμά ἐστιν, οὐ θέλεις δὲ τὴν μὴ ἁμαρτάνουσαν ψυχήν, τὴν ἑκουσίως καταβᾶσαν, τὴν μὴ ἁρπαγμὸν ἡγησαμένην τὸ εἶναι ἴσα θεῷ, ἓν πνεῦμα γεγονέναι καὶ ἓν γεγονέναι πρὸς τὸν πρωτότοκον πάσης κτίσεως; Προωρώμην οὖν τὸν κύριόν μου, ἐπεὶ ἐπαίδευσάν με οἱ νεφροί μου ἕως νυκτός.

44. Such lines of reasoning probably lie behind the later so-called *isochrists*, for whom see, E. M. Harding, "Origenist Controversies," in *The Westminster Handbook to Origen*, ed. John A. McGuckin (Louisville, KY: Westminster John Knox, 2004). The 13th Anti-Origenist Canon of 553 condemns those who maintained that in the eschaton all rational creatures would not differ in substance (οὐσία), knowledge (γνῶσις), potential (δύναμις), or activity (ἐνέργεια) from Christ. That is, all rational creatures would enjoy the same union with the divine *logos* as the human soul of Christ. This is probably close to Origen's teaching. If the canons may be trusted, however, they also believed in an incorporeal

The Soul's Preexistence

Though it is generally acknowledged as a feature of Origen's system, a number of recent scholars have rejected that Origen believed in the soul's preexistence, among whom are John Behr in the introduction to his recent translation of *princ*.[45] The homilies contradict this revisionary account, however, and thus it is worth examining them in some detail, especially *HPs15.2*. Here, Origen is confronted with the verse "I will praise the Lord who instructed me; even in the night, my kidneys taught me." The citations of this psalm in the New Testament establish it as a Christological psalm, and thus Origen must explain not only how Christ could be instructed but also the role of his kidneys in instruction. Origen's explication makes it clear throughout his career that he maintained a belief in the preexistence of the soul.

Christ's receiving teaching is simpler for Origen to explain. He observes that some statements about Christ in the scripture refer to his humanity, and some to his divinity. The picture is rather more complicated for Origen than for later exegetes, because Origen maintains that Christ's human soul preexisted his body. Thus, statements about his divinity may refer either to the "Firstborn of All Creation," or to "his soul before its body."[46]

Origen then must explain how kidneys play a role in Christ's instruction. He posits "kidneys of the soul" that have a function analogous to bodily kidneys. These soul-kidneys contain "concepts and the seeds of reasoning in potential before they rise to the heart."[47] He then asks us to consider the soul of Jesus before its incarnation, and to see how it "stores up within itself teachings and concepts (δόγματα καὶ νοήματα) and places them not in the heart, but in the kidneys." The soul of Jesus comes possessing in the kidneys of his soul things that "teach and direct him" (τὰ παιδεύοντα καὶ τὰ ἐπιστρέφοντα). Because Jesus entered the world with these things "stored in his soul-kidneys," he was able to live a sinless life. Preexistence also allows Origen to explain the

---

consummation in which individual natures were absorbed into divinity (canons 2, 14). Origen discusses this possibility in *princ.*, but never adopts it himself.

45. John Behr, *Origen: On First Principles* (Oxford: Oxford University Press, 2018), lxxxii. See also Mark J. Edwards, *Origen Against Plato* (Aldershot: Ashgate, 2002), 89–97 and Ramelli, "Evagrius and Gregory."

46. *HPs15.2*. καὶ τοιαῦτα περὶ αὐτοῦ δοξολογούμενα, νόει αὐτοῦ τὴν θεότητα, εἴτε κατὰ τὸν πρωτότοκον πάσης κτίσεως, εἴτε κατὰ τὴν πρὸ τοῦ σώματς ψυχὴν αὐτοῦ. Note, I have emended the punctuation of the edition.

47. *HPs15.2* sec. 3. τὰ πρὸ τοῦ ἀνατεῖλαι ἐπὶ τὴν καρδίαν νοήματα καὶ διαλογισμῶν σπέρματα, τὰ ἔνδον προόντα δυνάμει.

puzzling bit, "even in the night." He takes the night to be a symbol of life here on earth, paraphrasing the passage so:

> Therefore, he says, "*even in the night* my kidneys taught me," as if to say, "they were not just teaching and reminding me then about what I ought to do, but my kidneys would teach me even after my coming into the night of this age, after coming into this darkness."[48]

Origen thus explains that Christ came into the world with the "raw material" of ideas and teaching in potential within his soul. These would become actualized later and prevent him from sinning. A bit later Origen connects Christ's preexistence to humanity at large:

> For we also, after tending like a farmer to the seeds of the good we bore, came [sc. into this world] possessing certain principles of good, and these seeds that we have are said to be in our kidneys.[49]

Though not as explicit as he might be, Origen refers here to the preexistence of human souls. Our "coming" is described like Christ's coming (ἔρχομαι in the aorist in both instances). Moreover, the aorist participle γεωργήσαντες implies that we had "tended" to the seeds of good before our arrival in this world. How does this work out in the development of a child? Origen supposes that the law of God (i.e. moral principles) is not yet written on the heart when one is a child. Yet when one reaches an age where one can receive the law of God, it is inscribed on the heart by the Holy Spirit, using "seeds that had preexisted in the so-called kidneys."[50] The Spirit thus "reminds" the soul of dormant moral teachings and activates them. Blosser and Martens are thus both right to affirm Origen's belief in preexistence of the soul.[51]

Recollection

Origen's position on recollection has been more controversial. Von Stritzky has rightly affirmed that Origen held the doctrine, though she argues that it no longer carried the same epistemological weight in Origen's system that

---

48. *HPs15.2* sec. 3. Φησὶν οὖν ὅτι καὶ ἕως νυκτὸς ἐπαίδευσάν με οἱ νεφροί μου· οὐ μόνον καὶ <τότε> τὰ δέοντά με ἐπαίδευον καὶ ὑπεμίμνησκον, ἀλλὰ καὶ ἐλθόντα ἐπὶ τὴν νύκτα τοῦ αἰῶνος τούτου, ἐπὶ τὸν σκότον, ἐπαίδευσάν με οἱ νεφροί μου. Emphasis my own; I have supplied the τότε.

49. *HPs15.2* sec. 4. Ἤλθομεν γὰρ καὶ ἡμεῖς ἔχοντες τινὰς ἐν τοῖς νεφροῖς ἀγαθῶν ἀρχας [καὶ] γεωργήσαντες τὰ τῶν ἀγαγθῶν ὧν ἠνέγκαμεν σπέρματα, καὶ ταῦτα ἃ ἔχομεν, ἐν τοῖς νεφροῖς λέγεται.

50. *HPs15.2* sec. 5. προϋποκειμένων σπερμάτων ἐν τοῖς λεγομένοις νέφροις.

51. Blosser, *Become*, 160ff; Martens, "Embodiment," 594–620.

it did in Plato's.[52] Crouzel was considerably more skeptical, arguing that neither of the principal passages in Origen that deal with recollection (*Or.* 21 and *CJn* 20.51–53) require a doctrine of recollection.[53] Blosser does not completely follow Crouzel, but remarks that Origen's lack of interest in recollection is noteworthy.[54] Here, I would like to build upon an important observation made by Somos, who suggested that Origen's use of the stoic terminology of common conceptions (κοιναὶ ἔννοιαι) should be placed within a Platonic framework.[55] I argue that though Origen only rarely uses Platonic terminology for recollection, it is precisely a Platonic system that lies behind his much more common Stoic language. This suggests that recollection is more significant for Origen than it would first seem.

In *HPs15.2* sec. 3, Origen states that the soul of Jesus contains "ideas and seeds of reasonings in potential" that "instruct and direct" the incarnate Jesus.[56] The link with memory is made explicit when Origen restates the point a bit later, this time using ὑπομιμνῄσκω ("to remind") instead of ἐπιστρέφω ("to turn back or direct"): "Indeed, he [sc. Jesus] came having in his kidneys things that instructed and reminded him."[57] Jesus' soul has these principles not simply because they have been implanted by God, but because the soul has actively stored up for itself 'teachings and concepts' (δόγματα καί νοήματα) in its soul-kidneys before descending to the body.

"Look at how it stores up within itself teachings and concepts, and puts them not in the heart, but in the kidneys.[58] As Somos states, this passage is clearly of great importance for Origen's epistemology.[59] I would like to take this somewhat further, however, than Somos did, for Platonic recollection does not figure in his discussion of *HPs15.2* sec. 3. His reframing of

52. M. B. Von Stritzky, "Die Bedeutung der Phaidrosinterpretation für die Apokatastasislehre des Origenes," *Vigiliae Christianae* 31, no. 4 (1977): 287.

53. Henri Crouzel, "Idées Platoniciennes et Raisons Stoïciennes Dans La Théologie d'Origène," *Studia Patristica* 18, no. 3 (1989): 379–80.

54. Blosser, *Become*, 160.

55. Róbert Somos, "The Question of Innate Ideas in Origen," in *Origeniana Undecima: Origen and Origenism in the History of Western Thought*, ed. Anders-Christian Jacobsen (Leuven, Peeters, 2016), 862n20. He points to an important passage in Alcinous' *Didaskalikon* 4, in which the intellection (νόησις) of preexistent souls is contrasted with the intellection of embodied souls, which Alcinous calls "common conception" (φυχικὴ ἔννοια).

56. *HPs15.2* sec. 3. ὅρα μοι τὴν ψυχὴν Ἰησοῦ ἐρχομένην, ἐπὶ τῶν οὐ σωματικῶν νεφρῶν ἔχουσαν τὰ παιδεύοντα καὶ τὰ ἐπιστρέφοντα.

57. *HPs15.2* sec. 3. Καὶ ἦλθεν ἔχων ἐπὶ τῶν νεφρῶν δὴ τὰ παιδεύοντα αὐτὸν καὶ ὑπομιμνήσκοντα αὐτόν.

58. *HPs15.2* sec. 3. νοῶν μοι ταύτην τὴν ψυχήν, ὅρα αὐτὴν ἐναποθησαυρίζουσαν δόγματα καὶ νοήματα, καὶ ἐναποτιθεῖσαν οὐ τῇ καρδίᾳ ἀλλὰ τοῖς νεφροῖς.

59. Somos, "The Question," 869.

κοιναὶ ἔννοιαι within a Platonic framework, however, is quite important for our understanding of Origen's epistemology. Though Origen does not use the technical term κοιναὶ ἔννοιαι in the homily, he does adopt Stoic language, particularly seed language, to describe a largely Platonic scheme of recollection. Indeed, his expression, "seeds of ideas and thoughts," should probably be understood as a non-technical expression for κοιναὶ ἔννοιαι. Though Origen does not frequently speak openly of recollection, he does use the language of Stoic common conceptions quite often, and he is certainly fond of plant metaphors for mental life.[60] Not only does *HPs15.2* sec. 2–5 demonstrate that Origen continued to hold to a doctrine of recollection late in his life, but his terminology suggests that this doctrine is more important for Origen than previously recognized, for even those who have recognized that Origen held the doctrine, like Von Strizky, argued that the doctrine does not carry the same epistemological weight for Origen as it does for Plato.[61]

The Soul's Faculties and Parts

We now turn to the soul's faculties or parts. Origen treats the problem most extensively in *princ.* 3.4, where he gives three options for understanding the divisions within the soul: there are two distinct souls; the soul is simple; the soul consists of three parts. Scholars have understood Origen's presentation of the parts in a variety of ways. Schnitzer maintained that Origen had shown the absurdity of the two-soul theory and thus held to the unity of the soul.[62] Crouzel and Simonetti disagree, arguing that Origen actually held to a synthesis of the two views, where a unified soul is torn between two opposing tendencies, a vital principle that pulls it toward the body, and a principle of reason that pulls it toward the spirit.[63] Blosser goes still further and argues that a certain version of two souls doctrine characterizes Origen's views best.[64] It seems most likely to me that Origen consistently holds to a

---

60. *v.* Somos, "The Question," 862 and Origen, *Homilies on Genesis and Exodus*, trans. Ronald E. Heine. Fathers of the Church 71 (Washington, DC: The Catholic University of America Press, 1982), 8–12.

61. See above, note 56.

62. K. F. Schnitzer, trans., *Origenes über die Grundlehren der Glaubenswissenschaft* (Stuttgart: Imle und Krauss, 1835), 227n1.

63. Henri Crouzel and Manlio Simonetti, *Traité des principes. Livres 3 et 4, Commentaire et fragments 4*. Source Chrétiennes 269 (Paris: Cerf, 1980), 97–98n42.

64. "It seems, in conclusion, that the 'hierarchical' model of two souls does characterize Origen's thinking on the soul, although with the caution that he conceives this duality in a thoroughly Christian framework." Blosser, *Become*, 76.

simple soul, but incorporates elements from bipartition and tripartition in his system.

Despite Crouzel and Simonetti's warnings not to attribute one position to Origen,[65] Schnitzer probably has the best of it. Origen explains the two-souls theory at such length because it is popular and needs a full examination, not, as Blosser contends, because Origen ultimately finds it persuasive.[66] Parallels to other passages in *princ.*, or indeed, in later work, do not demonstrate that Origen held this view.[67] Crouzel and Simonetti are right to note that Origen's own view is a synthesis of the views laid out in the chapter, though here I would also say things a bit differently. We ought not to speak of a synthesis of two antitheses,[68] but rather of the incorporation of some aspects of bipartition and even tripartition, into a theory of simple soul. For instance, the basic continuum of *psyché-nous*, stressed by both Blosser and Crouzel-Simonetti, is set forth precisely in this final section on simple soul.[69]

How is this carried forward in the later work? Origen continues to hold

65. Crouzel and Simonetti, *Traité*, 97–98n42.

66. See Blosser, *Become*, 72. Origen, however, states that he has devoted so much time to the two-souls theory, "so that we may not be thought ignorant of these arguments that are often stirred up by those who investigate whether there is another soul besides the rational and heavenly soul." (…*uti ne latere nos putarentur ea, quae moueri solent ab his, qui quaerunt, utrum sit alia anima in nobis praeter hanc caelestem et rationabilem, quae etiam huic naturaliter aduersetur et uocetur uel caro uel sapientia carnis uel anima carnis princ* 3.4.3.).

"Stirred up" (Rufinus' *moueri* presumably translates the Greek κινέω) carries a negative connotation.

67. In addition to *princ.* 3.4.2, Blosser adduces *princ.* 2.8.1 to argue that Origen holds to a two-soul theory, at least in some form. There Origen cites Lev. 17:14 to show that all animals possess a vital soul, which is the same interpretation the two-soul proponents apply to humans in *princ.* 3.4.2. This interpretation is quite different from *dial.* 10–12, where Origen denies outright that the soul is the blood. Blosser resolves the contradiction with *dial.* 10–12 by noting that in *dial.* 10–12, Origen deals not with the vital principle, but with the mind (i.e. the "higher" soul). This does not quite work, however. In *dial.*, Origen is given free-reign to explain the meaning of Lev. 17:14. If he wished to put forth a two-souls doctrine, he could have, but instead chose to employ his body-part/soul-faculty parallel for his explanation. I would argue instead argue that *princ.* 2.8.1 deals with irrational souls, not rational ones, and so Origen's embrace of a "two-souls" theory is only apparent, not real. It is only in animals that Origen posits a material vital soul.

Crouzel and Simonetti point to *princ.* 2.10.7 to demonstrate that Origen posits two parts of the soul that correspond, at least in part, to the two-souls theory. The parallel is suggestive, but one should note that here we have two parts of a single soul, not two distinct entities.

68. "*En fait la doctrine des deux parties de l'âme que l'on trouve dans le reste de son oeuvre fait la synthèse des deux antithèses, dualiste et moniste, discutées dans ce chapitre*" Crouzel and Simonetti, *Traité*, 97–98n42.

69. *princ.* 3.4.5. *Quod vero inter 'carnis opera' descriptae sunt esse etiam 'haereses' et 'invidiae' et 'contentiones' vel cetera, ita accipiunt quod anima, cum crassioris sensus fuerit effecta, ex eo quod corporis sese passionibus subdit, oppressa vitiorum molibus et nihil subtile vel spiritale sentiens, caro dicitur effecta et inde nomen trahit, in quo plus studii vel propositi gerit.*

to a simple soul; he makes many of the same observations later that he does when describing the simple-soul position in *princ.* 3.4.5. The rich reflections on λογισμοί in *orat.* 8–10, for instance, reprise and develop many of the observations made in *princ.* 3.4.5. Origen also holds, throughout his career, to the notion that the soul becomes more and more fleshly by sinning, and more and more spiritual by virtuous action.[70] And yet, an explicit *psyché-nous* continuum seems to be dropped in his later work. Instead, Origen frequently speaks of both *psyché* and *nous* being present in humans. Though simple, the soul has numerous capacities (δυνάμεις), and mind (*nous*) is one of these capacities.[71] This coexistence of *nous* and *psyché* (or, more properly, the presence of *nous* within *psyché*) occurs in a wide variety of works, and not simply exegetical ones.[72] Moreover, Origen draws occasionally on St. Paul's phrase "futility of mind" to depict the *nous* as engaged in improper contemplation.[73] He even describes the divinization of the *psyché* in *HPs81.1* sec. 1 without any mention of transformation into *nous*. Origen thus seems to have abandoned this particular aspect of his theory, while retaining much of the underlying polarity of a soul torn between flesh and spirit.

Although the tripartition of the soul in *princ.* 3.4.1 receives short shrift from Origen, even this theory makes appearances in later work. However, we should understand *princ.* 3.4.1 not as an outright rejection of tripartition, but only an acknowledgment that it lacks much scriptural support.[74] The most prominent mention of tripartition is *HEz* 1.16. Here, Origen explains the four faces of Ezekiel's vision in Ez 1 as representing first the human spirit, and then the three parts of the soul: λόγος, θυμός and ἐπιθυμία. This division of the irrational part of the soul into θυμός and ἐπιθυμία occurs in other places too, even when a tripartite soul is not explicitly mentioned.[75] Origen nowhere, however, uses Plato's proposed mechanics of a tripartite soul, in which reason (λόγος) employs the spirited part (θυμός/θυμικόν/θυμοειδές) as a helper to overcome the desiring part (τὸ ἐπιθυμητικόν). Blosser is thus right to observe that

70. See, for example, *HPs77.7* sec. 2, discussed below.

71. The mind is explicitly called a faculty (δύναμις) in *HPs76.4* sec. 1.

72. For *psyché* and *nous* simultaneously present, see, for example, *orat.* 1.1, 13.3, 24.3; *cels.* 7.4; *HPs74.1* sec. 3.

73. See *HPs77.5* sec. 5.

74. Blosser states that Origen rejects the tripartite theory outright (Blosser, *Become*, 72), but *princ.* 3.4.1 states only that there is not much scriptural support for the doctrine. Paucity of scriptural support is different from outright falsehood, and this probably explains why we find Origen employing tripartite language later in practice.

75. See, for example, *HGen*, 1.17; 2.6; *HEx* 4.8; *HPs 36.2* sec. 1.

Origen's notion of tripartition is mediated through the Middle Platonists, and is not taken directly, necessarily, from Plato himself.[76] He also does not mention the tripartite division where one might expect it, for instance, when the psalmist mentions the kidneys (Plato located the desiring part of the soul near the kidneys in *Tim.* 69–71). Origen does in fact connect the kidneys with lust in *HPs37.1* sec. 6, but he does so on the basis of a medical metaphor,[77] not through recourse to a Platonic tripartite soul. He self-consciously departs from the Greek philosophical tradition in *HPs15.2* sec. 2–5, when he argues that the kidneys that instruct Christ are an intellectual faculty of his soul.[78] As such, the later works demonstrates that most elements of Origen's theory of soul-division remain constant: Origen incorporates elements of bipartition and tripartition into a simple soul. Though this soul is a single entity, it nevertheless possesses various faculties, or "parts", some of which pull it towards the spirit, and some of which pull it toward the flesh. Nowhere in the later work, however, do we see Origen reprise the theory that *psyché* is nothing but a "cooled" *nous*; this he seems to have set aside.

The Soul's "Spiritual Senses"

We now turn to Origen's so-called "spiritual senses." These figure in *HPs15.2* sec. 4, *HPs36.1* sec. 4, and *HPs76.4* sec. 1. Mark McInroy's recent treatment[79] is an important advance over the earlier work of John Dillon.[80] McInroy is

76. Blosser, *Become*, 27n34.

77. According to Hippocratic school, male seed came together in the kidneys before passing to the testes. See *Peri gonês* 1.17 (ed. Hippocrates 1840): "After the seed passes into this marrow, it arrives at the kidneys. Its road is through veins, and if the kidneys are constricted, sometimes blood forms. Then it goes from the kidneys through the testes to the genitals." (Ἐπὴν δὲ ἔλθῃ ἐς τοῦτον τὸν μυελὸν ἡ γονὴ, χωρέει παρὰ τοὺς νεφρούς· ταύτῃ γὰρ ἡ ὁδός ἐστι διὰ φλεβῶν, κἢν οἱ νεφροὶ ἑλκωθῶσιν, ἔστιν ὅτε καὶ αἷμα ξυμφέρεται· παρὰ δὲ τῶν νεφρῶν ἔρχεται διὰ τῶν ὀρχίων μεσάτων ἐς τὸ αἰδοῖον.).

For details on the Hippocratic and Galenic reproductive theories, see Michael Boylan, "Galen's Conception Theory," *Journal of the History of Biology* 19, no. 1 (1986): 47–77. For Origen's different approaches to scriptural mentions of kidneys, see Somos, "The Question," 868n44 and Perrone, "The Find of the Munich Codex: A Collection of 29 Homilies on the Psalms," in Anders-Christian Jacobsen, ed., *Origeniana Undecima. Origen and Origenism in the History of Western Thought* (Leuven: Peeters, 2016), 201–33.

78. Origen notes in *HPs15.2* sec. 3 that writings other than the scriptures do not connect kidneys with intellectual capacities.

79. Mark J. McInroy, "Origen of Alexandria," in *The Spiritual Senses: Perceiving God in Western Christianity*, ed. Paul L. Gavrilyuk and Sarah Coakley (Cambridge: Cambridge University Press, 2011), 20–35.

80. John M. Dillon, "Aisthèsis Noêtê. A Doctrine of Spiritual Senses in Origen and in Plotinus," in *Hellenica et Judaica: Hommage à Valentin Nikiprowetzky*, ed. A. Caquot, M. Hadas-Lebel, and J. Riaud (Leuven: Peeters, 1986), 443–55.

right to reject Dillon's developmental hypothesis, for he shows that Origen uses both metaphorical and analogical approaches to the spiritual senses throughout his career.[81] McInroy rightly concludes that Dillon's distinction between metaphor and analogy does not obtain for Origen. I would like to broaden the discussion by placing Origen's teaching on spiritual senses within Origen's wider theoretical framework; specifically, I contend that spiritual senses are rooted for Origen in "psychic" exegesis, the middle level in Origen's hierarchy of scriptural interpretation.[82]

Origen's doctrine of spiritual senses is one application of a broader correspondence between the inner and outer man, that is, between the body and the soul. Origen believes that bodily realities (like hands, feet, eyes, and ears) correspond by analogy to aspects or faculties of the soul. He uses this principle to explain passages that on the surface seem impossible or untrue, like Mt 5:8, where Jesus declares that the pure in heart will see God. Origen treats the principle most fully in *dial.* 15–24, where nearly every part of the human body is taken to refer to some aspect of the soul.[83] In *HPs36.1* sec. 4 the principle is even applied to clothing, for the soul "puts on the Lord Christ Jesus."[84] Origen appeals to this principle often, in both earlier and later works. For example, compare *princ.* 1.1.9 with *HPs15.2* sec. 5:

"For often the names of perceptible members are used for the soul, such that the soul is said to see with the eyes of the heart."[85]

81. Dillon argues that Origen moved from a metaphorical approach to spiritual senses in his early work to an analogical approach in his later work. In a metaphorical approach, the senses are taken altogether as a comparand for intellection. In an analogical approach, each sense is applied individually to the mind's grasp of intellectual realities. See McInroy, "Origen," 22–23.

We may add further passages from the *HPs* to those adduced by McInroy. For passages where the senses are compared collectively to intellection, see *HPs36.1* sec. 4 and *HPs76.4* sec. 1. For those which consider multiple senses individually, see *HPs15.2* sec. 4.

82. In *princ.* 4.2–3, Origen sets out an exegetical approach in which any text of scripture may have bodily, psychic, or pneumatic interpretations. The bodily sense is an edifying "literal" reading, while psychic and pneumatic interpretations are more figurative. Psychic interpretations properly deal with the individual soul, while spiritual interpretations have in view the entire community of rational creatures. Scholars have often argued that Origen fails to distinguish consistently between psychic and pneumatic interpretations but see Lauro's important rehabilitation of a distinct psychic sense: Elisabetta De Lauro, *The Soul and the Spirit of Scripture Within Origen's Exegesis* (Leiden: Brill, 2005).

83. Origen there develops the analogy in order to explain Lev. 17:14, "the soul of every living flesh is the blood."

84. *HPs 36.1* sec. 4, citing Gal. 3:27.

85. *Frequenter namque sensibilium membrorum nomina ad animam referuntur ita, ut 'oculis cordis' videre dicatur* (*princ.* 1.1.9).

Unlike other scholars (Butterworth, Crouzel/Simonetti, Schnitzer, Görgemanns/Karpp, and Behr), I understand *sensibilis* as passive ("perceptible") rather than active ("perceiving"). Either are possible

"For bodily names are often used by analogy of their bodily function for the faculties of the soul."[86]

In both passages Origen applies the same exegetical approach to explain a passage of scripture. Dillon has noted that Origen's concerns were primarily exegetical, but he does not incorporate Origen's exegetical theory into his discussion. Instead, he charged Origen with perversity:

> What must strike us about this assemblage of texts, and about the others which Origen gathers in the same cause at other passages to which we shall turn, is the extraordinarily perverse way in which he lumps together passages which are plainly allegorical or poetical with others which are plainly intended literally (e.g. 1 John 1:1, where John presumably means simply that he has touched Christ, who is the Logos)—and this from a man who is normally acutely alert to metaphor and allegory.[87]

This accusation of perversity fails to account for Origen's hierarchy of interpretation. For Origen, a given passage will have multiple valid interpretations. When Origen states that 1 Jn 1:1 means the apostle grasped the Logos with his mind, this by no means requires the exclusion of a lower somatic sense. This is nicely illustrated in *Cels.* 1.48, just after the passage cited by Dillon. Origen there explains how when Christ touches the leper in Mt. 8:3, there are two "touches." Not only does Christ cleanse the leper of his physical leprosy through a physical touch, but he also purifies the leper of spiritual leprosy (i.e. sin) through a divine or noetic touch. The purification from sin is more important, but this does not exclude the physical touch.[88]

---

construals of the Latin, but Origen's Greek is most likely something like πολλάκις γὰρ τῶν αἰσθητῶν μηλῶν τὰ ὀνόματα πρὸς τὴν ψυχὴν παραλαμβάνεται, and αἰσθητός can for Origen only bear the passive sense, not the active. For the juxtaposition of αἰσθητός with μέλος, *cf. dial.* 22: Ἐπεὶ ἔχεις ταῦτα πάντα τοῦ αἰσθητοῦ σώματος περὶ τὸν ἔσω ἄνθρωπον, μηκέτι δίσταζε καὶ περὶ τοῦ αἵματος **ὅτι ὁμωνύμως τῷ αἰσθητῷ αἵματι,** ὡς καὶ **τὰ ἄλλα μέλη τοῦ σώματος,** ἐστὶν κατὰ τὸν ἔσω ἄνθρωπον.

If Origen wanted to refer to the sense organs, he might have written μηλῶν αἰσθητικῶν, but the only attestation of αἰσθητικός in the non-fragmentary works is *CJn* 1.161, where it is clearly a mistake for αἰσθητός. Generally, Origen does not carefully distinguish sense organs from their corresponding faculties. This is seen best in his use of αἰσθητήριον, which is the *vox propria* in philosophical Greek for "sense organ." For Origen, however, it means "sense faculty" under the influence of Heb. 5:14; thus, Rufinus is right to translate it with the Latin *sensus*, as he does in *HPs 36.1* sec. 4.

86. *HPs 15.2* sec. 5. Σωματικὰ γὰρ ὀνόματα ἐπὶ τῶν δυνάμεων τῆς ψυχῆς παραλαμβάνεται κατὰ ἀναλογίαν τῶν σωματικῶν πραγμάτων.

87. Dillon, Aisthèsis Noêtê, 445.

88. Another good example of all three levels may be seen in *H76.4*. There Origen discusses Ps. 76:19, "the sound of your thunder is in the wheel." (φωνὴ τῆς βροντῆς σου ἐν τῷ τροχῷ). Origen offers to the best of his ability an appropriate somatic interpretation. The sound of the thunder is of course not physically in a wheel, but we do perceive a certain course of time elapsing at the sound of thunder. Later

Karl Rahner has also noted the exegetical roots of Origen's doctrine,[89] and does situate spiritual senses more broadly within Origen's broader theology.[90] But none of the modern treatments, his included, have placed spiritual senses within this broader inner man/outer man correspondence, nor have they made the connection to psychic exegesis. This is probably due to a misunderstanding of Origen's scheme. Though individual morality is the primary concern of psychic interpretation, a psychic account of a passage can treat any facet of an individual soul. So, in *HGen* 2.6, Origen declares in a psychic interpretation that the unclean animals on the ark, which come in "two by two," represent the two parts of the irrational soul, θυμός and ἐπιθυμία.[91] So construed, the connections in Origen's thinking become clearer. More immediately, spiritual senses are one application of a larger correspondence between the inner and outer man. This correspondence, in turn, should be viewed as a key feature in Origen's practice of psychic interpretation.

What bearing does this have on the traditional lines of debate? To use McInroy's question, "just how seriously should we take Origen's talk of 'perceiving' God?"[92] When we consider other instances of Origen's "inner-man/outer-man" correspondence, we see both that single parts of the body can refer to different faculties of the soul, and that different parts of the body can refer to one part of the soul. For example, the heart is the governing agent of the body (τὸ ἡγεμονικόν τοῦ σώματος), and as such corresponds to *hegemonikon* of the soul. Yet the eyes of the body correspond to the same faculty, this time called *nous*, for the *nous* is the "eye of the soul."[93] On the other hand, bodily kidneys normally signify the desiring part of the soul,[94] but can, as we have just seen, refer also to memory.[95] Such examples suggest that differentiation in the

---

he gives a psychic interpretation, whereby God's noetic thunder and lightning strike our souls and the "earth is shaken," that is, "our earthly members are shaken off." Finally, he offers a pneumatic interpretation in which various saints can be said to be "thunders." For further discussion on the various levels of interpretation, see Dively Lauro, *The Soul*.

89. Karl Rahner, "Le début d'une doctrine des cinq sens spirituels chez Origène," *Revue d'Ascétique et de Mystique* 13 (1932): 115, 117. "Comment Origène est-il parvenu à cette doctrine dont il nous faut préciser la signification? Autant qu'il est possible d'en juger, il n'a pas eu d'autre source que l'Ecriture Sainte" and "Une exégèse allégorique et en même temps systématique comme celle d'Origène était portée assez naturellement à tirer de ces textes une théorie des cinq sens spirituels"

90. Rahner, "Le début," 123–34.

91. Θυμός and ἐπιθυμία presumably stand behind Rufinus' *ira* and *concupiscentia*.

92. McInroy, "Origen," 22.

93. *HPs15.2* sec. 5. *Kardia, nous,* and *hegemonikon* all refer to same "highest part" of the soul for Origen.

94. v.*HPs37.1* sec. 6.

95. *HPs15.2* sec. 3–5.

perceptible realm does not necessarily imply differentiation in the realm of the soul. And yet, at least in *CJn* 20.405–406, Origen draws a sharp contrast between "seeing death" and "tasting death," and states that spiritual sight is distinct capacity (δύναμις) from spiritual taste.

For just as taste and sight are distinct corporeal senses, so with the senses called "divine" by Solomon: the visionary and contemplative faculty of the soul may be taken as distinct from the tasting faculty that receives the quality of spiritual foods.[96]

The spiritual senses refer to the different faculties at work in intellection. This passage also shows that the spiritual senses are not the sole prerogative of the righteous, as Rahner had argued.[97] In a certain manner, θεία αἴσθησις means "perception of the divine," and is probably why Origen sometimes reserves spiritual perception for the righteous.[98] But insofar as "divine perception" refers to a faculty or faculties of the soul, these are present in every rational being. As such, one can "see death" and "taste death" (i.e. the devil) just as one can "see God" and "taste God."[99] Though the result is quite different, the same faculties of the soul are used for both.

Soul, Mind, and Spirit

We now turn to the relationship between *psyché*, *nous*, and *pneuma*. After the work of Jacques Dupuis and Henri Crouzel, the scholarly consensus has been that for Origen, *nous* is the highest aspect of the soul. The *psyché* fluctuates between a higher aspect, called *nous*, *hegemonikon*, or *kardia*, and a lower aspect, called either *sarx* or φρόνημα τῆς σαρκός. The *pneuma*, by contrast, is the divine element present in the human person.[100] Earlier, Verbeke and others had argued that in Origen, *nous* and *pneuma* were equivalent.[101] Though I differ in some points of detail with Crouzel and Dupuis, their basic picture is

96. *CJn* 20.405–6. Ὥσπερ γὰρ ἐπὶ τοῦ σώματος διάφοροι αἰσθήσεις εἰσὶν γεῦσις καὶ ὅρασις, οὕτως κατὰ τὰς λεγομένας ὑπὸ τοῦ Σολομῶντος θείας αἰσθήσεις ἄλλη μέν τις ἂν εἴη <ἡ> ὁρατικὴ τῆς ψυχῆς δύναμις καὶ θεωρητική, ἄλλη δὲ ἡ γευστικὴ καὶ ἀντιληπτικὴ τῆς ποιότητος τῶν νοητῶν τροφῶν.

97. Rahner, "Le début," 119–20.

98. *e.g. Cels.* 2.72, where he explains that those who do not hear the Father's voice speaking to Jesus as "spiritually hard of hearing."

99. *v. CJn* 20.413; *HPs73.2* sec. 7.

100. Crouzel, *Théologie*, 130–33; Jacques Dupuis, *L'Esprit de l'homme: Étude sur l'anthropologie religieuse d'Origène* (Bruges: Desclée de Brouwer, 1967), 90–91. More recently, see Blosser, *Become*, 67–73 on the relationship between the higher and lower aspects of the soul, and 96–97 on the relationship between *pneuma* and *nous/psyché*.

101. Verbeke, *L'évolution de la doctrine du pneuma, du stoicisme à s. Augustin* (Paris: Desclée de Brouwer, 1945), 469. This position was later defended by Wolf-Dieter Hauschild, *Gottes Geist und der Mensch*

valid, if perhaps too tidy, for there are a number passages where their schema seems not to obtain. In some instances, the boundary between *nous* and *pneuma* is blurred. In others we have the reverse: *nous* seems to stand in for *psyché*. I will argue that Origen's apparent inconsistency is reasonably explained by two factors. The first is *homonymia*,[102] that is, the same term (*pneuma* or *nous*) can refer to different entities. The second is Origen's dynamic psychology, in which the soul may either "become spirit" by attending to virtue or "become flesh" by attending to vice.

Passages that identify Nous with Pneuma

In *HPs74.1* sec. 3, Origen explains the phrase, "this one he humbles, this one he exalts" (Ps. 74:8). After offering an historical explanation, he then gives a psychic interpretation:

Moreover, we understand this passage, "this one he humbles, and this one he exalts," also to refer to our tent here, as in the passage, "The earth has melted away, and all who dwell in it." For "this one he humbles," that is, the desire of the flesh and the flesh, since "I beat my body and make it my slave."[103] "This one he exalts," that is, the soul and the spirit. It is the opposite for sinners— their souls are humbled by sin, but its opposite [sc. the body] is exalted. The body of the righteous, however, is humbled as they fast, labor, keep vigils, and put to the death their earthly members, and their soul is exalted by being renewed "in accordance with the inner man" (Eph 3:16) and their mind is exalted "in the renewal of the mind" (Rom 12:2). God in his goodness "humbles this one and this one raises up."[104]

Origen's identification of mind and spirit is noteworthy. When he introduces the interpretation, he explains that God humbles the body and exalts

---

(Munich: Chr. Kaiser Verlag, 1972), 86–150. See also Crouzel's critique, Henri Crouzel, "Rev. Gottes Gest Und Der Mensch by Hauschild, W.D.," *Bulletin de Littérature Ecclésiastique* 77 (1976): 139–46.

102. Origen often explicitly appeals to this concept in his own exegesis. See for instance his distinction between different types of fear (*phobos*) in *HPs76.3* sec. 3.

103. 1 Cor. 9:27.

104. *HPs74.1* sec. 3: Καὶ ἐν τῇ κατασκευῇ δὲ ἡμῶν ἀκολούθως τῷ ἐτάκη ἡ γῆ, καὶ πάντες οἱ κατοικοῦντες ἐν αὐτῇ διηγησάμεθα τὸ τοῦτον ταπεινοῖ καὶ τοῦτον ὑψοῖ. Τοῦτον γὰρ ταπεινοῖ· τὸ φρόνημα τῆς σαρκὸς καὶ τὴν σάρκα· ὑπωπιάζω γὰρ τὸ σῶμα καὶ δουλαγωγῶ. Τοῦτον ὑψοῖ· τὴν ψυχὴν καὶ τὸ πνεῦμα. Τῶν μὲν γὰρ ἁμαρτωλῶν τὸ ἐναντίον ἡ ψυχὴ τεταπείνωται ὑπὸ τῆς ἁμαρτίας, τὸ δὲ ἕτερον ὕψωται. Τῶν δὲ δικαίων νηστευόντων, φιλοπονούντων, ἀγρυπνούντων, νεκρούντων τὰ μέλη τὰ ἐπὶ τῆς γῆς τὸ σῶμα τεταπείνωται, ἡ δὲ ψυχὴ ἀεὶ καινουμένη κατὰ τὸν ἔσω ἄνθρωπον, καὶ ὁ νοῦς ἐν τῇ ἀνακαινώσει τοῦ νοὸς ὑψοῦται. Ὁ θεὸς οὖν ὁ ἀγαθὸς τοῦτον ταπεινοῖ καὶ τοῦτον ὑψοῖ.

I've changed the punctuation slightly. Perrone provides no punctuation after ὕψωται, but there is a pause here in *M* (though slightly obscured), and the following δέ in τῶν δὲ δικαίων makes it clear we need a full stop. The full stop after τὰ μέλη τὰ ἐπὶ τῆς γῆς should be removed.

the soul and the spirit. Yet, when he rephrases the point, we have the body being humbled, the soul exalted by its "renewal in the inner man" and the mind "exalted in the renewal of the mind." The natural inference is that *pneuma* and *nous* refer to the same thing.

To these passages from the *HPs.* we may add a similar passage in *Cels.* 7.4, where Origen is discussing the difference between Hebrew prophets and the Delphic Pythia:

By assembling passages from the Holy Writings, we demonstrate that the prophets were illumined within by the Divine Spirit to such an extent that it allowed them to prophesy. As such, they experienced in advance the joy of the good coming to them. Because of this, so to speak, touching of their souls by the so-called Divine Spirit, they became extremely keen in their mind and soul, and even in their body, which was no longer vying against the virtuous life.[105]

As in our first passage in *HPs74.1*, we have a tripartite human consisting of *nous*, *psyché*, and *soma*. The *nous* and *psyché* are illumined by the divine Spirit (τὸ θεῖον πνεῦμα) which enables prophecy and progress in the moral life. We may also here note two passages preserved in Latin. In *CRom* 7.4.5, the Latin identifies "our spirit" (*noster spiritus*) with the mind (*mens*), and in *HGen* 1.6, the mind (*mens*) is called a *spiritus*. There was plenty of evidence, then, to support Verbeke's position that *nous* and *pneuma* were identical for Origen.

Passages where psyché and nous seem equivalent

There are, however, other passages where *nous* cannot be taken to refer to the human *pneuma*. The key passage for an "abject *nous*" is *HPs77.5* sec. 5. Here Origen uses St. Paul's phrase, "futility of mind" (ματαιότης τοῦ νοός) to explain Ps. 77:32–33 ("their days passed in futility"). He describes how time is not futile when it is spent at church, or at prayer, or in care for one's neighbor. But days are "in futility" when one becomes greedy and decides to build bigger barns, or when the soul (*psyché*) is wounded by the cares and concerns of this life. He connects this wounded soul to Eph. 4:17–18, where the gentiles are said to be "darkened in their understanding in the futility of their *nous*"[106] He elaborates so:

---

105. Origen, *Contra Celsum*. Ὅθεν ἡμεῖς ἀποδείκνυμεν συνάγοντες ἀπὸ τῶν ἱερῶν γραμμάτων ὅτι οἱ ἐν Ἰουδαίοις προφῆται, ἐλλαμπόμενοι ὑπὸ τοῦ θείου πνεύματος τοσοῦτον, ὅσον ἦν καὶ αὐτοῖς τοῖς προφητεύουσι χρήσιμον, προαπέλαυον τῆς τοῦ κρείττονος εἰς αὐτοὺς ἐπιδημίας· καὶ διὰ τῆς πρὸς τὴν ψυχὴν αὐτῶν, ἵν᾽ οὕτως ὀνομάσω, ἀφῆς τοῦ καλουμένου ἁγίου πνεύματος διορατικώτεροί τε τὸν νοῦν ἐγίνοντο καὶ τὴν ψυχὴν λαμπρότεροι ἀλλὰ καὶ τὸ σῶμα, οὐδαμῶς ἔτι ἀντιπρᾶττον τῷ κατ᾽ ἀρετὴν βίῳ.

106. *HPs77.5* sec. 5. ἐν ματαιότητι τοῦ νοός, ἐσκοτισμένοι τῇ διανοίᾳ ὄντες.

So then, it is also possible not to be "in the futility of *nous*" whenever the *nous* … pursues those things that lead to salvation. But "futility of *nous*" is when one busies oneself instead with the acquisition of wealth and increasing one's possessions. When someone doesn't contemplate how to understand the scriptures, or do good deeds … he acts in futility.[107]

Surprisingly, the *nous* is here described as an active agent in sin.[108] The moral battle of the *psyché*, so poignantly described, *e.g.* in *HPs77.8* sec. 9, is here also described, but attributed to *nous*.

HPs80.1 sec. 3–4 provides an important key for understanding this apparent identification of *nous* and *psyché*. Origen here comments on Ps. 80:3, "Take up a psalm and offer a drum, a happy harp with the kithara."[109] He understands the three different instruments as corresponding to the three aspects of a human being: body, soul, and spirit. A drum functions nicely as an image for the body, because it has a dead skin and thus may represent the "putting to death of the flesh and the desires of the flesh." After putting to death the members of the flesh, one is able to offer one's soul to God:

Then whenever sin is conquered and put to death and we can offer the drum, then we will be able to create harmony between the spirit and the soul, or, to call it what the apostle does, between the spirit and the mind, so that I can say, "I sing psalms with my spirit, and sing psalms with my mind," and so give the spirit as a harp, and my soul or mind as a lyre. For I offer them both to be joined together after the drum—a glad harp with the lyre. Now when I say "spirit," I mean the human spirit, of which Paul says, "for no one knows the thoughts of a man, except the spirit of the man within him."[110]

This passage suggests that the direct identification of soul and mind is something Origen does in some places under Pauline influence. He has to

---

107. *HPs77.5* sec. 5. Ἔστιν οὖν οὐ καὶ ἐν ματαιότητι εἶναι τοῦ νοός, ὅταν γὰρ ὁ νοῦς … ζητήσῃ τὰ πρὸς σωτηρίαν συντείνοντα· ἀλλ' ὡς πῶς ἐντρεχέστερον πραγματεύσηται περὶ τοῦ αὐξῆσαι τὸν πλοῦτον καὶ πῶς πλείονα ποιήσῃ τὰ ὑπάρχοντα, ματαιότης ἐστὶ τοῦ νοός. Ὅτε διαλογίζεταί τις οὐ πῶς νοήσει γραφήν, οὐ πῶς ἔργον ποιήσει ἀγαθόν, … ἐν ματαιότητι τὰ τοιαῦτα ποιεῖ.

108. Once translated into Latin, *vanitas mentis* could be explained through a privation argument, i.e., the issue is a lack of mind. But ματαῖος does not mean "empty" in a literal sense, only empty in the metaphorical sense. We would need something from κενός for such a privation argument to work in Greek.

109. λάβετε ψαλμὸν καὶ δότε τύμπανον, / ψαλτήριον τερπνὸν μετὰ κιθάρας.

110. *HPs80.1* sec. 3–4. Εἶθ' ὅταν νικηθῇ ἡ ἁμαρτία καὶ νεκρωθῇ, καὶ δυνηθῶμεν δοῦναι τὸ τύμπανον, τότε δυνησόμεθα συμφωνίαν ποιῆσαι τοῦ πνεύματος πρὸς τὴν ψυχὴν ἤ, ἵνα κατὰ τὸν ἀπόστολον ὀνομάσω, τοῦ πνεύματος πρὸς τὸν νοῦν, ἵνα εἴπω· ψαλῶ τῷ πνεύματι, ψαλῶ δὲ καὶ τῷ νοΐ, καὶ δῷ ψαλτήριον μὲν τὸ πνεῦμα, κιθάραν δὲ ἤτοι τὴν ψυχὴν ἢ τὸν νοῦν. Συζεύξασθαι δὲ ἀμφότερα δίδωμι μετὰ τὸ τύμπανον· ψαλτήριον τερπνὸν μετὰ κιθάρας. Πνεῦμα δὲ ἐὰν εἴπω, τὸ τοῦ ἀνθρώπου λέγω, περὶ οὗ ὁ Παῦλός φησιν· οὐδεὶς γὰρ οἶδεν τὰ τοῦ ἀνθρώπου, εἰ μὴ τὸ πνεῦμα τοῦ ἀνθρώπου τὸ ἐν αὐτῷ.

signal here the change to Pauline nomenclature—he cannot simply assume that the change from *psyché* to *nous* will be understood. Origen's picture has changed from *princ.*, for he no longer depicts the purified soul as a *nous*. Now any soul may be called a *nous*, even one thinking about sinful things.

Synthesis

Let us now bring this essay together. There are a number of reasons that make the identification of *nous* with human *pneuma* attractive. This affords a certain consistency between Origen's language of the purified soul: in *princ.* 2.8 this is narrated in terms of a transformation back into *nous*, but elsewhere this is explained as pneumatization. We have moreover seen passages in *cels.* and *HPs* where the human person is described as *nous*, *psyché* and *soma* instead of the expected *pneuma-psyché-soma*. To this we may add passages preserved in Latin that identify *mens* and *spiritus* (*HGen* 1.6, *CRom* 7.4.5). Finally, such an identification is strongly implied by *princ.* 2.10.7.

On the other hand, identifying *pneuma* with *nous* presents a number of problems, if taken univocally. The most difficult problem is that *psyché* and *pneuma* are separable for Origen. He states clearly in *dial.* 7 that Jesus deposits his human spirit with the Father before descending to Hades, and only reprises it upon the ascension. Clearly, we should not imagine an irrational *nous*-less Christ descending to Hades. Second, in *CJn* 32.218 Origen regards the human *pneuma* as impassible. Third, Origen quite clearly depicts the *nous* contemplating vice. By contrast, the human *pneuma* is also guiltless: *HPs77.6* sec. 2, among other passages, argues that the human *pneuma* returns to God during punishment and is thus not punished along with "us," who here comprise only body and soul.

Homonymia can help us in this impasse. Even if *nous* is not identical with the human *pneuma*, a *nous* certainly can be called a *pneuma*, simply by virtue of being an immaterial rational substance.[111] This is why fallen angels can be called "unclean spirits" (πνεύματα ἀκάθαρτα), or why humans can be called "those spirits that comprise the third order of rational creation."[112] This is clearly what Origen means in *HGen1.2*, when he says, "that is why the first

---

111. For the identification of pneumatic with immaterial, *v., inter alia, cels.* 6.70. This is a given for subsequent Christian thinkers, but not for Origen. *Pneuma* was highly refined, but nevertheless a material substance for the Greek philosophers of any school. Only Philo of Alexandria had posited an immaterial *pneuma*.

112. *princ.* 1.8.4. *Tertius vero creaturae rationabilis ordo est eorum spirituum...*

heaven, which we have called 'spiritual,' is our mind, which is also a spirit, that is, our spiritual man that sees and beholds God."[113]

We are still left with the problem of what Origen means when he says a person consists of "body, soul, and spirit." What is the identity of that spirit? Most frequently this refers to the human spirit proper, which Dupuis is right to characterize as a certain "transcendence" beyond the human personality. This is a part or piece, it seems, of the Holy Spirit, and it resides in all people to a greater or lesser degree.[114] But "our spirit" may sometimes refer to the mind, the highest aspect of our soul. This is not only justified by the polyvalence of the word *pneuma*, but by Origen's so-called "dynamic" anthropology, where the soul is divinized by progressively becoming more and more like God, and ultimately becomes "one spirit with Christ" (1 Cor 6:17).

Conclusion

A close reading of the homilies brings into clearer focus several key aspects of Origen's psychology. He simply expanded angelic administration from rational creatures to every aspect of the natural world. Rocks, snow, etc. do not possess their own souls, as do humans and animals, but do possess a rational guardian spirit present within. I have demonstrated on the basis of *HPs15.2* sec. 8 and *HPs73.1* sec. 1 that Origen does in fact believe that a soul can exist without a body. This represents a development from his view in *princ.* that the soul is necessarily embodied. We have also seen that Origen presumes in *HPs15.2* the preexistence of both the human soul of Christ and of humanity at large. Moreover, the delightfully strange image of "soul-kidneys" enriches our understanding of Origen's doctrine of recollection. While I have maintained here that Origen's picture of the soul is basically simple, he has nevertheless incorporated elements of bipartite and tripartite schemata into

---

113. *HGen1.2. Et ideo illud quidem primum coelum, quod spiritale diximus,* **mens nostra est, quae et ipsa spiritus est,** *id est spiritalis homo noster qui videt ac perspicit Deum.* Hauschild has cited this passage to support the identification of *nous* and *pneuma,* but it is clear that Origen is using *pneuma* here to mean 'immaterial.'

114. At *CRom 7.4.5,* the human spirit is called a "gift of the Holy Spirit imparted to people by God" (*gratiam Sancti Spiritus quae a Deo hominibus datur*). The genitive (*sancti Spiritus*) should probably be construed as objective, that is, the human spirit is a portion of the Spirit that God gives to people. Origen's teaches that this spirit has a certain συγγένεια with God (see *HPs81* sec. 1), and as such, we should locate this spirit on the "creator" side of the creator-creation dichotomy. This would also explain nicely why the human spirit is impassible for Origen. Συγγένεια is used, translated into Latin as *consanguinitas,* in *princ.* 4.4.10 to describe the virtues, which are all for Origen aspects of the Logos.

his model. This simple soul nevertheless possesses a number of faculties, most notably "spiritual senses." These I have placed within his larger exegetical framework, observing that they are a key feature "psychic" interpretation. In this instance, I have argued for continuity: Origen employs this analogy consistently, though with different emphases, from *princ.* onwards. Finally, we have seen that the relationship between *pneuma*, *nous*, *psyché*, and *soma* is more complicated in Origen's later work than it was in *princ.* The lovely depiction of the ascension in *HPs15.2* shows that Origen no longer holds that the resurrected body will be ethereal: Christ's wounds are still visible. Moreover, Christ brings flesh into heaven, something utterly unprecedented for the angelic spectators (and in Origen's earlier work too, it would seem). Dupuis and Crouzel's division between *nous* and human *pneuma* should be maintained, but I have shown that the *nous* may, on occasion, also be called a *pneuma* by virtue of its immateriality, and that Origen has probably set aside certain specifics his early theory about *nous* cooling into *psyché*.[115] In nearly all these instances, the positions taken by Origen in the new homilies can be found in some form in other late works, especially *Cels.* And yet, this new material has provided a much-needed impetus for us to reconsider what we know about this fascinating thinker. April 5, 2012 will indeed remain forever a *dies festus*, and we must extend our thanks to Lorenzo Perrone, Emanuela Prinzivalli, Antonio Cacciari, and Marina Molin Pradel for their tireless efforts in the preparation of the edition.

115. This renders more intelligible the reception of Origen's anthropology in Didymus the Blind, Evagrius of Pontus, and Gregory of Nyssa, for whom the tripartite person is primarily narrated in terms of *nous*, *psyché*, and *soma*. For the afterlife of Origen's anthropology, see Blosser, *Become*, 269–74.

6. FROM LEXIS TO LOGOS
Performing the Scriptures in Origen's
Homilies on the Psalms

It's a commonplace that early Christian interpretation of the Psalms took for granted that psalms were texts to be *performed,* texts that should live on the lips of Christians. According to Brian Daley in his introductory chapter to a 2015 volume of essays on early Christian psalm interpretation, "The psalms … do not simply command us to repent of our sins, to bear suffering patiently, or to praise God for his gifts; they actually give us the words by which we can come to say and do these things for ourselves."[1] Daley understands this performance as broadly liturgical in character, the recitation of a psalm as a literary unity, particularly in public or private prayer. (Daley, of course, is writing without the benefit of Origen's recently discovered homilies.)

For Origen, learning to perform the Psalms is not primarily a matter of liturgical performance. For one thing, his exegesis is predominantly sentence oriented. Consequently, when he describes the performance of a psalm, he tends to focus on the utterance of a single sentence, rather than the recital of the psalms as a literary whole. He also tends to focus on ways of using those sentences in a wide range of discursive contexts, rather than merely liturgical ones. I believe instead that for Origen, performing the Psalms is primarily a matter

---

1. Brian E. Daley, "Introduction" in The Harp of Prophecy: Early Christian Interpretation of the Psalms, eds. Brian E. Daley and Paul R. Kolbet (Notre Dame, IN: University of Notre Dame Press, 2015), 19.

of integrating the words of a psalm into one's own oral discourse, learning to speak its language by making its words part of one's own linguistic usage.

Scholars like Marguerite Harl, Catherine Chin, and Olivier Munnich have shown that Origen tends to approach scriptural words and sentences as samples of a coherent scriptural language. The *Homilies on the Psalms* offer a unique vantage point for examining Origen's interest in scriptural language because of the distinctive linguistic features of the psalms. Linguists distinguish between *semantic* and *pragmatic* aspects of an oral utterance. The semantic aspect is that which a sentence communicates irrespective of its context of use, such as the lexical meaning of a word. Its pragmatic aspect is that part of its function that depends on its actual use in a particular speech situation. For example, deictic terms like "I," "you," or "now" pick out a different referent each time they are uttered. When terms that function pragmatically are committed to writing, they force the interpreter to make decisions about the contexts to which one should refer the sentence. As a residue of their liturgical origin, the Psalms contain a high concentration of pragmatic linguistic devices, which, since their function is relative to their use, tend to foreground issues of linguistic performance.

I am interested in describing what we might call the logical substructure of Origen's exegetical procedures. I suggest that rather than thinking of Origen on the model of a text scholar determining the meaning or uses of a literary work, we should approach him as if he were a linguist, mapping the possible uses of a sentence. Ancient grammarians were themselves often more like linguists, particularly in their attempts to determine rules of correct Greek or Latin usage. Closer in spirit to Origen were the Stoic philosophers who, rejecting the Aristotelian account of conceptual thought as an extra-linguistic capacity, defended the older view of the wisdom traditions that rationality is displayed in *how* one uses language. Stoic logic in particular, the scientific study of λόγος, was in Michael Frede's apt formulation, "the doctrine of what somebody says who is guided by reason,"[2] that is, someone who speaks according to rational norms rather than the merely conventional norms of Greek or Latin. The Stoic project of what we might call a "rational linguistics" is, I believe, especially close to Origen's.

---

2. Michael Frede, "The Origins of Traditional Grammar" in Michael Frede, *Essays in Ancient Philosophy* (Minneapolis: University of Minnesota Press, 1987), 338–62, esp. 343.

Overview

I would like to begin by working through an illustrative example of Origen's performative exegesis. At the beginning of his second homily on Psalm 76, he interprets the words "Now I have begun" (Ps 76:11) through a rhetorical display of his own capacity to use them, an example of what Catherine Chin calls Origen's strategy of "hermeneutical exhaustion." But he is also making a kind of argument about how one ought to use them, describing a general rule governing their use and enumerating specific examples of this rule. To understand Origen's exegetical procedures is to understand the rationale for the rule of usage he commends.

The homily begins as follows:[3]

HomPs 76.2.1

Ὁ βιοὺς κατὰ θεὸν πολλάκις ἐν προοιμίοις ὢν τοῦ βίου τοῦ κατὰ θεὸν οἴεται τὴν ἀρχὴν πεποιῆσθαι τοῦ βιοῦν καθὸ χρὴ βιοῦν. ἐπὰν δὲ νοήσας τὴν διαφορὰν τοῦ προοιμίου τοῦ κατὰ θεὸν βίου γένηται μετὰ τὸ προοίμιον ἐπὶ τὴν ὁδὸν τοῦ κατὰ θεὸν βίου, ἐπιγινώσκων ὅτι πρότερον μὲν ἐδόκει ἄρχεσθαι, οὐκ ἦν δὲ ἀρξάμενος· ὕστερον δὲ ἔγνω τίς ἡ ἀρχή, φησὶ τὸ νῦν ἠρξάμην.

The one who aims to live a godly life frequently supposes that he has made a beginning of living as he ought to live, when he is only in the prelude of the godly life. But having come to understand the difference between the prelude of the godly life [and its beginning], he sets out after the prelude upon the way of the godly life, having come to recognize that though earlier he seemed to have begun, he had not [yet] begun. But later, when he knows what the beginning is, he says, "Now I have begun!"

Origen describes a type of person who has reached a new threshold in her spiritual life, in relation to which her earlier progress now seems to be merely a prelude. Under such circumstances, a person might say, "Now I have begun." He goes on to enumerate particular examples of this rule—one whose bad doctrine is corrected by good teachers; an Ebionite coming to recognize that the Law is shadows; a Jew becoming a Christian; and so on. In each case, the

---

3. In paragraphs 2–3, Origen argues that verses 11b-12 further explicate the particular conditions under which the words "now I will begin" are uttered. In paragraph 2, for example, Origen asks *why* one should say "now I will begin," and finds the answer in v. 11b: when one understands "the changing of the right hand of the highest." Origen takes this as a reference to the Incarnation. In paragraph 3, Origen further specifies *when* one should say, "now I will begin," and finds the answer in verse 12: when one remembers the works of the Lord and his wonders from the beginning. Since these works are written in scripture, Origen takes this as a reference to a new grasp of scripture's teaching.

person might say, "Now I have begun." While Origen does not explain what, if anything, puzzles him about these words, we might speculate that he is responding to the fact that they occur in the *middle* of the psalm, after many professions of piety that would seem to indicate that the psalmist has *already* begun.[4] The rule Origen proposes is intelligible as an answer to the question, how can someone say "now I have begun" if he is already in the middle?

After offering these hypothetical examples, Origen adds that some Christians in fact already speak according to this rule.

ἐγὼ πολλάκις ἤκουσα ὁμολογούντων πιστῶν πλείονα χρόνον ἐν τῇ πίστει πεποιηκότων καὶ μεμαθηκότων τὰ τῆς πίστεως μυστήρια, ἡνίκα ἐὰν περιτύχωσι διδασκάλῳ καλῶς τρανοῦντι, λεγόντων ὅτι νῦν ἠρξάμην Χριστιανὸς γενέσθαι, νῦν μανθάνω πρῶτον τί ἐστι Χριστιανισμός. ταῦτα δὲ λέγουσιν οὐχὶ τέλεον ἀθετοῦντες τὰ πρότερα, ἀλλ' ὁρῶντες ὅτι πρότερον μὲν οὐ συνίεσαν τῶν μυστηρίων, ἀρχὴν δὲ ἔχουσι τοῦ νοεῖν ὅτε τετεύχασι διδασκαλίας ἀγαθῆς.

I have frequently heard this sort of confession from believers who have practiced the faith for some time and have learned the mysteries of faith, when it happens that [they learn] some especially illuminating teaching, that they say, "now I have begun to be a Christian, now I am learning for the first time what Christianity is." But they say these things, not completely denying what came before, but seeing that before they did not understand the mysteries, but now they have a beginning of understanding when they are equipped with good teaching.

Finally, he ends with an exhortation to his hearers:

καὶ ἡμεῖς οὖν πειραθῶμεν τοιοῦτοι γενέσθαι ὥστε εἰπεῖν διὰ τὴν προκοπὴν ἡμῶν τῇ διαθέσει· νῦν ἀρηάμην.

Let us too, therefore, endeavor to be the sort of person who is able to say, on account of the progress in our disposition, "Now I have begun!"[5]

This example displays several aspects of Origen's exegetical attention to the performance of scriptural language. First, his aim is to determine how one ought to use a sentence of the psalm by determining the circumstances under which it would be appropriate to say it and its meaning or force when used under those circumstances—for example, that in confessing, "now I have begun," one is not completely denying what came before.[6] He does not assume these should be *liturgical* uses of the *whole* written text. Rather, he imagines

---

4. He has already, for example, cried to the Lord (v. 2), sought him in his suffering (v.3), and remembered the Lord with rejoicing (v. 4).

5. *HomPs* 76.2.1.

6. I speak of the "force" rather than the "meaning" of the sentence because Origen is describing a

integrating a single sentence into his everyday discourse with no reference to the surrounding sentences of the psalm, although he will go on to investigate why it is written in connection with subsequent sentences. This focus on the use of single sentences is characteristic of the oral orientation of a linguist, since the sentence is the basic unit of oral linguistic competence.

Second, Origen is not merely describing usage but making normative judgments about how one ought to speak. This normativity involves both the *words* themselves and the *circumstances* of their use. Origen assumes that these very words, "now I have begun," are words that one ought to say; and he assumes that one is able to say them only under particular conditions, namely, as the appropriate *person* on the appropriate *occasion*. (The demonstrative pronouns "I" and "now" likely invited this kind of consideration). Both norms are implicit in his concluding exhortation, "Let us too … endeavor to be the sort of person who is able to say, on account of the progress in our disposition, 'Now I have begun!'"[7]

Furthermore, this passage suggests that the criteria for determining the use of scriptural sentences involve what ordinary language philosophers call the "linguistic intuition" of his hearers. By "linguistic intuitions" I mean an intuitive capacity for judging the appropriateness of particular ways of using an expression and for discerning their force when so used. Since we appeal to linguistic intuitions when interpreting the utterances of others, we might think of it as a capacity to judge *by ear*. But linguistic intuition operates also when we judge in imagination what an expression *would* mean under certain *possible* circumstances. It is a capacity we use both when understanding others and when producing utterances of our own.

Two features of his discussion suggest that Origen is appealing to the linguistic intuitions of his hearers. First, his argument for each use case consists of little more than describing the case and announcing that such and such a person would say, "now I have begun." This implies that he expects his hearers to accept his proposals immediately upon hearing them, which would be by an intuitive judgment. Second and more revealingly, he also appeals to the actual linguistic practices of Christians in his community, pointing out that he has actually heard people speak in the way he commends. This implies that

---

pragmatic function, one that depends on their being used in a particular context, namely, under the particular circumstances he has described.

7. *HomPs* 76.2.1.

the criteria for his proposals are rules that already govern how his hearers actually speak. For this reason, the cases Origen enumerates do not go much beyond the rules already implicit and operative through their own linguistic intuitions. The result of his exegesis is primarily to make explicit what they already know.

Rules of Usage

What I want to do in the remainder of this paper is look in a more atomized way at Origen's attention to the use of scriptural sentences in his *Homilies on the Psalms*. One frequently finds Origen proposing rules that define the pragmatic conditions under which one may use a particular sentence of scripture. For example,

HomPs 15.1.7

… εἴπερ βούλει ταχύνειν ἐπὶ τὸ ὁδεῦσαι ἐπὶ τὰ ἀγαθά, μὴ ὄκνει εὐδοκεῖν ἐν ἀσθενείαις καὶ τοιοῦτος εἶναι ὡς φάσκειν· ὅταν ἀσθενῶ, τότε δυνατός εἰμι.

… *if you intend* to hurry on the way to good things, *do not shrink* from giving thanks in weakness and being such as to say, "When I am weak, then I am strong" (2 Cor. 12:10)."[8]

Being weak while intending to hurry towards good things is a condition for being able to say in the words of Paul, "When I am weak, then I am strong." Or:

HomPs 76.2.4

Ὥσπερ δὲ οἱ λόγοι κἂν ἐξίωσιν ἐκ στόματός μου, ὦσι δὲ ἀνεπίληπτοι καὶ θεῖοι, οὐκ εἰσὶν ἐμοῦ ἀλλὰ τοῦ θεοῦ, ὥστε θαρροῦντά με λέγειν· ἢ δοκιμὴν ζητεῖτε τοῦ ἐν ἐμοὶ λαλοῦντος Χριστοῦ.…

But just as the words that come out of my mouth, if they are blameless and divine, are not mine but God's, *so that I may boldly say,* "or do you seek proof that Christ speaks in me.…" (2 Cor. 13:3)

Here the rule is: if one's words are blameless and divine, one may say, "Christ speaks in me."

Instead of explicitly formulating a rule, Origen can also invite his hearers to imitate an exemplary speaker. For example:

8. *HomPs.* 15.1.7.

HomPs 67.1.1

Μαθητής ἐστι τοῦ εἰπόντος· *μάθετε ἀπ᾽ ἐμοῦ, ὅτι πραΰς εἰμι καὶ ταπεινὸς τῇ καρδίᾳ, ὁ τοσαῦτα περὶ ἑαυτοῦ ἐπὶ τὸ μετριώτερον εἰπών....*

The disciple of the one who says, "Learn from me, for I am meek and humble at heart" (Mt. 11:29) *says the same things about himself* in the proper measure....

Here the rule is: to the extent that one has become like Christ, one should say what Christ says of himself, and in particular, that "I am meek and humble at heart."

Making these sorts of judgments involves more than merely grammatical competence. They are judgments about the relation between words and things, requiring knowledge of both. To rightly say "I am meek and humble," for example, requires both some understanding of the words *and* an accurate measure of one's own character. Origen often uses the verbs ἁρμόζω (and its derivative ἐφαρμόζω) to refer to this relation of appropriateness between a sentence and its referent. Appropriateness is an aesthetic and normative relation between two particulars. By describing a rule of usage in terms of the appropriateness between a sentence and its referent, Origen suggests that determining these rules involves making an intuitive judgment about the relation between them. For example,

HomPs. 67.1.3

...καθέζεται ὅτε κρίνει. τῷ δὲ ἁγίῳ καὶ μακαρίῳ, ᾧ ἁρμόζει τὸ *ὁ πιστεύων εἰς ἐμὲ οὐ κρίνεται,* οὐ καθέζεται ἀλλὰ ἕστηκεν.

[God] sits when he judges. But for the one who is holy and blessed, to whom [the words,] "The one who believes in me is not judged" (John 3:18) are **appropriate,** he does not sit, but rather stands.

The words of John 3:18 are *appropriate* in that they may be asserted of the holy and blessed person. Or again:

HomPs. 36.3.1

Καὶ εἰ βούλει ἀπὸ παραδείγματος νοῆσαι πῶς *ῥομφαίαν ἐσπάσαντο οἱ ἁμαρτωλοί,* κατανόησον μαχομένους ἐθνικοὺς καὶ ῥήματα οὐ θεμιτὰ λέγοντας πρὸς ἀλλήλους μετὰ ὀργῆς καὶ ἔριδος. Τότε γὰρ ἐφαρμόσεις τὸ ῥητὸν αὐτοῖς καὶ ἐρεῖς· *ῥομφαίαν ἐσπάσαντο οἱ ἁμαρτωλοί.*

And if you intend to understand from this example how "the sinners draw a sword," (36:14a) consider how the Gentiles make war and speak lawless words to one another with anger and envy. For then you will **apply** the wording [of the text] to them and say, "The sinners draw a sword."

Origen uses the related verb ἐφαρμόζειν, "apply," for the act of fitting a sentence to a referent for which it is appropriate, in this case one that the sentence signifies allegorically. Origen is explicit that it is the wording—τὸ ῥητὸν—that may be fitted or applied to the Gentiles who speak lawlessly and that doing so involves *saying* the words "the sinners draw a sword" of them, in an allegorical sense. To recognize the appropriateness of this use requires "considering" the proposed referent—Gentiles, in their warlike use of language.

In this example his allegorical interpretation is in fact a proposal for a rule governing the allegorical use of the psalm by his hearers. We can observe something similar in the next example, which is noteworthy because it contains a fascinating discussion of the deictic mechanism by which a scriptural sentence may be used to select literal or allegorical referents when uttered.[9] Origen is commenting on Ps 77:54 (LXX):

καὶ εἰσήγαγεν αὐτοὺς εἰς ὄρος ἁγιάσματος αὐτου,
ὄρος τοῦτο, ὃ ἐκτήσατο ἡ δεξιὰ αὐτοῦ.

And he brought them to his mountain of holiness,
this mountain, which his right hand made.[10]

Origen comments:

HomPs 77.8.4

Καὶ ἐκεῖνον μὲν τὸν λαὸν τότε εἰς ὄρος, ἐπεὶ τυπικὰ ἐποίουν τὰ πράγματα,
εἰς ὄρος ἁγιάσματος σωματικοῦ, σὲ δὲ εἰς ὄρος ἁγιάσματος περὶ οὗ λέγει ὁ ἀπόστολος·
ἀλλὰ προσεληλύθατε Σιὼν ὄρει καὶ πόλει θεοῦ ζῶντος, Ιεροσαλὴμ ἐπουρανίῳ, καὶ
μυριάσιν ἀγγέλων, πανηγύρει. ἐκεῖνο τὸ ἀληθῶς ὄρος τοῦ ἁγιάσματός ἐστι τοῦ θεοῦ,
ὄρος τοῦτο ὃ ἐκτήσατο ἡ δεξιὰ αὐτοῦ. Τὸ μὲν τοῦτο σωματικῶς εἰκὸς δεδεῖχθαι ὑπὸ τοῦ
προφήτου ἐν Σιὼν καὶ νῦν δὲ τοῦτο τὸ ὄρος δείκνυται νῷ τῷ βλέποντι νοητὸν ὄρος.
Ὥσπερ ὀφθαλμοῖς σώματος ἡ δεῖξις σώματος γίνεται, οὕτως ὀφθαλμοῖς ψυχῆς ἡ
δεῖξις νοητὴ γίνεται, ὥστε τοῦτο μὴ ἐν κενοπαθείᾳ λέγεσθαι, νῷ βλέποντι οὐσίαν καὶ
ὑπόστασιν νοητοῦ.

---

9. Cf. CJ 2.66f; CM 12:19; 16:10; and see my discussions of these texts in the footnotes below.
10. Ps 77:54 (LXX).

[He led] that people in the past to a mountain, the mountain of bodily holiness, because they performed their acts as types; but [he leads] you to the mountain of holiness about which the apostle speaks: "but he has brought you to Mount Zion and the city of the living God, the heavenly Jerusalem, and to the assembly of countless angels" (Heb. 12:22). This is that which is truly "the mountain of God's holiness, this mountain which his right hand created" (Ps 77:54). The "this" was probably used by the prophet in Zion to indicate [by deixis] bodily; but even now the "this" indicates [by deixis] to the intellect which sees an intellectual mountain. As the deixis of the body occurs with respect to the eyes of the body, so the deixis of the intellect occurs to the eyes of the soul, so that "this" is said with respect to the intellect that sees the essence and subsistence of what is intellectual, not as an empty sensory affection.[11]

Origen's exegesis focuses on the deictic function of the demonstrative pronoun "τοῦτο" ("this"),[12] distinguishing an ordinary corporeal deixis from an intellectual deixis. The former "indicates [δεδεῖχθαι] bodily ... with respect to the eyes of the body," implying that the prophet accompanied the word "τοῦτο" with physical gestures directing the eyes of his hearers towards Mt. Zion. He recognizes its pragmatic function, that bodily deixis selects a corporeal object—in this case, Mt. Zion—as the referent of the utterance relative to its context of use. Since this can occur only when actually uttered, he presumably envisions the prophet actually saying these words, in the past, in sight of Mt. Zion.

Origen sketches his theory of intellectual deixis by analogy to its corporeal counterpart. As corporeal deixis designates a corporeal object as the referent of a demonstrative pronoun by presenting it to the eyes of the body, so intellectual deixis designates an intellectual object as the referent of the same pronoun by presenting it to the eyes of the soul. The analogy implies that spiritual deixis also operates only when these words are actually uttered in the present, which is further confirmed by the fact that Origen says that spiritual deixis "indicates now" and speaks of the word τοῦτο being "said" with respect to the eye of the soul. This theory, a linguistic adjunct to his theory of the spiritual senses, enables him to explain how the same physical words can be used literally or allegorically to refer to ontologically diverse entities.

---

11. *HomPs.* 77.8.4.

12. The only significant parallel in Origen of which I am aware is a scholion to Luke (PG 17.329). In a discussion of the fact that John's name signifies "ὁ δεικνύς," [the indicator], Origen says that John the Baptist would "indicate with his finger [τῷ δακτύλῳ δεικνύειν] the One who is present and say, 'Behold, the Lamb of God!'" Here too we have a deictic reference, in an actual speech situation, secured by the use of bodily gesture in relation to something present to the senses.

As a function of use, allegory is neither a property of the text in itself nor a "meaning" independent of the text. Rather, it is a relation between the sentence and a referent, determined by its use under certain conditions. This is why the question of whether allegory is legitimate is, for Origen, a matter of showing that a referent exists to which these words might appropriately be referred in an allegorical way. The function of his quotation from the book of Hebrews, which speaks of a *heavenly* Mt. Zion, is to establish the existence of such a referent, as Origen says using a deictic expression of his own, "*this* is that mountain...." The Pauline rule that Israel's acts were *types* then explains why there is an analogy between Israel's coming to the earthly Zion and the church's coming to the heavenly Zion. This analogy permits him to explain the relationship between the narrow rule of literal speech (observed by the psalmist) and the broader rule of allegorical speech (to be followed by Christians). If words that may be used of one thing may be used as well with respect to what is like it, then words that apply literally to one mountain may be applied allegorically to its antitype.

A more interesting case in which Origen examines the relation between potentially competing rules of speech—and one with no hint of allegory—can be found in Origen's 2nd homily on Psalm 36.

HomPs 36.2.1

Προστάσσοντος τοῦ λόγου καὶ λέγοντος· ὑποτάγηθι τῷ Κυρίῳ, ἀναγκαῖόν ἐστι τὸ ἀναπτύξαι καὶ παραστῆσαι τῷ λόγῳ, τίς μέν ἐστιν ὁ ὑποτασσόμενος τῷ Κυρίῳ, τίς δὲ ὁ μὴ ὑποτασσόμενος αὐτῷ. Ὥσπερ οὖν οὐ πᾶς ὁ λέγων μοι· κύριε, κύριε, εἰσελεύσεται εἰς τὴν βασιλείαν τῶν οὐρανῶν, ἀλλ᾽ ὁ ποιῶν τὸ θέλημα τοῦ Πατρός μου τοῦ ἐν τοῖς οὐρανοῖς, οὕτως οὐ πᾶς ὁ λέγων ὑποτάσσεσθαι τῷ Κυρίῳ, καὶ ὅσον ἐπὶ τῇ φωνῇ λέγων τοῦτο ποιεῖν· ἀληθῶς ὑποτάσσεσθαι τῷ Κυρίῳ ἀπὸ τῶν ἔργων χαρακτηρίζεται.

Since the Word [λόγου] commands and says, "submit to the Lord" (Psalm 36:7a), it is necessary to clarify and demonstrate by reason [λόγῳ] who it is that submits to the Lord, and who does not submit to him. For just as "Not all who say to me, 'Lord, Lord!' will enter into the kingdom of heaven, but only the one who does the will of my Father in heaven" (Matthew 7:21), so not everyone who says they submit to the Lord acts according to the word he says. Only from his works is he described truly as submitting to the Lord.[13]

It is characteristic of Origen's rationalist linguistics that he immediately transforms a problem of meaning into a problem of usage. For he assumes that

13. *HomPs.* 36.2.1.

to obey the command "submit to the Lord" is simply to become the kind of person of whom the words, "submitted to the Lord," can be said. To determine how to use this phrase, Origen argues by analogy with Matthew 7:21, itself a dominical rule about the conditions under which one may call Jesus "Lord." Origen argues that the grammar of submitting to the Lord should be analogous, that in both cases, submission is a matter of one's works.

However, Origen then points out that Paul says of Christ, "When all things are submitted to him, then the Son himself will submit to the one who submits all things to him" (1 Cor.15:28). If Origen's rule applied in this case, it would imply that the works of the Son himself were somehow imperfect. So, Origen must postulate a refinement to his general rule that can account for Paul's usage in this specific case.

> Ἀλλ' ὅρα αὐτοῦ τὴν πολλὴν φιλανθρωπίαν καὶ χρηστότητα· οὐδὲ αὐτὸν λογίζεται ὑποτετάχθαι, ὅσον ἔστι τι τῷ πατρὶ μὴ ὑποτεταγμένον. Τότε δὲ αὐτὸν ἐν ὑποτασσομένοις ἀριθμεῖ καὶ θαρρεῖ λέγειν ὑποτέταγμαι τῷ θεῷ, ὅτε πάντα παρίστησιν ὑποτεταγμένα τῷ λόγῳ.

> But see his great love of humanity and his kindness: he does not consider himself to be submitted, as long as anything is not submitted to the Father. But then he will number himself among those who are submitted and boldly say, "I am submitted to God," when he presents everything as submitted to the Word.[14]

Once again Origen transforms the problem of interpreting Paul's meaning into one of describing how Christ appropriately uses the expression, "I am submitted to God." Paul himself determines the appropriate occasions: Christ says this only after all things have submitted to God. The task Origen faces is thus to determine the force of Christ's language about submission, without contradicting the earlier rule or his commitments about Christ's character. Doing so leads Origen to a proposal that is at once linguistic and theological. Christ may identify himself with us in what he predicates of himself. In withholding or asserting that he is submitted to God, Christ's words signify by virtue of his identification with humanity rather than referring to the state of his own works. In this way, interpreting the psalmist's command "submit to the Lord" as implying a rule for the usage of scriptural language leads Origen not only to determine how to predicate submission of ourselves, but also to describe the extraordinary rules governing Christ's unique use of the same expression.

---

14. *HomPs.* 36.2.1.

Logos

The cases we have examined so far have focused on rules for the use of single sentences, but we have already seen that defining a rule for the use of one text may implicate others. This is not surprising, since Origen regards scripture as a rational unity, the body of the Logos. Consequently, Origen often attempts to formulate more general rules by induction, rules that organize the use of scriptural language over a range of particular cases, and by extension, determine in more general terms how Christians should speak in imitation of scripture.

This kind of argument can be used to organize a domain of allegorical discourse. A particularly clear and central case is his observation that scripture frequently uses the names of members of the body as metaphors for the soul. For example:

HomPs 15.2.4

Μιμηταὶ οὖν τοῦ Χριστοῦ γινόμενοι καὶ ἡμεῖς, ὅσα λέγει τὸ ἀνθρώπινον τοῦ Χριστοῦ φιλτιμούμεθα εἰπεῖν. Διὰ τοῦτο γὰρ ταῦτα λέγει, ἵν᾽ ἔχωμεν ὑπογραμμὸν τί μιμησόμεθα καὶ ἡμεῖς εἴπωμεν· εὐλογήσω τὸν κύριον τὸν συνετίσαντά με, ἵνα καὶ ἡμεῖς εἴπωμεν· ἔτι δὲ καὶ ἕως νυκτὸς ἐπαίδευσάν με οἱ νεφροί μου.

Therefore as we also are becoming imitators of Christ, it is worthy for us to say whatever the humanity of Christ says. For this reason [Christ] says these things, that we might have a kind of sketch of what we should imitate, that we might say, "I will bless the Lord who knit me together," that we also might say, "yet through the night my kidneys disciplined me."

The performative context is clear: Christ's words in Psalm 15 are a sketch (ὑπογραμμὸν) for us to imitate by taking up the very words of the psalm as our own. But what would we *mean* in saying that our kidneys disciplined us through the night? Origen approaches this question by situating scripture's use of the word "kidneys" in relation to its use of other bodily metaphors.

HomPs 15.2.5

Τοιαῦτά τινα νοήσεις, ἐὰν δυνηθῇς ἀκούειν καὶ συγκρίνειν πνευματικὰ πνευματικοῖς.... Σωματικὰ γὰρ ὀνόματα ἐπὶ τῶν δυνάμεων τῆς ψυχῆς παραλαμβάνεται κατὰ ἀναλογίαν τῶν σωματικῶν πραγμάτων.... Καὶ ὥσπερ ἡ καρδία <κατὰ> τὸ σῶμα ἔχει τὸ ἡγεμονικόν, οὕτως ἀνάλογον τῷ γινομένῳ ἐν τοῖς νεφροῖς γίνεται ἐν τοῖς νεφροῖς τῆς ψυχῆς.... Ἀκούων οὖν τοῦ κατὰ τὸν σωτῆρα ἀνθρώπου λέγοντος· εὐλογήσω τὸν κύριον τὸν συνετίσαντά με, ἔτι δὲ καὶ ἕως νυκτὸς ἐπαίδευσάν με οἱ νεφροί μου, καὶ σὺ ταῦτα λέγε....

> You will understand certain similar things, if you are able to hear and compare spiritual things with spiritual things.... For corporeal names are used for the powers of the soul by analogy with bodily things.... And just as the corporeal heart contains the ruling principle, so that which is produced in the kidneys is analogous to that which is produced in the kidneys of the soul.... Hearing then the humanity of the savior saying, "I will bless the Lord who knit me together, yet through the night my kidneys disciplined me," so you also should say the same things....

When he says that corporeal names "are applied" to the power of the soul, he means they are applied *by scripture,* and he demonstrates this point by enumerating several texts that use the word "heart" in an obviously metaphorical way. In this case, his oft-cited principle of "comparing spiritual things to spiritual things" means that one may determine a rule of usage in one case by scripture's example in other cases. Moreover, he assumes that scripture's allegorical example should guide *our own* speech as well: "you too should say the same things."

In other cases, however, Origen can commend for imitation a pattern of *literal* usage displayed in scripture. Origen himself calls attention to this possibility when discussing the scriptural habit of personifying apparently inanimate objects, as in Ps 76:17, "The waters saw and were afraid...."

HomPs 76.3.2

Μὴ παρέλθωμεν δὲ μηδὲ τὸ ῥητὸν κατ᾽ αὐτό, ἀλλ᾽ ἴδωμεν εἰ δύναται ἔχειν τινὰ νοῦν ἡ λέξις ἡ λέγουσα· εἴδοσάν σε ὕδατα καὶ ἐφοβήθησαν, ἐταράχθησαν ἄβυσσοι....[15]

Let us not pass by even the wording in itself, but let us consider whether it is possible that the [mere] text contains some [deeper] understanding when it says, "The waters saw and were afraid, the depths trembled...." (Ps 76:17)

Even τὸ ῥητὸν κατ᾽ αὐτό—that is, "the wording in itself," the words taken at face value by assuming that the waters really see and fear in their ordinary sense—contains "τινὰ νοῦν," a certain deeper understanding. Origen articulates this understanding as a general principle:

Ἐπέρχεται δή μοι λέγειν, ὅτι πάντα ἐψύχωται καὶ οὐδέν ἐστιν ἐν τῷ κόσμῳ κενὸν ψυχῆς· πάντα δὲ ἐψύχωται σώμασι διαφόροις.

It occurs to me to say that everything is ensouled, and there is nothing in the world devoid of soul; but everything is ensouled in different kinds of bodies.

Origen argues that this rule accounts not only for the present text, but for many similar texts in scripture, a number of which he goes on to enumerate,

---

15. *HomPs. 76* 3.2.

among them those that describe Christ as commanding the sea and the wind. This case particularly impresses Origen, since the imperative force of a command depends in part on its pragmatic relation to a hearer. "No one commands what is lifeless, but it is clear that he commands and speaks as Lord of all creation, 'Be silent…' And the sea was silent and became calm." Assuming that Christ's practice of commanding must be appropriate, Origen accounts for it by positing that those commanded must in fact be living beings with the capacity to obey. And once again, Origen argues that the Christian—at least, the one who is sufficiently advanced in the process of deification—should speak according to the same rule, not only in general by saying that all things have souls, but even by commanding creation as Christ does.

> Ἐὰν γένωμαι κἀγὼ ἄνθρωπος γνήσιος τοῦ θεοῦ, δύναμαι ἐν τῷ ἐν ἐμοὶ λαλοῦντι Χριστῷ Ἰησοῦ ἐπιτιμῆσαι τῇ κτίσει, ἵνα εἴπω τῷ ἡλίῳ· στῆθι κατὰ Γαβαώ.

> And if even I become a genuine man of God, I am able—with Christ Jesus speaking in me—to command creation, that I might say to the sun, "Be still over Gideon!" (Jos. 10:12)

These examples make it increasingly clear that, for Origen, our linguistic practices embody our rational commitments about the world. Linguistic usage involves judgments about how *words* may correctly be used of *things,* and hence involve an understanding of both words and things. Sometimes, as we have seen, Origen's exegesis involves little more than making explicit to his community some usage that they were already implicitly able to discern. In these cases, Origen's exegesis tends to presuppose what they already know how to do with words, and hence what they already believe about the world; and it has the effect of solidifying his community's grasp of their tradition (as embodied in their intuitive judgments).

But sometimes the words of scripture are such that the linguistic intuitions of his hearers cannot accommodate them—they are difficult, obscure, or simply offensive, the sorts of words that, in the hands of a Marcionite or Valentinian teacher, might lead a simple Christian away from Origen's proto-orthodox community. These kinds of texts play a crucial role in learning to perform the scriptures, since they provide the opportunity for correcting his hearer's linguistic intuitions to account for the difficult text, training their ears, as it were, to hear differently. Often this may lead to the discernment of an allegorical use. For example, Ps 77:65 compares the Lord to "one strong and drunk with wine." Origen comments:

HomPs 77.9.2

Ἐγὼ εἰ εἰρήκειν τὸν θεὸν ὡς δυνατὸν καὶ κεκραιπαληκότα ἐξ οἴνου ἀνίστασθαι,
τίς οὐκ ἂν ἐλάβετό μου τῶν φιλαιτίων λέγων ὅτι μέθην καὶ κραιπάλην φέρεις ἐπὶ
τὸν θεόν, ἄνθρωπος διδασκόμενος ὅτι οὐδὲ ἄνθρωποι μέθυσοι βασιλείαν θεοῦ
κληρονομήσουσιν; Ἀλλ’ ὅμως τὸ ἅγιον πνεῦμα ἐν τῇ ἐλευθέρῳ τοῦ λέγειν ἐξουσίᾳ
τυγχάνον εἶπεν τὸν θεὸν διανίστασθαί ποτε ὡς δυνατὸν καὶ κεκραιπαληκότα ἐξ
οἴνου. Τάχα γὰρ οἱονεὶ ἡμεῖς καροῦμεν καὶ μεθύειν ποιοῦμεν τὸν θεὸν ὡς καθεύδειν,
ὡς ὀργίζεσθαι, ὡς τὰ λοιπά, ἵνα μὴ νήφῃ ὁ θεὸς ἀλλὰ γένηται ὡς δυνατὸς καὶ
κεκραιπαληκώς. Ἀλλ’ ἐὰν ἐπιστρέψωμεν <ὡς> καὶ νηφαλίως ζῆν ... ἐγείρεται
ἡμῖν ὁ θεὸς ὡς δυνατὸν καὶ κεκραιπαληκότα ἐξ οἴνου. 3. Κολάζων μὲν γὰρ
κεκραιπαληκώς ἐστιν ἐξ οἴνου, παύων δὲ τὴν ὀργὴν διανίσταται ὡς δυνατὸς καὶ
κεκραιπαληκὼς ἐξ οἴνου.

If I had said that God arises "as one strong and drunk with wine," who among
those who love to find fault would not have censured me, saying, "You apply
intoxication and drunkenness to God, yet human beings are taught that, 'no
drunk person will inherit the kingdom of God' (1 Cor. 6:10)"? But the Holy
Spirit, having freedom to speak with authority, says that God sometimes awakes,
"as one strong and drunk with wine."[16] For perhaps when we are drunk, we also
make God drink, and (as it were) sleep, and get angry, and other [drunken
behaviors], so that God is not sober towards us but becomes like one strong and
drunk. But if we turn and, as it were, live soberly ... then God arises for us as one
strong and drunk with wine. 3. For when God punishes, he is drunk with wine,
but when he relents from his wrath, he awakes as one who is strong and drunk
with wine.

Again, his interpretation is oriented towards the performance of these
words in his own discourse. He points out that his hearers might find fault
with him for saying these words, had they not been already said by the Holy
Spirit, who possesses "freedom to speak with authority [ἐν τῇ ἐλευθέρῳ τοῦ
λέγειν ἐξουσίᾳ]."[17] The interpretive task is thus to propose a rule that accounts
for this way of speaking, a hypothesis introduced with the word ταχα, "perhaps." His proposal determines conditions under which we can speak of God
as drunk or sober by virtue of his relation to our *own* drunkenness or sobriety.
When we are drunk, God adopts the behavior of one who is drunk in punishing us. When we live soberly, God relents and ceases from punishing because we have returned to sobriety. Origen ends by putting the words of the

16. *HomPs.* 77.9.2; cf. Pitra 130.22–28.
17. See also *HomPs.* 76.4.6, in which Origen speaks of the Word "daring to speak" concerning his
flesh as food.

psalm on his lips—along with clarifying glosses—hopefully laden with new significance for his hearers. If they are able to hear the psalm in the way he has proposed, then their linguistic intuitions have been changed; they will have gained a new capacity for hearing.

To speak words like these is, for Origen, fraught with risk; it requires boldness. To speak boldly with understanding is an index of the progress of the more advanced Christian, for it shows that her own habits of speech are more and more conformed to those of scripture—especially in its obscurity. The following passage demonstrates this phenomenon and situates it in the context of a theology of deification through linguistic imitation—Origen imitating Paul, Paul imitating Christ, and Christ imitating God. We pick up Origen's text in the middle of an argument: while God is immutable in himself, Scripture speaks of God changing because his aspect changes in relation to us. Origen argues that Paul, in imitation of Christ himself, models the same divine pattern of gracious change in relation to those in need through his practice of becoming, in his words, "as one who is weak to the weak, that I might gain the weak" (1 Cor. 9:22). Origen argues that Paul does so in imitation of Christ, and hence that his practice is further proof of the divine humility it imitates.

> HomPs 67.1.3
>
> ἀλλὰ τίνος ὢν μιμητὴς Παῦλος ταῦτα ποεῖ; τολμῶ καὶ λέγω· Χριστοῦ, ὃς ἐγένετο ἀσθενέσιν ἀσθενής, ἵνα τοὺς ἀσθενεῖς κερδήσῃ. καὶ ἔστι τὸ ἀσθενὲς τοῦ θεοῦ ἰσχυρότερον τῶν ἀνθρώπων.
>
> But as whose imitator does Paul do these things? I am bold and say: [as an imitator] of Christ, who [also] became weak to the weak, that he might gain the weak. And "the weakness of God is stronger than human beings" (1 Cor. 1:25).

In speaking of Paul as an "imitator" of Christ, Origen is alluding to 1 Corinthians 11:1, in which Paul exhorts his readers to, "imitate me as I imitate Christ." These words imply that he and his readers should imitate the same pattern—not only by becoming weak to gain the weak, but also by imitating Paul's bold speech. Pressing the logic of imitation, Origen argues that the words Paul applies to his own ministry may also be applied to Christ, and by extension to God. Origen introduces this chain of reasoning using the formula, "I am bold and say" (τολμῶ καὶ λέγω). Origen's boldness consists, it would seem, not only in using Paul's words about becoming weak, but especially in his daring to use them in a new way, predicating weakness of Christ and of God as well. (Note that this bold proposal has nothing to do with allegory *per se*.) He uses the same formula to introduce *Paul's* words about the weakness of God, reiterating that he speaks in imitation of Paul's boldness.

> οὐ μόνον γὰρ τὰ ἀσθενὲς τοῦ Χριστοῦ, ὃ ἐσταυρώθη ἐξ ἀσθενείας, ἰσχυρότερόν ἐστιν τῶν ἀνθρώπων, ἀλλ᾽ ἐτόλμησεν ὁ ἀπόστολος εἰπεῖν - ὡς ἐξουσίαν ἔχων λέγειν τὰ ἀληθῆ καὶ εἰπὼν ὅτι τὸ ἀσθενὲς τοῦ θεοῦ ἰσχυρότερον τῶν ἀνθρώπων - παραβόλως πάνυ καὶ παρακεκινδυνευμένως ὡς πρὸς τοὺς ἀκροατὰς μὴ εἰδότας ἀκούειν.

> For not only the weakness of Christ, who was crucified out of weakness, is stronger than human beings, but the apostle was bold to speak, as one having freedom to speak the truth, even to say that "the weakness of God is stronger than human beings" — speaking very parabolically and with risk, as though to hearers that did not know how to hear.[18]

To say that Paul speaks "parabolically" (παραβόλως) to those who hear but "do not know how to hear" is also no doubt an allusion to Jesus' parabolic pedagogy and his refrain "he who has ears to hear, let him hear,"[19] another hint that Paul is simply imitating the pedagogical pattern of Christ, as by extension is Origen. This passage makes clear that the boldness of his speech is a function of its relation to his hearers: it is dangerous for them, since they "do not know how to hear," since they will automatically hear speech about God's weakness in the wrong way. Conversely, to be able to speak these bold words correctly, as Paul does, is an index of his great spiritual advancement and his conformity to Christ.

To summarize: in this paper I have shown how Origen characteristically determines specific rules for the use of single scriptural sentences and organizes these rules into broader rules that describe something more like a grammar of scriptural language. I have called attention to the central role played by linguistic intuitions in this process. Origen presupposes his hearers' capacity to make judgments about the appropriate relation between words and things; but he also regards this capacity as fallible and in need of correction. Deepening our own capacities to hear and use the language of scripture is central to the pedagogy of the Logos through scripture, and the boldest and most difficult sentences of scripture represent the leading edge of this pedagogy, where

---

18. *HomPs.* 67.1.3.

19. Mark 4:9, et al. This parallel is also not without difficulties, since parables are paradigmatically *obscure* discourse while the trouble with *bold* speech seems to be that it is all too open. But this problem is more apparent than real. Jesus' parables themselves involve many openly bold comparisons (such as when he compares God to an unjust judge), while Paul's utterance here is, despite its boldness, obscure or parabolic in the sense that it cannot be taken at face value.

our own fallible capacity for speech encounters its limit in the wise words of scripture. We might think of this process as a kind of rationalist linguistics.

I have taken pains to show that these procedures explain how Origen determines both literal and allegorical uses of scripture. This suggests that the dynamics of the scriptural pedagogy of the Logos (to use Torjesen's language) and their procedural manifestation as rationalist linguistics are more fundamental. I would suggest that instead of describing Origen's exegesis as a movement from one kind of meaning to another—from the literal to the spiritual senses—we should frame it instead as an increase of capacities from *lexis* to *logos,* from the words of the text to an account of their rational use in conformity with Christ. This means that interpretation begins prior to the literal sense, with the practice of memorizing the *lexis* of scripture—a necessary condition for being able to use its words in discourse. And the fruit of exegesis is more than spiritual understanding: it is the whole internalized capacity to perform scriptural language appropriately, in its literal and non-literal uses. The end of the movement from *lexis* to *logos* is the conformity of our rational discourse to Christ, the scripturalization and divinization of our own language, so that we can say in words Origen so often cites, "do you seek proof that Christ speaks in me."

Miriam DeCock

7. ORIGEN'S IDENTIFICATION OF THE PERSON IN HIS *HOMILIES ON THE PSALMS*

In 1985 Marie-Josèphe Rondeau published the second volume of her study of the Greek and Latin Church fathers' interpretation of the psalms.[1] In this volume, as in the first, Rondeau dedicated a major section of the work to Origen's treatment of the psalms, despite the fragmentary state of his lifelong work on the biblical text. A major emphasis of Rondeau's study was what she calls "*l'exégèse prosopologique*" of the Fathers, that is, their identifications of the psalm's narrator, its speaker, the characters present in the psalm's "scene," or its object of speech, often with recourse to the term "person" (τὸ πρόσωπον).[2] That is, this or that psalm is spoken "from the person" (ἐκ προσώπου) of whomever the interpreter determines is most fitting, given the psalm's content. Rondeau demonstrated that it was in fact Origen who first made systematic use of the method of identifying the person of a given text, for our purposes of the psalms, a method he learned from his training in the Greco-Roman grammatical-rhetorical schools where the method was used to interpret Homer or Plato.[3]

Rondeau conducted her study of Origen's "prosopological" Psalm exegesis based on the fragmentary evidence she had at her disposal: Rufinus' Latin

---

1. Marie-Josèphe Rondeau, *Exégèse prosopologique et théologie*, vol. 2, *Les commentaires patristiques du Psautier*, vol. 22, *Orientalia Christiana analecta* (Rome: Pontificium Institutum Studiorum Orientalium, 1985).

2. Rondeau, *Exegese Prosopologique et Theologie*, 10.

3. For a standard treatment of prosopology in the works of prior classical Hellenistic grammarians, see B. Neuschäfer, *Origenes als Philologue* (Basel: F. Reinhardt, 1987), 265.

translation of the nine homilies on Psalms 36–38, the small number of fragments found in the catenae, the Latin homilies attributed to Jerome that affirmed V. Peri's argument that they are substantially based on Origen's psalm exegesis,[4] Origen's use of the verses of isolated Psalms in the rest of his corpus,[5] and, finally, in what she describes as "echoes" of Origen discernible in authors that were dependent on him.[6] Rondeau observed that for Origen, the person of the psalms could be identified as God the Father,[7] God the Son,[8] the church,[9] the apostles,[10] the prophet himself (most often David),[11] the more general categories of "the just,"[12] the repentant sinner,[13] and in some instances, the psalms actually presented a conversation between characters, such as the Father and the Son,[14] or between God and his angelic counsel.[15]

Particularly insightful were Rondeau's observations about Origen's use of the "prosopological" method to identify the person of Christ in the psalms.[16] According to Rondeau, for Origen, in the Psalms from which it can be determined that Christ is the "person," we can actually understand Christ as providing information about himself in his speech (i.e. in the precise words of the psalm).[17] This approach, Rondeau observed, Origen adopted from the New Testament itself, for there we find examples in which Christ speaks the words of a handful of psalms in the first person.[18] Therefore, the interpreter is justified in understanding every verse of these psalms, namely, those quoted in

4. V. Peri, "Omelie origeniane sui Psalmi," Studi e Testi 289 (Vatican City, 1980).

5. She references such works as *Contra Celsum*; *Commentary on John*; *Homilies on Jeremiah*; *Commentary on the Song of Songs*; *Commentary on Romans*; *Homilies on Acts*.

6. Rondeau, *Exegese Prosopologique et Theologie*, 40.

7. Rondeau, *Exegese Prosopologique et Theologie*, 59. See for example, *Hom in Exodus* 3.2 on Ps 80.11; *Hom in Numbers* 7.1 on Ps 49.20; *Commentary on Romans* 9.1 80.13; "Jerome," *Tract. In Ps.* 81.2. (All examples in footnotes 6–14 cited by Rondeau, 59–72).

8. See for example: *Contra Celsus* 2.37 on Ps 68.22 and *Contra Celsus* 2.62 on Ps 15.10.

9. See for example: *Hom on Genesis* 3.4 on Ps 138.17; "Jerome," *Tract. in Ps* 5.1.

10. See for example: "Jerome," *Tract. in Ps* 66.2; 77.3; 78.13.

11. See for example his treatment of Ps 2.1–2 in the fragment of the Palestinian chain (PG 23, 84 A), and "Jerome," *Tract. in Ps* 105.1; 109.1; 133.3; 81.1; 86.1; 101.10; 103.24; 92.1.

12. See for example: *Hom in Num* 7.1 on Ps 100.5; *Hom in Gen* 5.1 on Ps 120.1.

13. See for example: *Hom in Gen* 11.1 on Ps 37.6; *Hom in Leviticus* 5.6 on Ps 37.6; *In Ps* 37 2.5 (SC 411) on Ps 37.18; "Jerome," *Tract. in Ps* 95; Ps 136.1, 7.

14. See his treatment of Ps 2.8, where he thinks the Father speaks to the Son. Cf. *Hom in Gen* 9.3; *Hom in Num* 17.5; *Hom in Iesu Naue* 11.3.

15. See for example *Hom in Ex* 8.2 on Ps 81.6–7.

16. Rondeau, *Exegese Prosopologique et Theologie*, 389.

17. Rondeau, *Exegese Prosopologique et Theologie*, 96, 101.

18. For example, Ps 21 in Matt 27:46 and Mark 15:34; Ps 40 in John 13:18, Ps 68 in John 15:25; Ps 117 in Matt 21:42, Mark 12:10–11; Luke 20:17.

the New Testament, as providing information about Christ.[19] However, when dealing with a psalm that is not quoted in the New Testament, Christ must be found in other ways. Not surprisingly, Rondeau observed that one of the most frequent ways Origen finds Christ in the psalms is by spiritual or anagogical exegesis of the psalm. So, for example, even if he identifies David as the speaker of the psalm at the level of the text, beyond the text, Christ is there to be discovered.[20] In these instances, Origen can determine that Christ is the *prosopon* or the speaker of either the whole psalm, or of only part of it, and sometimes of only single verses. When Origen finds Christ without recourse to spiritual exegesis, there are certain indicators in the text that tip him off, such as descriptions of the psalmist's death or descent into the underworld, indicators developed by analogy from psalms where Christ is identified with certainty.[21]

While Rondeau lamented the almost complete loss of Origen's exegetical work on the psalms as she conducted her study, she concluded based on her analysis of what was available to her that a precise or rigid assessment of the phenomenon of Origen's identification of Christ in the psalms is impossible for another reason. For Rondeau, the difficulty of describing the precise patterns of Origen's "prosopological" exegesis was less related to the fragmentary state of his work on the Psalms than it was to what she described as Origen's "*souple*" reading method.[22] That is, he often leaves the choice between two or even several *prosopa* open. For example, when Origen interprets Ps 3:4, he says, "if it is David who speaks," this is how we ought to understand the verse, "but if it is Christ," here is the sense.[23] Such flexibility around the identification of Christ in the psalms cannot be found in later authors, such as Augustine (or, in the case of Diodore of Tarsus, who is adamant that Christ ought not to be found in most psalms). What seemed clear to Rondeau, however, was that Origen heard the voice of Christ in the psalms that the New Testament imputes either explicitly or implicitly to Christ. In light of the new homilies of *Codex Monacensis Graecus* 314,[24] we are now in the fortunate position to be able to examine Rondeau's observations about Origen's use of "prosopological"

19. Rondeau, *Exegese Prosopologique et Theologie*, 97.

20. Rondeau, *Exegese Prosopologique et Theologie*, 100. E.g. Ps 3.

21. Rondeau, *Exegese Prosopologique et Theologie*, 112. E.g. Ps 29:10; 15:10.

22. Rondeau, *Exegese Prosopologique et* Theologie, 100.

23. Rondeau, *Exegese Prosopologique et Theologie*, 69. See also his treatment of Ps 3:6; 4:1–2, 9–10.

24. See Lorenzo Perrone's brief treatment of the Origen's prosopology within the newly discovered homilies in his "Origen Reading the Psalms: The Challenge of a Christian Interpretation," in the

exegesis to identity Christ, given that we have his full, sustained treatment of ten psalms in the 29 homilies.[25]

In fact, in the very first homily of the volume, his first homily on Psalm 15, Origen makes a very suggestive, even programmatic statement about identifying Christ in the psalms that confirms these two observations of Rondeau's. He explains that in the case of some psalms,

> if we were to say in the introduction that the person in the psalm is our Lord, it would either be because we had we discovered (εὑρίσκοντες) this, or apprehended it by intuition (ἐπιβάλλοντες), or had been enlightened (φωτιζόμενοι), or had guessed (στοχαζόμενοι), and we say this either correctly or not (ὑγιῶς ἢ οὐχ ὑγιῶς λέγομεν), but concerning other [psalms] we learn the person from Scripture (τῶν γραφῶν μανθάνομεν τὸ πρόσωπον).[26]

With this statement, Origen explicitly describes the flexibility in identifying Christ in the psalms that Rondeau observed, for he admits, whether rhetorically or not, that his identification of Christ in the case of the first category of psalms may or may not be correct. However, the statement also bears witness to his certainty about the psalms of the second group, whose person the New Testament indicates is Christ, again just as Rondeau observed in the limited material with which she had to work. Since we now have his sustained exegesis of the psalms in this collection, in this paper I will briefly explore some examples of how Origen identifies Christ in both categories of psalms he mentions in this passage: those psalms about which he may or may not be correct in identifying Christ as the person, and those psalms in which scripture teaches us the person. We will also look at how his identification of Christ in his introductory comments informs his interpretation of specific verses of the psalms, in order to observe how this theoretical statement works out in practice.

Let us turn first to a couple of examples from the group of psalms where Origen does operate with the flexibility we find him espousing in this theoretical statement regarding the identification of Christ in the psalms. We find one such example in his first homily on Ps 73. He claims that this psalm of Asaph

---

volume *Upholding Scripture, Rejecting Scripture: Strategies of Religious Subversion* (Tübingen: Mohr Siebeck, 2018).

25. Of course, we already had his homilies on three of these psalms (36–38) in Rufinus' Latin translation, one of the indicators that these Greek homilies were Origen's. See: Origen, *Homélies sur les Psaumes 36 à 38*, eds. Henri Crouzel, Luc Brésard, Emanuela Prinzivalli, Sources Chrétiennes 411 (Paris : Cerf, 1995).

26. *Origenes Werke* XIII, ed. L. Perrone, in collaboration with M. Molin Pradel, E. Prinzivalli and A. Cacciari, GCS NF 19 (Berlin: DeGruyter, 2015). Origen, *HPs15* 1 (Perrone, p. 280, ll. 7–11).

"deals with matters concerning Jerusalem" (συνειστήκει τὰ τῆς Ἰερουσαλήμ), and that it says, "as according to the wording (ὡς πρὸς τὸ ῥητόν) what had happened to the people after captivity." [27] So here we have Origen identifying the subject matter of Ps 73 as the Jewish people who were deported to Babylon. Here I should note that Origen does not always use the term *prosopon* when identifying the psalm's person or subject, as is the case here, but his method can still be described as "prosopological," a point Rondeau made as well.[28] Origen goes on to say that the words of this psalm, "fit, as far as the letter goes (ἁρμόζει, ὅσον ἐπὶ τῇ λέξει), the events after the captivity."[29] However, he does not stop there. He says in addition that "someone (τις) might say that it fits not only those events, but also those after the sojourn of our Savior, when the blood, according to their voice, was coming on them and their children" (an allusion to Matt 27:25, in which the evangelist has the Jews demand the release of Barrabas over Jesus in his passion narrative).[30] So for Origen, the events described in the words of the psalm refer not only to the Babylonian captivity of the historical southern kingdom of Judah, but also to the Jews' self-condemnation in their rejection of Christ, which led to his death, even if Origen relies on the hypothetical "someone" for the suggestion. Unlike other instances in Origen's scriptural exegesis, where "someone" tends to function for him as a hypothetical interpretive opponent to be refuted, in this instance he does not dismiss this "someone's" suggestion. Instead, he entertains it throughout his treatment of this psalm, to the point that one gets the distinct impression that the interpretive rebuttals of this "someone" in fact belong to Origen himself, for they seem to dictate his interpretation throughout his treatment of the entire psalm.[31] That he finds merit in this interpretation becomes clear immediately, for he goes on to add a third subject of the psalm, the souls of his hearers, by asking, "what else can be adapted according to the wording (δύνασαι κατὰ τὸ ῥητὸν ἐφαρμόσαι) and to the things recorded after the coming" (τὴν παρουσίαν)?[32] He does not use the language of allegorical or anagogical interpretation here, but his claim that "as far as the letter goes" the psalm

---

27. Origen, *HPs73* 1 (Perrone, p. 225, l.9–12). For a thorough treatment of *HPs73* 1 and 2, See Margaret M. Mitchell's article in this volume.

28. Rondeau, *Exegese Prosopologique et Theologie*, 134.

29. Origen, *HPs73* 1 (Perrone, p. 225, 1.12–15).

30. Origen, *HPs73* 1 (Perrone, p. 225, 1.15).

31. See for example the following passages: *HPs73* 1 (Perrone, p. 230, 5.17–28–p. 231, 5.1–7); *HPs73* 2 (Perrone, p. 239, 2.5ff); *HPs73* 2 (Perrone, p. 249, 7.19–20–p. 250, 7.1–14).

32. Origen, *HPs73* 1 (Perrone, p. 225, 1.19–20).

is concerned with the people of Jerusalem at the time of Babylonian captivity, implies that the other subjects he finds subsequently are "beyond the letter." So, in this example, we see Origen's flexibility in identifying two subjects, the one "according to the letter," and the other, namely, Christ, by "adapting," and thus perhaps by applying or fitting the psalm to the events surrounding the coming of Christ. We will see that when he turns to interpret specific verses of the psalm, he can find Christ there by searching for the deeper meaning, though his introductory identification of Christ in the psalm does not require it.

Let us turn to one such example now. When Origen comes to the words of Ps 73:1–2, "why God would you thrust us aside to the end?" we see again his flexibility in terms of the verses' referents. He begins with the understanding of "the simpler person" (ὁ ἁπλούστερος), who will say that the answer to the question of the verse is the general sins of the people, referring presumably the Jewish people of the Babylonian deportation, but perhaps simply to people generally.[33] For his second interpretation, Origen returns to the hypothetical "someone," who wants to look "to some deeper extent" (ἐπὶ ποσὸν βαθύτερον ὁρῶν) at the verse.[34] This interpreter will say that the people were "thrust aside" because they thrust aside Christ, causing him great suffering.[35] In fact, the second interpretation probably fits the words of the psalm more closely, for, Origen says, "certainly God had more reason to thrust aside the people after Christ's sojourn and the outrages he suffered."[36] In fact, there was no other time in which Jerusalem had been so bereft, says Origen, when the result of their actions was that sacrifices were no longer presented on their altars because God "thrust them aside."[37] We should note, before turning to the next example, that Origen found Christ here by going beyond the letter, and this will dictate his treatment of the rest of the psalm. Further, we even see him making the claim that it is this interpretation that best fits the words of the psalm. So, while he is flexible in allowing several referents or persons, he is confident that he has found Christ here, or at least that "someone" has.

---

33. Origen, *HPs73* 1 (Perrone, p. 226, 2.6–8). Cf. *Peri Archon* 4.2.1, 6 on the "simpler" of the church, who understand only the literal sense of scripture.

34. Origen, *HPs73* 1 (Perrone, p. 226, 2.8–9).

35. Origen, *HPs73* 1 (Perrone, p. 226, 2.10–12).

36. Origen, *HPs73* 1 (Perrone, p. 226, 2.11–13).

37. Origen will go on to provide another interpretation of "thrust aside," with regard to the individual soul, thrust aside in his union with the first Adam, but only to a certain extent, for in the second Adam, Christ, the human soul is made alive. Origen, *HPs73* 1 (Perrone, p. 226, 2.15–p. 227, 2.1–8).

The second example we will examine is his homily on Ps 75. He begins immediately with the first clause of Ps 75:2, "God is known in Judea." Concerning these words, he first admits that Judea clearly refers to the Jews/Judeans, who have "taken the name of the place of Judea," and thus who have supposed that "fear of God is with them only."[38] The psalm then is indeed about "the Jews." However, it is about "the Jews" only if understood "in a simpler way" (πρός τοὺς ἁπλούτερον).[39] But Origen then wonders (rhetorically) how the statement, "God is known in Judea" can be true if understood in this "simple" way, for, he asks, is God not known in Egypt, and in the desert, and in many other places also?[40] For, he observes, many signs and wonders occurred even in the wilderness, signs and wonders that clearly also made God known. This difficulty leads Origen to seek another explanation, and thus he asks the (rhetorical) question: "why then, if God is known in such numerous places, is it written, "God is known in Judea"?[41] He continues: "even if they[42] were unwilling (μὴ βούλωνται ἐκεῖνοι) unless compelled to accept (εἰ μὴ ἀωαγκάζονται παραδέξασθαι) [that] this statement was prophesied about the time of the Savior, was it not written because of the coming of Christ Jesus, himself God and Son of God, to Judea, when 'God became known in Judea'?"[43] Again, even though Origen admits that one can understand these words in a "simpler" (Jewish) way, he argues that the issue he finds at the level of text in this verse ought to point the careful reader to another, higher, interpretation. Again, we also see his flexibility demonstrated here. When he moves to address the words that follow in Ps 75:2, "your name is great in Israel," Origen extends this line of interpretation. The "God" mentioned in Ps 75:2a, from the words "God is known in Judea," Origen claims, actually refers to Christ, "whose name is great in Israel."[44] This in a manner reminiscent of his discussion in Book 4 of *Peri Archon*, where he claims that the apostle "raises our spiritual apprehension to a higher level" by distinguishing between an Israel of the flesh and an Israel of the spirit. He assumes here as there that the things promised in the Old Testament of Israel and Judah require a mystical interpretation, and that therefore we must hear the name "Israel" in accordance with Paul's principle

<hr>

38. Origen, *HPs75* 1 (Perrone, p. 280, 1.1–3).

39. Origen, *HPs75* 1 (Perrone, p. 280, 1.4).

40. Origen, *HPs75* 1 (Perrone, p. 280, 1.5–9).

41. Origen, *HPs75* 1 (Perrone, p. 280, 1.10–11).

42. Likely the "simple" Jews.

43. Origen, *Hom on Ps 75* 1 (Perrone, p. 280, 2.11–14). Here I am following Alex Poulos' reading of this passage.

44. Origen, *HPs75* 1 (Perrone, p. 280, 1.15–281, 1.1).

that "not all Israel are themselves Israel" (Rom 9:6), just as not all Gentiles are Gentiles.[45] So, he says, "Israel is reckoned as a Gentile nation not believing in the appearance of Jesus Christ our Lord"; however, if we understand Israel in this manner (that is, Israel understood inwardly), then it is "clear" (σαφὲς) how the words of Ps 75:2, "your name is great in Israel" can be understood to refer to the name of Jesus Christ, which is great, since he is God "according to Christians everywhere."[46] Again in this example, we see that his recourse to a spiritual interpretation assists him in understanding these specific words of Ps 75 as referring to Christ, and again, this will be the case for his treatment of the rest of the psalm. Again, we saw Origen's flexibility around identifying the psalm's person, but we also saw him argue that his discovery of Christ via his spiritual reading is actually quite "clear."

To conclude this section, admittedly based only on the example of two psalms, a couple of observations are necessary. In both of these examples from the first category of psalms that Origen mentions in his programmatic state-ment with which we began, we see him searching in the words of the psalm for the verses' deeper meaning in order that he might find Christ there. It seems that his uncertainty (even if feigned) about whether he has found Christ in these psalms allows for more flexibility in his identification of the *prosopon* in a given psalm, for in some cases he identifies as many as three. However, de-spite his claim above to be "either right or wrong" about his identification of Christ in the psalms belonging to the first category, he makes very confident claims about his discovery of Christ in his treatment of specific verses. Once he has inferred that he has found Christ in a given psalm, nearly every verse re-fers in some way to Christ or to the reality he imparts to the Christian in the incarnation.

For the remainder of this essay, let us return to the homilies on Psalm 15, the context in which we found Origen making his programmatic statement about the identification of Christ in the psalms. Again, I quote him:

> concerning some [psalms], if we were to say in the introduction that the person in the psalm is our Lord, it would either be because we had we discovered this, or apprehended it by intuition, or had been enlightened, or had guessed, and we say this either correctly or not, but concerning other [psalms] we learn the person from Scripture (τῶν γραφῶν μανθάνομεν τὸ πρόσωπον), just as is the case in this psalm (ὥσπερ ἐπὶ τούτο τοῦ ψαλμοῦ).[47]

45. *Peri Archon* 4.3.6, 9.
46. Origen, *HPs75* 1 (Perrone, p. 281, 1.2–12).
47. Origen, *HPs15* 1 (Perrone, p. 75, 2.7–12).

For Psalm 15, applied to Christ by Peter in Acts 2, provides us with an example where Origen's discovery of Christ in the psalm is authorized by the New Testament, and he says explicitly here, "the utterances cited from the Acts of the Apostles *prove* that the psalm was spoken from the person of our Lord Jesus Christ" (καὶ ἄλλα δὲ παρατεθέντα ὑπὸ τοῦ ἐν ταῖς Πράξεσιν τῶν ἀποστόλων Πέτρου ῥητὰ παραστήσει ὅτι ὁ ψαλμὸς ἐκ προσώπου λέγεται τοῦ κυρίου ἡμῶν Ἰησοῦ Χριστοῦ).[48] Origen's certainty about Christ as Psalm 15's *prosopon* comes not only from the fact that the Psalm is cited by the New Testament Acts text, but also from his understanding of inspired apostolic scriptural interpretation. For he says: "each apostle is a sacred witness clothed by the Holy Spirit whenever he interprets something from the scriptures," and this is the case because Jesus Christ "associated with the apostles" (συνέστησε γὰρ τοὺς ἀποστόλους), and God in turn was "in Jesus Christ."[49] This statement about the inspiration of the apostles confirms Karen Jo Torjesen's argument in her *Hermeneutical Procedure and Theological Method in Origen's Exegesis*, that the authors of both the Old and the New Testament "wrote by the spirit what the Logos taught them in order to teach us the same truth," and that "what they wrote and understood originates from their own experience with the pedagogy of the Logos."[50] In this passage Origen claims that Jesus "associated with them" and therefore they not only wrote out of this experience with him, but here it seems to be worked out with reference to scriptural interpretation, Christ himself having had some kind of influence on the apostles in this regard during his time with them. Moreover, says Origen, it is not just Peter who refers the Psalm to Christ in this way, but when Peter "raised his voice and he used" (ἐχρήσατο) Ps 15.8–10, he did so "with the other eleven apostles."[51] Now that we have seen just how Scripture teaches Origen that Christ is the speaker of this psalm, we will turn to specific examples in his treatment of the psalm's words.

There are two main features of Origen's interpretation of this category of psalm that I wish to focus on here: firstly, the extent to which he dwells on the difficulties involved with interpreting the words of the psalm despite, or

48. Origen, *HPs15* 1 (Perrone, p. 76, 2.12–14).

49. Origen, *HPs15* 2 (Perrone, p. 91, 1.1–4). Cf. *Peri Archon* 4.2.2 on the inspiration of the authors of scripture.

50. Karen Jo Torjesen, *Hermeneutical Procedure and Theological Method in Origen's Exegesis* (Berlin and New York: De Gruyter, 1986), 119.

51. Origen, *HPs15* 2 (Perrone, p. 91, 1.10–11).

perhaps even as a result of, his certainty about its "person" being Christ, and secondly, his solution to these difficulties, namely, his inclusion of humanity in the psalm's *prosopon*, as a result of Christ's union with humanity, and specifically with his body, the church. I will argue that he dwells on these difficulties for their rhetorical impact, in order to build up to his remarkable solution.[52]

We will begin with the difficulties resulting from the New Testament authorization of Christ as the psalm's person. It seems to me that it is precisely Origen's certainty that this psalm is spoken from the person of Christ that appears to cause him interpretive difficulties when he is faced with the task of explaining specific verses from the psalm. In other words, he has clarity about the person of this psalm from the outset. However, clarity on this level results in obscurity at the level of particular verses, obscurity that requires divine assistance, from God the Father and from his Logos, to provide clarity in order that they might be understood in light of the whole.[53]

For example, as he deals with the very first verse of the psalm, "protect me, Lord, for I have hoped in you" (15:1b–2a), he is faced with the difficult implications of assigning these words to Christ, who is divine. Origen deals with the verse in a couple of ways. He begins with the immediate statement that "the Savior explains for us his own prayer in order that he might teach us to pray."[54] Thus, these words serve as exemplary prayer for the one who wants to learn how to pray, similar to Jesus' exchange with his disciples in the Gospels. Origen moves on from this explanation quickly, however, and suggests implicitly that we ought not be surprised by Christ's praying these words; he does so "because the Savior is subordinate (ἐνδεὴς) to the Father," and it is only the Father who is not subordinate.[55] However, Origen assures his hearers, even though the Savior is subordinate, he has an "exceptional property" (ἐξαίρετόν),

<hr>

52. See Margaret M. Mitchell's "'Problems and Solutions' in Early Christian Biblical Interpretation: A Telling Case from Origen's Newly Discovered Greek Homilies on the Psalms (Codex Monacensis Graecus 314)" in *Adamantius* 24 (2018). She argues that the procedure of "problems and solutions" is the central to the unity of Origen's treatment of his first homily on Ps 77. There she explains that the goal of the exercise within liturgical oratory is to deflect the problems that are raised in order to pique the interest of one's audience. However, it is also the orator's responsibility to make sure no one leaves with any doubt that the problem has been completely resolved. We will see that this is the case in his treatment of Ps 15.

53. I should note here that in my attentiveness to Origen's oscillation between claims about a text's obscurity and clarity, I am indebted to Margaret M. Mitchell's notion of the "veil scale" of early Christian biblical interpreters. See her *Paul, the Corinthians, and the Birth of Christian Hermeneutics* (Cambridge: Cambridge University Press, 2010).

54. Origen, *HPs15* 1 (Perrone, p. 76, 3.15–16).

55. Origen, *HPs15* 1 (Perrone, p. 76, 3.17).

and is subordinate to only the Father, unlike us, who are "subordinate to more beings than he is."[56]

Having explained the verse in terms of its implications for Trinitarian doctrine, Origen provides another interpretation, dealing with the difficulty of fitting these words to Christ in "another way" (ἄλλως), indeed, in a way that he claims will be "more auspicious and pleasing to many" (εὐφημότερον καὶ ἀρεσκόντως πολλοῖς).[57] With the words, "protect me, Lord, for I have hoped in you," Jesus spoke to his Lord and Father "concerning those who are parts of himself" (περὶ τῶν ὄντων μελῶν ἑαυτοῦ).[58] The apostle helps him with this interpretation, for, as he says in 1 Cor 12:27, "you are the body of Christ," and thus, says Origen, Christ prays "for you, even as he speaks of himself" (εὐχόμενον περὶ σοῦ λέγειν περὶ ἑαυτοῦ).[59] We will look more closely at this text below, but for now it is enough to observe that Origen deals with the challenge of understanding these words as Christ's by claiming that despite their implication that Jesus is subordinate to the Father, they teach us how we ought to pray, and that they actually represent Jesus' prayer to the Father for his body, the church. We should note that in this example, none of his explanations of the verse require a move beyond the letter of the text.

We are given another example of the difficulties of understanding the words of Ps 15 as being spoken "from the person of Christ" as Origen turns to interpret the words of verse 5, "I shall bless the Lord who causes me to understand." This is the first verse Origen treats in his second homily on the psalm, but before he gets to them, he warns his readers of the difficulties presented by the New Testament indication of Christ as its "person." In the homily's introductory comments he says, "it is not very easy to refer the explanations, as to the Savior, which the apostles applied (οὐ πάνυ ἐστὶν εὐχερές τὰ μὲν οὖν ἐγκείμενα ἀναφέρειν ἐπὶ τὸν σωτῆρα, οἷς οἱ ἀπόστολοι ἐχρήσαντο), and for them to be explained by us vigorously according to the letter" (πρὸς λέξιν κεκρατημένως δι᾽ ἡμῶν διηγήσαθαι).[60] That is, he explains, identifying the psalm's person requires then that "the whole psalm must be made clear and fit textually to itself" (ὅλον δὲ τὸν ψαλμὸν σαφηνίσαι καὶ πρὸς λέξιν ἐφαρμόσαι ἑαυτῷ), meaning that each verse must be demonstrated to have been spoken

56. Origen, *HPs15* 1 (Perrone, p. 76, 3.17–18).
57. Origen, *HPs15* 1 (Perrone, p. 77, 3.14).
58. Origen, *HPs15* 1 (Perrone, p. 77, 3.14–16).
59. Origen, *HPs15* 1 (Perrone, p. 77, 3.20–22).
60. Origen, *HPs15* 2 (Perrone, p. 92, 1.5–6).

by or about the Savior, the psalm's person.[61] This endeavor is so difficult, Origen claims, that it "seems to require the Savior himself" (δοκεῖ μοι αὐτοῦ τοῦ σωτῆρος χρείαν ἔχειν).[62] In order that this take place, Origen asks those present to pray for God's assistance in helping him make the scriptures clear (πρὸς τὸ σαφηνίσαι τὴν γραφήν), and that God might "supply the Logos to us who thirst and request enlightenment on those matters that need to be made clear" (ἵν᾽ ὁ θεὸς διψῶσιν ἡμῖν καὶ αἰτοῦσι φωτισμὸν πραγμάτων δεομένων τρανώσεως ἐπιχορηγήσῃ λόγον), and further, that he himself may be "enlightened by the Logos" (φωτιζόμενοι ὑπὸ τοῦ λόγου).[63] Thus, in this passage we witness another confirmation of Torjesen's study, namely her articulation of the primary way in which Origen understands Christ's mediation at the present time: the interpretation of the written scriptural word is a form of the living and personal presence of the Word.[64]

Having warned his hearers of the difficulty of the interpretive endeavor before them, and the need for God's Logos to assist them, Origen finally turns to the first verse of focus in this homily, Ps 15:5a, "I shall bless the Lord who causes me to understand," which he claims Christ speaks. The issue to be dealt with here is how Christ can be said to be without understanding prior to the Lord causing him to understand. Origen deals with this issue by claiming, for the first time in his treatment of the psalm, that Christ speaks these words "according to his humanity" (κατὰ τὸ ἀνθρώπινον).[65] For, Origen instructs, "in the scriptures you separate when the Lord speaks, understood according to his divinity and when he speaks according to his humanity" (ἐν γὰρ ταῖς γραφαῖς διαστέλλεις πότε λέγει κύριος, ὁ κατὰ τὸ τὴν θεότητα νοούμενος, καὶ πότε λέγει Χριστός, ὁ κατὰ τὸ ἀνθρώπινον νοούμενος).[66] Note that he does not use the term *prosopon* in this instance, but that the principle that would dominate later Christological thought, that is, the differentiation of Jesus' words and actions as those he did and spoke "as God" and "as man," is present already here. It is more fitting that the human Christ can be said to lack understanding, thinks Origen, which is implied by these words of the psalm, and also by the words of verses 9 and 10, "but still my flesh will encamp in hope, nor will you allow your consecrated one to see corruption," which provide him with proof

61. Origen, *HPs15* 2 (Perrone, p. 92, 1.7–8).
62. Origen, *HPs15* 2 (Perrone, p. 92, 1.9–10).
63. Origen, *HPs15* 2 (Perrone, p. 92, 1.11–17).
64. Torjesen, *Hermeneutical Procedure*, 136.
65. Origen, *HPs15* 2 (Perrone, p. 92, 2.19).
66. Origen, *HPs15* 2 (Perrone, p. 92, 2.19–21).

that in all of Ps 15 it is the voice of the human Christ who speaks, for these are the words used by Peter in Acts.

Origen goes on in explanation of this verse to claim that the prophet Isaiah also spoke about Jesus "according to the flesh" with the words "there shall go forth a rod from the root of Jesse and a bloom shall ascend from the root, and the spirit of the Lord will rest upon him, the spirit of wisdom and understanding" (Is 11:1–2). Clearly it is the verbal and conceptual connection of "understanding" that elicits this citation, and concerning these words, Origen says, "if the spirit of understanding rests upon the one from the root of Jesse, ... the spirit of wisdom and understanding has been united to the Saviour understood according to the humanity."[67] What is it then that Christ has been given to understand by the Father? He speaks these words of the psalm, says Origen, because he is "apprehending the union" (τῆς ἑνώσεως ἀντιλαμβανόμενος) between his humanity and the divine "spirit of understanding."[68] Since Christ has been given this understanding of the union of the human and divine in him, he is therefore able to assist Origen, the interpreter, who participates in him. Origen has certainty that Christ is imparting to him this understanding and helping him to overcome these interpretive difficulties, for which he has asked his hearers to pray.

The words of Ps 15:7b, "yet also until night my kidneys have trained me," pose difficulties for Origen as well.[69] He begins his treatment of this phrase by saying of the verse, "the saying of this one and the next, require grace from God for clarification (τούτου δὲ ἐστι φωνὴ καὶ ἡ ἑξῆς, δεομένη τῆς ἀπὸ τοῦ θεοῦ χάριτος εἰς σαφήνειαν), for it is not easy to explain (οὐχ εὐχερὲς διηγήσασθαι) how Christ's kidneys trained him."[70] (Indeed, it is not easy to explain how anyone's kidneys have trained them, but this is particularly tricky in the case of Christ's kidneys, Origen claims). To solve this issue, Origen turns to scriptural examples where he finds the spiritual heart, one of the hidden things God searches, and makes clear that he thinks about the kidneys of this verse in a similar way. For he says, "these kidneys, the ones equivalent to the purity of

---

67. Origen, *HPs15* 2 (Perrone, p. 93, 2.10–17).

68. Origen, *HPs15* 2 (Perrone, p. 93, 2.17–p. 94, 2.11). Quite what one should make of this is unclear to this author at least. What is clear is that Origen is alert to some of the complexities of what would become the problem of the two natures and their union in subsequent centuries. For a closer treatment of Origen's Christology as it is developed in his homilies on Psalm 15, see Lorenzo Perrone's "Abstieg und Aufstieg Christi nach Origenes. Zur Auslegung von Psalm 15 in den Homilien von *Codex Monacensis Graecus 314*," *Theologie und Philosophie* 89 (2014), 321–40.

69. See Alex Poulos' treatment of the term νεφροί ("kidneys") in this clause in his paper in this volume.

70. Origen, *HPs15* 2 (Perrone, p. 94, 3.2–3).

heart having the roots and beginnings of thoughts … train the soul of Jesus."[71] Consider then, he says, "the soul of Jesus that came down from heaven" (John 3:13), that soul which "did not consider equality with God as something to be grasped, but emptied itself, taking the form of a slave" (Phil 2:6–7), and consider that soul as incarnating, storing teachings and thoughts, not in the heart, but in the kidneys, which train and maintain one's attention.[72] Consider also, says Origen, that these kidneys appear in Jesus' humanity, which did not sin, nor did it know sin (1 Pet 2:22).[73] That is, the kidneys have trained his soul in righteousness, so that he is free from sin in his humanity. In this way can Jesus be understood to say: "yet also until night my kidneys have trained me." There is much more that might be said about this passage, given its complexity, but I think it is enough to say for now that the verse provides one more example of the interpretive problems resulting from having to fit the psalm in its entirety to the person of Jesus. Again, we do not see Origen turning to the spiritual meaning of the text as a result of these difficulties. Instead, we see him repeatedly admitting the difficulties involved, and asking for assistance from Christ the Logos, the psalm's *prosopon*.

We will now turn to the second feature of these homilies on Ps 15 that I wish to focus on here, namely, what I will argue is part of Origen's overarching solution to the problems he has raised. According to Origen, the human believer is to be included in the person of Christ in the psalm. In fact, as he treats each verse of the psalm, it is often the case that he understands himself, his hearers, and Christians generally to actually speak the psalm's words through their union with Christ.

In his introductory comments to his second homily on Ps 15, Origen provides us with a statement in which he explains why it is necessary that he determine the psalm's "person." For he says, to "explain clearly the whole psalm and fit the text to itself, demonstrating that which is said is in the person of the Savior, and teaches worthily about the Savior, seems to require the Savior itself, in order that we will be enabled to speak with the Lord speaking within us" (a reference to 2 Cor 13:3).[74] Thus while it seems that one of his interpretive goals in these homilies is to interpret them in such a way as to provide his hearers with an understanding of the way in which the *human* Jesus spoke

---

71. Origen, *HPs15* 2 (Perrone, p. 94, 3.15–17).
72. Origen, *HPs15* 2 (Perrone, p. 95, 3.3–13).
73. Origen, *HPs15* 2 (Perrone, p. 95, 3.18–21).
74. Origen, *HPs15* 2 (Perrone, p. 92, 1.7–11).

the psalm's words, his primary interpretive goal, as stated explicitly here, is for Origen and his hearers to be "enabled to speak with the Lord" the words of the psalm. If it is clearly the Lord who spoke the words of the psalm according to his humanity, then his human body, that is, the church, is enabled to speak the words through him. Again, we must turn to Torjesen's study, particularly her treatment of Rufinus' translation of Origen's homily on Ps 37, from which she argued that, in interpreting the Psalms, Origen is "primarily interested in developing the relationship between his hearers and the content of the psalm."[75] This argument is confirmed by these homilies, and certainly by this statement here. In the psalm on which Torjesen worked, however, the speaker was identified by Origen simply as the psalmist, and in order to draw his hearers into the text so that they might be "acted upon" by the Logos, he had to find a common identity that would unite the psalmist and his hearers. In the case of Ps 37, it was the "repentant sinner."[76] However, in the case of Ps 15 in the homilies at hand, for Origen there is no need to search for a common identity that unites his hearers and the psalmist, for the Logos himself is the speaker, to whom his hearers are already mystically united. Here they do not need to be "acted upon," but instead they speak with Christ, as the speaking subjects of the psalm.

Thus, for almost every verse of Psalm 15, Origen ends his treatment of the verse by explaining how the human believer might also speak the words, as members of his body, the church. In fact, in these homilies, we find Origen claiming that a human prayer, which is offered "apart from the Savior," is actually "incomplete" (ἀτελῆ).[77] For, he explains, "it is necessary that my prayer be sent through Jesus Christ, the high priest and protector of our souls," since it is not possible for it to reach him "unless Jesus Christ offers it" (χωρὶς τοῦ προσφέροντος αὐτὴν Ἰησοῦ Χριστοῦ).[78] These statements are very similar to those found in his treatise *On Prayer*, where he provides the scriptural justification for this belief about prayer.[79] Therefore, if Psalm 15 presents Christ's actual speech, a hermeneutical supposition that Origen holds to be true, and if human prayer to God is only possible through Christ, then it only makes sense that the interpreter of this psalm would have the goal of understanding how humanity might join Christ in speaking these words to the Father.

75. Torjesen, *Hermeneutical Procedure*, 25.
76. Torjesen, *Hermeneutical Procedure*, 28, 47.
77. Origen, *HPs15* 1 (Perrone, p. 77, 3.3–5).
78. Origen, *HPs15* 1 (Perrone, p. 77, 3.6–9).
79. Origen, *On Prayer* 15.2–4; 23.1. He uses John 16:23–24 and Mark 10:18 to justify this.

So let us turn to some passages that exemplify this interpretive goal, a goal that also provides a solution to the problems raised by scripture's indication that Christ is the *prosopon* of the psalm. We will not be able to discuss every example, but we will examine three here. For the first example, we will return to Origen's treatment of the words of Ps 15:1b-2a, "protect me, Lord, for I have hoped in you." Once he explains how Christ speaks these words, that is, as a prayer to the Father for his own protection, and for the protection of his body, the church, Origen goes on to say that he himself is also able to speak the words. He says: "I dare to say to the Lord (Θαρρῶ εἰπεῖν τῷ κυρίῳ), 'protect me, Lord, for in you I have hoped' … because I, as a part of him, have hope in God through him" (καὶ ὅτι κἀγὼ τὸ μέλος αὐτοῦ δι' αὐτὸν ἐπὶ τὸν θεὸν ἐλπίζω).[80] Origen then explains how these words make sense coming from his and his audience's lips: "we need much of the Lord's protection and on every occasion."[81] Through the *prosopon* of Christ, Origen and his audience, and Christians generally, are able to pray these petitioning words of the psalm to the Father.

When Origen reaches the words, "the Lord is the portion of my inheritance and of my cup" of Ps 15:5, we see him making the same interpretive move. Once again, he determines that these words are spoken by Christ, and once again, he goes beyond this interpretation to demonstrate how it is that we are also able to speak these words. Again, Origen himself says directly, "the Lord is my portion of inheritance and my cup," in order to exemplify what he is claiming his hearers should say.[82] He goes on to explain that this is so because "we drink the Savior and we eat the Savior," for just as Christ has the Father as a portion of his inheritance, he is our nourishment and drink.[83] Of course the language of eating and drinking Christ sounds Eucharistic to us, but Origen goes on to explain what he means by these words in two different ways, neither of which is with reference to the Eucharist. He says explicitly that "prayer is the nourishment of the soul," and then he goes on to add that the soul is nourished as well when "the teaching Logos comes into the listener" (λόγος διδασκαλικὸς εἰσερχόμενος εἰς τὸν ἀκούντα).[84] It is not entirely

---

80. Origen, *HPs15* 1 (Perrone, p. 79, 4.8–10).

81. Origen, *HPs15* 1 (Perrone, p. 79, 4.10–11).

82. Origen, *HPs15* 1 (Perrone, p. 87, 8.1–2).

83. Origen, *HPs15* 1 (Perrone, p. 87, 9.4–5).

84. Origen, *HPs15* 1 (Perrone, p. 88, 9.13–15). I have not ruled out the possibility that he does allude to the soul's consumption of Christ in the sacrament of the Eucharist in this passage, but it is clear that he most certainly has in view the soul's nourishment in both prayer and in the hearing of the exegetical homily. The extent to which Origen ever has the Eucharist in view is a subject of dispute. See, however, the work of Elizabeth Dively Lauro on the topic: "The Eschatological Significance of Scripture According

clear what he means by the latter form of the soul's nourishment, but it seems to me that he hints at the soul's consumption of the Logos in the hearing of scripture, and perhaps also in hearing its explication in the form of Origen's own exegetical homily. This being so, therefore, Origen asks, "what sort of blessedness do we speak of before the Father?" (ποίαν μακαριότητα εἴπωμεν ἐπὶ τοῦ πατρός;). He answers his question: we speak the very words of the psalm, given our union with Christ in prayer and through participation in the hearing of scripture and its explanation.[85] However, just as Origen made clear that Jesus' subordination is different from our subordination when treating Christ's words of prayer in Ps 15:1–2, here too he warns his hearers that Jesus' nourishment by the Father is different from ours, in that Christ "is never neglectful of his own nourishment, but he is always wakeful and being nourished by the Father."[86] In our case, however, we can only speak these words if our souls are being nourished by him, and this is only the case if we do not neglect its nourishment, as we are want to do. However, if we are diligent in feeding our souls, we can speak with Christ the words of the psalm, "the Lord is the portion of my inheritance and of my cup." In this example then, Origen exhorts his hearers to the spiritual discipline of prayer, and to listen attentively to scripture and its explanation in his homilies. Only on the condition that they do these things, can they speak Christ's words.

The final example we will discuss comes at the end of his treatment of the psalm in the second homily, as he interprets the words, "you have made known to me the ways of life" of Ps 15:11. He begins again, by assigning these words to Christ's "human element" (τὸ ἀνθρώπινον αὐτοῦ), for he says, "it is the human who ascends on the ways of life."[87] From here he turns immediately to another possibility, along the lines of the examples we have observed in this section, saying, "perhaps he speaks of you" (τάχα δὲ καὶ περὶ σοῦ λέγει), "for Christ refers everything in you to himself (τὰ γὰρ ἐν σοὶ πάντα εἰς ἑαυτὸν ἀναφέρει), I tell you, being a body and a part of him" (ὄντι σώματι καὶ μέλει αὐτοῦ).[88] His treatment of this psalm is drawing to a close with this section, and so perhaps that is why he spends comparatively little time explaining his understanding of this verse, despite making such a profound statement.

---

to Origen," *Studia Patristica LVI* Vol. 4 (Leuven: Peeters, 2013), 83–201. She argues that Origen uses the consumption of Christ in the Eucharist as a basis for discussing the consumption of Christ in Scripture, both materially and intellectually.

85. Origen, *HPs15* 1 (Perrone, p. 87, 9.18–19).
86. Origen, *HPs15* 1 (Perrone, p. 89, 9.14–16).
87. Origen, *HPs15* 2 (Perrone, p. 111, 10.13–15).
88. Origen, *HPs15* 2 (Perrone, p. 111, 10.16–18).

Apparently by now the way this verse applies to Origen's hearers is self-evident. We might observe, however, that Origen describes here his understanding of Christ's recapitulation of every aspect of human nature in the incarnation, and thus as we are dealing in this psalm with the words of Jesus according to his humanity, he refers to the human soul's process or journey of ascension to the divine. Jesus took this on in himself too in the incarnation, and thus he speaks in this psalm of himself and of the human believer. His treatment of the next phrase of Ps 15:11, "you will fill me with rejoicing with your person" exhibits a similar pattern. Concerning these words, he argues that the Father "fills [Christ] with merry things and above all with his so-called person" (πληροῖ αὐτὸν εὐφροσυνῶν καὶ κατ᾽ ἐξοχὴν τὸ λεγόμενον πρόσωπον αὐτοῦ).[89] Thus as Christ speaks out of his participation in the person of the Father, so too does Origen claim that the human believer is able to speak these words in like participation in his union with Christ. However, even though the human believer may join with Jesus in speaking these words, Origen makes it clear that there is a limit to the way in which union with Christ is manifest in this life, for as he interprets the words, "delight in his right hand" of Ps 15:11, he says that "before she reaches the end, one does not succeed at participating in the 'delight in the right hand' of God."[90] This is then one more way in which the human person of Jesus is to be distinguished from the human believer; only to Christ do these words "delight in God's right hand" apply fully. They apply to his hearers only in the life to come.

In order to make some concluding comments about this section, let us return briefly to Rondeau and her arguments about Origen's Christology as articulated in the context of his exegesis of the Psalms. Again, based on the material with which she had to work, Rondeau made the important observation that Origen tends not to find Christ in the God addressed by the psalms, but rather in the human speaker.[91] Therefore, not only does Christ speak on his own behalf in these cases, but also on behalf of every person, *"qu'il assume et récapitule dans l'Incarnation,"* and specifically on behalf of his body, the church.[92] We have indeed seen that these two homilies on Ps 15 confirm these aspects of her argument too. In light of this interpretive tendency, Rondeau argued, the Christological implications of Origen's "prosopological" exegesis

---

89. Origen, *HPs15* 2 (Perrone, p. 112, 10.11–13).

90. Origen, *HPs15* 2 (Perrone, p. 112, 10.14–15).

91. Rondeau, *Exegese Prosopologique et Theologie*, 103.

92. Rondeau, *Exegese Prosopologique et Theologie*, 125, 134. This becomes one of the central threads of the early "Christianization" of the Psalter.

are perhaps better described as implications for his ecclesiology, for Origen deals less with the two natures of Christ than he does with Christ's role "according to the *oikonomia*" in salvation history.[93] As we saw again and again in these examples, when Origen identifies Christ as the speaker, he also identifies Christ's human body, the church, within this identification. Thus, to find Christ in the psalms is to find humanity, and specifically the church.

In conclusion, we have seen in these examples that, at least when Origen cannot claim with certainty that a psalm's *prosopon* is Christ, he is flexible in his identification of the person, finding Christ as one of several options. He can find Christ in these examples by way of examining the words of the psalm "in a deeper way," that is, by finding their spiritual meaning, about which he is frequently quite certain. Thus, his lack of certainty, even if rhetorical, about the psalm's overarching *prosopon*, provides him with the flexibility to find Christ beyond the letter of the text with great clarity. The opposite of this dynamic is true in the case of the homilies on Ps 15, whose person scripture taught us. Concerning this category of psalm, Origen's certainty about the psalm's overarching *prosopon* as Christ leads to difficulty and sometimes uncertainty at the level of individual psalm verses and phrases. Origen does not look beyond the letter of the text in order to solve these interpretive difficulties, however. For the inspired apostle Peter, who encountered the Logos and applied this psalm to him in light of this experience, has already found Christ there. Origen develops this by finding in Christ's psalmic words, with just as much certainty, the "person" of the human church.

Finally, Origen is not as rigid in his identification of Christ as the psalms' person as some later well-known Psalms commentators. Still, Origen's pioneering endeavor to identify the "person" of every psalm systematically would become commonplace for virtually every subsequent early Christian commentator, as was demonstrated by Rondeau. Further, the "prosopological" method does give Origen the framework to be able to specify if Christ speaks as man or as God, and we have seen this in one of the examples we have examined here, even if we see in his writings only the seeds of what becomes the later church's Christological discussions, in which the term *prosopon* is central.[94] Thus, one of Origen's contributions to subsequent Christological discussions is his introduction of the word *prosopon* by way of the "prosopological method."[95]

<hr>

93. Rondeau, *Exegese Prosopologique et Theologie*, 106, 121, 133.
94. Rondeau, *Exegese Prosopologique et Theologie*, 125.
95. Rondeau, *Exegese Prosopologique et Theologie*, 390.

Robin Darling Young

8. EVAGRIUS OF PONTUS SUMMARIZING ORIGEN

From Homily to Scholia on Psalm 76

Among the books of the Christian Old Testament, the Book of Psalms was particularly compelling for early Christian interpreters; they encountered the Psalms quoted extensively in the New Testament, and understood them not only to refer to Jesus, but to be his actual words, enunciated for the services of the ancient Temple, but discernible as his only later, during and after his lifetime. The Book of Psalms had been crucial for Origen's biblical interpretation from the beginning of his career, and some of his fourth-century readers made sure to preserve sections of that early commentary.[1] Likewise, at the end of his career, Origen added to his earlier interpretation the homilies delivered to a Christian congregation in Caesarea of Palestine—the subject of this volume, the recently-discovered Greek homilies that are now available in English translation.[2]

If the commentary had been preserved and made available, it is also likely that the Homilies on the Psalms likewise circulated widely among learned Christian teachers and presbyters, who themselves were interpreting the Psalms for their readers and listeners. Numerous Christian writers of the fourth and

1. See Origène, *Philocalie, 1–20 et Lettre à Africanus*, ed. Marguerite Harl and Nicholas De Lange (Paris: Cerf, 1983).

2. Perrone, Lorenzo, ed. with M. Molin Pradel, E. Prinzivalli und A. Cacciari, *Origenes Werke*, 13. Bd.: *Die neuen Psalmenhomilien. Eine kritische Edition des* Codex Monacensis Graecus 314, (Berlin: De Gruyter, 2015); Joseph W. Trigg, *Homilies on the Psalms: Codex Monacensis Graecus 314* (Washington, DC: The Catholic University of America Press, 2021).

fifth centuries likely read and used, at least in part, Origen's interpretation of the Psalms, both in the commentary and in the homilies. Certainly, Eusebius of Caesarea had done so, as did later interpreters, both Greek- and Latin-speaking. This essay traces how in one biblical interpreter of the late fourth century, Evagrius of Pontus, used Origen's earlier interpretation of the Psalms.

Evagrius' biblical interpretation has received relatively little attention, probably because scholars have been more interested in his role as a theoretician of the ascetic life associated with the monastic settlements of Egypt, and have not concentrated upon his activities as a scholar of the Bible. Yet Evagrius' exegesis, particularly in the form of his Biblical scholia, are of interest for the reception of Origen's work because they, like his, are the work of a teacher trained in philosophy as he adapts scriptural works to the stages of a Christianized paideia.

Beginning with his training as a scholar and philosopher, and associate of the three main fourth-century Christian writers from Cappadocia; then as a deacon in Constantinople and finally, an ascetic teacher residing in Kellia in Egypt, Evagrius was at the center of late-fourth-century Origenism.[3] His own *Scholia on the Psalms* reflect not only his reading and interpretation of Origen's homilies; they also show that Evagrius, like other prominent teachers of his era, wanted to preserve Origen's biblical interpretation for their own readers and successive generations, but without identifying them as his. Origen's work and reputation had encountered severe criticism even as Greek speakers were adapting it and western scholars were translating and making it available to Latin readers; at the same time, the recitation of the Psalms had begun to occupy a central part of Christian worship in urban churches—and were becoming a focal point for monastic thought and introspection.[4] These developments both rested upon, and required, Origen's work even as that same work gathered fierce opposition.

---

3. The most convenient general study of Evagrius' life and work remains Antoine Guillaumont, *Philosophe au désert Evagre le Pontique* (Paris: Vrin, 2004); of the controversy that led to the destruction of Origen's works in Greek, Elizabeth A. Clark, *The Origenist Controversy: The Cultural Construction of an Early Christian Debate* (Princeton: University Press, 1992) and an earlier work by Jon Dechow, *Dogma and Mysticism in Early Christianity: Epiphanius of Cyprus and the Legacy of Origen* (PhD dissertation, University of Pennsylvania, 1975). For a full bibliography of Evagrius' works and secondary studies, see the website evagriusponticus.net, created and maintained by Joel Kalvesmaki. It should be noted that this essay was completed before the publication of Paul Géhin's critical edition of Evagrius' Psalms scholia. Now see Evagre le Pontique, *Scholies aux Psaumes: Introduction, Edition princeps du texte Grec, traduction, note et annexes*, ed. Marie-Josèphe Rondeau, Paul Géhin and Matthieu Cassin (Paris: Cerf, 2021), vol. 2:57–68.

4. See Robert Taft, *The Liturgy of the Hours in East and West* (Collegeville, MN: Liturgical Press, 1993).

This essay presupposes that Evagrius knew of this controversy although he does not discuss it directly; and that, in his work as a teacher for much of his life, he thought that the work of Origen was both true and foundational. Further, it speculates as a hypothesis that Evagrius tried to forestall the disaster of rejection and partial destruction of that interpretation by reproducing Origen's interpretation in a new format. He did this, as I propose here, by reworking Origen's exegesis of the Psalms and encasing it in his own interpretive scholia, without explicitly giving Origen credit, but by pointing unmistakably to his work. To conclusively demonstrate this hypothesis would require a very large comparative study; and such a study would be hampered from the outset, because while this largest of Evagrius' works has survived in its original language, thanks to its preservation in later catenas, there are only twenty-nine of Origen's homilies remaining in Greek. Yet there is much to learn about Origen's value to later generations by comparing Evagrius' scholia to Origen's interpretive homilies. Here, then, it is enough to compare the two works where they treat the same Psalm, in order to suggest the potential usefulness of a much larger comparison in a later study.

My test case for the hypothesis is the interpretation of Psalm 76, on which Origen commented in four of his Greek homilies.[5] Did Evagrius copy and adapt the interpretation of Origen and insert it into his notes for his own study of this scriptural work? A comparison of the works of the two men shows that indeed, Evagrius did do that, and thus, by extension, is likely to have done so throughout his Psalms scholia, with the result that the missing homilies of Origen might still be found, reflected, in the scholia of Evagrius. Equally interesting is the presence of Clement of Alexandria's thought in the scholia. Evagrius frequently cites or outright copies Clement throughout his work, and he has done so as well in his Scholia on Psalm 76.[6]

Several previous studies have surveyed Evagrius' interpretation of the Psalms; Luke Dysinger has devoted a monograph and several articles to the subject; he has also provided a translation of a portion of the unedited Psalms scholia both in print and digitally. To Dysinger's study has been added

---

5. Perrone, ed. *Psalmenhomilien*, 293–350.

6. Antoine Guillaumont, "Le gnostique chez Clément d'Alexandrie et chez Evagre le Pontique," in *Alexandrina: Hellénisme, judaïsme et christianisme à Aexandrie. Mélanges offerts au P. Claude Mondésert* (Paris: Cerf, 1987), 195–201 and Robin Darling Young, "*Xeniteia* According to Evagrius of Pontus," in *Ascetic Culture: Essays in Honor of Philip Rousseau,* ed. Blake Leyerle and Robin Darling Young (Notre Dame, IN: University of Notre Dame Press, 2013), 229–52.

another survey of early monastic Psalms interpretation, half of which is devoted to Evagrius' scholia.[7]

Both scholars place Evagrius' scholia in the context of an organized communal monastic liturgical prayer, yet such a practice may have developed only later in his particular corner of the ascetic world. In the course of harmonizing the scholia with other works of Evagrius, neither explores the possibility that his scholia may not be directed toward the monastic life at all, and are not as much a reflection of monastic worship as a set of interpretive notes both for the Christian *gnostikoi* for whom Evagrius wrote, and for *later* use in works directed toward monks. It is notable that Evagrius' other scholia—on Proverbs, Ecclesiastes, and Job—do not mention the monastic life; instead, they are notes meant to aid in the decoding of books written by Solomon and Job, teachers of wisdom whose works Evagrius thought were crucial to the development of the Christian *gnostikos*. Perhaps the *Scholia on the Psalms* fit the same description.

Now that the entire collection of Evagrius' Psalms scholia has appeared in the *Sources Chrétiennes* series, a full exploration of the entire, lengthy Greek text can begin, thanks to the critical edition by Paul Géhin and Marie-Josephe Rondeau, with Matthieu Cassin.[8] In the meantime, however, a comparison of the pre-critical edition version of the scholia and of extracts from Origen's homilies points to just this conclusion: that Evagrius meant to preserve the thought of Origen by summarizing it and encoding it in his own scholia. The Psalms, in his view, were the site for that part of the path of gnosis that he called natural contemplation, *theôria physikê*.[9] His personal knowledge of the anti-heretical policies of the emperor Theodosius enacted while Evagrius was in Constantinople, and his awareness of the works and activities of Epiphanius of Salamis, the prime enemy of Origen and his followers, would likely have made him sense that his own work was urgent.[10]

<hr>

7. Luke Dysinger, *Psalmody and Prayer in the Writings of Evagrius Ponticus* (Oxford: Oxford University Press, 2005), and "Evagrius Ponticus: The Psalter as a Handbook for the Christian Contemplative," in *The Harp of Prophecy: Early Christian Interpretation of the Psalms*, ed. Brian E. Daley and Paul R. Kolbet (Notre Dame, IN: University of Notre Dame Press, 2015), 97–125. See also James Wellington, *Christe Eleison! The Invocatino of Christ in Eastern Monastic Psalmody c. 350–450* (Bern: Peter Lang, 2014).

8. Géhin, Paul, Marie-Josephe Rondeau and Matthieu Cassin, eds., *Évagre le Pontique, Scholies aux Psaumes, Tome I: Psaumes 1–70; Tome II: Psaumes 71–150.* Sources Chrétiennes (Paris: Cerf, 2021).

9. See Kevin Corrigan, *Evagrius and Gregory: Mind, Soul and Body in the 4th Century* (Farnham: Ashgate, 2009), 157–74, on Evagrius' description of the understanding of nature.

10. Evagrius likely knew of Epiphanius' *Panarion*, published before the Council of Constantinople at which they were both present. For Epiphanius' presence there, see most recently Andrew Kim,

The Diffusion of Origen's Psalms Interpretation

When Origen composed his *Homilies on the Psalms*, he had already written a commentary on the Psalms as a teacher in Alexandria[11]. Now as an older man returning to the Psalms as part of his work of instructing a Christian congregation in Caesarea, he could draw on his own past scriptural exegesis to examine some of the Psalms in detail, and by examining them, to teach their meaning to his congregation at the differing levels understandable to them. Because he was already considered an authority for Christian teaching thanks to his vast literary work, and had maintained a correspondence with other Christian leaders, it is likely that he knew his homilies would be copied and circulated.[12]

How did Evagrius come to read Origen's Homilies on the Psalms? They may have travelled to his native Asia Minor, or he may have encountered them in Jerusalem or Egypt. The earlier centers for the diffusion of Origen's works were Caesarea and Alexandria. Because Origen's library and his own works remained in Caesarea after his death, Eusebius could consider himself Origen's successor, and use the homilies in the composition of his own Psalms commentary.[13] From Caesarea they might have been made available to the episcopal library in Jerusalem, and at the end of the fourth century been put to use by Rufinus and Melania in their residence at the Mount of Olives beside Jerusalem.[14] But thanks to a strong connection with Asia Minor, many of Origen's works could have passed much earlier into the hands of Gregory Thaumaturgus, bishop of Neocaesarea, or Firmilian of Caesarea; the first was Origen's student, and the second, his correspondent. The next generation of early Christian thinkers indebted to Origen, the three main Cappadocian authors, also

---

Epiphanius of Cyprus: Imagining an Orthodox World (Ann Arbor: University of Michigan Press, 2015), 204–8.

11. Joseph W. Trigg, *Origen of Alexandria* (Abingdon: Routledge, 1998), 1–65.

12. For a recent account, see Alfons Fuerst, "Origen: Exegesis and Philosophy in Early Christian Alexandria," in *Interpreting the Bible and Aristotle in Late Antiquity: The Alexandrian Commentary Tradition Between Rome and Baghdad* (Farnham: Ashgate, 2011), 13–32.

13. See M. J. Hollerich, "Eusebius' Commentary on the Psalms and Its Place in the Origins of Christian Biblical Scholarship," in Aaron Johnson and Jeremy Schott, eds., *Eusebius of Caesarea: Tradition and Innovations*. (Washington, DC: Center for Hellenic Studies, 2013, and more recently, Tommaso Interi, "Origen and Eusebius Interpreting Psalm 77," *Studia Patristica* 61 (2021): 65–77. On the library of Eusebius, see Andrew Carriker, *The Library of Eusebius of Caesarea* (Leiden: Brill, 2003), 8–9, 240–43.

14. For details, see Catherine M. Chin, "Rufinus of Aquileia and Alexandrian Afterlives: Translation as Origenism," *Journal of Early Christian Studies* vol. 18 no 4 (Winter 2010): 617–47.

used Origen's interpretation of the Psalms in composing their own works.[15] It is possible, as well, that a Christian library in Alexandria possessed the homilies and commentary of Origen on the Psalms, and so would have been available for Didymus' use for the composition of scholia in his school there, or earlier to Athanasius in his Epistle to Marcellinus.[16] In other words, by the last quarter of the fourth century, these homilies are likely to have achieved a wide circulation among the scholars of eastern cities, and Evagrius might have read them either in Asia Minor or in one of his later residences.

But in these last decades of the fourth century, Origen's thought, and his biblical interpretation, were also growing more controversial. The Origenist controversy formally began with the condemnations of 400, but the preceding twenty-five-year campaign against Origen by Epiphanius of Salamis, may have bred caution among the next generation of those in the tradition of Origen or Alexandrian thought more generally, such as Melania, Rufinus and John of Jerusalem with their associates, and Didymus and Evagrius and his associates in Egypt. By the end of the fourth century, both Rufinus and Evagrius had found ways to preserve Origen's thought: Rufinus by translation primarily, and Evagrius by the reproduction of Origen's thought in a different literary form.[17]

Evagrius' Use of Origen's Psalms Homilies

As an ambitious scholar, and teacher in the Egyptian ascetic settlements of the late fourth century, Evagrius of Pontus encountered the Psalms in a setting vastly different from Origen's. Origen had preached his homilies on the Psalms to an urban congregation in a major city in Roman Palestine, and in an era of increasing state hostility to the church, but Evagrius worked nearly 150 years later and, after his arrival in Egypt, largely in connection with various ascetic

15. See most recently Mark del Cogliano, Basil of Caesarea's Homily on Psalm 115 (CPG 2910): Origen and Anti-Eunomian Polemic," *Sacris Erudiri* 57 (2018), 7–31, and for Gregory, Ronald Heine, *Gregory of Nyssa's Treatise on the Inscriptions of the Psalms* (Oxford: Clarendon Press, 1995).

16. Athansius of Alexandria, *A Letter to Marcellinus on the Interpretation of the Psalms*, trans. Robert Gregg in Athanasius, *Life of St. Anthony* (Mahwah, NJ: Paulist Press, 1980); Michael Gronewald, Didymus der Blinde, *Psalmenkommentar (Tura-Papyrus)* (Bonn: Rudolf Habelt, 1968); Albert-Kees Geljon, "Didymus the Blind: Commentary on Psalm 24 (23 LXX): Introduction, Translation and Commentary," *Vigiliae Christianae* 65 no. 1 (2011): 50–73. See also Blossom Stefaniw, *Mind, Text, and Commentary: Noetic Exegesis in Origen of Alexandria, Didymus the Blind, and Evagrius Ponticus* (Frankfurt am Main: Peter Lang, 2010).

17. The connection is discussed by Robin Darling Young in, "A Life in Letters," in *Melania: Early Christianity Through the Life of One Family*, ed. Catherine M. Chin and Caroline T. Schroeder (Berkeley: University of California Press, 2017), 153–70.

institutions. If he had been Basil's *anagnostês*, he might have compiled interpretive notes even earlier, in the 370s. Where Origen had crafted his thought as a pioneer in the use of philosophy for a coordinated and systematic exposition of Christian teaching, Evagrius could draw upon nearly a century and a half of later investigation based on Origen's work. He could have used libraries in at least four cities, from his student days under Gregory of Nazianzus (and perhaps under Libanius) to his sojourns in Constantinople and in Jerusalem, and very likely built his own library in Kellia, southeast of Alexandria. Taught by those who had read Origen's works before him—including Melania and Rufinus, as well as teachers he names in various works—, he came into contact more intensely with those books as he drew upon them in his own teaching.[18]

Before considering Evagrius' use of Origen in his own interpretation of the Psalms, however, it is helpful to review some previous scholarship that has placed Evagrius' interpretation squarely in the context of early monastic ritual use of the Psalms. Such an approach seems obvious, because, as both Evagrius and his biographers tell us, he spent the last period of his life in a monastic community; according to the History of the Monks of Egypt, the *Lausiac History* of Palladius, and the historians Sozomen and Socrates, Evagrius lived as a monk and wrote primarily for Christian ascetics. In particular, Palladius attests that Evagrius prayed one hundred prayers daily, although he does not mention that this prayer was from the Psalms or that it took place in the presence of others (and Evagrius does not himself mention the practice).[19] Furthermore, John Cassian, (a student of Evagrius although he lived in Scetis) describes in his *Conferences* and *Collations* the use of Psalms by the monks of Egypt during his stay in there in the last decade of the fourth century; his descriptions have been used retroactively to create the context for Evagrius' work on the Psalms. John Cassian's work is particularly important, since there is so little description left of how monks prayed the Psalms in the fourth century.[20]

The liturgical scholar Robert Taft, however, summarizing an earlier study

---

18. On the possibility that Evagrius had been a student of Libanius with John Chrysostom, now see Gabriel Bunge, "Evagre le Pontique fut-il un condisciple de saint Jean Chrysostome?" *Irénikon* vol. 91 no. 3 (2018): 163–83; 324–45.

19. See Columba Stewart, "Imageless Prayer and the Theological Vision of Evagrius Ponticus," *Journal of Early Christian Studies* 9 (2001), 185. Palladius does not mention Evagrius as praying Psalms at all. See Historia Lausiaca, ed Cuthbert Butler, The Lausiac History of Palladius, v. 2, Texts and Studies 6 (Cambridge: Cambridge University Press, 1904), section 38. English translation in Robert Meyer, *The Lausiac History* (New York: Newman Press, 1964), 110–14.

20. Columba Stewart, *Cassian the Monk* (Oxford: Oxford University Press, 1998), 100–105; 110–13.

of his, found no evidence for a monastic "office" at this time; rather, he described the knowledge of monastic psalmody as follows:

> Early monastic prayer was more a meditation in common on sacred scriptures than a "liturgical ceremony." The monastics paid no attention whatever to symbol or ceremonial, hymns or chant, or to ritualizing the hour or season or feast. Their interest was not in conforming their prayer to the time or season but in conforming their hearts to the word of God. This is quite different from the cathedral offices in which the psalmody is our praise of God rather than his saving word to us.

Taft further remarks that among monastics, a reader would recite the Psalms in order and listening monks absorb and meditate upon them, or a monastic brotherhood would recite the Psalms together or antiphonally.[21]

The surviving mentions of the use of the Psalms in the fourth century, as distinguished from fifth-century sources, tend to bear out Taft's observations. Athanasius' *Letter to Marcellinus* recommended praying the Psalms, but it is written to one person and claims the authority of an old man (geron) who may not necessarily be a monk.[22] Eusebius wrote a *Commentary on the Psalms*, but it is a scholarly work, not reflecting an ascetic context. Likewise, Basil of Caesarea directed his *Homilies on the Psalms* toward a congregation, and his *Letter to Neocaesarea* mentions a dispute about the proper way to recite the Psalms, but this dispute reflects the practice in a cathedral church in which his addressees are apparently claiming a tradition to which he objects. [23] Gregory of Nyssa's *On the Inscriptions of the Psalms* considers the Psalms in their relationship to the ascent of the soul; its relationship to Evagrius' work has yet to be assessed. Finally, Didymus the Blind's *Commentary on the Psalms* is a collection of notes dictated to a scribe while the author was in the course of lecturing on the Psalms, presumably for students in a school in which he taught. Detailed comparisons of these works might well find common themes of interpretation, even common themes dating back to Origen's Psalm Homilies, but such work remains to be done in the future.

---

21. Robert Taft, "Christian Liturgical Psalmody: Origins, Development, Decomposition, Collapse," in *Psalms in Community: Jewish and Christian Textual, Liturgical and Artistic Traditions*, ed. Harold W. Attridge and Margot E. Fassler, 7–32 (Leiden: Brill, 2004). See also Taft, *The Liturgy of the Hours in East and West*.

22. Athanasius of Alexandria, *A Letter to Marcellinus on the Interpretation of the Psalms*, trans. Robert Gregg in Athanasius, *Life of St. Anthony* (Mahwah, NJ: Paulist Press, 1980).

23. Basil of Caesarea, *Homiliae super Psalmos Patrologia Graeca* 29.209–424. To the Neocaesareans: Letter 207 in *Letters*, ed Yves Courtonne, *Saint Basile. Lettres*, 3 vols. (Paris: Les Belles Lettres, 1957–1966).

Evagrius' *Scholia on the Psalms* have, so far, been examined primarily in the context of a presumed monastic psalmody, on the basis of the later witnesses mentioned above, and because Evagrius mentions the Psalms in other works as being effective in the life of the monk. For instance, in Kephalaion 15 of the *Praktikos*, a work applying his teaching to the initial training of a monk, Evagrius remarks:

> When the mind wanders, reading, vigils, and prayer bring it to a standstill. When desire bursts into flame, hunger, toil, and anachoresis extinguish it. When the irascible part becomes agitated, psalmody, patience, and mercy calm it...[24]

Likewise, a later passage in the same treatise discusses the opposition arising from demonic opposition to monastic practice, with its goal of dispassion (*apatheia*) and love:

> The demonic songs set our desire in motion and cast the soul into shameful fantasies, but "psalms, hymns, and spiritual songs" (Eph.5:19) call the mind to the constant remembrance of virtue, cooling our boiling irascibility and extinguishing our desires.[25]

In each case, however, Evagrius does not refer either to communal recitation or to solitary recitation; he is speaking of the role of the Psalms in the process of his own description of ascetic warcraft against demons; this is the object of the entire *Praktikos* in which these two remarks appear. Such combat, however, is not limited to ascetics and solitaries; resistance to the demonic was a universal art in late antiquity.[26]

Furthermore, in Evagrius' treatise *On Prayer*, a collection of 153 kephalaia that owes much to Origen's treatise *On Prayer*, it is clear that psalmody is a preparatory activity actually inferior to prayer itself. Chapters 82–86 compare prayer and psalmody, making it clear that psalmody belongs both to the

---

24. *Praktikos* 15. It is clear from the remainder of the kephalaion that Evagrius is discussing personal recitation of a Psalm or psalms: "But these practices are to be engaged in at the appropriate times and in due measure, for what is done without due measure or not at the opportune moment lasts but a little while; and what is short-lived is more harmful than it is profitable." Robert Sinkewicz, *Evagrius of Pontus. The Greek Ascetic Corpus* (Oxford: Oxford University Press, 2003), 100. Greek text in Antoine and Claire Guillaumont, *Evagre le Pontique, Traité pratique, ou Le moine*, t. II (Paris: Cerf, 1971), 536–39.

25. Guillaumonts, *op.cit.*, 658–59. Sinkewicz, *Evagrius*, 109 Cf. To a Virgin 48 (tr. Sinkewicz, 134, and *Scholia on Psalms* 101.10: "*For I ate ashes as bread and mingled my drink with weeping.* This verse is useful for those who take enjoyment in flute-playing and songs while drinking." Unless ascetics were enjoying civic rituals with customary musical performances, this is another Psalm scholion that points away from an ascetic context (see below).

26. See, recently, Dayna S. Kalleres, *City of Demons: Violence, Ritual and Power in Late Antique Christianity* (Berkeley: University of California Press, 2015).

achievement of *apatheia* and hence the dispassionate observation of the natural world, while prayer itself is the approach to divine knowledge:

> 82. Pray suitably and without disturbance, and sing Psalms intelligently (Ps 46.8), and in good rhythm, and you will be like an eaglet, raising yourself up to the heights.
>
> 83. Psalmody lulls the passions and completes the calming of the body, but prayer prepares the mind to exercise its own activity (*energeia*).
>
> 84. Prayer is the activity that prepares for the proper rank of the mind, that is, its activity and its better and purer use.
>
> 85. Psalmody is "of the variegated wisdom" (Eph 3.10), but prayer is the prelude to immaterial and unvariegated knowledge.
>
> 86. Knowledge is excellent, for it is the co-worker of prayer, awakening the intellectual power of the mind for contemplation of divine knowledge.[27]

But the passages cited above appear in works that Evagrius meant for those who were pursuing the ascetic life at the highest level, those who had arrived at the borders of *theoria theologikê,* intellective unity with the divine being.[28] The *Praktikos,* on the other hand, among various other works such as his *To Monks in Monasteries,* outlined the ascetic combat against demons in pursuit of calm, apatheia, and love—a state unattainable without thorough self-control. Numerous other places in Evagrius' works repeat his teaching on the subject of psalmody, and its effect on the soul.[29]

The Psalms also reflect the "wisdom full of variety" that provides the objects for contemplation on the part of the one in training to become a *gnostikos.* In a recent essay, Dysinger has grouped the scholia into four categories that allow the Psalms to be a kind of bridge between the beginnings of the ethical life and the state of *theôria theologikê* that, according to Evagrius, is the most complete state of the human being, and the contemplation that accompanies the state of being a *gnostikos,*—a teacher capable of guiding others to contemplation as they reach the unity of the nous with the divine.[30] According to Evagrius, Dysinger writes, the Psalms can have a literal sense: often

27. Paul Géhin, ed. and trans., *Evagre le Pontique, Chapitres sur la prière,* Sources chrétiennes 589 (Paris: Cerf, 2017), 299–301. Cf. Sinkewicz, *Evagrius,* 183–209.

28. See Gabriel Bunge, "In Geist und Wahrheit." *Studien zu den 153 Kapiteln Über das Gebet des Evagrios Pontikos* (Bonn: Borengässer, 2010), 28–35.

29. See Géhin's list in 299n83 of his translation of the *On Prayer* (op. cit.). In addition to the *Praktikos* passages, *Exhortation* 1.3, *Thoughts* 27, *Monks* 98; *Antirrhetikos* 4.22; and *Letter on Faith* 12.

30. Luke Dysinger, O.S.B., "Evagrius Ponticus: The Psalter as a Handbook for the Christian Contemplative," 97–125 in *The Harp of Prophecy: Early Christian Interpretation of the Psalms,* ed. Brian E. Daley, S.J., and Paul R. Colbet (Notre Dame, IN: University of Notre Dame Press, 2015).

they are meant to spur compunction or repel a demon. At the level of "ascetical wisdom," the Psalms can help their reader (or one who recites them) to conquer vice and regain the virtues; on occasion this wisdom includes the recognition of "providential abandonment," to prod a Christian to regain the humility necessary for progress. Third, some of the scholia "interpret the words and events of the psalms as symbols and allegories of the great cosmic drama of the Fall, the Incarnation, and the ultimate eschatological reunion of all reasoning beings with God." Evagrius' understanding of the "logoi of providence and judgment" summarize the divine *oikonomia* at which Clement had hinted, but Origen first described clearly in *On First Principles*. Finally, Evagrius finds the figure of Christ in the Psalms; he "explicitly mentions [him] at least once in 107 of the 149 psalms on which he comments, referring to Christ by name, by title, or by citation of Christ's words from the Gospels."[31]

As we have seen, Evagrius' *Scholia on the Psalms* have been interpreted as reflecting the practice of psalmody in fourth-century monasteries:

> In the liturgical practice of the late fourth century, and especially in monastic communities, opportunities for such prayer recurred regularly, frequently throughout the day and night. The term *psalmodia* referred to corporate or private chanting of psalms, interrupted at regular intervals by pauses for prayer.... The prayer offered during these pauses could be vocal or silent and of variable duration (although generally not protracted), depending on circumstances, local practice, and whether the monk lived alone as a hermit or with others in a community (coenobium).[32]

James Wellington follows Dysinger in placing Evagrius' teaching on the Psalms in the monastic context and taking Cassian's later depiction of communal monastic prayer in Egypt as a useable description not only of Evagrius' primary context, but as the proper interpretive context for the scholia.

Yet even apart from their context, the dating of the scholia is far from certain. Gehin, and Guillaumont before him, thought the scholia were written during Evagrius' monastic career. Yet it stands to reason that if these longest of

31. Dysinger, "Evagrius Ponticus," 109.

32. Dysinger, "Evagrius Ponticus," 116. In the note to this passage, Dysinger cites Cassian's Institutes 2.5–8 as the source for the description of monastic psalmody, as well as discussions by Gabriel Bunge in Das Geistgebet (which posted either a corporate or private recitation) and in a later article "'Der Mystische Sinn der Schrift'" in which Bunge, according to Dysinger, "concludes that these texts and Evagrius's recommendations of undistracted psalmody are less applicable to the common recitation of the monastic office in communities than to the more leisurely solitary meditation on the Psalter practiced by hermits like Evagrius in the privacy of their cell."

Evagrius' works were written for monks, then later works that mention Evagrius' works would have mentioned at least those Scholia—and probably the other scholia as well. Or, on the other hand, it is reasonable to suppose that the scholia would contain references to the monastic life, which they do not.

The Development of Scholia in Christian Exegesis

The *scholion*, or short interpretive note, had already been used by literary scholars since the early third century BCE, and recent scholarship has made progress in discussing their use and development in the grammar schools of Alexandria and elsewhere in the cities of the eastern Mediterranean.[33] Evagrius appears to have been a pioneer in transferring the genre of scholia into Christian literary culture.[34] Although Paul Géhin[35] followed other scholars in attributing the adoption of scholia to Origen—based on a remark of Jerome's—Eric Junod, has on the contrary, argued that Origen did not use the form, and thus Jerome was mistaken. Nonetheless, Marie-Josèphe Rondeau further isolated and reassigned to Evagrius, almost sixty years ago, those scholia once attributed to Origen.[36] An English edition and translation, as stated above, has now appeared.[37]

The editor of the critical edition of Evagrius' other Scholia, Paul Géhin, identified six types of scholia used by Evagrius: paraphrase, pastiche, syllogism, Biblical parallel, question and response, and antirrhetical scholia. In his

33. See Eleanor Dickey, *Ancient Greek Scholarship: A Guide to Finding, Reading, and Understanding Scholia, Commentaries, Lexica, and Grammatical Treatises, from Their Beginnings to the Byzantine Period* (Oxford: Oxford University Press, 2007).

34. The first to study Evagrius' scholia was Hans Urs von Balthasar, in *"Die Hiera* des Evagrius,"* Zeitschrift für katholische Theologie* 63 (1939): 31–47 and Evagrius wrote separate biblical commentaries only in this form, doubtless after he had been exposed to them in his own education is indicated by his familiarity with this form. Marie-Josèphe Rondeau, "Le commentaire sur les Psaumes d'Evagre le Pontique," *Orientalia Christiana Periodica* 26 (1960): 307–48. See also her later volume, *Les commentaires patristiques du Psautier (IIIe-Ve siècles) 1* Orientalia Christiana Analecta 219 (Rome: Pontificium Institutum Studiorum Orientalium, 1982).

35. Scholies au proverbes.

36. Eric Junod, "Que savons-nous du "Scholies" (σχόλια-σημειώσις) d'Origène?," 133–49 in *Origeniana Sexta: Origène et la Bible/Origen and the Bible. Actes du Colloquium Origenianum Sextum. Chantilly 30 août – 3 septembre 1993,* ed. Gilles Dorival et al., (Leuven: Leuven University Press, 1995). For a short description of Evagrius' Scholia and other exegetical works attributed to him, see Guilaumont, *Un philosophe au désert,* 136–40.

37. Carl Vennerstrom ispreparing a translation of all the scholia for publication. See Vennerstrom, "Homeric Scholia, Hellenistic Education, and Ascetic Pedagogy: The Scholia of Evagrius Ponticus" (Early Christian Seminar, 04/02/19) https://cua.academia.edu/CarlVennerstrom last accessed November 10, 2019. More recently, Vennerstrom, "A Spiritual Scholiast in a Changing World: Evagrius Ponticus and His Spiritual Exegesis," for the Mundelein Seminary Graduate Student Conference (October, 2019).

introduction to the *Scholia on Proverbs*, he describes an approach that characterizes all the exegetical works of Evagrius.[38]

In a paraphrase, Evagrius merely restated or expanded a biblical lemma, presumably because it had a moral import or metaphysical significance he did not need to modify or comment upon. In the second, "pastiche," Evagrius composes a scholion imitating the style of Proverbs, and uses the form of antithetical distichs or parallels, comparisons, or enigmas. For instance, in composing a scholion on Prov 30:4 LXX, "Who has risen to the heaven and descended," Evagrius responds with a quotation from John 3:13, "No one has risen to the heaven above, if not the son of man, who has come down from heaven."[39]

The third form of the scholion is the syllogism, or proof, in which Evagrius employs a biblical quotation as a demonstration to support another point of his own teaching. For instance, on Scholion 27, on Proverbs 3.1 "My son, do not forget my laws, and let your heart guard my words," Evagrius writes:

> If it is true that the one who does not live according to it forgets the law, the one who lives according to it remembers the law. And if it is true that he who keeps the words of God does them, he who does not will to observe them loses them. "For the hearers of the law are not those who are righteous before God," he says, "but those who keep the law will be made righteous." (Rom 2:13)[40]

The fourth type of scholion Evagrius employs is the biblical parallel. Although Géhin does not cite Origen as the source of Evagrius' view, he mentions the principle of the unity and non-contradiction of scripture, and thus it is not hard to see Origen as the source of Evagrius' exegetical practice. In Géhin's view, though, Evagrius' exegesis differs from Origen's, because he does not employ the historical sense and take much of scripture literally, as did Origen. But Evagrius reflects the purposes of a very specific kind of exegesis, and it is likely that he read and agreed with much of the scriptural interpretation outlined in *Peri Archon*, while employing it in his own scholia in a more restricted or focused sense.[41]

Two more kinds of scholia complete Géhin's list: the question-and-response form, presumably mirroring a classroom experience. Here, notes Gehin, Evagrius uses the *aporiai kai luseis* method already long practiced by Hellenistic

---

38. Paul Géhin, *Scholies aux proverbes* (Paris: Cerf, 1987), 16–18. See accompanying footnotes for the category to which each scholion of the commentary belongs.

39. Géhin, *Scholies au proverbes*, Scholion 291, p. 382.

40. Géhin, *Scholies au proverbes*, 120.

41. Géhin, *Scholies au proverbes*, 228.

grammarians, and this is noted by a copyist of Patmiacus 270. In this form of
the scholion, a puzzle in the text can be solved; Scholion 71 on Proverbs, for instance, takes up Proverbs 6:6 ("Consider the ant") and connects wisdom with
the "natural and harmonious movement of the ant," to turn the verse toward a
consideration of God as creator from the wisdom of created works.[42]

The final category of scholia Evagrius employs is the antirrhetical, such as
scholia against those "who despise knowledge, false spiritual teachers, those
who despise the body, who lose sight of spiritual teaching, who choose unworthy candidates for clerical positions, evil bishops" These scholia, Géhin notes,
begin with the phrase, "it is necessary to use this proverb against those who …"
This kind of scholion not only corresponds to the intent, and partially to the
form, of Evagrius' *Antirrhetikos*, a handbook of scriptural sayings culled to provide ammunition in the fight against logismoi, or tempting thoughts; but the
form also appears very frequently in the Psalms scholia, presumably because
numerous Psalms voice the distress of the speaker.[43]

In all their forms, the scholia of Evagrius obviously are meant to provide the materials for interpretation, either his own, or someone else's. They
could have been composed when he was still in Caesarea as Basil's *anagnostês*,
or again, as an aid to the interpretation of Origen that went on in Jerusalem,
in the studium of Rufinus and Melania. Elsewhere I will provide a more detailed argument to support this proposal. In this essay, however, I will show
how Evagrius incorporated Clement and Origen's thought as he crafted scholia. In particular, I examine Evagrius' scholia on Psalm 76(77). Such an examination shows that Evagrius knew Origen's homilies on the Psalms, just as he
knew and used other works of Origen.

If these scholia were not intended for ascetics alone, for whom else were
they meant? Evagrius' works frequently allude to philosophical sources and
the works of other Christian teachers in addition to Origen; it is likely, then,
that they were meant for learned readers, both men and women. Since the
Psalms, like Proverbs and Ecclesiastes, were spoken in the voice of the Logos,
they are meant to be a guide to the world of rational beings, and their salvation made possible through the Logos' *oikonomia*. To help his students and
readers understand the Psalms in this way, Evagrius had no better resource

---

42. Géhin, *Scholies au proverbes*, 166.

43. Géhin connects these kinds of scholia to Evagrius' works directed specifically at ascetics in
need of a mode of combat against *logismoi* deceptive thoughts or reasonings often prompted by demons;
cf. *Praktikos* 6–33, identifying the *logismoi* and their remedies. Sinkewicz, *Evagrius*, 97–103.

than the Psalms homilies of Origen. In the scholia Evagrius does not refer to a congregation of an urban church, as Origen does; but he certainly knew that his scholia would circulate among a wider "congregation" of those interested in Christian gnosis, whether in the context of an ascetic or monastic community, or not. Unlike Origen, Evagrius likely did not deliver his Psalms scholia at ecclesial gatherings on Sundays, but crafted them as literary works, meant to train the mind in hearing the Psalms, properly, i.e. according to the interpretation Evagrius had adopted from Clement and Origen and earlier, perhaps, from Basil of Caesarea and Gregory of Nazianzus, or perhaps, according to a recent interpretation, Gregory of Nyssa.[44]

The remainder of this essay will show how Evagrius used and rearranged the thought of Origen in the Psalms homilies and elsewhere to reiterate and update, and to make necessary shifts in, the teaching of Origen—to which he joined the teaching of Clement as a kind of postscript.

Evagrius' Scholia on Psalm 76

Based on the collation by Marie-Josèphe Rondeau, the following text represents the Greek of the Scholia on Psalm 76 as presented by Luke Dysinger.[45] The first two verses of the psalm have not been supplied with scholia by Evagrius, who begins with verse 3:

3 ἐν ἡμέρᾳ θλίψεώς μου τὸν Θεὸν ἐξεζήτησα

> 1. διὰ τῆς πρακτικῆς ἐν τῷ νῦν αἰῶνι τὸν Θεὸν ἐκζητοῦμεν. [=*PG* 12.1537] [*cf.Ant* 6.24]

3(3) ²'Ἀπηνήνατο παρακληθῆναι ἡ ψυχή μου
> [ἐμνήσθην τοῦ Θεοῦ καὶ εὐφράνθην.]

> 2. Οὐδὲν οὕτω παρακαλεῖ ψυχὴν ὡς μνήμη Θεοῦ. [=*PG* 12.1537]

4(1) ἐμνήσθην τοῦ θεοῦ καὶ εὐφράνθην

> 3. μνήμη θεοῦ εὐφραίνει ψυχήν. ὁ δὲ ἐπιλαθόμενος αὐτῆς πενθήσει πικρῶς. [cf Pitra 76.4]

---

44. Ilaria Ramelli, "Evagrius and Gregory: Nazianzen or Nyssen? A Remarkable Issue that Bears on the Cappadocian (and Origenian) Influence on Evagrius," *Greek, Roman and Byzantine Studies* 53 (2013): 117–37. See also eadem, *Evagrius's Kephalaia Gnostika: A New Translation of the Unreformed Text from the Syriac, Translated with Introduction and Commentary* (Atlanta: SBL Press, 2015), xvi–xvii and notes.

45. Accessed online at http://www.ldysinger.com/Evagrius/08_Psalms/00a_start.htm (last accessed 11/7/2019).

5(1) **προκατελάβοντο φυλακὰς οἱ ὀφθαλμοί μου**

> **4.** τοῦτο γνώρισμά ἐστι πολλῆς ἀγρυπνίας. [=*PG* 12.1537]

9(1) **ἢ εἰς τέλος τὸ ἔλεος αὐτοῦ ἀποκόψει**

> **6.** ὡς κόπτοντος αὐτοῦ τὸ ἔλεος ἐπί τισιν, εἴρηται ἀλλαχοῦ τὸ, «παράτεινον τὸ
> ἔλεός σου τοῖς γινώσκουσί σε.» [=*PG* 12.1540]

11(2) **αὕτη ἡ ἀλλοίωσις τῆς δεξιᾶς τοῦ ὑψίστου**

> **7.** ἀλλοίωσιν λέγει ἐνταῦθα τὴν ἀπὸ κακίας καὶ ἀγνωσίας ἐπ᾽ ἀρετὴν καὶ γνῶσιν
> ἐπάνοδον. [=*PG* 12.1540]

13(2) **καὶ ἐν τοῖς ἐπιτηδεύμασίν σου ἀδολεσχήσω**

> **8.** ἀδολεσχία ἐστὶν ἡ περί τι συνεχὴς διατριβὴ καὶ ὁμιλία. [= Pitra 76.13]

14(1) **ὁ θεὸς, ἐν τῷ ἁγίῳ ἡ ὁδός σου·**

> **9.** ἤτοι ἐν παντὶ ἁγίῳ ἡ ὁδὸς τοῦ θεοῦ, ἢ ἐν τῷ Χριστῷ ὁ λόγος αὐτοῦ.
> [=*PG* 12.1540]

15 **σὺ εἶ ὁ θεὸς ὁ ποιῶν θαυμάσια**
 ἐγνώρισας ἐν τοῖς λαοῖς τὴν δύναμίν σου

> **10.** τουτέστι τὸν Χριστόν· Χριστὸς γὰρ θεοῦ δύναμις καὶ θεοῦ σοφία.
> [cf *PG* 12.1540.34]

16(1) **ἐλυτρώσω ἐν τῷ βραχίονί σου τὸν λαόν σου**

> **11.** βραχίων τοῦ θεοῦ ὁ Χριστὸς δι᾽ οὗ ἠνέργησεν τὰ ἐν ἡμῖν ἀγαθά, τὰ κατὰ τὴν
> ἐπιθυμίαν αὐτοῦ γεγονότα. [=Pitra 76, 16.1]

17(1–2) **εἴδοσάν σε ὕδατα, ὁ θεὸς,**
 εἴδοσάν σε ὕδατα.

> **12.** νῦν τὰ ὕδατα λογικὰς φύσεις σημαίνει. [=Pitra 76, 17.1–2]

76:17(3) **καὶ ἐταράχθησαν ἄβυσσοι, πλῆθος ἤχους ὑδάτων**

> **13.** αἱ ἄβυσσοι τὰς καταχθονίους δυνάμεις δηλοῦσιν, αἵτινες ἐν τῇ παρουσίᾳ τοῦ
> Χριστοῦ ἐταράχθησαν. [=*PG* 12.1540]

19(1). **φωνὴ τῆς βροντῆς σου ἐν τῷ τροχῷ**

> **14.** ὁ τροχὸς ἢ τὸν αἰῶνα σημαίνει τοῦτο ἢ τὸν κόσμον τὸν αἰσθητὸν, ἢ τὴν
> καθαρὰν καὶ αἰώνιον ψυχὴν, εἴπερ ἡ κακία παρὰ γωνίαν παρεδρεύει.
> [=*PG* 12.1540.43]

76:21 **ὡδήγησας ὡς πρόβατα τὸν λαόν σου**
 ἐν χειρὶ Μωϋσῆ καὶ Ἀαρών.

15. ἡ κατὰ Μωσέα φιλοσοφία τετραχῇ τέμνεται, εἰς τὸ ἱστορικὸν, καὶ τὸ κυρίως λεγόμενον νομοθετικὸν, ἅπερ ἂν εἴη τῆς ἠθικῆς πραγματείας ἴδια, τὸ τρίτον τε εἰς τὸ ἱερουργικὸν, ὅ ἐστιν ἤδη τῆς φυσικῆς θεωρίας, καὶ τέταρτον ἐπὶ πᾶσι τὸ θεολογικὸν εἶδος.

Translation:

3(1) On the day of my affliction I sought God

In the present aeon/age we seek God through the praktikê

3(3) My soul refused to be comforted

Nothing so comforts the soul as the memory of God.

4(1) I remembered God and rejoiced

Memory of God rejoices the soul; the forgetfulness of him will grieve it bitterly.

5(1) My eyes were preoccupied with watches of the night

This is a token of much wakefulness.

6 I considered the ancient days, and an aeonic year I remembered and meditated

The one knowing the obscure and the hidden matters of God (Ps 50:8) also holds the memories of passing aeons and of the years in them, and the ancient days from which he composed them.

9(1) Or will he cut off his mercy forever?

If he has cut off his mercy to some, it is said elsewhere that "he extends his mercy to those who know you" (Ps 35:11).

11(2) And I said, "now I have begun." This is the change of the right hand of the Most High.

[David] speaks here of the ascent from evil and ignorance to virtue and knowledge.

13(2) And upon your customs I will meditate

Continual study and conversation about someone is meditation.

14(1) Oh God, your road is in the holy place

Either the road of God surely is in every holy place, or his logos is in the Christ.

15 You are the God who is working wonders, you have indicated your power in the peoples.

That is, the Christ, for a Christ is the power of God and the wisdom of God (1Cor. 1:24)

16(1) You redeemed your people with your right arm.

> *The Christ is the right arm of God, through whom he effects the good things in us, the things coming about according to his desire.*

17 (1–2) Waters saw you, oh God, waters saw you and were afraid.

> *Now he signals that the waters are reasoning natures.*

17 (3) and the abysses were shaken, a great reverberation of waters

> *"The abysses" signify the subterranean powers, which were shaken at the presence of the Christ.*

19 (1) A voice of your thunder in the wheel.

> *The wheel signifies either this aeon or the sense-perceptible cosmos, or the pure and aeonic soul, if indeed evil is always near a corner (cf. Prov 17:12).*

21 You guided your people like sheep, by the hand of Moses and Aaron.

> *The philosophy according to Moses is divided* tetrachôs *(into four parts) (Clement str. 1.28): one the historical, and [second] the precisely termed legislative part, which two especially belong to an ethical treatise; but the third is about the divine worship, which is now of the natural contemplation, and a fourth generally the theological form. It is necessary for us also to grasp in a fourfold way the intention of the law as clarifying some type, or as showing some sign, or as confirming a law for the purpose of upright governance or declaring by an oracle, as prophecy. By such a method Moses and Aaron will lead the people traveling from evil to virtue.*

Scholion 1 on Ps 76 3.1, "We seek God through the *praktikê* in the present aeon."

This scholion raises the question of how anyone among his readers ("we") can seek God; and Evagrius' answer is through training, to which many of his treatises and collections of kephalaia are devoted—in the very age in which we live in our bodies, the *aeon* that is present to us. *Aeon* here I have translated "age" instead of "time" even though the Greek word can mean either, according to context. But because he accepts Origen's account of the fall and return of minds to God, Evagrius here uses the word *aeon* to refer to a time span in which the mind lives, having gained a soul, in a particular kind of body—human, angelic, or demonic—that is its *katastasis*, or state. God's providence and judgment has placed it in this state, and in the human state the *praktikê*, training in ethics and insight, enables it to begin its return to God.

In Homily 1 on Psalm 76, Origen writes "I remember saying elsewhere that 'with the hands' is the same as 'with conduct.' For this is to seek God, in your conduct, from which God is found."[46]

Thus, the first two topics, appearing in the scholion to verse 3(1), are the *praktikê* and the present *aeon*. Evagrius depends upon Origen's description of time and the cosmos in *Peri Archon* 3.3.5 to frame the human lifespan as "the day of my affliction," where "day" is equivalent to our lives from birth to death, but also means a particular longer timespan which could be succeeded by another, as part of the divine *oikonomia*. In our present *aeon* we have the chance to employ a specific ethical training incumbent upon baptized Christians. The thought of both Clement and Origen lie behind the idea of this training, but because Evagrius was involved in the crafting of a discipline adaptable to those who were trainings to become *gnostikoi*, this scholion shows how Evagrius regards affliction as a disease requiring as a cure the application of his particular program—a program schematized in the *Praktikos* but appearing in other works, for example in the *Sentences to Monks in Monasteries*.[47] (see Homily 1 on Ps 76, section 2–3).

In this state of acquiring a discipline Evagrius likens to the work that all young men would have encountered, in their educations, in the gymnasium and preparation for the sports of wrestling and racing, a person also has to remember God. Evagrius describes this in his *To a Virgin* as a matter of solitary prayer and study.

Scholion 2, on Psalm 76.3.3, "Nothing so comforts the soul as the memory of God."

The memory is an ambivalent faculty, in Evagrius' view. On the one hand, as Evagrius details extensively in the treatise *On Thoughts*, it produces "recollection of evil," *mnêsikakia*, a resentful and continuous awareness of wrongs suffered, that leads backwards into encounters with demons and further vice through the *logismoi*, thoughts that prompt a person to engage in a particular vice. On the other hand, remembering one's own sin is useful[48] (*Eulogius* 14:13, "hold on to the memory of your sin"), and when the memory does not stir up the *pathê*—disturbances of the soul—it can "move you toward the knowledge of your presence (before God)," as Evagrius remarks in *On Prayer*.[49]

---

46. Homily 1 on Ps 76, section 4 (Trigg translation, 206, Homilia, 298).
47. Trigg, 205, Homilia, 296.
48. See *To Eulogius* 14.13, Sinkewicz, *Evagrius*, 41.
49. *On Prayer* 44–46; Sinkewicz, *Evagrius*, 197.

Origen comments, on Ps 76:3, that the cure of the passions is the memory of God:

> Two passions occurring to a man in difficult situations are discussed, so that we can get help by learning what we say at first and how, when we are undergoing them, we may be cured from passions. Whenever something is painful or when, at times, we come wholly under the domination of pain and affliction, we do not even listen to the one who comforts us, but say, "My soul refused to be comforted." But if we want, after being dominated by [a disturbance of the soul/emotion] and refusing to be comforted, to be comforted and to rejoice, it suffices to remember God ... If ever something painful happens to you, as you pray to be a man of the church, and you see yourself darkened by pain and dominated by the pain itself, remember his *logoi* of hope, the blessedness in Christ, and immediately the pain will fall away.[50]

In the next scholion, **Scholion 3, on Ps 76:4(1)**, Evagrius reinforces this teaching: the soul gains happiness (*chara*) from the memory of God (meaning, also the memory of the nous' presence before God, before the creation of the cosmos and time) but bitter grief from forgetting God, which latter state entails thinking that the struggles of the visible world, and of the soul's warfare with the demonic vices, is the sum and substance of the world and life as it is. Here, again, he follows Origen: "Where there is remembering God, passion has been put to flight. Where there is passion, someone has not remembered God." [51]

Scholion 4, on Ps 76.5(1) "This is a token of much wakefulness"
Evagrius, directing his reader to the ascetic practice of wakefulness, *agrypnia*, uses the word *gnôrisma*, "sign, mark, token" in the sense in which it was used in a criminal trial: as a *corpus delicti*—as in *Praktikos* 55:

> When the natural movements of the body during sleep are free of images, they reveal that the soul is healthy to a certain extent. The formation of images is an indication of ill health. If it is a matter of indistinct faces, consider this a sign of an old passion; if the faces are distinct, it is a sign of a current wound.[52]

"Wakefulness" is a quality of angelic life—the highest possible form of life for the nous still awaiting reunion with God—but it is also a practice for beginning monks, as in Foundations 11:

---

50. Homily 1 on Ps 76, 208.

51. Hom 1 Ps 76/7.

52. Sinkewicz, *Evagrius*, 107.Following David Brakke, Sinkiewiecz believes that Evagrius refers to seminal emissions. See Brakke, "The Problematization of Nocturnal Emissions in Early Christian Syria, Egypt and Gaul," *Journal of Early Christian Studies* 3 (1995): 419–60.

Prayer, petition and supplication become truly empty and profitless when they are not carried out, as we said, in fear and trembling, with vigilance and wakefulness. If then someone approaches a human king with fear, trembling and vigilance and presents a petition in this way, should not one all the more present himself in similar fashion to God the Lord of all and to Christ the King of Kings and Prince of Princes, and so make his petition and supplication?[53]

Scholion 5 on Ps 76. 6.1 "The one knowing the obscure and the hidden matters of God (Ps 50:8) also holds the memories of passing aeons and of the years (*etôn*) in them, and the ancient days (*aiônôn*) from which he composed them."

This scholion and the next two after it have to do with *gnosis*, the knowledge that both leads to God and makes a *gnostikos*, a sage or philosopher, and the leader of Christians in their return to the knowledge of God. This knowledge has no content; instead, it is a knowing that unites the mind with God in a state of knowing beyond any distinction observed in the human being or the natural world:

> When the mind has put off the old self and shall put on the one born of grace (Col 3:9–10) then it will see its own state (*katastasis*) in the time of prayer resembling sapphire or the color of heaven: this state scripture calls the place of God that was seen by the elders on Mt. Sinai (Ex 24:9–11).[54]

Thus, the next scholion, **Scholion 6 on Ps 76.9.1**, reads "If he has cut off his mercy to some, it is said elsewhere that "he extends his mercy to those who know you." (Ps 35:11)

Here Evagrius underlines the role of the *gnostikos* in reconciling minds divided from God by vice or forgetfulness; they manifest the mercy of God to those whom they train, and create images of the Logos in their students.

Addressing this verse in Homily 76.1, Origen says:

> "Shall he cut off his mercy to the end from generation to generation? And I reviewed this and my spirit stirred." (Ps 76.6a,7b) When God is giving us over to punishments, does he cut off his mercy from us, so that he will never reverse himself and be merciful to us, but, cutting off his mercy, abandon us from generation to generation? … Is he possibly going to forget us in travails and sufferings and never have compassion?

Origen does not answer his own question directly; instead, he refers to Paul's having heard "unspeakable utterances" and John's having heard "the seven

---

53. Sinkewicz, *Evagrius*, 11.
54. Sinkewicz, *Evagrius*, 180.

thunders;" yet neither of them wrote down these sounds; likewise the Psalm-ist, "as he was wailing and raising new doubts saw the secret, but, seeing the secret, he hid it, since it was better to hide it than say all these things that he had understood. So much is the multitude of your kindness, Lord, which you hid for those who fear you in Christ Jesus...."[55] Origen seems not to want his listeners to rely on the mercy of divine *oikonomia,* even though he alludes to Paul and John as authorities for *apokatastasis.*

Scholion 7, on Psalm 76.11.2 enlists the Psalmist as a witness: "[David] speaks here of the ascent from evil and ignorance to virtue and knowledge." Evagrius thought of all Christian *gnostikoi* as performing the same service as Moses, David, or Christ: to instruct people in the *praktikê* by various means so that they could arrive at "virtue and gnosis," the preconditions for the contem-plation of the invisible and visible world, and the knowledge of God described above. Once again, Evagrius follows Origen—now in the second homily on Psalm 76—who applied this verse to someone who has been misled by "teach-ers who do not have it straight." "Darkness and ignorance in the soul," follow-ing the Jewish law, or not "understand[ing] the clarity of the truth" are all ex-amples of false beginnings.

> I have often heard believers testifying that they have been deemed to be in the faith for a long time, and to have been taught the secrets of the faith, at some point finding a teacher who makes it clear, saying "now I have begun to become a Christian, now I am learning for the first time what Christianity is." They say these things not to take away from their earlier practice, but seeing that earlier they had not gotten to the point of the secrets....[56]

Scholion 8, in Ps 76. 13.2 "Meditation is continual study and conversation about someone."

Evagrius uses the word *adoleschia* here not in its original sense, as "chatter" or "prattling," but as conversation or meditation, and he may have given the word the sense it has in later monastic writings. But it reflects Plato's use of the word for subtlety in *Phaedrus* 269e, and for conversation in the LXX itself (4 Kingdoms 9:11 and Ps 55.2). (The *tis* in the scholion is "someone"—namely, the Logos).

Diatribê and *homilia,* words I have translated as "continual study" and "conversation," are not words Evagrius used frequently; but in his Scholia

<hr>

55. Hom 1 on Ps 76, Trigg translation, 206 (Homilia, 312).
56. Homily 2 on Ps 76, 219 (Homilia, 315).

on Proverbs, each appears with some frequency because the Septuaging uses them, and Evagrius connects them to the program of study he proposes for his students.[57]

Again, Evagrius seems here to be recasting Origen's comment, in Homily 2 section 4, "This study is blessed, when one studies, not catchphrases or verbal formulas, but 'all God's works....'"[58]

Scholion 9 on Ps 76.14.1 "Either the road of God surely is in every holy place, or his logos is in the Christ."

Here Evagrius uses equivalent terms to decode the Psalm verse, "Oh God, your road is in the holy [place, or perhaps person]." His Proverbs scholia speak often of "road," since the term is used frequently in the OT to signify not only a journey but conduct over time. Here Evagrius makes "every holy place/person" equivalent to "Christ" and "road" equivalent to "logos." Evagrius has several possibilities in mind: either the logos has created all things, and therefore is available everywhere, or is in every person becoming holy, meaning that all are potentially Christ. Origen writes, in Homily 2.5 on Ps 76, "What is God's road, leading to God, but the one who says 'I am the road and the truth and the life.' Where is God's road? In the holy one, if you are holy.... It is a most surprising matter, his road is in you just as God's kingdom is not outside you.... If we travel on it, it is within us."[59]

Scholion 10 on Ps 76.15 "That is, the Christ, for a Christ is 'the power of God and the wisdom of God.'" (1 Cor 7.1)

Origen writes, "What sort of power has he made known among the peoples? Christ, for Christ is the power of God and the wisdom of God (1 Cor 7.1). The power of Jesus is here and when the power is present, you are all gathered and we are united every day by his power, for 'he who is joined to the Lord is one sprit.'"[60]

Scholion 11 on Ps 76.16.1 "The Christ is the right arm of God, through whom he effects the good things in us, the good things coming about according to his desire (*epithumia*)"

---

57. On Proverbs 21.19, 227, and 31.21 (p .380).
58. Homily 2 on Ps 76, 222 (Homilia, 319).
59. Homily 2 on Ps 76, 223 (Homilia, 320).
60. Homily 2 on Ps 76, 226 (Homilia, 325).

Although *epithumia* generally has a negative sense in Evagrius' thought, since without proper training a person's "desire" is associated with carnality and covetousness, here Evagrius gives the term a positive valence.

Again, Evagrius follows Origen, who writes on this verse:

> "You redeemed your people with your arm," the Savior stretching out his own arm has redeemed his people from the hand of the enemies, he gathered them from the countries, he redeemed the "children of Jacob."

But where Origen continues to emphasize that the Jews are not these children, because they had denied both Jacob and Abraham "through their works and through their unbelief in my God, Jesus Christ," Evagrius is silent on the subject. Unlike Origen, Evagrius almost never mentions contemporary Jews as a presence for his readers; and likewise, he only alludes to heretical teachers—he does not confront them directly—seemingly a feature of his pedagogical setting—some version of a schoolroom—contrasted with Origen's setting in these homilies as a teacher of the whole community.[61]

Scholion 12 on Ps 76.17.1–2, "Now he signals (*sêmainei*) that the waters are reasoning natures (*logikas physeis*),"

This reflects Origen's interpretation that the waters above the firmament are angelic beings, in contrast to those below the earth, which are demonic. Thus, in the next scholion, **Scholion 13 on Ps 17.3**, Evagrius writes, "The abysses' signify the subterranean powers, which were shaken at the presence of the Christ." Like Origen, Evagrius accepts the teaching that Christ in death descended to Hell and plundered it, thus dislodging the reign of Satan and death in Hell.

Here Origen expresses some caution about the interpretation of these verses, but once again is the source of Evagrius' interpretation:

> I myself, seeing in the beginning of the making of the cosmos both a "spirit of God," as the prophet says, borne, in the arrangement of the universe, "above the water" and a "darkness" not "above the water" (for that is where the spirit of God was), but "above the abyss" is where the darkness was, beseeching God, after much prayer, I was moved to seek concerning these references to places—since also the firmament is produced on account of waters, so that some may stay above and some may stay below—if "Israel" is not about sensible waters but about more divine powers that stay below the firmament, those that were the abyss above

---

61. Origen, Hom. 2 on Ps 76, (Trigg, 227) (Homilia, 325).

which was the darkness (for we even fight against world-dominators of this darkness) but the water above which the spirit of God was were better powers.[62]

As my colleague Joseph Trigg points out in the footnote to this passage, Origen speaks here about demons yoked to human beings, as the waters below the firmament, and the powers above the firmament as the angels who see the face of God, recalling Ephesians 5:8, "you were once darkness... ." Trigg also remarks that the passage in the homily is compact and probably would not have been understood except by Origen's students. Evagrius, working with a copy of the homilies before him, seems to further encode Origen's teaching for the benefit of his own students and readers, implying that the passage speaks both about the creation of the cosmos and the two states of rational beings toward which a human can move: angelic and demonic. Finally, Evagrius has compressed a lengthy discussion in Origen's third homily on Ps 76 into two short scholia—perhaps assuming that his readers would also have known the earlier work.

Scholion 13, on Ps 76.21, interprets "the voice of your thunder in the wheel" as Christ's voice: "The wheel signifies either this aeon or the sense-perceptible cosmos, or the pure and aeonic soul, if indeed evil is always near a corner (cf. Prov 7:12)."

This scholion, like numerous others in Evagrius' corpus, is constructed as a syllogism: if x, then y. So, the first part of the syllogism is the condition of sexual temptation—the effect, in untrained souls, of an untrained and improper response to stimuli. Although Gehin thinks, in his commentary on the Proverbs scholia, this sexual temptation is a homosexual one[63] (n. to scholion 93, 193) In the Scholia on Proverbs, Evagrius interprets the passage from Proverbs 7 in the following way: "Those who wander in the streets" have thoughts of adultery, fornication, and fraud. Those who 'wander outside' them have movements against nature—they try to seek a bed with men and harbor fantasies of certain forbidden matters." In the next scholion, also on Prov 7,12,

---

62. Hom 3 on Ps 76 (Trigg, 229). (Homilia, 328).

63. Géhin writes that "This scholia classes the graver sins in two categories: they ward against homosexuality, and more particularly against pederasty, so frequent in the Egyptian monastic literature; Evagrius himself in Foundations 5, warns a hermit not to have at his side a young slave who might be an occasion of a fall. It should be noted that the first stich of Prof. 7,12 is cited in Thoughts 26, concerning sins of which perversity is even more great than the matter (hyle) necessary to their realization makes a default. He has equally made an illusion to 'the imagination of forbidden things' (*pros tas apeiremenas phantasias*) in Praktikos 46, but the context is different."

Evagrius goes on to say that "if certain thoughts are pure, others are impure, and if certain lines are called straight ones, and others broken, and if a 'corner' might be a broken line, intelligible 'corner' is an impure thought. Consequently, let malice 'always near a corner' signify that she abuses the soul by all the impure thoughts. The demoniacal 'kiss' is the passionate *noêma* (representation) that summons the soul to shameful working."

But what does this corner have to do with a "wheel"?

Again, the answer is likely to be in Origen, Homily 4 on Psalm 76, section 3:

> Hear how it is "in a wheel": the holy person is not angular, nor does he have any roughness in him, but he imitates heaven, seeing that it has "the image of the heavenly" (1 Cor. 15.49) and just as heaven is not angular, but is curved and spherical, and the spirit is not angular—"Circling it would circle, the spirit goes about and the spirit returns in its circle" (Ecc 1.6), in the same way also the holy person, imitating the spirit, going about circling circles, but also imitating heaven, belongs to wisdom, so, on this account, it is said "a voice of your thunder is in the wheel"[64]

Origen also adds to this a further interpretation, "If someone is able to see stronger things than these, because the holy spirit is rich when it comes to hiding deep things and great things and things not tracked down, let his [interpretation] be heard rather than these, if they are found to be more excellent than these." Evagrius may have read this passage as an invitation to his own—and others'—further speculation.

Evagrius' final scholion on Ps 76 reads: "The philosophy according to Moses is divided *tetrachôs* (into four parts): one the historical, and [second] the properly-termed legislative part, which two especially belong to an ethical treatise; but the third is about the divine worship, which is now about the natural contemplation, and a fourth especially the theological vision." It is necessary for us also to grasp in a fourfold way the intention of the law as clarifying some type, or as showing some sign, or as confirming a law for the purpose of upright governance or declaring by an oracle, as prophecy. By such method Moses and Aaron will lead the people traveling from evil to virtue.

The first part of the scholion is a quotation, slightly altered, from Clement of Alexandria's *Stromateis*. Clement ascribes the fourfold meaning of the

---

64. Hom 4 on Ps 76 (Trigg, 246) (Homilia, 345).

law to Moses as a way to show, against dualist Christian interpreters, that the Jewish law was a "merciful anticipation" of the Gospel: "For both the law and the Gospel are the energy of one Lord, who is 'the power and wisdom of God.'"[65] Evagrius' intention, however, was to show how the Psalms function as part of the training for the cultivation of *theôria*. He collapses parts one and two into an "ethical treatise," i.e. the *praktikê*, and associates the third and fourth parts with the life of the *gnostikos* devoted, first, to natural contemplation and second to the contemplation of God. The "intention of the Law" (Greek) is also typological or prophetic, i.e. referring to the exodus from Egypt to the land of Promise—a pattern advanced more clearly in the works of Origen than in Clement's.

Conclusion

In the foregoing examination of Evagrius' scholia on Psalm 76, we have seen that his interpretation closely follows that of Origen's homilies on the same Psalm. So closely does Evagrius' work follows Origen's, in fact, that it suggests a deliberate attempt to copy and adapt not only the general approach of Origen, but the precise meaning of each Psalm. Subsequent examination of the entire corpus of Origen's exegesis of Psalms might well discover a similar mirroring. Such a result would confirm that Evagrius used his own position as teacher in Egypt to preserve Origen's approach and his specific interpretations for another generation of students; but as it stands, Evagrius' project looks increasingly like a careful and thoroughgoing attempt to provide not only a biblical exegesis, but an understanding of Christian life dating from a much earlier period, and distinctly different from either the authority of the bishop and his teaching, or portrait of the monastic life that emphasized the miraculous at the expense of the learned. These scholia may have been an early step in the preservation of the Origen homilies rediscovered in 2012; a full examination, once the critical edition is available, may provide an invaluable witness, abbreviated though it is, to the entire collection.

---

65. Clement of Alexandria, *Stromateis* 1.28.176.1–2; cf. 1.28.179.3–4. P. Caster, Les Stromates, Stromate I (Paris: Cerf, 1951). See now, on the tetraktys, Jeremiah Coogan, "Reading (in) a Quadriform Cosmos: Gospel Books in the Early Christiani Imagination," *Journal of Early Christian Studies* 31.1 (2023), 85–103.

Altar, Richard. *The Art of Bible Translation*. Princeton, NJ: Princeton University Press, 2019.

Athanasius, *Life of St. Anthony*. Translated by Robert Gregg. Mahwah, NJ: Paulist Press, 1980.

Attridge, Harold W. and Margot E. Fassler, eds. Psalms *in Community: Jewish and Christian Textual, Liturgical and Artistic Traditions*. Leiden: Brill, 2004.

Bandt, C. "Origen in the Catenae on Psalms: II. The Rather Complicated Case of Psalms 51 to 76." *Adamantius* 20 (2014): 14–26.

———. "The Reception of Origen's *Homilies on Psalms* in the Catenae." In Jacobsen, *Origeniana Undecima: Origen and Origenism in the History of Western Thought*, 235–46.

Basil of Caesarea. *Homiliae super Psalmos*. Patrologia Graeca 29. Paris: J. P. Migne, 1857.

Basil of Caesarea. *Saint Basile. Lettres*. Edited by Yves Courtonne. 3 vols. Paris: Les Belles Lettres, 1957–1966.

Barilli, C. and L Perrone. "Origene commentatore dei Salmi: dai frammenti catenari al Codice di Monaco." *Adamantius* 20 (2014): 8–286.

Behr, John. *Origen: On First Principles*. Oxford: Oxford University Press, 2018.

Berliner, Avraham, ed. *Midrash Rabbah. Bereshit Rabbah*. Jerusalem: Wahrmann Books, 1990.

Bellos, David. *Is that a Fish in Your Ear: Translation and the Meaning of Everything*. New York: Faber and Faber, 2011.

Berger, Klaus. *Identity and Experience in the New Testament*. Minneapolis, MN: Fortress Press, 2003.

Bienert, Wolfgang A. and Uwe Kühneweg, eds. *Origeniana Septima: Origenes in den Auseinandersetzungen des 4. Jahrhunderts*. Leuven: Leuven University Press, 1999.

Blosser, Philip. *Become Like the Angels: Origen's Doctrine of the Soul*. Washington, DC: The Catholic University of America Press, 2012.

Bondanella, Peter, and Mark Musa, eds. and trans. *The Portable Machiavelli*. New York: Penguin, 1979.

Bottini, Giovanni C. and Chrupcala, L. Daniel, eds. *Knowledge and Wisdom. Archaeological and Historical Essays in Honour of Leah Di Segni*. Milan: Terra Santa, 2014.

Boulnois, Marie-Odile. "Chronique d'une découverte et de ses retombées scientifiques: les nouvelles Homélies sur les Psaumes d'Origène" *Revue des Études Tardo-Antiques* 5 (2015–16): 351–62.

Boylan, Michael. "Galen's Conception Theory." *Journal of the History of Biology* 19, no. 1 (1986): 47–77.

Bunge, Gabriel. "Evagre le Pontique fut-il un condisciple de saint Jean Chrysostome?" *Irénikon* 91 no. 3 (2018): 163–83; 324–45.

Bunge, Gabriel. *"In Geist und Wahrheit." Studien zu den 153 Kapiteln Über das Gebet des Evagrios Pontikos.* Bonn: Borengässer, 2010.

Brakke, David. "The Problematization of Nocturnal Emissions in Early Christian Syria, Egypt and Gaul." *Journal of Early Christian Studies* 3 (1995): 419–60.

Brown, Raymond E. *The Gospel According to John I–XII.* Anchor Bible Series 29. New York: Doubleday, 1966.

Buber, Shmuel, ed. *Midrash Tanhuma.* Vilna: Romm, 1885–1886.

Butler, Cuthbert, ed. *The Lausiac History of Palladius.* 2 vols. Texts and Studies 6. Cambridge: Cambridge University Press, 1904.

Cacciari, Antonio. "Lingua e stile nel Commento a Matteo: sondaggi e osservazioni." In *Il Commento a Matteo di Origene: atti del X Convegno di Studi del Gruppo Italiano di ricerca su Origene e la tradizione alessandrina, Napoli, 24–26 settembre 2008,* edited by Teresa Piscitelli, 162–77. Brescia: Morcelliana, 2011.

———. "Nuova luce sull'officina origeniana. I LXX e gli 'altri.'" *Adamantius* 20 (2014): 217–25.

Capone, Alessandro. "Folia vero in verbis sunt": parola divina e lingua umana nei Tractatus in psalmos attribuiti a Gerolamo." *Adamantius* 19 (2013): 437–56.

Carriker, Andrew. *The Library of Eusebius of Caesarea.* Leiden: Brill, 2003.

Caster, Marcel. *Les Stromates, Stromate I.* Paris: Cerf, 1951.

Chantraine, Pierre. *Dictionnaire étymologique de la langue grecque: Histoire des mots.* New Edition. Paris: Klincksieck, 2009.

Chin, Catherine M. "Rufinus of Aquileia and Alexandrian Afterlives: Translation as Origenism." *Journal of Early Christian Studies* 18, no. 4 (Winter 2010): 617–47.

Chin, Catherine M. and Caroline T. Schroeder. *Melania: Early Christianity Through the Life of One Family.* Berkeley: University of California Press, 2017.

Clark, Elizabeth A. *The Origenist Controversy: The Cultural Construction of an Early Christian Debate.* Princeton, NJ: Princeton University Press, 1992.

Crouzel, Henri. *Théologie de l'image de Dieu chez Origène.* Paris: Aubier, 1956.

———. "Rev. Gottes Gest Und Der Mensch by Hauschild, W. D." *Bulletin de Littérature Ecclésiastique* 77 (1976): 139–46.

———. "Idées Platoniciennes et Raisons Stoïciennes Dans La Théologie d'Origène." *Studia Patristica* 18, no. 3 (1989): 365–83.

Crouzel, Henri, and Manlio Simonetti. *Traité des principes. Livres 3 et 4, Commentaire et fragments 4.* Source Chrétiennes 269. Paris: Cerf, 1980.

Coullet, Magali. "Eusèbe de Césarée – Commentaire sur les Psaumes." Thesis, Université d'Aix-Marseille 2016.

Curti, Carmelo et al., eds. *La terminologia esegetica nell'antichità: Atti del Primo Seminario di antichità cristiane Bari, 25 ottobre 1984.* Bari: Edipuglia, 1987.

Daley, Brian E. and Paul R. Kolbet, eds. *The Harp of Prophecy: Early Christian Interpretation of the Psalms.* Notre Dame, IN: University of Notre Dame Press, 2015.

Daniélou, Jean. *Origen.* Translated by Walter Mitchell. London and New York: Sheed & Ward, 1955.

de Lange, Nicholas. *Origen and the Jews: Studies in Jewish-Christian Relations in Third-Century Palestine.* Cambridge: Cambridge University Press, 1976.

de Lubac, Henri. *Histoire et esprit: L'intelligence de l'écriture d'après Origène.* Paris: Aubier, 1950.

des Places, Édouard. *Suggeneia: La parenté de l'homme avec Dieu d'Homère à la patristique.* Paris: Klincksiek, 1965.

Dillon, John M. "Aisthèsis Noêtê. A Doctrine of Spiritual Senses in Origen and in Plotinus." In *Hellenica et Judaica: Hommage à Valentin Nikiprowetzky*, edited by A. Caquot, M. Hadas-Lebel, and J. Riaud, 443–55. Leuven: Peeters, 1986.

Dechow, Jon. "Dogma and Mysticism in Early Christianity: Epiphanius of Cyprus and the Legacy of Origen." PhD diss., University of Pennsylvania, 1975.

del Cogliano, Mark. "Basil of Caesarea's Homily on Psalm 115 (CPG 2910): Origen and Anti-Eunomian Polemic." *Sacris Erudiri* 57 (2018): 7–31.

Dickey, Eleanor. *Ancient Greek Scholarship: A Guide to Finding, Reading, and Understanding Scholia, Commentaries, Lexica, and Grammatical Treatises, from Their Beginnings to the Byzantine Period.* Oxford: Oxford University Press, 2007.

Dively Lauro, Elizabeth Ann. *The Soul and Spirit of Scripture within Origen's Exegesis.* Leiden: Brill, 2005.

______. "The Meaning and Significance of Scripture's Sacramental Nature." *Studia Patristica* (2017) 94:153–85.

______. "The Eschatological Significance of Scripture According to Origen." *Studia Patristica* (2013) 56:83–102.

Dorival, Gilles. "Origen in the Catenae on Psalms: I. An Overall Outline." *Adamantius* 20 (2014): 8–13.

Dorival, Gilles et al., eds. *Origeniana Sexta: Origène et la Bible/Origen and the Bible. Actes du Colloquium Origenianum Sextum. Chantilly 30 août – 3 septembre 1993.* Leuven: Leuven University Press, 1995.

Dysinger, Luke. *Psalmody and Prayer in the Writings of Evagrius Ponticus.* Oxford: Oxford University Press, 2005.

Dupuis, Jacques. *L'Esprit de l'homme: Étude sur l'anthropologie religieuse d'Origène.* Bruges: Desceé de Brouwer, 1967.

Edwards, Mark J. *Origen Against Plato.* Aldershot: Ashgate, 2002.

Epstein, Isidore, ed. *Babylonian Talmud.* London: The Soncino Press, 1935–1948.

Fitzmyer, Joseph A. *Romans.* Anchor Bible Series 33. New York: Doubleday, 1993.

Frede, Michael. *Essays in Ancient Philosophy.* Minneapolis: University of Minnesota Press, 1987.

Fürst, A. "Judentum, Judenchristentum und Antijudaismus in den neu entdeckten Psalmenhomilien." *Adamantius* 20 (2014): 275–86.

Géhin, Paul, ed. and trans. *Evagre le Pontique, Chapitres sur la prière*. Sources chrétiennes 589. Paris: Cerf, 2017.

Géhin, Paul. *Scholies aux proverbs*. Paris: Cerf, 1987.

Geljon, Albert-Kees. "Didymus the Blind: Commentary on Psalm 24 (23 LXX): Introduction, Translation and Commentary." *Vigiliae Christianae* 65, no. 1 (2011): 50–73.

Grafton, Anthony and Megan Williams. *Christianity and the Transformation of the Book*. Cambridge, MA: Harvard University Press, 2006.

Gregory of Nyssa: The Life of Moses. Translated by Abraham J. Malherbe and Everett Ferguson. New York: Paulist Press, 1978.

Greer, Rowan A. *Origen: An Exhortation to Martyrdom, Prayer and Selected Works*. New York: Paulist Press, 1979.

Gronewald, Michael. *Didymus der Blinde, Psalmenkommentar (Tura-Papyrus)*. Bonn: Rudolf Habelt GmbH, 1968.

Guillaumont, Antoine and Claire Guillaumont. *Evagre le Pontique, Traité pratique, ou Le moine, tome II*. Paris: Cerf, 1971.

Guillaumont, Antoine. "Le gnostique chez Clément d'Alexandrie et chez Evagre le Pontique." In *Alexandrina: Hellénisme, judaïsme et christianisme à Aexandrie. Mélanges offerts au P. Claude Mondésert*, edited by Claude Mondésert, 195–201. Paris: Cerf, 1987.

———. *Un Philosophe au désert Evagre le Pontique*. Paris: Vrin, 2004.

Hällström, Gunnar. *Charismatic Succession: A Study of Origen's Concept of Prophecy*. Helsinki: Publications of the Finnish Exegetical Society, 1985.

Hanson, R. P. C. *Allegory and Event: A Study of the Sources and Significance of Origen's Interpretation of Scripture*. London: SDCM Press, 1959.

Harding, E. M. "Origenist Controversies." In *The Westminster Handbook to Origen*, edited by John A. McGuckin, 162–67. Louisville, KY: Westminster John Knox Press, 2004.

Harl, Marguerite, ed. *La chaîne palestinienne sur le Psaume 118 (Origène, Eusèbe, Didyme, Apollinaire, Athanase, Théodoret)*. 2 vols. Paris: Cerf, 1972.

———. *La langue de Japhet: Quinze études sur la Septante et le grec des Chrétiens*. Paris: Cerf, 1994.

———. "La mort salutaire du Pharaon." In *Studi e materiali di storia delle religioni* 38 (1967) 260–68; reprinted in Harl, Marguerite. *Le déchiffrement su sens: études sur l'herméneutique d'Origène à Grégoire de Nysse*. Paris: Institut d'Études Augustiniennes, 1993.

Harl, Marguerite and Gilles Dorival and Olivier Munnich. *La Bible grecque des Septante: du Judaisme hellénistique au Christianisme ancient*. Paris: Cerf, 1994.

Hart, David Bentley. *The New Testament: A Translation*. New Haven, CT: Yale University Press, 2017.

Hauschild, Wolf-Dieter. *Gottes Geist und der Mensch*. Munich: Chr. Kaiser Verlag, 1972.

Heine, Ronald. *Gregory of Nyssa's Treatise on the Inscriptions of the Psalms*. Oxford: Clarendon Press, 1995.

Littré, Émile. *Oeuvres complètes d'Hippocrate*. 7 vols. Paris: Bailliere, 1839.

Interi, Tommaso. "Origen and Eusebius Interpreting Psalm 77." *Studia Patristica* 61 (2021): 65–77.

Jacobsen, Anders-Christian., ed. *Origeniana Undecima: Origen and Origenism in the History of Western Thought*. Leuven: Peeters, 2016.

Johnson, Aaron and Jeremy Schott, eds. *Eusebius of Caesarea: Tradition and Innovations*. Washington DC: Center for Hellenic Studies, 2013.

Kalleres, Dayna S. *City of Demons: Violence, Ritual and Power in Late Antique Christianity*. Berkeley: University of California Press, 2015.

Kim, Andrew. *Epiphanius of Cyprus: Imagining an Orthodox World*. Ann Arbor: University of Michigan Press, 2015.

Lau, D. *Origenes' tropologische Hermeneutik und die Wahrheit des biblischen Wortes*. Frankfurt am Main: Peter Lang, 2016.

Lauro, Elisabetta De. *The Soul and Spirit of Scripture Within Origen's Exegesis*. Leiden: Brill, 2005.

Leemans, Johan. "Angels." *The Westminster Handbook to Origen*. Edited by John Anthony McGuckin. Louisville, KY: Westminster John Knox Press, 2004.

Le Boulluec, A. "La polémique contre les hérésies dans les Homélies sur les Psaumes d'Origène (*Codex Monacensis Graecus* 314)." *Adamantius* 20 (2014): 256–74.

Leyerle, Blake and Robin Darling Young, eds. *Ascetic Culture: Essays in Honor of Philip Rousseau*. Notre Dame, IN: University of Notre Dame Press, 2013.

Lies, Lambert. "Origenes Und Reinkarnation." *Zeitschrift Für Katholische Theologie* 121, no. 2 (1999): 139–58.

Lipatov-Chicherin, N. "Preaching as the Audience Heard it: Unedited Transcripts of Patristic Homilies." *Studia Patristica* 64 (2013): 277–97.

Lössl, Joseph and John W. Watt. *Interpreting the Bible and Aristotle in Late Antiquity: The Alexandrian Commentary Tradition Between Rome and Baghdad*. Farnham: Ashgate, 2011.

Martens, Peter W. "Embodiment, Heresy, and the Hellenization of Christianity: The Descent of the Soul in Plato and Origen." *Harvard Theological Review* 108, no. 4 (2015): 594–620. doi:10.1017/S0017816015000401.

———. *Origen and Scripture. The Contours of the Exegetical Life*. Oxford: Oxford University Press, 2012.

———. "Revisiting the Allegory/Typology Distinction: The Case of Origen." *Journal of Early Christian Studies* 16, no. 3 (2008): 283–317.

McGuckin, John Anthony. "Origen on the Jews." In *Christianity in Relation to Jews, Greeks, and Romans*, edited by Everett Ferguson, 23–35. 2 vols. Hamden, CT: Garland, 1999. First printed in *Studies in Church History* 29 (1992): 1–13.

———. "Origen's Use of the Psalms in the Treatise *On First Principles*." In *Meditations of the Heart: The Psalms in Early Christian Thought and Practice. Essays in Honour of Andrew Louth*, edited by A. Andreopoulos, A. Casiday, C. Harrison, 97–118. Turnhout: Brepols, 2011.

———, ed. *The Westminster Handbook to Origen*. Louisville, KY: Westminster John Knox Press, 2004.

McInroy, Mark J. "Origen of Alexandria." In *The Spiritual Senses: Perceiving God in Western Christianity*, edited by Paul L. Gavrilyuk and Sarah Coakley, 20–35. Cambridge: Cambridge University Press, 2011.

Melzer, Arthur M. *Philosophy Between the Lines: The Lost History of Esoteric Writing.* Chicago: University of Chicago Press, 2014.

Metzler, K. "Tachygraphen-Fehler in den neu entdeckten Homilien des Origenes." *Adamantius* 19 (2013): 463–65.

Meyer, Robert. *The Lausiac History.* New York: Newman Press, 1964.

Mitchell, Margaret M. "Patristic Rhetoric on Allegory: Origen and Eustathius Put 1 Samuel 28 on Trial." *Journal of Religion* 85 (2005): 414–45, reprinted with add. in *The "Belly-Myther" of Endor. Interpretations of First Kingdoms 28 in the Early Church. Translation with introduction and notes by R. A. Greer and M. M. Mitchell.* Atlanta: SBL Press, 2007.

———. *Paul, the Corinthians and the Birth of Christian Hermeneutics.* Cambridge: Cambridge University Press, 2010.

———. "Problems and Solutions in Early Christian Biblical Interpretation: A Telling Case from Origen's Newly Discovered Greek Homilies on the Psalms (*codex Monacensis Graecus* 314)." *Adamantius* 22 (2016): 40–55.

Mithen, Steven. *The Singing Neanderthals: The Origins of Music, Language, Mind, and Body.* Cambridge, MA: Harvard University Press, 2006.

Molin Pradel, M. "Novità origeniane dalla Staatsbibliothek di Monaco di Baviera: il Cod. graec. 314." *Adamantius* 18 (2012): 16–40.

Monaci Castagno, Adele, "Origene e Ambrogio: l'indipendenza dell'intellettuale e le pretese del patronato." In *Origeniana Octava: Origen and the Alexandrian Tradition*, edited by Lorenzo Perrone, 165–93. Leuven: Peeters, 2003.

———. "Contesto liturgico e cronologia della predicazione origeniana alla luce delle nuove Omelie sui Salmi." *Adamantius* 20 (2014): 238–54.

———. *Origene predicatore e il suo pubblico*, F. Angeli, Milano 1987.

Morin, D. Germanus. *Hieronymus. Tractatus sive Homiliae in Psalmos.* CChSL, 78. Turnhout: Brepols, 1958.

Morlet, Sébastien. *Symphonia: La concorde des textes et des doctrines dans la littérature grecque jusqu'à Origène.* Paris: Les Belles Lettres, 2019.

Nautin, Pierre. *Origène: sa vie et son œuvre.* Paris: Beauchesne, 1977.

———. *Homélies sur Jérémie, tome II: Homélies XII–XX et Homélies latines.* Sources Chretiennes. Paris: Cerf, 1977.

Neuschäfer, Bernhard. *Origenes als Philologe.* Basel: Friedrich Reinhardt, 1987.

Origen. *Commentaire sur Saint Jean.* Edited by Cécile Blanc. Vols. 4: books 19–20. Paris: Cerf, 1982.

———. *Contra Celsum: Libri VIII.* Edited by Miroslav Marcovich. Leiden: Brill, 2001.

———. *Die neuen Psalmenhomilien: Eine kritische Edition des* Codex Monacensis Graecus 314. Edited by Lorenzo Perrone, Emanuela Prinzivalli, and Antonio Cacciari. Origenes Werke 13. Berlin, New York: Walter de Gruyter, 2015.

———. *Extraits des Livres I et II du Contre Celse d'Origène, d'après la papyrus no 88747 du Musée du Caire, par Jean Scherer.* Edited by Jean Scherer (Cairo: Imprimerie de l'Institut français d'archéologie orientale, 1956).

———. *Homilies on Genesis and Exodus.* Translated by Ronald E. Heine. Fathers of the Church 71. Washington, DC: The Catholic University of America Press, 1982.

———. *Homélies sur la Genèse.* Edited and translated by Louis Doutreleau. Sources Chrétiennes 7. Paris: Cerf, 1985.

———. *Homélies sur L'Exode.* Edited and translated by Marcel Borret. Sources Chrétiennes 321. Paris: Cerf, 1985.

———. *Homilies on Leviticus 1–16.* Translated by Gary Wayne Barkley. Fathers of the Church 83. Washington, DC: The Catholic University of America Press, 1990.

———. *Homélies sur Le Lévitique, Tome 2.* Edited and translated by Marcel Borret. Sources Chrétiennes 287. Paris: Cerf, 1981.

———. *Homilies on Judges.* Translated by Elizabeth Ann Dively Lauro. Fathers of the Church 119. Washington, DC: The Catholic University of America Press, 2010.

———. *Homélies sur les Juges.* Edited and translated by Pierre Messié, Louis Neyrand, and Marcel Borret. Sources Chrétiennes 389. Paris: Cerf, 1993.

———. *Homélies sur les Psaumes 36 á 38.* Edited and translated by Henri Crouzel, Luc Brésard, Emanuela Prinzivalli. Sources Chrétiennes 411. Paris: Cerf, 1995.

———. *Homilies on Isaiah.* Translated by Elizabeth Ann Dively Lauro. Fathers of the Church 142. Washington, DC: The Catholic University of America Press, 2021.

———. *Omelie sui Salmi, Homiliae in Psalmos XXXVI – XXXVII – XXXVIII.* Edited by E. Prinzivalli. Firenze: Nardini, 1991.

———. *On First Principles.* Translated by G. W. Butterworth. Gloucester, MA: Peter Smith, 1973.

———. *Philocalie, 1–20 et Lettre à Africanus.* Edited by Marguerite Harl and Nicholas De Lange. Paris: Cerf, 1983.

———. *Origenis Hexaplorum quae supersunt.* Edited by F. Field, I–II, Oxford, 1875.

———. *Origenes Werke,* 13. Bd.: *Die neuen Psalmenhomilien. Eine kritische Edition des* Codex Monacensis Graecus 314. Edited by L. Perrone with M. Molin Pradel, E. Prinzivalli and A. Cacciari. Griechischen Christlichen Schriftsteller NF 19. Berlin: De Gruyter, 2015.

———. *Sur la Päque.* Edited by Octave Guérand and Pierre Nautin. Paris: Beauchesne, 1979.

———. *Traité Des Principes,* Tome 3. Edited and translated by Henri Crouzel and Manlio Simonetti. *Sources Chrétiennes,* 268. Paris: Cerf, 1980.

Pace, Nicola. *Ricerche sulla traduzione di Rufino del "De principiis" di Origene.* Florence: La Nuova Italia Editrice, 1990.

Pavan, M. *"Ricordavano che Dio è la loro roccia" (Sal 78,38). Il Salterio come libro della e per la memoria.* Assisi: Cittadella, 2017.

Pazzini, Domenico. *Lingua e teologia in Origene: Il Commento a Giovanni.* Brescia: Paideia, 2009.

Peri, V. "Omelie origeniane sui Psalmi." Studi e Testi 289. Vatican City, 1980.

Perrone, Lorenzo "Abstieg und Aufstieg Christi nach Origenes. Zur Auslegung von Psalm 15 in den Homilien von *Codex Monacensis Graecus* 314." *Theologie und Philosophie,* 89 (2014): 321–40.

———. "Aspetti dottrinali delle nuove omelie di Origene sui salmi: le tematiche cristologiche a confronto col Perì archôn," *Teología y Vida*, 55 (2014): 209–43.

———. *Discovering Origen's Lost Homilies on the Psalms*, Auctores Nostri 15 (2015): 19–46.

———. "Doctrinal Traditions and Cultural Heritage in the newly Discovered Homilies of Origen on the Psalms (*Cod. Mon. Graec. 314*)," *Phasis* 18 (2015): 191–212.

———. "'I Cuori E I Reni': Note Sull'interpretazione Origeniana Di Sal 7,10." *Adamantius* 22 (2016): 87–104.

———. "'La mia gloria è la mia lingua': per un ritratto dell'autore delle *Omelie sui Salmi* nel Codice Monacense Greco 314," *Adamantius* 20 (2014): 177–92.

———. *La preghiera secondo Origene. L'impossibilità donata*, Brescia: Morcelliana, 2011

———. "*Ne corrumpas* (Sal 74, 1): l'omelia di Origene sul Salmo 74 nel codice di Monaco." In *Amicorum Munera: Studi in onore di Antonio V. Nazzaro*, edited by Gennaro Luongo, 99–113. Napoli: Satura Editrice, 2016.

———. "Origenes rediuiuus: La découverte des homélies sur les Psaumes dans le Cod. Gr. 314 de Munich," in *Revue d'études augustiniennes et patristiques* 59 (2013): 55–93.

———. "Origen's 'Confessions': Recovering the Traces of a Self-Portrait." *Studia Patristica* 56 no. 4 (2013): 3–27.

———. "Origen's Interpretation of the Psalter Revisited: The Nine Homilies on Psalm 77(78) in the Munich Codex." Lecture at the NAPS Conference, Chicago 2017.

———. "Rediscovering Origen Today: First Impressions of the New Collection of Homilies on the Psalms in the *Codex Monacensis Graecus* 314." In Vinzent, *Studia Patristica 56*, 103–22.

———. "Scrittura e cosmo nelle nuove Omelie di Origene sui Salmi: L'interpretazione del Salmo 76." In *Patrística, Biblia Y Teología: Caminos de diálogo*, edited by Francisco Bastitta-Harriet, 45–72. Buenos Aires: Agape Libros, 2017.

———. "The Find of the Munich Codex: A Collection of 29 Homilies on the Psalms." In Jacobsen, *Origeniana Undecima. Origen and Origenism in the History of Western Thought*, 201–33.

Pietersma, Albert, and Benjamin G. Wright, eds. *A New English Translation of the Septuagint*. Oxford: Oxford University Press, 2007.

Prinzivalli, E. "Vinea. spiritualis intellegentiae. L'interpretazione omiletica dei salmi in Origene. Un'indagine a partire dalle omelie sui salmi 36 37 38." *Annali di storia dell'esegesi* 7 (1990): 397–416.

Rahner, K. "Le début d'une doctrine des cinq sens spirituels chez Origène." *Revue d'Ascétique et de Mystique* 13 (1932): 113–45.

Ramelli, Ilaria. "Evagrius and Gregory: Nazianzen or Nyssen? A Remarkable Issue that Bears on the Cappadocian (and Origenian) Influence on Evagrius." *Greek, Roman and Byzantine Studies* 53 (2013): 117–37.

———. *Evagrius's Kephalaia Gnostika: A New Translation of the Unreformed Text from the Syriac, Translated with Introduction and Commentary*. Atlanta: SBL Press, 2015.

———. "Preexistence of Souls? The ἀρχή and τέλος of Rational Creatures in Origen and Some Origenians." In *Studia Patristica 56. Papers Presented at the Sixteenth International Conference on Patristic Studies Held in Oxford 2011: Volume 4: Rediscovering Origen*, 167–226.

———. *The Christian Doctrine of Apokatastasis: A Critical Assessment from the New Testament to Eriugena.* VCSup 120. Leiden: Brill, 2013.

Rondeau, Marie-Josèphe. *Exégèse prosopologique et théologie 2, Les commentaires patristiques du Psautier 22, Orientalia Christiana analecta.* Rome: Pontificium Institutum Studiorum Orientalium, 1985.

———. "Le commentaire sur les Psaumes d'Evagre le Pontique." *Orientalia Christiana Periodica* 26 (1960): 307–48.

———. *Les commentaries patristiques du Psautier (IIIe-Ve siècles).* Volume 1. Orientalia Christiana Analecta 219. Rome: Pontificium Institutum Studiorum Orientalium, 1982.

Schérer, Jean. *Le commentaire d'Origène sur Rom. III.5–V.7.* Cairo: L'Institut Français d'Archéologie Orientale, 1957.

Schnitzer, K. F., trans. *Origenes über die Grundlehren der Glaubenswissenschaft.* Stuttgart: Imle und Krauss, 1835.

Seidman, Naomi. *Faithful Renderings: Jewish-Christian Difference and the Politics of Translation.* Chicago: University of Chicago Press, 2006.

Sinkewicz, Robert. *Evagrius of Pontus. The Greek Ascetic Corpus.* Oxford: Oxford University Press, 2003.

Somos, Róbert. *Logic and Argumentation in Origen. Adamantiana 7.* Münster: Aschendorff, 2013.

———. "The Question of Innate Ideas in Origen." In Jacobsen, *Origeniana Undecima: Origen and Origenism in the History of Western Thought,* 857–70.

Stefaniw, Blossom. *Mind, Text, and Commentary: Noetic Exegesis in Origen of Alexandria, Didymus the Blind, and Evagrius Ponticus.* Frankfurt am Main: Peter Lang, 2010.

Steiner, George. *After Babel: Aspects of Language and Translation,* 2nd ed. Oxford: Oxford University Press, 1992.

Stewart, Columba. *Cassian the Monk.* Oxford: Oxford University Press, 1998.

Stewart, Columba. "Imageless Prayer and the Theological Vision of Evagrius Ponticus." *Journal of Early Christian Studies* 9 (2001): 173–204.

Taft, Robert. *The Liturgy of the Hours in East and West.* Collegeville, MN: Liturgical Press, 1993.

Tanguay, Daniel. *Leo Strauss: an Intellectual Biography.* Translated by Christopher Nadon. New Haven, CT: Yale University Press, 2007.

Torjesen, Karen Jo. *Hermeneutical Procedure and Theological Method in Origen's Exegesis.* Patristische Texte und Studien, 28. Berlin: Walter de Gruyter, 1986.

Trigg, Joseph W. *Homilies on the Psalms: Codex Monacensis Graecus 314.* Washington, DC: The Catholic University of America Press, 2020.

———. *Origen of Alexandria.* Abingdon: Routledge, 1998.

———. "The Angel of Great Counsel: Christ and the Angelic Hierarchy in Origen's Theology." *The Journal of Theological Studies* 42 no. 1 (1991): 35–51.

Vennerstrom, Carl. "A Spiritual Scholiast in a Changing World: Evagrius Ponticus and His Spiritual Exegesis," for the Mundelein Seminary Graduate Student Conference (October, 2019).

Verbeke, G. *L'evolution de la doctrine du pneuma, du stoicisme à s. Augustin.* Paris: Desclée de Brouwer, 1945.

Vinzent, Markus, ed. *Studia Patristica 56. Papers Presented at the Sixteenth International Conference on Patristic Studies Held in Oxford 2011: Volume 4: Rediscovering Origen.* Leuven: Peeters, 2013.

Vogt, Hermann Josef. *Origenes als Exeget.* Paderborn: Schöningh, 1999.

von Balthasar, Hans Urs. "Die Hiera des Evagrius." *Zeitschrift für katholische Theologie* 63 (1939): 31–47.

Von Stritzky, M. B. "Die Bedeutung der Phaidrosinterpretation für die Apokatastasislehre des Origenes." *Vigiliae Christianae* 31 no. 4 (1977): 282–97. doi:10.2307/1583573.

Wellington, James. *Christe Eleison! The Invocatino of Christ in Eastern Monastic Psalmody c. 350–450.* Bern: Peter Lang, 2014.

Young, Frances M. *Biblical Exegesis and the Formation of Christian Culture.* Peabody, MA: Hendrickson Publishers, 2002.

CONTRIBUTORS

Miriam De Cock is a member of the faculty of the School of Theology, Philosophy and Music, Dublin City, Ireland.

Mark Randall James is an independent scholar and coeditor of the *Journal of Textual Reasoning*, and a minister at Christ Church Parish in Washington, DC.

Elizabeth Dively Lauro is Professor in the Department of Theological Studies at Loyola Marymount University, Los Angeles, California.

Margaret Mitchell is Shailer Mathews Distinguished Service Professor at the University of Chicago Divinity School, Chicago, Illinois.

Lorenzo Perrone is Emeritus Professor in the Department of Classical and Italian Philology, University of Bologna, Italy.

Alex Poulos holds a PhD from the Department of Greek and Latin at the Catholic University of America and is currently a Senior Backend Engineer at Spotify.

Joseph Trigg (PhD U. Chicago) is the Rector Emeritus of Christ Church, Port Tobacco Parish (La Plata, Maryland) and the translator of *Homilies on the Psalms*: Codex Monacensis Graecus 314, Fathers of the Church series (Washington, DC: The Catholic University of America Press, 2021).

Robin Darling Young is Ordinary Professor of Church History at The Catholic University of America and a member of the International Theological Commission.

Law, 135, 150, 205 Jewish, 8, 69, 70–120, 168
Lexis, 56–62, 183

Metempsychosis, 146, 148
Mind. *See Nous*
Music and musical instruments, 6, 26–27,
    33n80. 52, 69n137, 162, 211n25

Nourishment, spiritual, 55, 131–32
Nous, 153–62; of Christ, 142n22; presence
    before God, 212, 222

Pamphilus, *Apology of*, 3, 12, 40
Paul, 9; authority for *apokatastasis*, 224; on
    church, 32; imitating Christ, 33, 134–36,
    181–82; influence of, 162; on Israel, 8, 175, 191;
    Origen reading, 37; Origen using, 52, 63–102,
    106–7, 112–13, 115–20, 131, 161; strength in
    weakness in, 171; submission to God in, 176;
    unspeakable utterances in, 58, 223
Persona (*Prosopon*), 8, 122–23, 133–35, 137,
    184–202
Personification, 178
Philo, 43, 58, 68, 163n111
Philosophy, 1–2; and grammarians, 33; esoter-
    ism in, 41; Origen trained in, 7; Origen's use
    of, 61, 146; zetetic method in, 40, 73
Plato, 27, 152, 184
Platonism, 138, 148, 151–52
Prayer, 3, 5, 9; use of, in homilies 25
Preexistence. *See* Soul, preexistence of;
    Kidneys
Preface. *See* Prologue
Prologue, 18–27, 33–34
Protology, 144, 148
Prosopology, 184, 186n24. *See also* Persona
Providence, 49, 52–53, 68, 213, 220
Psychology, 1, 6, 137–38, 160, 164. *See also* Soul
Punishment, divine, 21, 76, 86, 163, 180, 223;
    of Jews, 8, 100, 102, 119

Resurrection, 54, 57, 124; Christ's, 130, 146;
    body, 136, 147, 165. *See also* Body, Deification
Rhetoric, 18–27, 74, 104, 125n16, 193–97
Rufinus of Aquileia, 2–4, 7–9, 11–12, 14–16,
    36, 38–44, 56, 63, 142, 145, 153, 157–58. 184,
    187, 198, 207–8, 216

Schism, 31–32
Scripture, 21–22, 24–25, 123; body of the logos,
    56, 68; Evagrius's interpretation of, 215;
    hidden meanings in, 32–33; interpreting by
    scripture, 79; literal sense of, 139; medita-
    tion on, 210; multiple senses of, 22, 58, 156;
    nourishment through, 32, 56–57, 135; per-
    forming, 8, 136; power of, 122; proof from,
    77, 95, 154; *prosopon* in, 184–202; reliability
    of, 74; text of, 69; understanding of, 90;
    word usage in, 28
Septuagint (LXX), 5, 28, 36, 41–49, 51–52,
    68–69, 74, 84, 124, 138, 224
Sin, atonement for, 90; conquest of, 162; cure
    of, 31n71; fall into, 131n46; Jesus free from,
    197; of Jews, 102–3; purification from, 157;
    remembering, 221
Soul, 6–7, 138–65; ascent of, 210; deification of,
    65; effect of Psalmody on, 212–22; demons
    work on, 228; eye of, 118, 174; of Jesus,
    129–30, 197; Logos as food of, 54–55, 132,
    199–200; parts of the body homologous to,
    177–78; preexistence of, 143–46, 149–51,
    164
Spiritual senses, 156
Suborinationism, 40–41
Synagogue, 89

Tatian, 62
Teacher: Christ as, 56, 193–94; Evagrius on,
    204, 209, 212, 216, 226, 229; finding a, 24,
    34, 168–69, 224; Logos as, 55; needing a, 30;
    Origen as, 1, 7, 9, 11, 20, 32–33, 53
Temple, 23, 97, 100, 105, 203
Theology, 19, 70, 72, 136, 158; as a term, 16;
    of deification, 181; of the Trinity, 121
Translation, 35–69, 122n5; by Jerome, 14;
    by Rufinus, 2–6, 9, 15–16, 36–41, 125, 185,
    187n25, 198, 208; of Bible, 29, 102, 104
Tura Papyri, 4, 145, 208n16
Typology, 91n78, 101n106. *See also* Figurative
    interpretation

Visitation. *See Epidēmia*

Zētēsis. See Philosophy, zetetic method in

To Train His Soul in Books:
Syriac Asceticism in Early Christianity
Edited by Robin Darling Young and Monica J. Blanchard

Breaking the Mind: New Studies in the Syriac "Book of Steps"
Edited by Kristian S. Heal and Robert A. Kitchen

Group Identity and Religious Individuality in Late Antiquity
Edited by Éric Rebillard and Jörg Rüpke

Reading Patristic Texts on Social Ethics: Issues and Challenges
for Twenty-First-Century Christian Social Thought
Edited by Johan Leemans, Brian Matz and Johan Verstraten